United States Congress

The tariff and administrative customs acts of 1890

Indexed

United States Congress

The tariff and administrative customs acts of 1890
Indexed

ISBN/EAN: 9783337154592

Printed in Europe, USA, Canada, Australia, Japan

Cover: Foto ©ninafisch / pixelio.de

More available books at **www.hansebooks.com**

53D CONGRESS, }
2d Session.

THE TARIFF AND ADMINISTRATIVE CUSTOMS ACTS OF 1890,

AND THE

BILL H. R. 4864,

AS REPORTED TO THE SENATE FROM THE FINANCE COMMITTEE MARCH 20, 1894.

INDEXED.

PREPARED UNDER THE DIRECTION OF THE COMMITTEE ON FINANCE APRIL 2, 1894.

INDEX TO SCHEDULES.

SCHEDULES: Page.
A: Chemicals, oils, and paints 1
B: Earths, earthenware, and glassware 9
C: Metals and manufactures of 15
D: Wood and manufactures of 29
E: Sugar 30
F: Tobacco and manufactures of 32
G: Agricultural products and provisions 33
H: Spirits, wines, and other beverages 40
I: Cotton manufactures 43
J: Flax, hemp, and jute, and manufactures of 47
K: Wool and manufactures of wool 50
L: Silks and silk goods 56
M: Pulp, papers, and books 57
N: Sundries 58
Free list 65

WASHINGTON:
GOVERNMENT PRINTING OFFICE.
1894.

53D CONGRESS, }
2D SESSION. }

THE TARIFF, AND ADMINISTRATIVE CUSTOMS ACTS OF 1890,

COMPARED WITH THE

BILL H. R. 4864 AS REPORTED TO THE SENATE FROM THE FINANCE COMMITTEE MARCH 20, 1894,

INDEXED.

[Present law large type and numbered paragraphs romans.]
[Proposed House amendments follow in smaller type romans.]
Senate Finance Committee amendments are indicated as follows: Additions in italics; Omissions in romans inclosed in brackets [ ].

AN ACT to reduce the revenue and equalize duties on imports, and for other purposes.

Be it enacted by the Senate and House of Representatives of the United States of America in Congress assembled, That on and after the sixth day of October, eighteen hundred and ninety, unless otherwise specially provided for in this act, there shall be levied, collected, and paid upon all articles imported from foreign countries, and mentioned in the schedules herein contained, the rates of duty which are, by the schedules and paragraphs, respectively prescribed, namely:

A BILL to reduce taxation, to provide revenue for the Government, and for other purposes.

Be it enacted by the Senate and House of Representatives of the United States of America in Congress assembled, That [on and] after the [first] thirtieth day of June, eighteen hundred and ninety-four, unless otherwise specially provided for in this act, there shall be levied, collected, and paid upon all articles imported from foreign countries, or withdrawn for consumption, and mentioned in the schedules herein contained, the rates of duty which are, by the schedules and paragraphs, respectively prescribed, namely:

SCHEDULE A.—CHEMICALS, OILS, AND PAINTS.

ACIDS.—

1. Acetic or pyroligneous acid, not exceeding the specific gravity of one and forty-seven one-thousandths, one and one-half cents per pound; exceeding the specific gravity of one and forty-seven one-thousandths, four cents per pound.

ACIDS:
1. Acetic or pyroligneous acid, twenty per centum ad valorem.

TA——1

2. Boracic acid, five cents per pound.
>2. Boracic acid, twenty per centum ad valorem.

3. Chromic acid, six cents per pound.
>3. Chromic acid, ten per centum ad valorem.

4. Citric acid, ten cents per pound.
>4. Citric acid twenty per centum ad valorem.

5. Sulphuric acid or oil of vitriol, not otherwise specially provided for, one-fourth of one cent per pound.
>Placed upon free list. Par. 643.

6. Tannic acid or tannin, seventy-five cents per pound.
>5. Tannic acid or tannin, thirty-five cents per pound.

7. Tartaric acid, ten cents per pound.
>6. Tartaric acid, [twenty] *ten* per centum ad valorem.

8. Alcoholic perfumery, including cologne-water and other toilet waters, two dollars per gallon and fifty per centum ad valorem; alcoholic compounds not specially provided for in this act, two dollars per gallon and twenty-five per centum ad valorem.
>7. Alcoholic perfumery, including cologne-water and other toilet waters and alcoholic compounds not specially provided for in this act, two dollars per gallon and twenty-five per centum ad valorem.

9. Alumina, alum, alum cake, patent alum, sulphate of alumina, and aluminous cake, and alum in crystals or ground, six-tenths of one cent per pound.
>8. Alumina, ten per centum ad valorem; alum, alum cake, patent alum, sulphate of alumina and aluminous cake, and alum in crystals or ground, [twenty] *thirty* per centum ad valorem.

10. AMMONIA.—Carbonate of, one and three-fourths cents per pound; muriate of or sal-ammoniac, three-fourths of one cent per pound; sulphate of, one-half of one cent per pound.
>Placed upon free list. Par. 391.

11. Blacking of all kinds, twenty-five per centum ad valorem.
>9. Blacking of all kinds, twenty per centum ad valorem. *Bone char suitable for use in decolorizing sugars, twenty per centum ad valorem.*

12. Blue vitriol, or sulphate of copper, two cents per pound.
>Placed upon free list. Par. 405.

13. Bone-char, suitable for use in decolorizing sugars, twenty-five per centum ad valorem.
>Placed upon free list by House. Par. 409.
>*See paragraph 11 for action in Senate.*

14. Borax, crude, or borate of soda, or borate of lime, three cents per pound; refined borax, five cents per pound.
>10. Borax, crude, or borate of soda, or borate of lime, placed upon free list (see Par. 415); refined borax, twenty per centum ad valorem.

15. Camphor, refined, four cents per pound.
>Placed upon free list. Par. 429.

16. Chalk, prepared, precipitated, French, and red, one cent per pound; all other chalk preparations not specially provided for in this act, twenty per centum ad valorem.
>11. Chalk, prepared, precipitated, French, red, and all other chalk preparations not specially provided for in this act, twenty per centum ad valorem.
>12. Chloral hydrate, twenty-five per centum ad valorem.

17. Chloroform, twenty-five cents per pound.
   13. Chloroform, twenty-five cents per pound.

COAL-TAR PREPARATIONS—
18. All coal-tar colors or dyes, by whatever name known, and not specially provided for in this act, thirty-five per centum ad valorem.
   COAL-TAR PREPARATIONS:
   14. All coal-tar colors or dyes, by whatever name known, and not specially provided for in this act, twenty per centum ad valorem.

19. All preparations of coal-tar, not colors or dyes, not specially provided for in this act, twenty per centum ad valorem.
   Placed upon free list. Par. 443.

20. Cobalt, oxide of, thirty cents per pound.
   Placed upon free list. Par. 444.

21. Collodion and all compounds of pyroxyline, by whatever name known, fifty cents per pound; rolled or in sheets, but not made up into articles, sixty cents per pound; if in finished or partly finished articles, sixty cents per pound and twenty-five per centum ad valorem.
   15. Collodion and all compounds of pyroxyline, by whatever name known, forty cents per pound; rolled or in sheets, but not made up into articles, fifty cents per pound; if in finished or partly finished articles, forty-five per centum ad valorem.

22. Coloring for brandy; wine, beer, or other liquors, fifty per centum ad valorem.
   16. Coloring for brandy, wine, beer, or other liquors, [fifty] *thirty* per centum ad valorem.

23. Copperas or sulphate of iron, three-tenths of one cent per pound.
   Placed upon free list. Par. 455.

24. Drugs, such as barks, beans, berries, balsams, buds, bulbs, and bulbous roots, and excrescences, such as nut-galls, fruits, flowers, dried fibers, grains, gums, and gum resins, herbs, leaves, lichens, mosses, nuts, roots and stems, spices, vegetables, seeds (aromatic, not garden seeds), and seeds of morbid growth, weeds, woods used expressly for dyeing, and dried insects, any of the foregoing which are not edible, but which have been advanced in value or condition by refining or grinding, or by other process of manufacture, and not specially provided for in this act, ten per centum ad valorem.
   Placed upon free list. Par. 470.

25. Ethers sulphuric, forty cents per pound; spirits of nitrous ether, twenty-five cents per pound; fruit ethers, oils, or essences, two dollars and fifty cents per pound; ethers of all kinds not specially provided for in this act, one dollar per pound.
   17. Ethers sulphuric, thirty-five cents per pound; spirits of nitrous ether, twenty cents per pound; fruit ethers, oils, or essences, one dollar per pound; ether of all kinds not specially provided for in this act, one dollar per pound.

26. Extracts and decoctions of logwood and other dye-woods, extract of sumac, and extracts of barks, such as are commonly used for dyeing or tanning, not specially provided for in this act, seven-eighths of one cent per pound; extracts of hemlock bark one-half of one cent per pound.
   18. Extracts and decoctions of logwood and other dye-woods, extract of sumac, and extracts of barks, such as are commonly used for dyeing or tanning, not specially provided for in this act, and extracts of hemlock bark, ten per centum ad valorem.

27. Gelatine, glue, and isinglass, or fish-glue, valued at not above seven cents per pound, one and one-half cents per pound valued at above seven cents per pound and not above thirty cents per pound, twenty-five per centum ad valorem; valued at above thirty cents per pound, thirty per centum ad valorem.
> 19. Gelatine, glue, isinglass or fish-glue, and prepared fish-sounds, twenty-five per centum ad valorem.

28. Glycerine, crude, not purified, one and three-fourths cents per pound. Refined, four and one-half cents per pound.
> 20. Glycerine, crude, [not] purified, one cent per pound. Refined, three cents per pound.

29. Indigo, extracts, or pastes of, three-fourths of one cent per pound; carmined, ten cents per pound.
> Placed upon free list. Par. 514.

30. Ink and ink-powders, printers' ink, and all other ink not specially provided for in this act, thirty per centum ad valorem.
> 21. Ink and ink-powders, printers' ink, and all other ink not specially provided for in this act, twenty per centum ad valorem.

31. Iodine, resublimed, thirty cents per pound.
> Placed upon free list. Par. 515.

32. Iodoform, one dollar and fifty cents per pound.
> 22. Iodoform, [one dollar per pound] *twenty-five per centum ad valorem*.

33. Licorice, extracts of, in paste, rolls, or other forms, five and one-half cents per pound.
> 23. Licorice, extracts of, in paste, rolls, or other forms, [five] *four cents per pound.*

34. Magnesia, carbonate of, medicinal, four cents per pound calcined, eight cents per pound; sulphate of, or Epsom salts, three-tenths of one cent per pound.
> 24. Magnesia, carbonate of, medicinal, [three cents per pound;] *and* calcined, [seven cents per pound;] *thirty per centum ad valorem;* sulphate of or Epsom salts, free.

35. Morphia, or morphine, and all salts thereof, fifty cents per ounce.
> 25. Morphia, or morphine, and all salts thereof, seventy-five cents per ounce.

OILS.—

36. Alizarine assistant, or soluble oil, or oleate of soda, or Turkey red oil, containing fifty per centum or more of castor oil, eighty cents per gallon; containing less than fifty per centum of castor oil, forty cents per gallon; all other, thirty per centum ad valorem.
> OILS:
> 26. Alizarine assistant, or soluble oil, or oleate of soda, or Turkey red oil, thirty per centum ad valorem.

37. Castor oil, eighty cents per gallon.
> 27. Castor oil, thirty-five cents per gallon.

38. Cod-liver oil, fifteen cents per gallon.
> 28. Cod-liver oil, twenty per centum ad valorem.

39. Cotton-seed oil, ten cents per gallon of seven and one-half pounds weight.
> Placed upon free list. Par. 568.

40. Croton oil, thirty cents per pound
> Placed upon free list. Par. 568.

41. Flaxseed or linseed and poppy-seed oil, raw, boiled, or oxidized, thirty-two cents per gallon of seven and one-half pounds weight.
>29. Flaxseed or linseed and poppy-seed oil, raw, boiled, or oxidized, fifteen cents per gallon of seven and one-half pounds weight.

42. Fusel oil, or amylic alcohol, ten per centum ad valorem.
>30. Fusel oil, or amylic alcohol, ten per centum ad valorem.

43. Hemp-seed oil and rape-seed oil, ten cents per gallon.
>31. Hemp-seed oil and rape-seed oil, ten cents per gallon.

44. Olive oil, fit for salad purposes, thirty-five cents per gallon.
>32. Olive oil, fit for salad purposes, [thirty-five cents per gallon] *twenty-five per centum ad valorem.*

45. Peppermint oil, eighty cents per pound.
>33. Peppermint oil, [twenty-five] *twenty* per centum ad valorem.

46. Seal, herring, whale, and other fish oil, not specially provided for in this act, eight cents per gallon.
>34. Seal, herring, whale, and other fish oil not specially provided for in this act, [twenty-five] *twenty* per centum ad valorem. [Cod oil, fifteen per centum ad valorem.]

47. Opium, aqueous extract of, for medicinal uses, and tincture of, as laudanum, and all other liquid preparations of opium, not specially provided for in this act, forty per centum ad valorem.
>35. Opium, aqueous extract of, for medicinal uses, and tincture of, as laudanum, and all other liquid preparations of opium, not specially provided for in this act, [twenty-five] *twenty* per centum ad valorem.

48. Opium containing less than nine per centum of morphia, and opium prepared for smoking, twelve dollars per pound; but opium prepared for smoking and other preparations of opium deposited in bonded warehouse shall not be removed therefrom without payment of duties, and such duties shall not be refunded.
>36. Opium, crude or unmanufactured, and not adulterated, containing nine per centum and over of morphia, one dollar per pound. Opium containing less than nine per centum of morphia, and opium prepared for smoking, six dollars per pound; but opium prepared for smoking and other preparations of opium deposited in bonded warehouse shall not be removed therefrom without payment of duties, and such duties shall not be refunded. [See also Par. 663.]

PAINTS, COLORS, AND VARNISHES.—
49. Baryta, sulphate of, or barytes, including barytes earth, unmanufactured, one dollar and twelve cents per ton; manufactured, six dollars and seventy-two cents per ton.
>PAINTS, COLORS, AND VARNISHES:
>37. Baryta, sulphate of, or barytes, manufactured, [three dollars per ton] *twenty-five per centum ad valorem.*

50. Blues, such as Berlin, Prussian, Chinese, and all others, containing ferrocyanide of iron, dry or ground in or mixed with oil, six cents per pound; in pulp or mixed with water six cents per pound on the material contained therein when dry.
>38. Blues, such as Berlin, Prussian, Chinese, and all others, containing ferrocyanide of iron, dry or ground in or mixed with oil, six cents per pound; *and* in pulp or mixed with water, six cents per pound on the material contained therein when dry.

51. Blanc-fixe, or satin white, or artificial sulphate of barytes, three-fourths of one cent per pound.
>39. Blanc-fixe, or satin white, or arificial sulphate of baytes, twenty-five per centum ad valorem.

52. Black, made from bone, ivory, or vegetable, under whatever name known, including bone black and lamp-black, dry or ground in oil or water, twenty-five per centum ad valorem.

>40. Black, made from bone, ivory, or vegetable, under whatever name known, including bone black and lampblack, dry or ground in oil or water, twenty per centum ad valorem.

53. Chrome yellow, chrome green, and all other chromium colors in which lead and bichromate of potash or soda are component parts, dry, or ground in or mixed with oil, four and one-half cents per pound; in pulp or mixed with water, four and one-half cents per pound on the material contained therein when dry.

>41. Chrome yellow, chrome green, and all other chromium colors in which lead and bichromate of potash or soda are component parts, dry, or ground in or mixed with oil, or in pulp or mixed with water, two and one-quarter cents per pound on the material contained therein when dry.

54. Ocher and ochery earths, sienna and sienna earths, umber and umber earths not specially provided for in this act, dry, one-fourth of one cent per pound; ground in oil, one and one-half cents per pound.

>42. Ocher and ochery earths, sienna and sienna earths, umber and umber earths, ground in oil, [one and one-fourth of one cent per pound] *twenty-five per centum ad valorem.*
>NOTE.—Ocher, etc., dry. See free list. Par. 566.

55. Ultramarine blue, four and one-half cents per pound.

>43. Ultramarine blue, whether dry, in pulp or mixed with water, and wash blue containing ultramarine, twenty per centum ad valorem.

56. Varnishes, including so-called gold size or japan, thirty-five per centum ad valorem; and on spirit varnishes for the alcohol contained therein, one dollar and thirty-two cents per gallon additional.

>44. Varnishes, including so-called gold size or japan, twenty-five per centum ad valorem; and on spirit varnishes for the alcohol contained therein, one dollar and thirty-two cents per gallon additional.

57. Vermilion red, and colors containing quicksilver, dry or ground in oil or water, twelve cents per pound.

>45. Vermilion red, and other colors containing quicksilver, dry or ground in oil or water, twenty per centum ad valorem. Vermilion red, not containing quicksilver, but made of lead or containing lead, six cents per pound.

58. Wash blue, containing ultramarine, three cents per pound.

>NOTE.—Consolidated with paragraph 43, ultramarine blue.

59. Whiting and Paris white, dry, one-half of one cent per pound; ground in oil, or putty, one cent per pound.

>46. Whiting and Paris white, dry, and ground in oil, or putty, [twenty-five] *thirty-five* per centum ad valorem.

60. Zinc, oxide of, and white paint, containing zinc, but not containing lead, dry, one and one-fourth cents per pound; ground in oil, one and three-fourth cents per pound.

>47. Zinc, oxide of, and white zinc paint or pigment, dry or ground in oil, [twenty] *twenty-five* per centum ad valorem.

61. All other paints and colors, whether dry or mixed, or ground in water or oil, including lakes, crayons, smalts, and frostings, not specially provided for in this act, and artists' colors of all kinds, in tubes or otherwise, twenty-five per centum ad valorem; all paints and colors, mixed or ground with water or solutions other than oil, and commercially known as artists' water color paints, thirty per centum ad valorem.

> 48. All other paints, colors, and pigments, whether dry or mixed, or ground in water or oil, or other solutions, including all colors in tubes, lakes, crayons, smalts, and frostings, and not specially provided for in this act, twenty-five per centum ad valorem.

LEAD PRODUCTS.—

62. Acetate of lead, white, five and one-half cents per pound; brown, three and one-half cents per pound.

> LEAD PRODUCTS:
> 49. Acetate of lead, white, two and three-quarters cents per pound; brown, one and three-quarter cents per pound;

63. Litharge, three cents per pound.

> 49. Litharge, one and one-half cents per pound.

64. Nitrate of lead, three cents per pound.

> 50. Nitrate of lead, one and one-half cents per pound.

65. Orange mineral, three and one-half cents per pound.

> 51. Orange mineral, one and three-quarters cents per pound;

66. Red lead, three cents per pound.

> 51. Red lead, one and one-half cents per pound.

67. White lead, and white paint containing lead, dry or in pulp, or ground or mixed with oil, three cents per pound.

> 52. White lead, and white paint and pigment containing lead, dry or in pulp, or ground or mixed with oil, one and one-half cents per pound.

68. Phosphorus, twenty cents per pound.

> 53. Phosphorus, twenty-five per centum ad valorem.

POTASH.—

69. Bichromate and chromate of, three cents per pound.

> POTASH:
> 54. Bichromate and chromate of, [twenty] *twenty-five* per centum ad valorem.

70. Caustic or hydrate of, refined in sticks or rolls, one cent per pound.

> Placed upon free list. Par. 595.

71. Hydriodate, iodide, and iodate of, fifty cents per pound.

> 55. Hydriodate, iodide, and iodate of, [twenty-five cents per pound] *ten per centum ad valorem.*

72. Nitrate of, or saltpeter, refined, one cent per pound.

> 56. Nitrate of, or saltpeter, refined, [one-half of one cent per pound] *ten per centum ad valorem.*

73. Prussiate of, red, ten cents per pound; yellow, five cents per pound.

> 57. Prussiate of, red, or yellow, twenty per centum ad valorem.

PREPARATIONS.—

74. All medicinal preparations, including medicinal proprietary preparations, of which alcohol is a component part, or in the preparation of which alcohol is used, not specially provided for in this act, fifty cents per pound.

> PREPARATIONS:
> 58. All medicinal preparations, including medicinal proprietary preparations, of which alcohol is a component part, or in the preparation of which alcohol is used, not specially provided for in this act, fifty cents per pound. *Provided,* That no such preparation shall pay less than twenty-five per centum ad valorem.

75. All medicinal preparations, including medicinal proprietary preparations, of which alcohol is not a component part, and not specially provided for in this act, twenty-five per centum ad valorem; calomel and other mercurial medicinal preparations, thirty-five per centum ad valorem.

> 59. All medicinal preparations, not specially provided for in this act, twenty-five per centum ad valorem.

76. Products or preparations known as alkalies, alkaloids, distilled oils, essential oils, expressed oils, rendered oils, and all combinations of the foregoing, and all chemical compounds and salts, not specially provided for in this act, twenty-five per centum ad valorem.

> 60. Products or preparations known as alkalies, alkaloids, distilled oils, essential oils, expressed oils, rendered oils, and all combinations of the foregoing, and all chemical compounds and salts, not specially provided for in this act, twenty-five per centum ad valorem.

77. Preparations used as applications to the hair, mouth, teeth, or skin, such as cosmetics, dentifrices, pastes, pomades, powders, and tonics, including all known as toilet preparations, not specially provided for in this act, fifty per centum ad valorem.

> 61. Preparations used as applications to the hair, mouth, teeth, or skin, such as cosmetics, dentifrices, pastes, pomades, powders, and all toilet preparations and articles of perfumery, not specially provided for in this act, [forty] *thirty* per centum ad valorem.

78. Santonine, and all salts thereof containing eighty per centum or over of santonine, two dollars and fifty cents per pound.

> 62. Santonine, and all salts thereof containing eighty per centum or over of santonine, one dollar per pound.

79. Soap: Castile soap, one and one-fourth cents per pound; fancy perfumed, and all descriptions of toilet soap, fifteen cents per pound; all other soaps, not specially provided for in this act, twenty per centum ad valorem.

> 63. Soap: Castile soap, twenty per centum ad valorem; fancy, perfumed and all descriptions of toilet soap, [thirty-five] *thirty* per centum ad valorem; all other soaps, not specially provided for in this act, ten per centum ad valorem.

SODA.—

80. Bicarbonate of soda or supercarbonate of soda or saleratus, one cent per pound.

> SODA:
> 64. Bicarbonate of soda or supercarbonate of soda or saleratus, [one-half cent per pound] *thirty per centum ad valorem.*

81. Hydrate of or caustic soda, one cent per pound.

> 65. Hydrate of, or caustic soda, [one-half of one cent per pound] *twenty-five per centum ad valorem.*

82. Bichromate and chromate of, three cents per pound.
> 66. Bichromate and chromate of, [twenty] *twenty-five* per centum ad valorem.

83. Sal-soda, or soda-crystals, and soda-ash, one-fourth of one cent per pound.
> 67. Sal-soda, or soda-crystals, [one-eighth of one cent per pound;] *and* soda-ash, [one-fourth of one cent per pound] *twenty per centum ad valorem.*

84. Silicate of soda, or other alkaline silicate, one-half of one cent per pound.
> 68. Silicate of soda, or other alkaline silicate, [one-fourth of one cent per pound] *twenty per centum ad valorem.*

85. Sulphate of soda, or salt-cake or niter-cake, one dollar and twenty-five cents per ton.
> Placed upon the free list. Par. 622.

86. Sponges, twenty per centum ad valorem.
> 69. Sponges, ten per centum ad valorem.

87. Strychnia, or strychnine, and all salts thereof, forty cents per ounce.
> 70. Strychnia, or strychnine, and all salts thereof, thirty per centum ad valorem.

88. Sulphur, refined, eight dollars per ton; sublimed or flowers of ten dollars per ton.
> 71. Sulphur, sublimed, or flowers of, twenty per centum ad valorem.
> NOTE.—Sulphur refined on free list. See paragraph 642.

89. Sumac, ground, four-tenths of one cent per pound.
> 72. Sumac, ground, ten per centum ad valorem.

90. Tartar, cream of, and patent tartar, six cents per pound.
> 73. Tartar, cream of, and patent tartar, [twenty-five] *twenty* per centum ad valorem.

91. Tartars and lees crystals, partly refined, four cents per pound.
> 74. Tartars and lees crystals, partly refined, [twenty-five] *twenty* per centum ad valorem.

92. Tartrate of soda and potassa, or Rochelle salts, three cents per pound.
> 75. Tartrate of soda and potassa, or Rochelle salts, ten per centum ad valorem.

SCHEDULE B.—EARTHS, EARTHENWARE, AND GLASSWARE.

BRICK AND TILE—
93. Fire-brick, not glazed, enameled, ornamented, or decorated in any manner, one dollar and twenty-five cents per ton; glazed, enameled, ornamented, or decorated, forty-five percentum ad valorem.
> BRICK AND TILE:
> 76. Brick, not glazed, enameled, ornamented, or decorated in any manner, [twenty] *Twenty-five* per centum ad valorem; glazed, enameled, ornamented, or decorated, thirty per centum ad valorem.
> 77. Magnesic fire-brick, one dollar per ton.

94. Tiles and brick, other than fire brick, not glazed, ornamented, painted, enameled, vitrified, or decorated, twenty-five per centum ad valorem; ornamented, glazed, painted, enameled, vitrified, or decorated, and all encaustic, forty-five per centum ad valorem.

> 78. Tiles, plain and encaustic, not glazed, ornamented, painted, enameled, vitrified, or decorated, twenty-five per centum ad valorem; ornamented, glazed, painted, enameled, vitrified, or decorated, forty per centum ad valorem.

CEMENT, LIME, AND PLASTER—

95. Roman, Portland, and other hydraulic cement, in barrels, sacks, or other packages, eight cents per one hundred pounds, including weight of barrel or package; in bulk, seven cents per one hundred pounds; other cement, twenty per centum ad valorem.

CEMENT, LIME, AND PLASTER:
> 79. Roman, Portland, and other hydraulic cement, in barrels, sacks, or other packages, eight cents per one hundred pounds, including weight of barrel or package; in bulk, seven cents per one hundred pounds; other cement, ten per centum ad valorem.

96. Lime, six cents per one hundred pounds, including weight of barrel or package.

> 80. Lime, *including the value of the covering or barrel*, [ten] *fifteen* per centum ad valorem.

97. Plaster of Paris, or gypsum, ground, one dollar per ton; calcined, one dollar and seventy-five cents per ton.

> 81. Plaster of Paris, or gypsum, ground, [ten per centum ad valorem] *one dollar per ton*; calcined, [fifteen per centum ad valorem] *one dollar and twenty-five cents per ton.*

CLAYS OR EARTHS—

98. Clays or earths, unwrought or unmanufactured, not specially provided for in this act, one dollar and fifty cents per ton; wrought or manufactured, not specially provided for in this act, three dollars per ton; china, clay, or kaolin, three dollars per ton.

CLAYS OR EARTHS:
> 82. Clays or earths, wrought or manufactured, not specially provided for in this act, one dollar per ton; china clay, or kaolin, two dollars per ton.
> NOTE.—Clays or earths, unwrought or unmanufactured, not specially provided for in this act, free list.

EARTHENWARE AND CHINA—

99. Common brown earthenware, common stoneware, and crucibles, not ornamented or decorated in any manner, twenty-five per centum ad valorem.

EARTHENWARE AND CHINA:
> 83. Common yellow and brown earthenware, plain or embossed, common stoneware, and crucibles, not decorated in any manner, twenty per centum ad valorem.

100. China, porcelain, parian, bisque, earthen, stone, and crockery ware, including plaques, ornaments, toys, charms, vases, and statuettes, painted, tinted, stained, enameled, printed, gilded, or otherwise decorated or ornamented in any manner, sixty per centum ad valorem if plain white, and not ornamented or decorated in any manner, fifty-five per centum ad valorem.

> 84. China, porcelain, parian, bisque, earthen, stone, and crockery ware, including plaques, ornaments, toys, charms, vases, and statuettes, plain white, and not decorated in any manner, [thirty-five] *forty* per centum ad valorem.

85. China, porcelain, parian, bisque, earthen, stone, and crockery ware, including plaques, ornaments, toys, charms, vases, and statuettes, painted, tinted, stained, enameled, printed, gilded, or otherwise decorated in any manner, [forty] *forty-five* per centum ad valorem.

101. All other china, porcelain, parian, bisque, earthen, stone, and crockery ware, and manufactures of the same, by whatsoever designation or name known in the trade, including lava tips for burners, not specially provided for in this act, if ornamented or decorated in any manner, sixty per centum ad valorem; if not ornamented or decorated, fifty-five per centum ad valorem.

86. All other china, porcelain, parian, bisque, earthen, stone, and crockery ware, including lava tips for burners, not specially provided for in this act, if decorated in any manner, forty per centum ad valorem; if not decorated, thirty-five per centum ad valorem.

102. Gas-retorts, three dollars each.

87. Gas-retorts, twenty per centum ad valorem.

GLASS AND GLASSWARE—

103. Green, and colored, molded or pressed, and flint, and lime glass bottles, holding more than one pint, and demijohns, and carboys (covered or uncovered), and other molded or pressed green and colored and flint or lime bottle glassware, not specially provided for in this act, one cent per pound. Green, and colored, molded or pressed, and flint, and lime glass bottles, and vials holding not more than one pint and not less than one-quarter of a pint, one and one-half cents per pound; if holding less than one-fourth of a pint, fifty cents per gross.

GLASS AND GLASSWARE:
88. Plain green, and colored, molded or pressed, and flint, and lime glassware, including bottles, vials, demijohns, and carboys (covered or uncovered), whether filled or unfilled, and whether their contents be dutiable or free, not specially provided for in this act, [thirty] *forty* per centum ad valorem.

104. All articles enumerated in the preceding paragraph, if filled, and not otherwise provided for in this act, and the contents are subject to an ad valorem rate of duty, or to a rate of duty based upon the value, the value of such bottles, vials, or other vessels shall be added to the value of the contents for the ascertainment of the dutiable value of the latter; but if filled, and not otherwise provided for in this act, and the contents are not subject to an ad valorem rate of duty, or to rate of duty based on the value, or are free of duty, such bottles, vials, or other vessels shall pay, in addition to the duty, if any, on their contents, the rates of duty prescribed in the preceding paragraph: *Provided,* That no article manufactured from glass described in the preceding paragraph shall pay a less rate of duty than forty per centum ad valorem.

105. Flint and lime, pressed glassware, not cut, engraved, painted, etched, decorated, colored, printed, stained, silvered, or gilded, sixty per centum ad valorem).

106. All articles of glass, cut, engraved, painted, colored, printed, stained, decorated, silvered, or gilded, not including plate glass, silvered, or looking-glass plates, sixty per centum ad valorem.

89. All articles of glass, cut, engraved, painted, colored, printed, stained, decorated, silvered, or gilded, not including plate glass, silvered, or looking-glass plates, [thirty-five] *forty* per centum ad valorem.

107. Chemical glassware for use in laboratory, and not otherwise specially provided for in this act, forty-five per centum ad valorem.

108. Thin blown glass, blown with or without a mold, including glass chimneys and all other manufactures of glass, or of which glass shall be the component material of chief value, not specially provided for in this act, sixty per centum ad valorem.

109. Heavy blown glass, blown with or without a mold, not cut or decorated, finished or unfinished, sixty per centum ad valorem.

110. Porcelain or opal glassware, sixty per centum ad valorem.

111. All cut, engraved, painted, or otherwise ornamented or decorated glass bottles, decanters, or other vessels of glass shall, if filled, pay duty in addition to any duty chargeable on the contents, as if not filled, unless otherwise specially provided for in this act.

> 90. All glass bottles, decanters, or other vessels or articles of glass, when cut, engraved, painted, colored, printed, stained, etched, or otherwise ornamented or decorated, except such as have ground necks and stoppers only, not specially provided for in this act, including porcelain or opal glassware, [thirty-five] *forty* per centum ad valorem: *Provided*, That if such articles shall be imported filled, the same shall pay duty, in addition to any duty chargeable upon the contents as if not filled, unless otherwise specially provided for in this act.

112. Unpolished cylinder, crown, and common window glass, not exceeding ten by fifteen inches square, one and three-eighths cents per pound); above that, and not exceeding sixteen by twenty-four inches square, one and seven-eighths cents per pound; above that, and not exceeding twenty-four by thirty inches square, two and three-eighths cents per pound; above that, and not exceeding twenty-four by thirty-six inches square, two and seven-eighths cents per pound; all above that, three and one-eighths cents per pound: *Provided*, That unpolished, cylinder, crown, and common window glass, imported in boxes, shall contain fifty square feet, as nearly as sizes will permit, and the duty shall be computed thereon according to the actual weight of glass.

> 91. Unpolished cylinder, crown, and common window glass, not exceeding sixteen by twenty-four inches square, one *and one-eighth* [cent] *cents* per pound; above that, and not exceeding twenty-four by thirty inches square, one and [one-eighth] *one-fourth* cents per pound; above that, and not exceeding twenty-four by thirty-six inches square, one and [three-eighths] *one-half* cents per pound; all above that, one and [one-half] *five-eighths* cents per pound.

113. Cylinder and crown glass, polished, not exceeding sixteen by twenty-four inches square, four cents per square foot; above that, and not exceeding twenty-four by thirty inches square, six cents per square foot; above that, and not exceeding twenty-four by sixty inches square, twenty cents per square foot; above that, forty cents per square foot.

> 92. Cylinder and crown glass, polished, not exceeding sixteen by twenty-four inches square, two and one-half cents per square foot; above that, and not exceeding twenty-four by thirty inches square, four cents per square foot; above that, and not exceeding twenty-four by sixty inches square, fifteen cents per square foot; above that, twenty cents per square foot.

114. Fluted, rolled, or rough plate glass, not including crown, cylinder, or common window glass, not exceeding ten by fifteen inches square, three-fourths of one cent per square foot; above that, and not exceeding sixteen by twenty-four inches square, one cent per square foot; above that, and not exceeding twenty-four by thirty inches square, one and one-half cents per square foot; all above that, two cents per square foot; and all fluted, rolled, or rough plate glass, weighing over one hundred pounds per one hundred square feet, shall pay an additional duty on the excess at the same rates herein imposed: *Provided*, That all of the above plate glass, when ground, smoothed, or otherwise obscured, shall be subject to the same rate of duty as cast polished plate glass unsilvered.

93. Fluted, rolled, or rough plate glass, not including crown, cylinder, or common window glass, not exceeding sixteen by twenty-four inches square, three-fourths of one cent per square foot; above that, and not exceeding twenty-four by thirty inches square, one cent per square foot; all above that, one and one-half cents per square foot; and all fluted, rolled, or rough plate glass, weighing over one hundred pounds per one hundred square feet, shall pay an additional duty on the excess at the same rates herein imposed: *Provided*, That all of the above plate glass, when ground, smoothed, or otherwise obscured, shall be subject to the same rate of duty as cast polished plate glass unsilvered.

115. Cast polished plate-glass, finished or unfinished and unsilvered, not exceeding sixteen by twenty-four inches square, five cents per square foot; above that, and not exceeding twenty-four by thirty inches square, eight cents per square foot; above that, and not exceeding twenty-four by sixty inches square, twenty-five cents per square foot; all above that, fifty cents per square foot.

94. Cast polished plate-glass, finished or unfinished and unsilvered, not exceeding sixteen by twenty-four inches square, five cents per square foot; above that, and not exceeding twenty-four by thirty inches square, eight cents per square foot; above that, and not exceeding twenty-four by sixty inches square, [eighteen] *twenty* cents per square foot; all above that, [thirty] *thirty-five* cents per square foot.

116. Cast polished plate-glass, silvered, and looking-glass plates, not exceeding sixteen by twenty-four inches square, six cents per square foot; above that, and not exceeding twenty-four by thirty inches square, ten cents per square foot; above that, and not exceeding twenty-four by sixty inches square, thirty-five cents per square foot; all above that, sixty cents per square foot.

95. Cast polished plate-glass, silvered, and looking-glass plates, exceeding in size one hundred and forty-four square inches and not exceeding sixteen by twenty-four inches square, six cents per square foot; above that, and not exceeding twenty-four by thirty inches square, ten cents per square foot; above that, and not exceeding twenty-four by sixty inches square, twenty cents per square foot; all above that, thirty-five cents per square foot.

117. But no looking-glass plates, or plate glass silvered, when framed, shall pay a less rate of duty than that imposed upon similar glass of like description not framed, but shall pay in addition thereto upon such frames the rate of duty applicable thereto when imported separate.

96. But no looking-glass plates or plate glass, silvered, when framed, shall pay a less rate of duty than that imposed upon similar glass of like description not framed, but shall pay in addition thereto upon such frames the rate of duty applicable thereto when imported separate.

118. Cast polished plate glass, silvered or unsilvered, and cylinder, crown, or common window glass, when ground, obscured, frosted, sanded, enameled, beveled, etched, embossed, engraved, stained, colored, or otherwise ornamented or decorated, shall be subject to a duty of ten per centum ad valorem in addition to the rates otherwise chargeable thereon.

> 97. Cast polished plate glass, silvered or unsilvered, and cylinder, crown, or common window glass, when ground, obscured, frosted, sanded, enameled, beveled, etched, embossed, engraved, flashed, stained, colored, painted, or otherwise ornamented or decorated, shall be subject to a duty of ten per centum ad valorem in addition to the rates otherwise chargeable thereon.

119. Spectacles and eye-glasses, or spectacles and eye glass frames, sixty per centum ad valorem.

> 98. Spectacles, eyeglasses, goggles, opera glasses, and other optical instruments, and frames for the same, thirty-five per centum ad valorem.

120. On lenses costing one dollar and fifty cents per gross pairs or less, sixty per centum ad valorem.

> 99. Glass beads, loose, strung or carded, ten per centum ad valorem.

121. Spectacle and eyeglass lenses with their edges ground or beveled to fit frames, sixty per centum ad valorem.

> 100. Lenses of glass or pebble, wholly or partly manufactured, thirty-five per centum ad valorem.

122. All stained or painted window-glass and stained or painted glass windows, and hand, pocket or table mirrors not exceeding in size one hundred and forty-four square inches, with or without frames or cases, of whatever material composed, lenses of glass or pebble, wholly or partly manufactured, and not specially provided for in this act, and fusible enamel, forty-five per centum ad valorem.

> 101. Fusible enamel, and glass slides for magic lanterns, twenty-five per centum ad valorem.
> 102. All stained or painted window-glass and stained or painted glass windows, and all mirrors not exceeding in size one hundred and forty-four square inches, with or without frames or cases, and all manufactures of glass, or of which glass is the component of chief value, not specially provided for in this act, thirty-five per centum ad valorem: *Provided,* That bent glass shall pay the same rates of duty as the like glass when flat.

MARBLE AND STONE, AND MANUFACTURES OF—

123. Marble of all kinds in block, rough or squared, sixty-five cents per cubic foot.

> MARBLE AND STONE, AND MANUFACTURES OF:
> 103. Marble of all kinds in block, rough or squared only, forty cents per cubic foot.

124. Veined marble, sawed, dressed, or otherwise, including marble slabs and marble paving tiles, one dollar and ten cents per cubic foot (but in measurement no slab shall be computed at less than one inch in thickness).

> 104. Marble, sawed, dressed, or otherwise, including marble slabs, mosaic cubes, and marble paving tiles, seventy-five cents per cubic foot (no slab to be computed at less than one inch in thickness).

125. Manufactures of marble not specially provided for in this act, fifty per centum ad valorem.

> 105. Manufactures of marble, onyx, or alabaster, not specially provided for in this act, thirty per centum ad valorem.

STONE—
126. Burr-stones manufactured or bound up into mill-stones, fifteen per centum ad valorem.
> STONE:
> Placed upon free list. Par. 638.

127. Freestone, granite, sandstone, limestone, and other building or monumental stone, except marble, unmanufactured or undressed, not specially provided for in this act, eleven cents per cubic foot.
> Placed upon free list. Par. 638.

128. Freestone, granite, sandstone, limestone, and other building or monumental stone, except marble, not specially provided for in this act, hewn, dressed, or polished, forty per centum ad valorem.
> 106. Freestone, granite, sandstone, limestone, and other building or monumental stone, except marble, not specially provided for in this act, hewn, dressed, or polished, twenty per centum ad valorem.

129. Grindstones, finished or unfinished, one dollar and seventy-five cents per ton.
> 107. Grindstones, finished or unfinished, [one dollar and seventy-five cents per ton] *ten per centum ad valorem.*

SLATE—
130. Slates, slate chimney pieces, mantels, slabs for tables, and all other manufactures of slate, not specially provided for in this act, thirty per centum ad valorem.
> SLATE:
> 108. Slates, slate chimney-pieces, mantels, slabs for tables, and all other manufactures of slate, not specially provided for in this act, twenty per centum ad valorem.

131. Roofing slates, twenty-five per centum ad valorem.
> 109. Roofing slates, [ten] *twenty* per centum ad valorem.

SCHEDULE C.—METALS AND MANUFACTURES OF.

IRON AND STEEL.

132. Chromate of iron, or chromic ore, fifteen per centum ad valorem.
> Placed upon free list. Par. 438.

133. Iron ore, including manganiferous iron ore, also the dross or residuum from burnt pyrites, seventy-five cents per ton. Sulphur ore, as pyrites, or sulphuret of iron in its natural state, containing not more than three and one-half per centum copper, seventy-five cents per ton: *Provided,* That ore containing more than two per centum of copper shall pay, in addition thereto, one-half of one cent per pound for the copper contained therein: *Provided, also,* That sulphur ore as pyrites or sulphuret of iron in its natural state, containing in excess of twenty-five per centum of sulphur, shall be free of duty, except on the copper contained therein, as above provided: *And provided further,* That in levying and collecting the duty on iron ore no deduction shall be made from the weight of the ore on account of moisture which may be chemically or physically combined therewith.
> [HOUSE ACTION.—Iron ore, including manganiferous iron ore, also the dross or residuum from burnt pyrites and sulphur ore, as pyrites, or sulphuret of iron in its natural state, placed upon free list. Par. 518.]
> SENATE ACTION, 109½.—*Iron ore, including manganiferous iron ore, also the dross or residuum from burnt pyrites, forty cents per ton.*

134. Iron in pigs, iron kentledge, spiegeleisen, ferro-manganese ferro-silicon, wrought and cast scrap iron, and scrap steel, three-tenths of one cent per pound; but nothing shall be deemed scrap iron or scrap steel except waste or refuse iron or steel fit only to be remanufactured.

> 110. Iron in pigs, iron kentledge, spiegeleisen, ferro-silicon, [twenty] *twenty-two and one-half* per centum ad valorem; wrought and cast scrap iron, and scrap steel, ten per centum ad valorem; but nothing shall be deemed scrap iron or scrap steel except waste or refuse iron or steel fit only to be remanufactured; ferro-manganese, ten per centum ad valorem.

135. Bar-iron, rolled or hammered, comprising flats not less than one inch wide, nor less than three-eighths of one inch thick, eight-tenths of one cent per pound; round iron not less than three-fourths of one inch in diameter, and square iron not less than three-fourths of one inch square, nine-tenths of one cent per pound; flats less than one inch wide, or less than three-eighths of one inch thick; round iron less than three-fourths of one inch and not less than seven-sixteenths of one inch in diameter; and square iron less than three-fourths of one inch square, one cent per pound.

> 112. Bar-iron, rolled or hammered, round iron in coils or rods, and bars or shapes of rolled iron, [twenty-five] *twenty-eight* per centum ad valorem.

136. Round iron, in coils or rods, less than seven-sixteenths of one inch in diameter, and bars or shapes of rolled iron, not specially provided for in this act, one and one-tenth cents per pound: *Provided*, That all iron in slabs, blooms, loops, or other forms less finished than iron in bars, and more advanced than pig-iron, except castings, shall be rated as iron in bars, and be subject to a duty of eight-tenths of one cent per pound; and none of the iron above enumerated in this paragraph shall pay a less rate of duty than thirty-five per centum ad valorem: *Provided further*, That all iron bars, blooms, billets, or sizes or shapes of any kind, in the manufacture of which charcoal is used as fuel, shall be subject to a duty of not less than twenty-two dollars per ton.

> 111. All iron in slabs, blooms, loops, or other forms more advanced than pig-iron, and less finished than iron in bars, [twenty-two and one-half] *twenty-five* per centum ad valorem.

137. Beams, girders, joists, angles, channels, car-truck channels, TT, columns and posts or parts or sections of columns and posts, deck and bulb beams, and building forms, together with all other structural shapes of iron or steel, whether plain or punched, or fitted for use, nine-tenths of one cent per pound.

> 113. Beams, girders, joists, angles, channels, car-truck channels, TT, columns and posts or parts or sections of columns and posts, deck and bulb beams, and building forms, together with all other structural shapes of iron or steel, whether plain or punched, or fitted for use, [thirty] *thirty-five* per centum ad valorem.

138. Boiler or other plate iron or steel, except saw-plates hereinafter provided for, not thinner than number ten wire gauge, sheared or unsheared, and skelp iron or steel sheared or rolled in grooves, valued at one cent pound or less, five-tenths of one cent per pound; valued above one cent and not above one and four-tenths cents per pound, sixty-five hundredths of one cent per pound; valued above one and four-tenths cents and not above two cents per pound, eight-tenths of one cent per pound; valued above two cents and not above three cents per pound, one and one-tenth cents per pound; valued above three cents and not above four cents per pound, one and five-tenths cents per pound; valued above four cents and not above seven cents per

pound, two cents per pound; valued above seven cents and not above ten cents per pound, two and eight-tenths cents per pound; valued above ten cents and not above thirteen cents per pound, three and one-half cents per pound; valued above thirteen cents per pound, forty-five per centum ad valorem: *Provided*, That all plate iron or steel thinner than number ten wire gauge shall pay duty as iron or steel sheets.

    114. Boiler or other plate iron or steel, except saw plates hereinafter provided for, not thinner than number ten wire gauge, sheared or unsheared, and skelp iron or steel sheared or rolled in grooves, [twenty-five] *thirty* per centum ad valorem.

139. Forgings of iron or steel, or forged iron and steel combined, of whatever shape, or in whatever stage of manufacture, not specially provided for in this act, two and three-tenths cents per pound: *Provided*, That no forgings of iron or steel, or forgings of iron and steel combined, by whatever process made, shall pay a less rate of duty than forty-five per centum ad valorem.

    115. Forgings of iron or steel, or forged iron or steel combined, of whatever shape, or in whatever stage of manufacture, not specially provided for in this act, [twenty-five] *thirty* per centum ad valorem.

140. Hoop, or band, or scroll, or other iron or steel, valued at three cents per pound or less, eight inches or less in width, and less than three-eighths of one inch thick and not thinner than number ten wire gauge, one cent per pound; thinner than number ten wire gauge and not thinner than number twenty wire gauge, one and one-tenth cents per pound; thinner than number twenty wire gauge, one and three-tenths cents per pound: *Provided*, That hoop or band iron, or hoop or band steel, cut to length, or wholly or partially manufactured into hoops or ties for baling purposes, barrel hoops of iron or steel, and hoop or band iron or hoop or band steel flared, splayed or punched, with or without buckles or fastenings, shall pay two-tenths of one cent per pound more duty than that imposed on the hoop or band iron or steel from which they are made.

    116. Hoop, band, or scroll iron or steel, except as otherwise provided for in this act, [twenty-five] *thirty* per centum ad valorem.

141. Railway-bars, made of iron or steel, and railway-bars made in part of steel, T-rails, and punched iron or steel flat rails, six-tenths of one cent per pound.

    117. Railway bars, made of iron or steel, and railway bars made in part of steel, T-rails, and punched iron or steel flat rails, [twenty] *twenty-two and one-half* per centum ad valorem.

142. Sheets of iron or steel, common or black, including all iron or steel commercially known as common or black taggers iron or steel, and skelp iron or steel, valued at three cents per pound or less: Thinner than number ten and not thinner than number twenty wire gauge, one cent per pound; thinner than number twenty wire gauge, and not thinner than number twenty-five wire gauge, one and one-tenth cents per pound; thinner than number twenty-five wire gauge, one and four-tenths cents per pound; corrugated or crimped, one and four-tenths cents per pound: *Provided*, That all common or black sheet-iron or sheet-steel not thinner than number ten wire gauge shall pay duty as plate iron or plate steel.

    118. Sheets of iron or steel, common or black, excepting as hereinafter provided for, thinner than number ten wire gauge, and not thinner than number twenty-five wire gauge, including sheets which have been pickled or cleaned by acid, or by any other material or process, or which is cold rolled, smoothed only, not polished, shall pay a duty of thirty-five per

centum ad valorem. All sheets of iron or steel common or black, excepting as hereinafter provided for, thinner than number twenty-five wire gauge and all iron or steel commercially known as common or black taggers iron or steel or which have been pickled or cleaned by acid or by any other material or process or which is cold rolled, smoothed only, not polished, shall pay a duty of [nine-tenths] *three-fourths* of one cent per pound: *Provided*, That the reduction herein provided for as to sheets of iron or steel thinner than number twenty-five wire gauge shall take effect on and after October first, eighteen hundred and ninety-four.

143. All iron or steel sheets or plates, and all hoop, band, or scroll iron or steel, excepting what are known commercially as tin plates, terne plates, and taggers tin, and hereinafter provided for, when galvanized or coated with zinc or spelter, or other metals, or any alloy of those metals, shall pay three-fourths of one cent per pound more duty than the rates imposed by the preceding paragraph upon the corresponding gauges, or forms, of common or black sheet or taggers iron or steel; and on and after July first, eighteen hundred and ninety-one, all iron or steel sheets, or plates, or taggers iron coated with tin or lead or with a mixture of which these metals or either of them is a component part, by the dipping or any other process, and commercially known as tin plates, terne plates, and taggers tin, shall pay two and two-tenths cents per pound: *Provided*, That on and after July first, eighteen hundred and ninety-one, manufactures of which tin, tin plates, terne plates, taggers tin or either of them, are component materials of chief value, and all articles, vessels, or wares manufactured, stamped or drawn from sheet-iron or sheet-steel, such material being the component of chief value, and coated wholly or in part with tin or lead or a mixture of which these metals or either of them is a component part shall pay a duty of fifty-five per centum ad valorem: *Provided, further*, That on and after October first, eighteen hundred and ninety-seven, tin plates and terne plates lighter in weight than sixty-three pounds per hundred square feet shall be admitted free of duty, unless it shall be made to appear to the satisfaction of the President (who shall thereupon by proclamation make known the fact) that the aggregate quantity of such plates lighter than sixty-three pounds per hundred square feet produced in the United States during either of the six years next preceding June thirtieth, eighteen hundred and ninety-seven, has equaled one third the amount of such plates imported and entered for consumption during any fiscal year after the passage of this act, and prior to said October first, eighteen hundred and ninety-seven: *Provided*, That the amount of such plates manufactured into articles exported, and upon which a drawback shall be paid, shall not be included in ascertaining the amount of such importations: *And provided further*, That the amount or weight of sheet iron or sheet steel manufactured in the United States and applied or wrought in the manufacture of articles or wares tinned or terneplated in the United States, with weight allowance as sold to manufacturers or others, shall be considered as tin and terne plates produced in the United States within the meaning of this act.

119. All iron or steel sheets or plates, and all hoop, band, or scroll iron or steel, excepting what are known commercially as tin plates, terne plates, and taggers tin, and hereinafter provided for, when galvanized or coated with zinc or spelter, or other metals, or any alloy of those metals, thirty-five per centum ad valorem.

144. Sheet-iron or sheet-steel, polished, planished, or glanced, by whatever name designated, two and one-half cents per pound: *Provided*, That plate or sheet or taggers iron or steel, by whatever name designated, other than the polished, planished, or glanced herein provided for, which has been pickled or cleaned by acid, or by any other

material or process, or which is cold-rolled, smoothed only, not polished, shall pay one-quarter of one cent per pound more duty than the corresponding gauges of common or black sheet or taggers iron or steel.

> 120. Sheet-iron or sheet-steel, polished, planished, or glanced, by whatever name designated, thirty-five per centum ad valorem.

145. Sheets or plates of iron or steel, or taggers iron or steel, coated with tin or lead, or with a mixture of which these metals, or either of them, is a component part, by the dipping or any other process, and commercially known as tin plates, terne plates, and taggers tin, one cent per pound until July first, eighteen hundred and ninety-one.

> 121. Sheets or plates of iron or steel, or taggers iron or steel, coated with tin or lead, or with a mixture of which these metals, or either of them, is a component part, by the dipping or any other process, and commercially known as tin plates, terne plates, and taggers tin, one [and one-fifth cents] *cent* per pound : *Provided,* That the reduction of duty herein provided for shall take effect on and after October first, eighteen hundred and ninety-four. No article not specially provided for in this act, wholly or partly manufactured from tin plate, terne plate, or the sheet, or plate iron or steel herein provided for, or of which such tin plate, terne plate, sheet, or plate iron or steel shall be the material of chief value, shall pay a lower rate of duty than that imposed on the tin plate, terne plate, or sheet, or plate iron or steel from which it is made, or of which it shall be the component thereof of chief value.

146. Steel ingots, cogged ingots, blooms, and slabs, by whatever process made; die blocks or blanks; billets and bars and tapered or beveled bars; steamer, crank, and other shafts; shafting; wrist or crank pins; connecting-rods and piston rods; pressed, sheared, or stamped shapes; saw-plates, wholly or partially manufactured; hammer-molds or swaged steel; gun-barrel molds not in bars; alloys used as substitutes for steel tools; all descriptions and shapes of dry sand, loam, or iron-molded steel castings; sheets and plates not specially provided for in this act, and steel in all forms and shapes not specially provided for in this act; all of the above valued at one cent per pound or less, four-tenths of one cent per pound; valued above one cent and not above one and four-tenths cents per pound, five-tenths of one cent per pound; valued above one and four-tenths cents and not above one and eight-tenths cents per pound, eight-tenths of one cent per pound; valued above one and eight-tenths cents and not above two and two-tenths cents per pound, nine-tenths of one cent per pound; valued above two and two-tenths cents, and not above three cents per pound, one and two-tenths cents per pound; valued above three cents and not above four cents per pound, one and six-tenths cents per pound; valued above four cents and not above seven cents per pound, two cents per pound; valued above seven cents and not above ten cents per pound, two and eight-tenths cents per pound; valued above ten cents and not above thirteen cents per pound, three and one-half cents per pound; valued above thirteen cents and not above sixteen cents per pound, four and two-tenths cents per pound; valued above sixteen cents per pound, seven cents per pound.

> 122. Steel ingots, cogged ingots, blooms, and slabs, by whatever process made; die blocks or blanks; billets and bars and tapered or beveled bars; steamer, crank, and other shafts; shafting; wrist, or crank pins; connecting-rods and piston-rods; pressed, sheared, or stamped shapes; saw-plates, wholly or partially manufactured; hammer molds or swaged steel; gun-barrel molds not in bars; alloys used as substitutes for steel in the manufacture of tools; all descriptions and shapes of dry sand, loam, or iron-molded steel castings; sheets and plates not specially provided for in this act; and steel in all forms and shapes not specially provided for in this act, twenty-five per centum ad valorem.

WIRE—

147. Wire rods: Rivet, screw, fence, and other iron or steel wire rods, and nail rods, whether round, oval, flat, square, or in any other shape, in coils or otherwise, not smaller than number six wire gauge, valued at three and half cents or less per pound, six-tenths of one cent per pound; and iron or steel, flat, with longitudinal ribs for the manufacture of fencing, valued at three cents or less per pound, six-tenths of one cent per pound: *Provided*, That all iron or steel rods, whether rolled or drawn through dies, smaller than number six wire gauge, shall be classed and dutiable as wire.

> WIRE—
> 123. Wire rods: Rivet, screw, fence and other iron or steel wire rods, and nail rods, whether round, oval, flat, square, or in any other shape, in coils or otherwise, twenty-five per centum ad valorem.

148. Wire: Wire made of iron or steel; not smaller than number ten wire gauge, one and one-fourth cents per pound; smaller than number ten, and not smaller than number sixteen wire gauge, one and three-fourths cents per pound; smaller than number sixteen and not smaller than number twenty-six wire gauge, two and one-fourth cents per pound; smaller than number twenty-six wire gauge, three cents per pound: *Provided*, That iron or steel wire covered with cotton, silk, or other material, and wires or strip steel, commonly known as crinoline wire, corset-wire, and hat-wire, shall pay a duty of five cents per pound: *And provided further*, That flat steel wire, or sheet steel in strips, whether drawn through dies or rolls, untempered or tempered, of whatsoever width, twenty-five one thousandths of an inch thick or thinner (ready for use or otherwise), shall pay a duty of fifty per centum ad valorem: *And provided further*, That no article made from iron or steel wire, or of which iron or steel wire is a component part of chief value, shall pay a less rate of duty than the iron or steel wire from which it is made either wholly or in part: *And provided further*, That iron or steel wire cloths, and iron or steel wire nettings made in meshes of any form, shall pay a duty equal in amount to that imposed on iron or steel wire used in the manufacture of iron or steel wire cloth, or iron or steel wire nettings, and two cents per pound in addition thereto.

There shall be paid on iron or steel wire coated with zinc or tin, or any other metal (except fence-wire and iron or steel, flat, with longitudinal ribs, for the manufacture of fencing), one-half of one cent per pound in addition to the rate imposed on the wire of which it is made; on iron wire rope and wire strand, one cent per pound in addition to the rate imposed on the wire of which it is made; on steel wire rope and wire strand, two cents per pound in addition to the rate imposed on the wire of which they or either of them are made: *Provided further*, That all iron or steel wire valued at more than four cents per pound shall pay a duty of not less than forty-five per centum ad valorem except that card wire for the manufacture of card clothing shall pay a duty of thirty-five per centum ad valorem.

> 124. Wire: Iron or steel wire, and wire or strip steel, commonly known as crinoline wire, corset-wire, drill rods, needle wire, and all steel rods or bars, whether polished or unpolished, in coils or straightened and cut to length, drawn cold through dies, and hat-wire, flat steel wire, or sheet steel

in strips, uncovered or covered with cotton, silk, or other material, iron or steel wire cloths, and iron or steel wire nettings made in meshes of any form, iron or steel wire coated with zinc or tin, or any other metal, thirty per centum ad valorem; wire rope and wire strand, thirty-five per centum ad valorem.

GENERAL PROVISIONS.

149. No allowance or reduction of duties for partial loss or damage in consequence of rust or of discoloration shall be made upon any description of iron or steel, or upon any article wholly or partly manufactured of iron or steel, or upon any manufacture of iron and steel.

> 125. No allowance or reduction of duties for partial loss or damage in consequence of rust or of discoloration shall be made upon any description of iron or steel, or upon any article wholly or partly manufactured of iron or steel.

150. All metal produced from iron or its ores, which is cast and malleable, of whatever description or form, without regard to the percentage of carbon contained therein, whether produced by cementation, or converted, cast, or made from iron or its ores, by the crucible, Bessemer, Clapp-Griffith, pneumatic, Thomas-Gilchrist, basic, Siemens-Martin, or open-hearth process, or by the equivalent of either, or by a combination of two or more of the processes, or their equivalents, or by any fusion or other process which produces from iron or its ores a metal either granular or fibrous in structure, which is cast and malleable, excepting what is known as malleable-iron castings, shall be classed and denominated as steel.

151. No article not specially provided for in this act, wholly or partly manufactured from tin plate, terne plate, or the sheet, plate, hoop, band, or scroll iron or steel herein provided for, or of which such tin plate, terne plate, sheet, plate, hoop, band, or scroll iron or steel shall be the material of chief value, shall pay a lower rate of duty than that imposed on the tin plate, terne plate, or sheet, plate, hoop, band, or scroll iron or steel from which it is made, or of which it shall be the component thereof of chief value.

152. On all iron or steel bars or rods of whatever shape or section, which are cold rolled, cold hammered, or polished in any way in addition to the ordinary process of hot rolling or hammering, there shall be paid one-fourth of one cent per pound in addition to the rates provided in this act, and on all strips, plates, or sheets of iron or steel of whatever shape, other than the polished, planished, or glanced sheet-iron or sheet-steel hereinbefore provided for, which are cold rolled, cold hammered, blued, brightened, tempered, or polished by any process to such perfected surface finish, or polish better than the grade of cold rolled, smooth only, hereinbefore provided for, there shall be paid one and one-fourth cents per pound in addition to the rates provided in this act upon plates, strips, or sheets of iron or steel of common or black finish; and on steel circular saw plates there shall be paid one cent per pound in addition to the rate provided in this act for steel saw plates.

MANUFACTURES OF IRON AND STEEL.

153. Anchors, or parts thereof, of iron or steel, mill-irons and mill-cranks of wrought-iron, and wrought-iron for ships, and forgings of iron or steel, or of combined iron and steel, for vessels, steam-engines, and locomotives, or parts thereof, weighing each twenty-five pounds or more, one and eight-tenths cents per pound.

> 126. Anchors, or parts thereof, of iron or steel, mill irons and mill cranks of wrought iron, and wrought iron for ships, and forgings of iron or steel, or of combined iron and steel, for vessels, steam engines, and locomotives, or parts thereof, twenty-five per centum ad valorem.

154. Axles, or parts thereof, axle-bars, axle-blanks, or forgings for axles, whether of iron or steel, without reference to the stage or state of manufacture, two cents per pound: *Provided,* That when iron or steel axles are imported fitted in wheels, or parts of wheels, of iron or steel, they shall be dutiable at the same rate as the wheels in which they are fitted.

> 127. Axles, or parts thereof, axle bars, axle blanks, or forgings for axles, whether of iron or steel, without reference to the stage or state of manufacture, twenty-five per centum ad valorem.

155. Anvils of iron or steel, or of iron and steel combined, by whatever process made, or in whatever stage of manufacture, two and one-half cents per pound.

> 128. Anvils of iron or steel, or of iron and steel combined, by whatever process made, or in whatever stage of manufacture, twenty-five per centum ad valorem.

156. Blacksmiths' hammers and sledges, track tools, wedges, and crowbars, whether of iron or steel, two and one-fourth cents per pound.

> 129. Blacksmiths' hammers and sledges, track tools, wedges, and crowbars, whether of iron or steel, twenty-five per centum ad valorem.

157. Boiler or other tubes, pipes, flues, or stays of wrought-iron or steel, two and one-half cents per pound.

> 130. Boiler or other tubes, pipes, flues, or stays of wrought iron or steel, [twenty-five] *twenty* per centum ad valorem.

158. Bolts, with or without threads or nuts, or bolt-blanks, and finished hinges or hinge-blanks, whether of iron or steel, two and one-fourth cents per pound.

> 131. Bolts, with or without threads or nuts, or bolt-blanks, and finished hinges or hinge-blanks, whether of iron or steel, twenty-five per centum ad valorem.

159. Card-clothing manufactured from tempered steel wire, fifty cents per square foot; all other, twenty-five cents per square foot.

> 132. Card-clothing, made of leather and iron or steel wire, twenty-five per centum ad valorem; all other card-clothing, thirty-five per centum ad valorem.

160. Cast-iron pipe of every description, nine-tenths of one cent per pound.

> 133. Cast-iron pipe of every description, [twenty-five] *twenty-two and one-half* per centum ad valorem.

161. Cast-iron vessels, plates, stove-plates, andirons, sad-irons, tailors' irons, hatters' irons, and castings of iron, not specially provided for in this act, one and two-tenths cents per pound.

> 134. Cast-iron vessels, plates, stove-plates, andirons, sad-irons, tailors' irons, hatters' irons, and castings of iron, not finished parts of machinery, and not specially provided for in this act, twenty-five per centum ad valorem.

162. Castings of malleable iron not specially provided for in this act, one and three-fourths cents per pound.

> 135. Castings of malleable iron not specially provided for in this act, twenty-five per centum ad valorem.

163. Cast hollow-ware, coated, glazed, or tinned, three cents per pound.

> 136. Cast hollow ware coated, glazed, or tinned, thirty per centum ad valorem.

164. Chain or chains of all kinds, made of iron or steel, not less than three-fourths of one inch in diameter, one and six-tenths cents per pound less than three-fourths of one inch and not less than three-eighths

of one inch in diameter, one and eight-tenths cents per pound less than three-eighths of one inch in diameter, two and one-half cents per pound but no chain or chains of any description shall pay a lower rate of duty than forty-five per centum ad valorem.

    137. Chains of all kinds, made of iron or steel, thirty per centum ad valorem.

CUTLERY—

165. Pen-knives or pocket-knives of all kinds, or parts thereof, and erasers, or parts thereof, wholly or partly manufactured, valued at not more than fifty cents per dozen, twelve cents per dozen valued at more than fifty cents per dozen and not exceeding one dollar and fifty cents per dozen, fifty cents per dozen valued at more than one dollar and fifty cents per dozen and not exceeding three dollars per dozen, one dollar per dozen valued at more than three dollars per dozen, two dollars per dozen and in addition thereto on all the above, fifty per centum ad valorem. Razors and razor blades, finished or unfinished, valued at less than four dollars per dozen, one dollar per dozen valued at four dollars or more per dozen, one dollar and seventy-five cents per dozen and in addition thereto on all the above razors and razor-blades, thirty per centum ad valorem.

    138. Penknives or pocketknives of all kinds, or parts thereof, and erasers, or parts thereof, wholly or partly manufactured, razors and razor blades, finished or unfinished, and shears and scissors, forty-five per centum ad valorem.

166. Swords, sword-blades, and side-arms, thirty-five per centum ad valorem.

    139. Swords, sword-blades, and side-arms, thirty-five percentum ad valorem.

167. Table-knives, forks, steels, and all butchers', hunting, kitchen, bread, butter, vegetable, fruit, cheese, plumbers', painters" palette, and artists' knives of all sizes, finished or unfinished, valued at not more than one dollar per dozen pieces, ten cents per dozen valued at more than one dollar and not more than two dollars, thirty-five cents per dozen valued at more than two dollars and not more than three dollars, forty cents per dozen valued at more than three dollars and not more than eight dollars, one dollar per dozen valued at more than eight dollars, two dollars per dozen and in addition upon all the above-named articles, thirty per centum ad valorem. All carving and cooks' knives and forks of all sizes, finished or unfinished, valued at not more than four dollars per dozen pieces, one dollar per dozen valued at more than four dollars and not more than eight dollars, two dollars per dozen pieces valued at more than eight dollars and not more than twelve dollars, three dollars per dozen pieces valued at more than twelve dollars, five dollars per dozen pieces and in addition upon all the above named articles, thirty per centum ad valorem.

    140. Table knives, forks, steels, and all hunting, kitchen, bread, butter, vegetable, fruit, cheese, plumbers', painters', palette and artists' knives; also all carving, cooks' and butchers' knives, forks, and steels; all sizes of all of the above, finished or unfinished, thirty-five per centum ad valorem.

168. Files, file-blanks, rasps, and floats, of all cuts and kinds, four inches in length and under, thirty-five cents per dozen; over four inches in length and under nine inches, seventy-five cents per dozen; nine inches in length and under fourteen inches, one dollar and thirty cents per dozen; fourteen inches in length and over, two dollars per dozen.

    141. Files, file blanks, rasps, and floats, of all cuts and kinds, thirty-five per centum ad valorem.

FIREARMS—
169. Muskets and sporting rifles, twenty-five per centum ad valorem.
> FIREARMS:
> 142. Muskets, muzzle loading shot-guns, and sporting rifles, and parts thereof, twenty-five per centum ad valorem.

170. All double-barrelled, sporting, breech-loading shot-guns valued at not more than six dollars each, one dollar and fifty cents each; valued at more than six dollars and not more than twelve dollars each, four dollars each; valued at than more twelve dollars each, six dollars each; and in addition thereto on all the above, thirty-five per centum ad valorem. Single-barrel breech-loading shot-guns, one dollar each and thirty-five per centum ad valorem. Revolving pistols valued at not more than one dollar and fifty cents each, forty cents each; valued at more than one dollar and fifty cents, one dollar each; and in addition thereto on all the above pistols, thirty-five per centum ad valorem.
> 143. Sporting, breech-loading shotguns and pistols, and parts thereof, thirty per centum ad valorem.

171. Iron or steel sheets, plates, wares, or articles, enameled or glazed with vitreous glasses, forty-five per centum ad valorem.
> 144. Sheets, plates, wares, or articles of iron, steel, or other metal, enameled or glazed with vitreous glasses, thirty-five per centum ad valorem.

172. Iron or steel sheets, plates, wares, or articles, enameled or glazed as above with more than one color, or ornamented, fifty per centum ad valorem.

NAILS, SPIKES, TACKS, AND NEEDLES—
173. Cut nails and cut spikes of iron or steel, one cent per pound.
> NAILS, SPIKES, TACKS, AND NEEDLES:
> 145. Cut nails and cut spikes of iron or steel, [twenty-five] *twenty-two and one-half* per centum ad valorem.

174. Horseshoe nails, hob nails, and all other wrought iron or steel nails not specially provided for in this act, four cents per pound.
> 146. Horseshoe nails, hob nails, and all other wrought iron or steel nails not specially provided for in this act, thirty per centum ad valorem.

175. Wire nails made of wrought iron or steel, two inches long and longer, not lighter than number twelve wire gauge, two cents per pound; from one inch to two inches in length, and lighter than number twelve and not lighter than number sixteen wire gauge, two and one-half cents per pound; shorter than one inch and lighter than number sixteen wire gauge, four cents per pound.
> 147. Wire nails made of wrought iron or steel, twenty-five per centum ad valorem.

176. Spikes, nuts, and washers, and horse, mule, or ox shoes, of wrought iron or steel, one and eight-tenths cents per pound.
> 148. Spikes, nuts, and washers, and horse, mule, or ox shoes of wrought iron or steel, twenty-five per centum ad valorem.

177. Cut tacks, brads, or sprigs, not exceeding sixteen ounces to the thousand, two and one-fourth cents per thousand; exceeding sixteen ounces to the thousand, two and three-fourths cents per pound.
> 149. Cut tacks, brads, or sprigs, of all kinds, twenty-five per centum ad valorem.

178. Needles for knitting or sewing machines, crochet-needles and tape-needles and bodkins of metal, thirty-five per centum ad valorem.
> 150. Needles for knitting or sewing machines, crochet-needles and tape-needles and bodkins of metal, twenty-five per centum ad valorem.

179. Needles, knitting, and all others not specially provided for in this act, twenty-five per centum ad valorem;
> knitting and all other needles, not specially provided for in this act, twenty-five per centum ad valorem.
> NOTE.—This and preceding paragraph consolidated.

PLATES—

180. Steel plates engraved, stereotype plates, electrotype plates, and plates of other materials, engraved or lithographed, for printing, twenty-five per centum ad valorem.
> PLATES:
> 151. Steel plates engraved, stereotype plates, electrotype plates, and plates of other materials, engraved or lithographed, for printing, twenty-five per centum ad valorem.

181. Railway fish-plates or splice-bars, made of iron or steel, one cent per pound.
> 152. Railway fish-plates or splice-bars, made of iron or steel, twenty-five per centum ad valorem.

182. Rivets of iron or steel, two and one-half cents per pound.
> 153. Rivets of iron or steel, [thirty] *twenty-five* per centum ad valorem.

183. SAWS: Cross-cut saws, eight cents per linear foot; mill, pit, and drag-saws, not over nine inches wide, ten cents per linear foot; over nine inches wide, fifteen cents per linear foot; circular saws, thirty per centum ad valorem; hand, back, and all other saws, not specially provided for in this act, forty per centum ad valorem.
> 154. SAWS: Crosscut saws, mill, pit, and drag saws, *fifteen per centum ad valorem;* circular saws, hand, back, and all other saws, twenty-five per centum ad valorem.

184. Screws, commonly called woodscrews, more than two inches in length, five cents per pound; over one inch and not more than two inches in length, seven cents per pound; over one-half inch and not more than one inch in length, ten cents per pound; one-half inch and less in length, fourteen cents per pound.
> 155. Screws, commonly called wood screws, [thirty-five] *thirty* per centum ad valorem.

•185. Wheels or parts thereof, made of iron or steel, and steel-tired wheels for railway purposes, whether wholly or partly finished, and iron or steel locomotive, car, or other railway tires or parts thereof, wholly or partly manufactured, two and one-half cents per pound; and ingots, cogged ingots, blooms, or blanks for the same, without regard to the degree of manufacture, one and three-fourth cents per pound: *Provided*, That when wheels or parts thereof, of iron or steel, are imported with iron or steel axles fitted in them, the wheels and axles together shall be dutiable at the same rate as is provided for the wheels when imported separately.
> 156. Wheels, or parts thereof, made of iron or steel, and steel-tired wheels for railway purposes, whether wholly or partly finished, and iron or steel locomotive, car, or other railway tires or parts thereof, wholly or partly manufactured, and ingots, cogged ingots, blooms, or blanks for the same, without regard to the degree of manufacture, thirty per centum ad valorem.

MISCELLANEOUS METALS AND MANUFACTURES OF.

186. Aluminium, or aluminum, in crude form, alloys of any kind in which aluminum is the component material of chief value, fifteen cents per pound.
> 157. [Aluminium, or aluminum.] *Aluminum* in crude form, alloys of any kind in which aluminum is the component material of chief value, [twenty-five] *fifteeen* per centum ad valorem.

187. Antimony, as regulus or metal, three-fourths of one cent per pound.
> Placed upon free list. Par. 376.

188. Argentine, albata, or German silver, unmanufactured, twenty-five per centum ad valorem.
> 158. Argentine, albata, or German silver, unmanufactured, fifteen per centum ad valorem.

189. Brass, in bars or pigs, old brass, clippings from brass or Dutch-metal, and old sheathing, or yellow metal, fit only for remanufacture, one and one-half cents per pound.
> 159. Brass, in bars or pigs, old brass, clippings from brass or Dutch-metal, and old sheathing, or yellow metal, fit only for remanufacture, ten per centum ad valorem.

190. Bronze powder, twelve cents per pound; bronze or Dutch-metal or aluminum, in leaf, eight cents per package of one hundred leaves.
> 160. Bronze powder, metallics or flitters, bronze or Dutch-metal, or aluminum, in leaf, thirty per centum ad valorem.

COPPER—
191. Copper imported in the form of ores, one-half of one cent per pound on each pound of fine copper contained therein.
> COPPER—
> Placed upon the free list. Par. 451.

192. Old copper, fit only for remanufacture, clippings from new copper, and all composition metal of which copper is a component material of chief value, not specially provided for in this act, one cent per pound.
> Placed upon the free list. Par. 452.

193. Regulus of copper and black or coarse copper, and copper cement, one cent per pound on each pound of fine copper contained therein.
> Placed upon the free list. Par. 453.

194. Copper in plates, bars, ingots, Chili or other pigs, and in other forms, not manufactured, not specially provided for in this act, one and one-fourth cents per pound.
> Placed upon the free list. Par. 454.

195. Copper in rolled plates, called braziers' copper, sheets, rods, pipes, and copper bottoms, also sheathing or yellow metal of which copper is the component material of chief value, and not composed wholly or in part of iron ungalvanized, thirty-five per centum ad valorem.
> 161. Copper in rolled plates, called braziers' copper, sheets, rods, pipes, and copper bottoms, also sheathing or yellow metal of which copper is the component material of chief value, and not composed wholly or in part of iron ungalvanized, twenty per centum ad valorem.

GOLD AND SILVER.—
196. Bullions and metal thread of gold, silver, or other metals, not specially provided for in this act, thirty per centum ad valorem.
> GOLD AND SILVER.—
> 162. Bullions and metal thread of gold, silver, or other metals, not specially provided for in this act, twenty-five per centum ad valorem.

197. Gold leaf, two dollars per package of five hundred leaves.
> 163. Gold leaf, [thirty-five] *thirty* per centum ad valorem.

198. Silver leaf, seventy-five cents per package of five hundred leaves.
> 164. Silver leaf, [thirty-five] *thirty* per centum ad valorem.

LEAD.—
199. Lead ore and lead dross, one and one-half cents per pound. *Provided*, That silver ore and all other ores containing lead shall pay a duty of one and one-half cents per pound on the lead contained therein, according to sample and assay at the port of entry.
> LEAD.—
> 165. [Lead ore and lead dross 15 per centum ad valorem upon the lead contained therein according to sample and assay at the port of entry, provided that all ores containing silver and lead, in which the value of the silver contents shall be greater than the value of lead contents, according to sample and assay at the port of entry, shall be considered silver ores.] *Lead ore and lead dross, three-fourths of one cent per pound: Provided, That silver ore and all other ores containing lead shall pay a duty of three-fourths of one cent per pound on the lead contained therein, according to sample and assay at the port of entry.*

200. Lead in pigs and bars, molten and old refuse lead run into blocks and bars, and old scrap-lead fit only to be remanufactured, two cents per pound.
> 166. Lead in pigs and bars, molten and old refuse lead run into blocks and bars and old scrap lead fit only to be remanufactured one cent per pound: *Provided*, That in case any foreign country shall impose an export duty upon lead ore or lead dross or silver ores containing lead, exported to the United States from such country, then the duty upon *such ores and* lead in pigs and bars, molten and old refuse lead run into blocks and bars, and old scrap lead fit only to be remanufactured, herein provided for, when imported from such country, shall remain the same as fixed by the law in force prior to the passage of this act.

201. Lead in sheets, pipes, shot, glaziers' lead, and lead wire, two and one-half cents per pound.
> 167. Lead in sheets, pipes, shot, glaziers' lead, and lead wire, one and one-quarter cents per pound.

202. Metallic mineral substances in a crude state and metals unwrought, not specially provided for in this act, twenty per centum ad valorem; mica, thirty-five per centum ad valorem.
> Placed upon free list. Par. 552.

NICKEL.—
203. Nickel, nickel oxide, alloy of any kind in which nickel is the component material of chief value, ten cents per pound.
> NICKEL.—
> Placed upon free list. Par. 563.

204. Pens, metallic, except gold pens, twelve cents per gross.
> 168. Pens, metallic, except gold pens, [thirty-five] *thirty* per centum ad valorem.

205. Pen-holder tips, pen-holders or parts thereof, and gold pens, thirty per centum ad valorem.
> 169. Pen-holder tips, pen-holders or parts thereof, and gold pens, twenty-five per centum ad valorem.

206. Pins, metallic, solid-head or other, including hair-pins, **safety-pins**, and hat, bonnet, shawl, and belt pins, thirty per centum ad valorem.

> 170. Pins, metallic, including *pins with solid or glass heads*, hair-pins, safety-pins, and hat; bonnet, shawl, and belt pins, not [commercially known] *suitable for use* as jewelry, twenty per centum ad valorem.

207. Quicksilver, ten cents per pound. The flasks, bottles, or other vessels in which quicksilver is imported shall be subject to the same rate of duty as they would be subjected to if imported empty.

> Placed upon free list. Par. 599.

208. Type metal, one and one-half cents per pound for the lead contained therein; new types, twenty-five per centum ad valorem.

> 171. Type metal, and new types, fifteen per centum ad valorem.

209. Tin: On and after July first, eighteen hundred and ninety-three, there shall be imposed and paid upon cassiterite or black oxide of tin, and upon bar, block, and pig tin, a duty of four cents per pound: *Provided*, That unless it shall be made to appear to the satisfaction of the President of the United States (who shall make known the fact by proclamation) that the product of the mines of the United States shall have exceeded five thousand tons of cassiterite, and bar, block, and pig tin in any one year prior to July first, eighteen hundred and ninety-five, then all imported cassiterite, bar, block, and pig tin shall after July first, eighteen hundred and ninety-five, be admitted free of duty.

> TIN:
> Placed upon free list. Par. 653.

WATCHES.—

210. Chronometers, box or ship's, and parts thereof, ten per centum ad valorem.

> WATCHES.—
> 172. Chronometers, box or ship's, and parts thereof, ten per centum ad valorem.

211. Watches, parts of watches, watch-cases, watch movements, and watch-glasses, whether separately packed or otherwise, twenty-five per centum ad valorem.

> 173. Watches, and clocks, or parts thereof, whether separately packed or otherwise, twenty-five per centum ad valorem.

ZINC OR SPELTER.—

212. Zinc in blocks or pigs, one and three-fourths cents per pound.

> ZINC OR SPELTER.—
> 174. Zinc in blocks or pigs, twenty per centum ad valorem.

213. Zinc in sheets, two and one-half cents per pound.

> 175. Zinc in sheets, twenty-five per centum ad valorem.

214. Zinc, old and worn out, fit only to be remanufactured, one and one-fourth cents per pound.

> 176. Zinc, old and worn out, fit only to be remanufactured, fifteen per centum ad valorem.

215. Manufactures, articles, or wares, not specially enumerated or provided for in this act, composed wholly or in part of iron, steel, lead, copper, nickel, pewter, zinc, gold, silver, platinum, aluminum, or any other metal, and whether partly or wholly manufactured, forty-five per centum ad valorem.

> 177. Manufactured articles, or wares, not specially provided for in this act, composed wholly or in part of any metal, and whether partly or wholly manufactured, [thirty-five] *thirty* per centum ad valorem.

Schedule D.—Wood and Manufactures of.

216. Timber, hewn and sawed, and timber used for spars and in building wharves, ten per centum ad valorem.
  Placed upon free list. Par. 674.

217. Timber, squared or sided, not specially provided for in this act, one-half of one cent per cubic foot.
  Placed upon free list. Par. 675.

218. Sawed boards, plank, deals, and other lumber of hemlock, white wood, sycamore, white pine and basswood, one dollar per thousand feet board measure; sawed lumber, not specially provided for in this act, two dollars per thousand feet board measure; but when lumber of any sort is planed or finished, in addition to the rates herein provided, there shall be levied and paid for each side so planed or finished fifty cents per thousand feet board measure; and if planed on one side and tongued and grooved, one dollar per thousand feet board measure; and if planed on two sides, and tongued and grooved, one dollar and fifty cents per thousand feet board measure; and in estimating board measure under this schedule no deduction shall be made on board measure on account of planing, tongueing and grooving: *Provided*, That in case any foreign country shall impose an export duty upon pine, spruce, elm, or other logs, or upon stave bolts, shingle wood, or heading blocks exported to the United States from such country, then the duty upon the sawed lumber herein provided for, when imported from such country, shall remain the same as fixed by the law in force prior to the passage of this act.

  168. Lumber of any sort, planed or finished, for each side so planed or finished, fifty cents per thousand feet, board measure; and if planed on one side and tongued and grooved, one dollar per thousand feet, board measure; and if planed on two sides and tongued and grooved, one dollar and fifty cents per thousand feet, board measure; and in estimating board measure under this schedule no deduction shall be made on board measure on account of planing, tongueing, and grooving.
  Note.—Sawed boards, plank, deals, and other lumber, free. Par. 676.

219. Cedar: That on and after March first, eighteen hundred and ninety-one, paving posts, railroad ties, and telephone and telegraph poles of cedar, shall be dutiable at twenty per centum ad valorem.
  Placed upon free list. Par. 684.

220. Sawed boards, planks, deals, and all forms of sawed cedar, lignum-vitae, lancewood, ebony, box, granadilla, mahogany, rosewood, satinwood, and all other cabinet-woods not further manufactured than sawed, fifteen per centum ad valorem; veneers of wood, and wood, unmanufactured, not specially provided for in this act, twenty per centum ad valorem.
  Placed upon free list. Par. 684.

221. Pine clapboards, one dollar per one thousand.
  Placed upon free list. Par. 677.

222. Spruce clapboards, one dollar and fifty cents per one thousand.
  Placed upon free list. Par. 678.

223. Hubs for wheels, posts, last-blocks, wagon-blocks, oar-blocks, gun-blocks, heading-blocks, and all like blocks or sticks, rough-hewn or sawed only, twenty per centum ad valorem.
  Placed upon free list. Par. 679.

224. Laths, fifteen cents per one thousand pieces.
  Placed upon free list. Par. 680.

225. Pickets and palings, ten per centum ad valorem.
> Placed upon free list. Par. 681.

226. White pine shingles, twenty cents per one thousand; all other, thirty cents per one thousand.
> Placed upon free list. Par. 682.

227. Staves of wood of all kinds, ten per centum ad valorem.
> Placed upon free list. Par. 683.

228. Casks and barrels (empty), sugar-box shooks, and packing-boxes and packing-box shooks, of wood, not specially provided for in this act, thirty per centum ad valorem.
> 180. Casks and barrels, empty, sugar-box shooks, and packing-boxes and packing-box shooks, of wood, not specially provided for in this act, twenty per centum ad valorem.

229. Chair cane, or reeds wrought or manufactured from rattans or reeds, and whether round, square, or in any other shape, ten per centum ad valorem.
> 179. Osier or willow prepared for basketmakers' use, twenty per centum ad valorem; manufactures of osier or willow, twenty-five per centum ad valorem; chair cane, or reeds wrought or manufactured from rattans or reeds, [seven] ten per centum ad valorem.
> See also Par. 684.

230. House or cabinet furniture, of wood, wholly or partly finished manufactures of wood, or of which wood is the component material of chief value, not specially provided for in this act, thirty-five per centum ad valorem.
> 181. House or cabinet furniture, of wood, wholly or partly finished, manufactures of wood, or of which wood is the component material of chief value, not specially provided for in this act, twenty-five per centum ad valorem.

Schedule E.—Sugar.

231. That on and after July first, eighteen hundred and ninety-one, and until July first, nineteen hundred and five, there shall be paid, from any moneys in the Treasury not otherwise appropriated, under the provisions of section three thousand six hundred and eighty-nine of the Revised Statutes, to the producer of sugar testing not less than ninety degrees by the polariscope, from beets, sorghum, or sugar-cane grown within the United States, or from maple sap produced within the United States, a bounty of two cents per pound; and upon such sugar testing less than ninety degrees by the polariscope, and not less than eighty degrees, a bounty of one and three-fourths cents per pound, under such rules and regulations as the Commissioner of Internal Revenue, with the approval of the Secretary of the Treasury, shall prescribe.

> Schedule E.—Sugar.
> 182. That so much of the act entitled "An act to reduce revenue, equalize duties, and for other purposes," approved October first, eighteen hundred and ninety, as provides for and authorizes the issue of licenses to produce sugar, and for the payment of a bounty to the producers of sugar from beets, sorghum, or sugar cane, grown in the United States, or from maple sap produced within the United States, be, and the same is hereby, repealed, to take effect July first, eighteen hundred and ninety-four, and thereafter it shall be unlawful to issue any license to produce sugar or to pay any bounty for the production of sugar of any kind under the said act.

232. The producer of said sugar to be entitled to said bounty shall have first filed prior to July first of each year with the Commissioner of Internal Revenue a notice of the place of production, with a general

description of the machinery and methods to be employed by him, with an estimate of the amount of sugar proposed to be produced in the current or next ensuing year, including the number of maple trees to be tapped, and an application for a license to so produce, to be accompanied by a bond in a penalty, and with sureties to be approved by the Commissioner of Internal Revenue, conditioned that he will faithfully observe all rules and regulations that shall be prescribed for such manufacture and production of sugar.

233. The Commissioner of Internal Revenue, upon receiving the application and bond. hereinbefore provided for, shall issue to the applicant a license to produce sugar from sorghum, beets, or sugar-cane grown within the United States, or from maple sap produced within the United States at the place and with the machinery and by the methods described in the application; but said license shall not extend beyond one year from the date thereof.

234. No bounty shall be paid to any person engaged in refining sugars which have been imported into the United States, or produced in the United States upon which the bounty herein provided for has already been paid or applied for, nor to any person unless he shall have first been licensed as herein provided, and only upon sugar produced by such person from sorghum, beets, or sugar-cane grown within the United States, or from maple sap produced within the United States. The Commissioner of Internal Revenue, with the approval of the Secretary of the Treasury, shall from time to time make all needful rules and regulations for the manufacture of sugar from sorghum, beets, or sugar cane grown within the United States, or from maple sap produced within the United States, and shall, under the direction of the Secretary of the Treasury, exercise supervision and inspection of the manufacture thereof.

235. And for the payment of these bounties the Secretary of the Treasury is authorized to draw warrants on the Treasurer of the United States for such sums as shall be necessary, which sums shall be certified to him by the Commissioner of Internal Revenue, by whom the bounties shall be disbursed, and no bounty shall be allowed or paid to any person licensed as aforesaid in any one year upon any quantity of sugar less than five hundred pounds.

236. That any person who shall knowingly refine or aid in the refining of sugar imported into the United States or upon which the bounty herein provided for has already been paid or applied for, at the place described in the license issued by the Commissioner of Internal Revenue, and any person not entitled to the bounty herein provided for, who shall apply for or receive the same, shall be guilty of a misdemeanor, and, upon conviction thereof, shall pay a fine not exceeding five thousand dollars, or be imprisoned for a period not exceeding five years, or both, in the discretion of the court.

237. All sugars above number sixteen Dutch standard in color shall pay a duty of five-tenths of one cent per pound: *Provided*, That all such sugars above number sixteen Dutch standard in color shall pay one-tenth of one cent per pound in addition to the rate herein provided for, when exported from, or the product of any country when and so long as such country pays or shall hereafter pay, directly or indirectly, a bounty on the exportation of any sugar that may be included in this grade which is greater than is paid on raw sugars of a lower saccharine strength; and the Secretary of the Treasury shall prescribe suitable rules and regulations to carry this provision into effect: *And provided further*, That all machinery purchased abroad and erected in a beet-

sugar factory and used in the production of raw sugar in the United States from beets produced therein shall be admitted duty free until the first day of July, eighteen hundred and ninety-two: *Provided*, That any duty collected on any of the above-described machinery purchased abroad and imported into the United States for the uses above indicated since January first, eighteen hundred and ninety, shall be refunded.

> 182½. *All sugars, tank bottoms, sirups of cane juice or of beet juice, melada, concentrated melada, concrete and concentrated molasses testing by the polariscope not above eighty degrees shall pay a duty of one cent per pound, and for every additional degree or fraction of a degree above eighty and not above ninety degrees shown by the polariscope test, shall pay one one-hundredth of a cent per pound additional, and above ninety and not above ninety-eight degrees, for every additional degree or fraction of a degree shown by the polariscope test, shall pay a duty of two one-hundredths of a cent per pound additional, and upon all sugar testing above ninety-eight degrees by polariscope test, or above number sixteen by the Dutch standard in color, there shall be levied and collected a duty of one-eighth of one cent per pound in addition to the duty imposed upon sugars testing above ninety-eight degrees; molasses testing not above fifty-six degrees by the polariscope shall pay a duty of two cents per gallon; molasses testing above fifty-six degrees shall pay a duty of four cents per gallon.*

238. Sugar candy and all confectionery, including chocolate confectionery, made wholly or in part of sugar, valued at twelve cents or less per pound, and on sugars after being refined, when tinctured, colored, or in any way adulterated, five cents per pound.

239. All other confectionery, including chocolate confectionery, not specially provided for in this act, fifty per centum ad valorem.

240. Glucose, or grape sugar, three-fourths of one cent per pound.

> 183. Sugar candy and all confectionery, made wholly or in part of sugar, and on sugars after being refined, when tinctured, colored, or in any way adulterated, thirty per centum ad valorem; glucose, or grape sugar, fifteen per centum ad valorem.

NOTE.—Paragraphs 238, 239, and 240 consolidated.

241. That the provisions of this act providing terms for the admission of imported sugars and molasses and for the payment of a bounty on sugars of domestic production shall take effect on the first day of April, eighteen hundred and ninety-one: *Provided*, That on and after the first day of March, eighteen hundred and ninety-one, and prior to the first day of April, eighteen hundred and ninety-one, sugars not exceeding number sixteen Dutch standard in color may be refined in bond without payment of duty, and such refined sugars may be transported in bond and stored in bonded warehouse at such points of destination as are provided in existing laws relating to the immediate transportation of dutiable goods in bond, under such rules and regulations as shall be prescribed by the Secretary of the Treasury.

SCHEDULE F.—TOBACCO AND MANUFACTURES OF.

242. Leaf tobacco suitable for cigar-wrappers, if not stemmed, two dollars per pound; if stemmed, two dollars and seventy-five cents per pound: *Provided*, That if any portion of any tobacco imported in any bale, box, or package, or in bulk, shall be suitable for cigar-wrappers, the entire quantity of tobacco contained in such bale, box, or package, or bulk shall be dutiable; if not stemmed, at two dollars per pound; if stemmed, at two dollars and seventy-five cents per pound.

> 184. On all leaf tobacco, on such part thereof as is wrapper tobacco and suitable for cigar wrappers, if unstemmed, one dollar per pound; if stemmed, one dollar and twenty-five cents per pound.

243. All other tobacco in leaf, unmanufactured and not stemmed, thirty-five cents per pound; if stemmed, fifty cents per pound.
> 185. All other leaf tobacco, if unstemmed, thirty-five cents per pound; if stemmed, fifty cents per pound.

244. Tobacco, manufactured, of all descriptions, not specially enumerated or provided for in this act, forty cents per pound.
> 186. Tobacco, manufactured, or unmanufactured, of all descriptions, not specially enumerated or provided for in this act, forty cents per pound.

245. Snuff and snuff flour, manufactured of tobacco, ground dry, or damp, and pickled, scented, or otherwise, of all descriptions, fifty cents per pound.
> 187. Snuff and snuff flour, manufactured of tobacco, ground dry, or damp, and pickled, scented, or otherwise, of all descriptions, forty cents per pound.

246. Cigars, cigarettes, cheroots of all kinds, four dollars and fifty cents per pound and twenty-five per centum ad valorem; and paper cigars and cigarettes, including wrappers, shall be subject to the same duties as are herein imposed upon cigars.
> 188. Cigars, cheroots and cigarettes, of all kinds, including wrappers, three dollars per pound and twenty-five per centum ad valorem.

SCHEDULE G.—AGRICULTURAL PRODUCTS AND PROVISIONS.

ANIMALS, LIVE—
247. Horses and mules, thirty dollars per head: *Provided*, That horses valued at one hundred and fifty dollars and over shall pay a duty of thirty per centum ad valorem.
248. Cattle, more than one year old, ten dollars per head; one year old or less, two dollars per head.
249. Hogs, one dollar and fifty cents per head.
250. Sheep, one year old or more, one dollar and fifty cents per head; less than one year old, seventy-five cents per head.
251. All other live animals, not specially provided for in this act twenty per centum ad valorem.
> 189. All other live animals, not specially provided for in this act, twenty per centum ad valorem.

NOTE.—Paragraphs 247 to 251, inclusive, consolidated in paragraph 189.

BREADSTUFFS AND FARINACEOUS SUBSTANCES—
252. Barley, thirty cents per bushel of forty-eight pounds.
253. Barley-malt, forty-five cents per bushel of thirty-four pounds.
254. Barley, pearled, patent, or hulled, two cents per pound.
> 191. Barley, and barley, pearled, patent, or hulled, [twenty-five] *thirty* per centum ad valorem; barley malt, [thirty-five] *forty* per centum ad valorem.

NOTE.—Paragraphs 252, 253, and 254 consolidated.

255. Buckwheat, fifteen cents per bushel of forty-eight pounds.
256. Corn or maize, fifteen cents per bushel of fifty-six pounds.
257. Corn-meal, twenty cents per bushel of forty-eight pounds.
258. Macaroni, vermicelli, and all similar preparations, two cents per pound.
> 192. Macaroni, vermicelli, and all similar preparations, [twenty-five] *twenty* per centum ad valorem.

259. Oats, fifteen cents per bushel.
260. Oatmeal, one cent per pound.

261. Rice, cleaned, two cents per pound; uncleaned rice, one and one-quarter cents per pound; paddy, three-quarters of one cent per pound; rice-flour, rice-meal, and rice, broken, which will pass through a sieve known commercially as number twelve wire sieve, one-fourth of one cent per pound.

> 193. Rice, cleaned, one and one-half cents per pound; uncleaned rice, or rice free of the outer hull and still having the inner cuticle on, one cent per pound; rice flour, and rice meal and rice broken which will pass through a sieve known commercially as number twelve wire sieve, one-fourth of one cent per pound; paddy, or rice having the outer hull on, three-fourths of one cent per pound.

262. Rye, ten cents per bushel.
263. Rye-flour, one-half of one cent per pound.
264. Wheat, twenty-five cents per bushel.
265. Wheat-flour, twenty-five per centum ad valorem.

> 190. Buckwheat, corn or maize, corn meal, oats, [oat meal,] rye, rye flour, wheat, and wheat flour, twenty per centum ad valorem, but each of the above products shall be admitted free of duty from any country which imposes no import duty on the like product when exported from the United States; *oat meal, fifteen per centum ad valorem.*
>
> NOTE.—Paragraphs 255, 256, 257, 259, 260, 262 to 265, inclusive, consolidated.

DAIRY PRODUCTS—

266. Butter, and substitutes therefor, six cents per pound.
> DAIRY PRODUCTS—
> 194. Butter, and substitutes therefor, [four cents per pound] *twenty per centum ad valorem.*

267. Cheese, six cents per pound.
> 195. Cheese, twenty-five per centum ad valorem.

268. Milk, fresh, five cents per gallon.
> Placed upon free list. Par. 554.

269. Milk, preserved or condensed, including weight of packages, three cents per pound; sugar of milk, eight cents per pound.
> 196. Milk, preserved or condensed, two cents per pound, including weight of packages; sugar of milk [twenty per centum ad valorem], *five cents per pound.*

FARM AND FIELD PRODUCTS—

270. Beans, forty cents per bushel of sixty pounds.
> FARM AND FIELD PRODUCTS—
> 197. Beans, twenty per centum ad valorem.

271. Beans, pease, and mushrooms, prepared or preserved, in tins, jars, bottles, or otherwise, forty per centum ad valorem.
> 198. Beans, pease, mushrooms and other vegetables prepared or preserved, in tins, jars, bottles, or otherwise, and pickles and sauces of all kinds, thirty per centum ad valorem.

272. Broom-corn, eight dollars per ton.
> Placed upon free list. Par. 422.

273. Cabbages, three cents each.
> Placed upon free list. Par. 425.

274. Cider, five cents per gallon.
> Placed upon free list. Par. 430.

275. Eggs, five cents per dozen.
> Placed upon free list. Par. 471.

276. Eggs, yolk of, twenty-five per centum ad valorem.
> Placed upon free list. Par. 471.

277. Hay, four dollars per ton.
    199. Hay, [two dollars per ton] *twenty per centum ad valorem.*
278. Honey, twenty cents per gallon.
    200. Honey, [ten cents per gallon] *twenty per centum ad valorem.*
279. Hops, fifteen cents per pound.
    201. Hops, [eight cents per pound] *twenty per centum ad valorem.*
280. Onions, forty cents per bushel.
    202. Onions, [twenty cents per bushel] *twenty per centum ad valorem.*
281. Pease, green, in bulk or in barrel, sacks, or similar packages, forty cents per bushel of sixty pounds; pease, dried, twenty cents per bushel, split pease, fifty cents per bushel of sixty pounds; pease in cartons, papers, or other small packages, one cent per pound.
    203. Pease, dried, [twenty cents per bushel;] split pease, [fifty cents per bushel of sixty pounds;] *and* pease in cartons, papers, or other small packages, [one cent per pound] *twenty per centum ad valorem.*
    NOTE.—Pease, green, in bulk or in barrel, sacks, or similar packages, free list. Par. 580.
282. Plants, trees, shrubs, and vines of all kind, commonly known as nursery stock, not specially provided for in this act, twenty per centum ad valorem.
    Placed upon free list. Par. 587.
283. Potatoes, twenty-five cents per bushel of sixty pounds.
    204. Potatoes, [ten cents per bushel of sixty pounds] *thirty per centum ad valorem.*

SEEDS—
284. Castor beans or seeds, fifty cents per bushel of fifty pounds.
    SEEDS—
    205. Castor beans or seeds, twenty-five cents per bushel of fifty pounds
285. Flaxseed or linseed, poppy seed and other oil seeds, not specially provided for in this act, thirty cents per bushel of fifty-six pounds; but no drawback shall be allowed on oil-cake made from imported seed.
    206. Flaxseed or linseed, poppy seed and other oil seeds, not specially provided for in this act, twenty cents per bushel of fifty-six pounds; but no drawback shall be allowed on oil-cake made from imported seed.
286. Garden seeds, agricultural seeds, and other seeds, not specially provided for in this act, twenty per centum ad valorem.
    Placed upon free list. Par. 611.
287. Vegetables of all kinds, prepared or preserved, including pickles, and sauces of all kinds, not specially provided for in this act, forty-five per centum ad valorem.
    NOTE.—Consolidated with paragraph 198, proposed law.
288. Vegetables in their natural state, not specially provided for in this act, twenty-five per centum ad valorem.
    207. Vegetables in their natural state, not specially provided for in this act, ten per centum ad valorem.
289. Straw, thirty per centum ad valorem.
    Placed upon free list. Par. 637.
290. Teazles, thirty per centum ad valorem.
    Placed upon free list. Par. 649.

FISH—
291. Anchovies and sardines, packed in oil or otherwise, in tin boxes measuring not more than five inches long, four inches wide, and three and one-half inches deep, ten cents per whole box; in half boxes, measuring not more than five inches long, four inches wide, and one and five-eighths inches deep, five cents each; in quarter boxes, measuring not more than four and three-fourths inches long, three and one-half inches wide, and one and one-fourth inches deep, two and one-half cents each; when imported in any other form, forty per centum ad valorem.

FISH—
208. Anchovies, sardines, and other fish packed in oil, in tin boxes or in any other form, [thirty] *twenty-five* per centum ad valorem.

292. Fish, pickled, in barrels or half barrels, and mackerel or salmon, pickled or salted, one cent per pound.

NOTE.—Provided for in paragraphs 209 and 210, proposed law.

293. Fish, smoked, dried, salted, pickled, frozen, packed in ice, or otherwise prepared for preservation, and fresh fish, not specially provided for in this act, three-fourths of one cent per pound.

209. Fish, smoked, dried, salted, pickled, or otherwise prepared for preservation, [three-fourths of one cent per pound] *fifteen per centum ad valorem.* See also 481.

294. Herrings, pickled or salted, one-half of one cent per pound; herrings, fresh, one-fourth of one cent per pound.

210. Herrings, pickled, frozen or salted, and salt-water fish, frozen or packed in ice, [one-half of one cent per pound] *fifteen per centum ad valorem.*

295. Fish in cans or packages made of tin or other material, except anchovies and sardines and fish packed in any other manner, not specially enumerated or provided for in this act, thirty per centum ad valorem.

211. Fish in cans or packages made of tin or other material, except anchovies and sardines and fish packed in any other manner, not specially enumerated or provided for in this act, twenty-five per centum ad valorem.

296. Cans or packages, made of tin or other metal, containing shell fish admitted free of duty, not exceeding one quart in contents, shall be subject to a duty of eight cents per dozen cans or packages; and when exceeding one quart, shall be subject to an additional duty of four cents per dozen for each additional half quart or fractional part thereof: *Provided,* That until June thirtieth, eighteen hundred and ninety-one, such cans or packages shall be admitted as now provided by law.

212. [Cans or packages, made of tin or other metal, containing shellfish admitted free of duty, not exceeding one quart in contents, shall be subject to a duty of eight cents per dozen cans or packages; and when exceeding one quart, shall be subject to an additional duty of four cents per dozen for each additional half quart or fractional part thereof.]

FRUITS AND NUTS—
Fruits:
297. Apples, green or ripe, twenty-five cents per bushel.

[NOTE.—Placed upon free list by House.] Par. 378.

298. Apples, dried, desiccated, evaporated, or prepared in any manner, and not otherwise provided for in this act, two cents per pound.

[Placed upon free list by House.] Par. 370.

213. *Apples, green or ripe, dried, desiccated, evaporated, or prepared in any manner, twenty per centum ad valorem.*
213a. Currants, [Zante or other, ten,] *twenty per centum ad valorem.*
213b. Dates, *twenty per centum ad valorem.*

299. Grapes, sixty cents per barrel of three cubic feet capacity or fractional part thereof; plums, and prunes, two cents per pound.
214. Grapes, [plums, and prunes,] twenty per centum ad valorem.

300. Figs, two and one-half cents per pound.
215. [Figs, twenty per centum ad valorem.]
215½. *Olives, green or prepared, twenty per centum ad valorem.*

301. Oranges, lemons, and limes, in packages of capacity of one and one-fourth cubic feet or less, thirteen cents per package; in packages of capacity exceeding one and one-fourth cubic feet and not exceeding two and one-half cubic feet, twenty-five cents per package; in packages of capacity exceeding two and one-half cubic feet and not exceeding five cubic feet, fifty cents per package; in packages of capacity exceeding five cubic feet, for every additional cubic foot or fractional part thereof, ten cents; in bulk, one dollar and fifty cents per one thousand; and in addition thereto a duty of thirty per centum ad valorem upon the boxes or barrels containing such oranges, lemons, or limes.
216. Oranges, lemons, and limes, in packages, at the rate of eight cents per cubic foot of capacity; in bulk, one dollar and fifty cents per one thousand and in addition thereto a duty of thirty per centum ad valorem upon the boxes or barrels containing such oranges, lemons, or limes.

302. Raisins, two and one-half cents per pound.
217. [Raisins] *Plums, prunes, figs, raisins,* and other dried grapes, *including Zante currants,* [one and one-half cents per pound.] *thirty per centum ad valorem:*

303. Comfits, sweetmeats, and fruits preserved in sugar, sirup, molasses, or spirits not specially provided for in this act, and jellies of all kinds, thirty-five per centum ad valorem.
218. Comfits, sweetmeats, and fruits preserved in sugar, sirup, molasses, or spirits not specially provided for in this act, and jellies of all kinds, thirty per centum ad valorem.

304. Fruits preserved in their own juices, thirty per centum ad valorem.
219. Fruits preserved in their own juices, twenty per centum ad valorem.

305. Orange-peel and lemon-peel, preserved or candied, two cents per pound.
220. Orange peel and lemon peel, preserved or candied, thirty per centum ad valorem.

Nuts:
306. Almonds, not shelled, five cents per pound; clear almonds, shelled, seven and one-half cents per pound.
Nuts:
221. Almonds, [not] shelled, [three cents per pound; clear almonds, shelled, five cents per pound] *or unshelled, twenty-five per centum ad valorem.*

307. Filberts and walnuts of all kinds, not shelled, three cents per pound; shelled, six cents per pound.
222. Filberts and walnuts of all kinds, [not shelled, two cents per pound; shelled, four cents per pound] *thirty-five per centum ad valorem; cream or Brazil nuts, twenty per centum ad valorem.*

308. Peanuts or ground beans, unshelled, one cent per pound; shelled, one and one-half cents per pound.
> 223. Peanuts or ground beans, [unshelled, one cent per pound; shelled, one and one-half cents per pound] *twenty per centum ad valorem.*

309. Nuts of all kinds, shelled or unshelled, not specially provided for in this act, one and one-half cents per pound.
> 224. Nuts of all kinds, shelled or unshelled, not specially provided for in this act, [one cent per pound] *twenty per centum ad valorem.*

MEAT PRODUCTS—

310. Bacon and hams, five cents per pound.
> MEAT PRODUCTS:
> Placed upon free list. Par. 392.

311. Beef, mutton, and pork, two cents per pound.
> [NOTE.—Placed upon free list by House.]
> 224½. *Fresh beef, mutton, and pork, twenty-five per centum ad valorem.*

312. Meats of all kinds, prepared or preserved, not specially provided for in this act, twenty-five per centum ad valorem.
> Placed upon free list. Par. 392.

313. Extract of meat, all not specially provided for in this act, thirty-five cents per pound; fluid extract of meat, fifteen cents per pound; and no separate or additional duty shall be collected on such coverings unless as such they are suitable and apparently designed for use other than in the importation of meat extracts.
> 225. Extract of meat, twenty per centum ad valorem.

314. Lard, two cents per pound.
> Placed upon free list. Par. 530.

315. Poultry, live, three cents per pound; dressed, five cents per pound.
> 226. Poultry [two cents per pound; dressed, three cents per pound] *dressed or undressed, twenty per centum ad valorem.*

316. Tallow, one cent per pound; wool grease, including that known commercially as degras or brown wool grease, one-half of one cent per pound.
> Placed upon free list. Par. 645.

MISCELLANEOUS PRODUCTS—

317. Chicory-root, burnt or roasted, ground or granulated, or in rolls, or otherwise prepared, and not specially provided for in this act, two cents per pound.
> 227. Chicory-root, burnt or roasted, ground or granulated, or in rolls, or otherwise prepared, and not specially provided for in this act [two cents per pound] *thirty per centum ad valorem.*

318. Chocolate, (other than chocolate confectionery and chocolate commercially known as sweetened chocolate,) two cents per pound.
> 228. Chocolate, and sweetened chocolate, [worth] *valued at* not exceeding thirty-five cents per pound, [two cents per pound] *ten per centum ad valorem;* chocolate confectionery, twenty-five per centum ad valorem.

319. Cocoa, prepared or manufactured, not specially provided for in this act, two cents per pound.
> 229. Cocoa, prepared or manufactured, not specially provided for in this act [two cents per pound], *five per centum ad valorem.*

320. Cocoa-butter or cocoa-butterine, three and one-half cents per pound.
>230. Cocoa-butter or cocoa-butterine [three and one-half cents per pound], *fifteen per centum ad valorem.*

321. Dandelion-root and acorns prepared, and other articles used as coffee, or as substitutes for coffee not specially provided for in this act, one and one-half cents per pound.
>231. Dandelion-root and acorns prepared, and other articles used as coffee, or as substitutes for coffee, not specially provided for in this act [one and one-half cents per pound], *thirty per centum ad valorem.*

SALT—
322. Salt in bags, sacks, barrels, or other packages twelve cents per one hundred pounds; in bulk, eight cents per one hundred pounds: *Provided,* That imported salt in bond may be used in curing fish taken by vessels licensed to engage in the fisheries, and in curing fish on the shores of the navigable waters of the United States, under such regulations as the Secretary of the Treasury shall prescribe; and upon proof that the salt has been used for either of the purposes stated in this proviso, the duties on the same shall be remitted: *Provided further,* That exporters of meats, whether packed or smoked, which have been cured in the United States with imported salt, shall, upon satisfactory proof, under such regulations as the Secretary of the Treasury shall prescribe, that such meats have been cured with imported salt, have refunded to them from the Treasury the duties paid on the salt so used in curing such exported meats, in amounts not less than one hundred dollars.
>NOTE.—Placed on free list. Par. 608.

323. Starch, including all preparations, from whatever substance produced, fit for use as starch, two cents per pound.
>232. Starch, including all preparations, from whatever substance produced, commonly used as starch [one cent per pound], *thirty per centum ad valorem.*

324. Dextrine, burnt starch, gum substitute, or British gum, one and one-half cents per pound.
>233. Dextrine, burnt starch, gum substitute, or British gum [one cent per pound], *thirty per centum ad valorem.*

325. Mustard, ground or preserved, in bottles or otherwise, ten cents per pound.
>234. Mustard, ground or preserved, in bottles or otherwise [ten cents per pound], *twenty-five per centum ad valorem.*
>234½. Orchids, *lily of the valley, azaleas, palms, and other plants used for forcing under glass for cut flowers or decorative purposes, ten per centum ad valorem.*

326. Spices, ground or powdered, not specially provided for in this act, four cents per pound; cayenne pepper, two and one-half cents per pound, unground; sage, three cents per pound.
>235. Spices, ground or powdered [not specially provided for in this act, three cents per pound]; capsicum or red pepper [two and one-half cents per pound], unground; sage [one cent per pound], *thirty per centum ad valorem.*

327. Vinegar, seven and one-half cents per gallon. The standard for vinegar shall be taken to be that strength which requires thirty-five grains of bicarbonate of potash to neutralize one ounce troy of vinegar.
>236. Vinegar [seven and one-half cents per gallon. The standard for vinegar shall be taken to be that strength which requires thirty-five grains of bicarbonate of potash to neutralize one ounce troy of vinegar], *twenty per centum ad valorem.*

328. There shall be allowed on the imported tin-plate used in the manufacture of cans, boxes, packages, and all articles of tin ware, exported, either empty or filled with domestic products, a drawback equal to the duty paid on such tin-plate, less one per centum of such duty, which shall be retained for the use of the United States.

SCHEDULE H.—SPIRITS, WINES, AND OTHER BEVERAGES.

SPIRITS.—

329. Brandy and other spirits manufactured or distilled from grain or other materials, and not specially provided for in this act, two dollars and fifty cents per proof gallon.

> 237. Brandy and other spirits manufactured or distilled from grain or other materials, and not specially provided for in this act, one dollar and eighty cents per proof gallon. *But when imported in bottles or jugs no separate or additional duty shall be assessed on the bottles or jugs.*

330. Each and every gauge or wine gallon of measurement shall be counted as at least one proof gallon; and the standard for determining the proof of brandy and other spirits or liquors of any kind imported shall be the same as that which is defined in the laws relating to internal revenue; but any brandy or other spirituous liquors, imported in casks of less capacity than fourteen gallons, shall be forfeited to the United States: *Provided*, That it shall be lawful for the Secretary of the Treasury, in his discretion, to authorize the ascertainment of the proof of wines, cordials, or other liquors, by distillation or otherwise, in case where it is impracticable to ascertain such proof by the means prescribed by existing law or regulations.

> 238. Each and every gauge or wine gallon of measurement shall be counted as at least one proof gallon; and the standard for determining the proof of brandy and other spirits or liquors of any kind imported shall be the same as that which is defined in the laws relating to internal revenue; but any brandy or other spirituous liquors, imported in casks of less capacity than fourteen gallons, shall be forfeited to the United States: *Provided*, That it shall be lawful for the Secretary of the Treasury, in his discretion, to authorize the ascertainment of the proof of wines, cordials, or other liquors, by distillation or otherwise, in cases where it is impracticable to ascertain such proof by the means prescribed by existing law or regulations.

331. On all compounds or preparations of which distilled spirits are a component part of chief value, not specially provided for in this act, there shall be levied a duty not less than that imposed upon distilled spirits.

> 239. [On all compounds or preparations of which distilled spirits are a component part of chief value, not specially provided for in this act, there shall be levied a duty not less than that imposed upon distilled spirits.] *Upon all compounds or preparations containing alcohol there shall be levied a duty at the rate of one dollar and eighty cents per proof gallon upon the distilled spirits contained therein in addition to the duty provided by law upon the other ingredients contained in such compounds or preparations.*

332. Cordials, liquors, arrack, absinthe, kirschwasser, ratafia, and other spirituous beverages or bitters of all kinds containing spirits, and not specially provided for in this act, two dollars and fifty cents per proof gallon.

> 240. Cordials, liquors, arrack, absinthe, kirschwasser, ratafia, and other spirituous beverages or bitters of all kinds containing spirits, and not specially provided for in this act, one dollar and eighty cents per proof gallon. *But when imported in bottles or jugs no separate or additional duty shall be assessed on the bottles or jugs.*

333. No lower rate or amount of duty shall be levied, collected, and paid on brandy, spirits, and other spirituous beverages than that fixed by law for the description of first proof; but it shall be increased in proportion for any greater strength than the strength of first proof, and all imitations of brandy or spirits or wines imported by any names whatever shall be subject to the highest rate of duty provided for the genuine articles respectively intended to be represented, and in no case less than one dollar and fifty cents per gallon.

> 241. No lower rate or amount of duty shall be levied, collected, and paid on brandy, spirits, and other spirituous beverages than that fixed by law for the description of first proof; but it shall be increased in proportion for any greater strength than the strength of first proof, and all imitations of brandy or spirits or wines imported by any names whatever shall be subject to the highest rate of duty provided for the genuine articles respectively intended to be represented, and in no case less than one dollar per gallon.

334. Bay-rum or bay-water, whether distilled or compounded, of first proof, and in proportion for any greater strength than first proof, one dollar and fifty cents per gallon.

> 242. Bay-rum or bay-water, whether distilled or compounded, of first proof, and in proportion for any greater strength than first proof, one dollar per gallon.

WINES:
335. Champagne and all other sparkling wines, in bottles containing each not more than one quart and more than one pint, eight dollars per dozen; containing not more than one pint each and more than one-half pint, four dollars per dozen; containing one-half pint each or less, two dollars per dozen; in bottles or other vessels containing more than one quart each, in addition to eight dollars per dozen bottles, on the quantity in excess of one quart, at the rate of two dollars and fifty cents per gallon.

> 243. Champagne and all other sparkling wines, in bottles containing each not more than one quart and more than one pint, eight dollars per dozen; containing not more than one pint each and more than one-half pint, four dollars per dozen; containing one-half pint each or less, two dollars per dozen; in bottles or other vessels containing more than one quart each, in addition to eight dollars per dozen bottles, on the quantity in excess of one quart, at the rate of two dollars and fifty cents per gallon; *but no separate or additional duty shall be assessed on the bottles.*

336. Still wines, including ginger wine or ginger cordial and vermuth, in casks, fifty cents per gallon; in bottles or jugs, per case of one dozen bottles or jugs, containing each not more than one quart and more than one pint, or twenty-four bottles or jugs containing each not more than one pint, one dollar and sixty cents per case; and any excess beyond these quantities found in such bottles or jugs shall be subject to a duty of five cents per pint or fractional part thereof, but no separate or additional duty shall be assessed on the bottles or jugs: *Provided,* That any wines, ginger-cordial, or vermuth imported containing more than twenty-four per centum of alcohol shall be forfeited to the United States: *And provided further,* That there shall be no constructive or other allowance for breakage, leakage, or damage on wines, liquors, cordials, or distilled spirits. Wines, cordials, brandy, and other spirituous liquors imported in bottles or jugs shall be

packed in packages containing not less than one dozen bottles or jugs in each package; and all such bottles or jugs shall pay an additional duty of three cents for each bottle or jug unless specially provided for in this act.

244. Still wines, including ginger wine or ginger cordial and vermuth in casks, or packages other than bottles or jugs, *if containing fourteen per centum or less of absolute alcohol, thirty cents per gallon; if containing more than fourteen per centum of absolute alcohol,* fifty cents per gallon: [*Provided,* That no such still wines in casks shall pay a higher rate of duty than one hundred per centum ad valorem;] in bottles or jugs, per case of one dozen bottles or jugs, containing each not more than one quart and more than one pint, or twenty-four bottles or jugs containing each not more than one pint, one dollar and sixty cents per case; and any excess beyond these quantities found in such bottles or jugs shall be subject to a duty of five cents per pint or fractional part thereof, but no separate or additional duty shall be assessed on the bottles or jugs: *Provided,* That any wines, ginger cordial, or vermnth imported containing more than twenty-five per centum of alcohol shall be classed as spirits and pay duty accordingly: *And provided further,* That there shall be no constructive or other allowance for breakage, leakage, or damage on wines, liquors, cordials, or distilled spirits. Wines, cordials, brandy, and other spirituous liquors imported in bottles or jugs shall be packed in packages containing not less than one dozen bottles or jugs in each package, or duty shall be paid as if such package contained at least one dozen bottles or jugs.

337. Ale, porter, and beer, in bottles or jugs, forty cents per gallon, but no separate or additional duty shall be assessed on the bottles or jugs; otherwise than in bottles or jugs, twenty cents per gallon.

245. Ale, porter, and beer, in bottles or jugs, thirty cents per gallon but no separate or additional duty shall be assessed on the bottles or jugs; otherwise than in bottles or jugs, [fifteen] *ten* cents per gallon.

338. Malt extract, fluid, in casks, twenty cents per gallon; in bottles or jugs, forty cents per gallon; solid or condensed, forty per centum ad valorem.

246. Malt extract, including all preparations bearing the name and commercially known as such fluid, in casks, fifteen cents per gallon; in bottles or jugs, thirty cents per gallon; solid or condensed, thirty per centum ad valorem.

339. Cherry juice and prune juice, or prune wine, and other fruit juice not specially provided for in this act, containing not more than eighteen per centum of alcohol, sixty cents per gallon; if containing more than eighteen per centum of alcohol, two dollars and fifty cents per proof gallon.

247. Cherry juice and prune juice, or prune wine, and other fruit juice not specially provided for in this act, containing eighteen per centum or less of alcohol, fifty cents per gallon; if containing more than eighteen per centum of alcohol, one dollar and eighty cents per proof gallon.

340. Ginger-ale, ginger-beer, lemonade, soda-water, and other similar waters in plain green or colored molded or pressed glass bottles, containing each not more than three-fourths of a pint, thirteen cents per dozen; containing more than three-fourths of a pint each and not more than one and one-half pints, twenty-six cents per dozen; but no separate or additional duty shall be assessed on the bottles; if imported otherwise than in plain green or colored molded or pressed glass bottles, or in such bottles containing more than one and one-half pints each, fifty cents per gallon and in addition thereto,

duty shall be collected on the bottles, or other coverings, at the rates which would be chargeable thereon if imported empty.

<blockquote>
248. Ginger-ale or ginger-beer, twenty per centum ad valorem, but no separate or additional duty shall be assessed on the bottles.

NOTE.—Lemonade and soda water placed on free list. Par. 555.
</blockquote>

341. All mineral waters, and all imitations of natural mineral waters, and all artificial mineral waters not specially provided for in this act, in green or colored glass bottles, containing not more than one pint, sixteen cents per dozen bottles. If containing more than one pint and not more than one quart, twenty-five cents per dozen bottles. But no separate duty shall be assessed upon the bottles. If imported otherwise than in plain green or colored glass bottles, or if imported in such bottles containing more than one quart, twenty cents per gallon, and in addition thereto duty shall be collected upon the bottles or other covering at the same rates that would be charged if imported empty or separately.

<blockquote>
249. All imitations of natural mineral waters, and all artificial mineral waters, thirty per centum ad valorem.
</blockquote>

SCHEDULE I.—COTTON MANUFACTURES.

342. Cotton thread, yarn, warps, or warp-yarn, whether single or advanced beyond the condition of single, by grouping or twisting two or more single yarns together, whether on beams or in bundles, skeins, or cops, or in any other form, except spool-thread of cotton, hereinafter provided for, valued at not exceeding twenty-five cents per pound, ten cents per pound; valued at over twenty-five cents per pound and not exceeding forty cents per pound, eighteen cents per pound; valued at over forty cents per pound and not exceeding fifty cents per pound, twenty-three cents per pound; valued at over fifty cents per pound and not exceeding sixty cents per pound, twenty-eight cents per pound; valued at over sixty cents per pound and not exceeding seventy cents per pound, thirty-three cents per pound; valued at over seventy cents per pound and not exceeding eighty cents per pound, thirty-eight cents per pound; valued at over eighty cents per pound and not exceeding one dollar per pound, forty-eight cents per pound; valued at over one dollar per pound, fifty per centum ad valorem.

SCHEDULE I.—COTTON MANUFACTURES.

<blockquote>
250. Cotton thread, yarn, warps, or warp yarn, whether single or advanced beyond the condition of single, by grouping or twisting two or more single yarns together, whether on beams or in bundles, skeins, or cops, or in any other form, except spool thread of cotton, hereinafter provided for, valued at not exceeding twelve cents per pound, twenty per centum ad valorem; valued at over twelve cents per pound and not exceeding twenty cents per pound, twenty-five per centum ad valorem; valued at over twenty cents per pound and not exceeding thirty cents per pound, thirty per centum ad valorem; valued at over thirty cents per pound, and not exceeding forty cents per pound, thirty-five per centum ad valorem; valued at over forty cents per pound, forty per centum ad valorem.
</blockquote>

343. Spool-thread of cotton, containing on each spool not exceeding one hundred yards of thread, seven cents per dozen; exceeding one hundred yards on each spool, for every additional one hundred yards

of thread or fractional part thereof in excess of one hundred yards, seven cents per dozen spools.

> 251. Spool-thread of cotton, containing on each spool not exceeding one hundred yards of thread, four and one-half cents per dozen; exceeding one hundred yards on each spool, for every additional one hundred yards of thread or fractional part thereof in excess of one hundred yards, four and one-half cents per dozen spools.

344. Cotton cloth not bleached, dyed, colored, stained, painted, or printed, and not exceeding fifty threads to the square inch, counting the warp and filling, two cents per square yard; if bleached, two and one-half cents per square yard; if dyed, colored, stained, painted, or printed, four cents per square yard.

> 252. Cotton cloth not bleached, dyed, colored, stained, painted, or printed, and not exceeding fifty threads to the square inch, counting the warp and filling, one cent per square yard; if bleached, one and one-fourth cents per square yard; if dyed, colored, stained, painted, or printed, two cents per square yard.

345. Cotton cloth, not bleached, dyed, colored, stained, painted, or printed, exceeding fifty and not exceeding one hundred threads to the square inch, counting the warp and filling, two and one-fourth cents per square yard; if bleached, three cents per square yard; if dyed, colored, stained, painted, or printed, four cents per square yard : *Provided*, That on all cotton cloth not exceeding one hundred threads to the square inch, counting the warp and filling, not bleached, dyed, colored, stained, painted, or printed, valued at over six and one-half cents per square yard; bleached, valued at over nine cents per square yard; and dyed, colored, stained, painted or printed, valued at over twelve cents per square yard, there shall be levied, collected, and paid a duty of thirty-five per centum ad valorem.

> 253. Cotton cloth not bleached, dyed, colored, stained, painted, or printed, exceeding fifty and not exceeding one hundred threads to the square inch, counting the warp and filling, one and one-fourth cents per square yard; if bleached, one and one-half cents per square yard; if dyed, colored, stained, painted, or printed, two and three-fourths cents per square yard: *Provided*, That on all cotton cloth not exceeding one hundred threads to the square inch, counting the warp and filling, not bleached, dyed, colored, stained, painted, or printed, valued at over six and one-half cents per square yard, twenty per centum ad valorem; bleached, valued at over nine cents per square yard, twenty-five per centum ad valorem; and dyed, colored, stained, painted, or printed, valued at over twelve cents per square yard, there shall be levied, collected, and paid a duty of thirty per centum ad valorem.

346. Cotton cloth, not bleached, dyed, colored, stained, painted, or printed, exceeding one hundred and not exceeding one hundred and fifty threads to the square inch, counting the warp and filling, three cents per square yard; if bleached, four cents per square yard; if dyed, colored, stained, painted, or printed, five cents per square yard: *Provided*, That on all cotton cloth exceeding one hundred and not exceeding one hundred and fifty threads to the square inch, counting the warp and filling, not bleached, dyed, colored, stained, painted, or printed, valued at over seven and one-half cents per square yard; bleached, valued at over ten cents per square yard; dyed, colored, stained, painted, or printed, valued at over twelve and one-half cents per square yard, there shall be levied, collected, and paid a duty of forty per centum ad valorem.

> 254. Cotton cloth, not bleached, dyed, colored, stained, painted, or printed, exceeding one hundred and not exceeding one hundred and fifty threads to the square inch, counting the warp and filling, one and one-half cents per square yard; if bleached, two and one-half cents per square yard; if

dyed, colored, stained, painted, or printed, three and one-half cents per square yard: *Provided*, That on all cotton cloth exceeding one hundred and not exceeding one hundred and fifty threads to the square inch, counting the warp and filling, including all cotton duck, not bleached, dyed, colored, stained, painted, or printed, valued at over seven and one-half cents per square yard, twenty-five per centum ad valorem; bleached, including all cotton duck, valued at over ten cents per square yard, thirty per centum ad valorem; dyed, colored, stained, painted, or printed, valued at over twelve and one-half cents per square yard, there shall be levied, collected, and paid a duty of thirty-five per centum ad valorem.

347. Cotton cloth, not bleached, dyed, colored, stained, painted, or printed, exceeding one hundred and fifty and not exceeding two hundred threads to the square inch, counting the warp and filling, three and a half cents per square yard; if bleached, four and one-half cents per square yard; if dyed, colored, stained, painted, or printed, five and one-half cents per square yard: *Provided*, That on all cotton cloth exceeding one hundred and fifty and not exceeding two hundred threads to the square inch, counting the warp and filling, not bleached, dyed, colored, stained, painted, or printed, valued at over eight cents per square yard; bleached valued at over ten cents per square yard; dyed, colored, stained, painted, or printed, valued at over twelve cents per square yard, there shall be levied, collected, and paid a duty of forty-five per centum ad valorem.

255. Cotton cloth, not bleached, dyed, colored, stained, painted, or printed, exceeding one hundred and fifty and not exceeding two hundred threads to the square inch, counting the warp and filling, two cents per square yard; if bleached, two and three-quarter cents per square yard; if dyed, colored, stained, painted, or printed, four and one-fourth cents per square yard: *Provided*, That on all cotton cloth exceeding one hundred and fifty and not exceeding two hundred threads to the square inch, counting the warp and filling, not bleached, dyed, colored, stained, painted, or printed, valued at over eight cents per square yard, thirty per centum ad valorem; bleached, valued at over ten cents per square yard, thirty-five per centum ad valorem; dyed, colored, stained, painted, or printed, valued at over twelve cents per square yard, there shall be levied, collected, and paid a duty of forty per centum ad valorem.

348. Cotton cloth, not bleached, dyed, colored, stained, painted, or printed, exceeding two hundred threads to the square inch, counting the warp and filling, four and one-half cents per square yard; if bleached, five and one-half cents per square yard; if dyed, colored, stained, painted, or printed, six and three-fourths cents per square yard: *Provided*, That on all such cotton cloths not bleached, dyed, colored, stained, painted, or printed, valued at over ten cents per square yard; bleached, valued at over twelve cents per square yard; and dyed, colored, stained, painted, or printed, valued at over fifteen cents per square yard, there shall be levied, collected, and paid a duty of forty-five per centum ad valorem: *Provided further*, That on cotton cloth, bleached, dyed, colored, stained, painted or printed, containing an admixture of silk, and not otherwise provided for, there shall be levied, collected, and paid a duty of ten cents per square yard, and in addition thereto thirty-five per centum ad valorem.

256. Cotton cloth, not bleached, dyed, colored, stained, painted, or printed, exceeding two hundred threads to the square inch, counting the warp and filling, three cents per square yard; if bleached, four cents per square yard; if dyed, colored, stained, painted, or printed, five and three-fourths cents per square yard: *Provided*, That on all such cotton cloths not bleached, dyed, colored, stained, painted, or printed, valued at over ten cents per square yard, thirty per centum ad valorem; bleached, valued at over twelve cents per square yard, thirty-five per centum ad valorem; and dyed, colored, stained, painted, or printed, valued at over fifteen cents per square yard, there shall be levied, collected, and paid a duty of forty per centum ad valorem.

257. The term cotton cloth or cloth, wherever used in the foregoing paragraphs of this schedule shall be held to include all woven fabrics of cotton in the piece, whether figured, fancy or plain, not specially provided for in this act, the warp and filling threads of which can be counted by unraveling or other practicable means.

349. Clothing ready made, and articles of wearing apparel of every description, handkerchiefs, and neckties or neck wear, composed of cotton or other vegetable fiber, or of which cotton or other vegetable fiber is the component material of chief value, made up or manufactured wholly or in part by the tailor, seamstress, or manufacturer, all of the foregoing not specially provided for in this act, fifty per centum ad valorem: *Provided*, That all such clothing ready made and articles of wearing apparel having India rubber as a component material (not including gloves or elastic articles that are specially provided for in this act), shall be subject to a duty of fifty cents per pound, and in addition thereto fifty per centum ad valorem.

258. Clothing ready made, and articles of wearing apparel of every description, handkerchiefs, and neckties or neck wear, composed of cotton or other vegetable fiber, or of which cotton or other vegetable fiber is the component material of chief value, made up or manufactured wholly or in part by the tailor, seamstress, or manufacturer, all of the foregoing not specially provided for in this act, forty per centum ad valorem.

350. Plushes, velvets, velveteens, corduroys, and all pile fabrics composed of cotton or other vegetable fiber, not bleached, dyed, colored, stained, painted, or printed, ten cents per square yard and twenty per centum ad valorem; on all such goods if bleached, twelve cents per square yard and twenty per centum ad valorem; if dyed, colored, stained, painted, or printed, fourteen cents per square yard and twenty per centum ad valorem; but none of the foregoing articles in this paragraph shall pay a less rate of duty than forty per centum ad valorem.

259. Plushes, velvets, velveteens, corduroys, and all pile fabrics composed of cotton or other vegetable fiber, not bleached, dyed, colored, stained, painted, or printed, thirty-five per centum ad valorem; on all such goods if bleached, dyed, colored, stained, painted, or printed, forty per centum ad valorem.

351. Chenille curtains, table covers, and all goods manufactured of cotton chenille, or of which cotton chenille forms the component material of chief value, sixty per centum ad valorem.

260. Chenille curtains, table covers, and all goods manufactured of cotton chenille, or of which cotton chenille forms the component material of chief value, forty per centum ad valorem.

352. Stockings, hose and half-hose, made on knitting machines or frames, composed of cotton or other vegetable fiber and not otherwise specially provided for in this act, and shirts and drawers composed of cotton, valued at not more than one dollar and fifty cents per dozen, thirty-five per centum ad valorem.

261. Stockings, hose and half-hose, made on knitting machines or frames, composed of cotton or other vegetable fiber and not otherwise specially provided for in this act, and shirts and drawers composed of cotton, valued at not more than one dollar and fifty cents per dozen, thirty per centum ad valorem.

353. Stockings, hose, and half-hose, selvedged, fashioned, narrowed, or shaped wholly or in part by knitting machines or frames, or knit by hand, including such as are commercially known as seamless stockings, hose or half-hose, all of the above composed of cotton or other vegetable fiber, finished or unfinished, valued at not more than sixty cents

per dozen pairs, twenty cents per dozen pairs, and in addition thereto twenty per centum ad valorem; valued at more than sixty cents per dozen pairs and not more than two dollars per dozen pairs, fifty cents per dozen pairs, and in addition thereto thirty per centum ad valorem; valued at more than two dollars per dozen pairs, and not more than four dollars per dozen pairs, seventy-five cents per dozen pairs, and in addition thereto, forty per centum ad valorem; valued at more than four dollars per dozen pairs, one dollar per dozen pairs, and in addition thereto, forty per centum ad valorem; and all shirts and drawers composed of cotton or other vegetable fiber, valued at more than one dollar and fifty cents per dozen and not more than three dollars per dozen, one dollar per dozen, and in addition thereto, thirty-five per centum ad valorem; valued at more than three dollars per dozen and not more than five dollars per dozen, one dollar and twenty-five cents per dozen, and in addition thereto, forty per centum ad valorem; valued at more than five dollars per dozen, and not more than seven dollars per dozen, one dollar and fifty cents per dozen, and in addition thereto, forty per centum ad valorem; valued at more than seven dollars per dozen, two dollars per dozen, and in addition thereto, forty per centum ad valorem.

> 262. Stockings, hose and half-hose, selvedged, fashioned, narrowed, or shaped wholly or in part by knitting machines or frames, or knit by hand, including such as are commercially known as seamless or clocked stockings, hose or half-hose, all of the above composed of cotton or other vegetable fiber, finished or unfinished, forty per centum ad valorem.

354. Cotton cords, braids, boot, shoe, and corset lacings, thirty-five cents per pound; cotton gimps, galloons, webbing, goring, suspenders, and braces, any of the foregoing which are elastic or nonelastic, forty per centum ad valorem: *Provided*, That none of the articles included in this paragraph shall pay a less rate of duty than forty per centum ad valorem.

> 263. Cords, braids, boot, shoe, and corset lacings, tape, gimps, galloons, webbing, goring, suspenders, and braces, made of cotton or other vegetable fiber and whether composed in part of India rubber or otherwise, and cotton damask, in the piece or otherwise, thirty-five per centum ad valorem.

355. Cotton damask, in the piece or otherwise, and all manufactures of cotton not specially provided for in this act, forty per centum ad valorem.

> 264. All manufactures of cotton not specially provided for in this act, including cloth having India-rubber as a component material, thirty-five per centum ad valorem.

SCHEDULE J.—FLAX, HEMP, AND JUTE, AND MANUFACTURES OF.

356. Flax straw, five dollars per ton.
> Placed upon free list. Par. 497.

357. Flax, not hackled or dressed, one cent per pound.
> Placed upon free list. Par. 497.

358. Flax, hackled, known as "dressed line," three cents per pound.
> 265. Flax, hackled, known as "dressed line," one and one-half cents per pound.

359. Tow, of flax or hemp, one-half of one cent per pound.
> Placed upon free list. Par. 497.

360. Hemp twenty-five dollars per ton; hemp, hackled, known as line of hemp, fifty dollars per ton.

> 266. Hemp, hackled, known as "dressed line," one cent per pound.
> NOTE.—Hemp placed on free list. Par. 497.

361. Yarn, made of jute, thirty-five per centum ad valorem.

> 267. Yarn, made of jute, twenty per centum ad valorem.

362. Cables, cordage, and twine (except binding twine) composed in whole or in part of istle or Tampico fiber, manila, sisal grass, or sunn, one and one-half cents per pound; all binding twine manufactured in whole or in part from istle or Tampico fiber, manila, sisal grass, or sunn, seven-tenths of one cent per pound; cables and cordage made of hemp, two and one-half cents per pound; tarred cables and cordage, three cents per pound.

> 268. Cables, cordage, and twine (except binding twine) composed in whole or in part of New Zealand hemp, istle or Tampico fiber, manila, sisal grass, or sunn, ten per centum ad valorem; all binding twine manufactured in whole or in part from New Zealand hemp, istle or Tampico fiber, manila, sisal grass, or sunn, of single ply and measuring not exceeding six hundred feet to the pound, free. Par. 399.

363. Hemp and jute carpets and carpetings, six cents per square yard.

> 269. Hemp and jute carpets and carpetings, twenty per centum ad valorem.

364. Burlaps, not exceeding sixty inches in width, of flax, jute or hemp, or of which flax, jute, or hemp, or either of them, shall be the component material of chief value (except such as may be suitable for bagging for cotton), one and five-eighths cents per pound.

365. Bags for grain made of burlaps, two cents per pound.

> 270. Burlaps, not exceeding sixty inches in width, containing not over forty threads to the square inch counting warp and filling, fifteen per centum ad valorem; bags for grain made of such burlaps, [twenty] *twenty-two and one-half* per centum ad valorem.
> NOTE.—Paragraphs 364 and 365 of present law consolidated.

366. Bagging for cotton, gunny cloth, and all similar material suitable for covering cotton, composed in whole or in part of hemp, flax, jute, or jute butts, valued at six cents or less per square yard, one and six-tenths cents per square yard; valued at more than six cents per square yard, one and eight-tenths cents per square yard.

> 271. Bagging for cotton, gunny cloth, and all similar material suitable for covering cotton, composed in whole or in part of hemp, flax, jute, or jute butts, fifteen per centum ad valorem.

367. Flax gill-netting, nets, webs, and seines, when the thread or twine of which they are composed is made of yarn of a number not higher than twenty, fifteen cents per pound, and thirty-five per centum ad valorem; when made of threads or twines, the yarn of which is finer than number twenty, twenty cents per pound and in addition thereto forty-five per centum ad valorem.

> 272. Flax gill-netting, nets, webs, and seines [thirty] *thirty-five* per centum ad valorem.

368. Linen hydraulic hose, made in whole or in part of flax, hemp or jute, twenty cents per pound.

> NOTE.—This paragraph consolidated with paragraph 275 proposed law.

369. Oil cloth for floors, stamped, painted, or printed, including linoleum, corticene, cork-carpets, figured or plain, and all other oil-cloth (except silk oil-cloth), and water-proof cloth, not specially provided for in this act, valued at twenty-five cents or less per square yard, forty

per centum ad valorem; valued above twenty-five cents per square yard, fifteen cents per square yard and thirty per centum ad valorem.

<blockquote>273. Oil-cloth for floors, stamped, painted, or printed, including linoleum, corticene, cork-carpets, figured or plain, and all other oil-cloth (except silk oil-cloth), and water-proof cloth, not specially provided for in this act, valued at twenty-five cents or less per square yard, twenty per centum ad valorem; valued above twenty-five cents per square yard, [thirty] thirty-five per centum ad valorem.</blockquote>

370. Yarns or threads composed of flax òr hemp, or of a mixture of either of these substances, valued at thirteen cents or less per pound, six cents per pound; valued at more than thirteen cents per pound, forty-five per centum ad valorem.

<blockquote>274. Yarns or threads composed of flax or hemp, or of a mixture of either of these substances, valued at thirteen cents or less per pound, twenty-five per centum ad valorem, valued at more than thirteen cents per pound, thirty per centum ad valorem.</blockquote>

371. All manufactures of flax or hemp, or of which these substances, or either of them, is the component material of chief value, not specially provided for in this act, fifty per centum ad valorem: *Provided*, That until January first, eighteen hundred and ninety-four, such manufactures of flax containing more than one hundred threads to the square inch, counting both warp and filling, shall be subject to a duty of thirty-five per centum ad valorem in lieu of the duty herein provided.

<blockquote>NOTE.—This paragraph consolidated with paragraph 277 proposed law.</blockquote>

372. Collars and cuffs, composed entirely of cotton, fifteen cents per dozen pieces and thirty-five per centum ad valorem composed in whole or in part of linen, thirty cents per dozen pieces and forty per centum ad valorem; shirts, and all articles of wearing apparel of every description, not specially provided for in this act, composed wholly or in part of linen, fifty-five per centum ad valorem.

<blockquote>275. Collars and cuffs, [and shirts] composed wholly or in part of linen, fifty-five per centum ad valorem; shirts and all other articles of wearing apparel of every description, not specially provided for in this act, composed wholly or in part of linen, [and linen hydraulic hose] [thirty-five] fifty per centum ad valorem.</blockquote>

373. Laces, edgings, embroideries, insertings, neck rufflings, ruchings, trimmings, tuckings, lace window-curtains, and other similar tamboured articles, and articles embroidered by hand or machinery, embroidered and hem-stitched handkerchiefs, and articles made wholly or in part of lace, rufflings, tuckings, or ruchings, all of the above-named articles, composed of flax, jute, cotton, or other vegetable fiber, or of which these substances or either of them, or a mixture of any of them is the component material of chief value, not specially provided for in this act, sixty per centum ad valorem: *Provided*, That articles of wearing apparel, and textile fabrics, when embroidered by hand or machinery, and whether specially or otherwise provided for in this act, shall not pay a less rate of duty than that fixed by the respective paragraphs and schedules of this act upon embroideries of the materials of which they are respectively composed.

<blockquote>276. Laces, edgings, embroideries, insertings, neck rufflings, ruchings, trimmings, tuckings, lace window-curtains, and other similar tamboured articles, and articles embroidered by hand or machinery, embroidered or hem-stitched handkerchiefs, and articles made wholly or in part of lace, rufflings, tuckings, or ruchings, all of the above-named articles, composed of flax, jute, cotton, or other vegetable fiber, or of which these substances or either of them, or a mixture of any of them is the component material of chief value, not specially provided for in this act, forty per centum ad valorem.</blockquote>

374. All manufactures of jute, or other vegetable fiber, except flax, hemp or cotton, or of which jute, or other vegetable fiber, except flax, hemp or cotton, is the component material of chief value, not specially provided for in this act, valued at five cents per pound or less, two cents per pound; valued above five cents per pound, forty per centum ad valorem.

277. All manufactures of flax, hemp, jute, or other vegetable fiber, except cotton, or of which flax, hemp, jute, or other vegetable fiber, except cotton, is the component material of chief value, not specially provided for in this act, thirty per centum ad valorem.

SCHEDULE K.—WOOL AND MANUFACTURES OF WOOL.

NOTE.—Paragraphs 375 to 387 see free list.

375. All wools, hair of the camel, goat, alpaca, and other like animals shall be divided for the purpose of fixing the duties to be charged thereon into the three following classes:

376. Class one, that is to say, Merino, mestiza, metz, or metis wools, or other wools of Merino blood, immediate or remote, Down clothing wools, and wools of like character with any of the preceding, including such as have been heretofore usually imported into the United States from Buenos Ayres, New Zealand, Australia, Cape of Good Hope, Russia, Great Britain, Canada, and elsewhere, and also including all wools not hereinafter described or designated in classes two and three.

377. Class two, that is to say, Leicester, Cotswold, Lincolnshire, Down combing wools, Canada long wools, or other like combing wools of English blood, and usually known by the terms herein used, and also hair of the camel, goat, alpaca, and other like animals.

378. Class three, that is to say, Donskoi, native South American, Cordova, Valparaiso, native Smyrna, Russian camels hair, and including all such wools of like character as have been heretofore usually imported into the United States from Turkey, Greece, Egypt, Syria, and elsewhere, excepting improved wools hereinafter provided for.

379. The standard samples of all wools which are now or may be hereafter deposited in the principal custom-houses of the United States, under the authority of the Secretary of the Treasury, shall be the standards for the classification of wools under this act, and the Secretary of the Treasury shall have the authority to renew these standards and to make such additions to them from time to time as may be required, and he shall cause to be deposited like standards in other custom-houses of the United States when they may be needed.

380. Whenever wools of class three shall have been improved by the admixture of Merino or English blood from their present character as represented by the standard samples now or hereafter to be deposited in the principal custom-houses of the United States, such improved wools shall be classified for duty either as class one or as class two, as the case may be.

381. The duty on wools of the first class which shall be imported washed shall be twice the amount of the duty to which they would be subjected if imported unwashed; and the duty on wools of the first and second classes which shall be imported scoured shall be three times the duty to which they would be subjected if imported unwashed.

382. Unwashed wools shall be considered such as shall have been shorn from the sheep without any cleansing; that is, in their natural condition. Washed wools shall be considered such as have been washed with water on the sheep's back. Wool washed in any other manner than on the sheep's back shall be considered as scoured wool.

383. The duty upon wool of the sheep or hair of the camel, goat, alpaca, and other like animals which shall be imported in any other than ordinary condition, or which shall be changed in its character or condition for the purpose of evading the duty, or which shall be reduced in value by the admixture of dirt or any other foreign substance, or which has been sorted or increased in value by the rejection of any part of the original fleece, shall be twice the duty to which it would be otherwise subject: *Provided*, That skirted wools as now imported are hereby excepted. Wools on which a duty is assessed amounting to three times or more than that which would be assessed if said wool was imported unwashed, such duty shall not be doubled on account of its being sorted. If any bale or package of wool or hair specified in this act imported as of any specified class, or claimed by the importer to be dutiable as of any specified class shall contain any wool or hair subject to a higher rate of duty than the class so specified, the whole bale or package shall be subject to the highest rate of duty chargeable on wool of the class subject to such higher rate of duty, and if any bale or package be claimed by the importer to be shoddy, mungo, flocks, wool, hair, or other material of any class specified in this act, and such bale contain any admixture of any one or more of said materials, or of any other material, the whole bale or package shall be subject to duty at the highest rate imposed upon any article in said bale or package.

384. The duty upon all wools and hair of the first class shall be eleven cents per pound, and upon all wools or hair of the second class twelve cents per pound.

385. On wools of the third class and on camel's hair of the third class the value whereof shall be thirteen cents or less per pound, including charges, the duty shall be thirty-two per centum ad valorem.

386. On wools of the third class, and on camel's hair of the third class, the value whereof shall exceed thirteen cents per pound, including charges, the duty shall be fifty per cent ad valorem.

387. Wools on the skin shall pay the same rate as other wools, the quantity and value to be ascertained under such rules as the Secretary of the Treasury may prescribe.

NOTE.—Paragraphs 375 to 387 see free list as follows:

685. All wool of the sheep, hair of the camel, goat, alpaca, and other like animals, and all wool and hair on the skin, yarn waste, card waste, bur waste, rags and flocks, including all waste, or rags composed wholly or in part of wool: *Provided*, That this paragraph shall take effect on and after August second, eighteen hundred and ninety-four.

388. On noils, shoddy, top waste, slubbing waste, roving waste, ring waste, yarn waste, garnetted waste, and all other wastes composed wholly or in part of wool, the duty shall be thirty cents per pound.

389. On woolen rags, mungo, and flocks, the duty shall be ten cents per pound.

278. Wool of the sheep, hair of the camel, goat, alpaca and other like animals in the form of slubbing waste, roving waste, ring waste, mungo, shoddies, garnetted or carded waste, carbonized noils or other waste product, any of which is composed wholly or in part of wool, the hair of the camel, goat, alpaca and other like animals, which has been improved or advanced beyond its original condition as waste by the use of machinery or the application of labor, or both, and carbonized wool, shall be subject to a duty of fifteen per centum ad valorem.

390. Wools and hair of the camel, goat, alpaca, or other like animals, in the form of roping, roving, or tops, and all wool and hair which have been advanced in any manner or by any process of manufacture beyond the washed or scoured condition, not specially provided for in this act, shall be subject to the same duties as are imposed upon manufactures of wool not specially provided for in this act.

> 279. On wool of the sheep, hair of the camel, goat, alpaca, or other like animals in the form of roving, roping, or tops, [valued at not more than thirty-five cents per pound, the duty shall be] twenty-five per centum ad valorem; [valued at over thirty-five cents per pound, the duty shall be thirty per centum ad valorem.]

391. On woolen and worsted yarns made wholly or in part of wool, worsted, the hair of the camel, goat, alpaca, or other animals, valued at not more than thirty cents per pound, the duty per pound shall be two and one-half times the duty imposed by this act on a pound of unwashed wool of the first class, and in addition thereto, thirty-five per centum ad valorem; valued at more than thirty cents and not more than forty cents per pound, the duty per pound shall be three times the duty imposed by this act on a pound of unwashed wool of the first class, and in addition thereto thirty-five per centum ad valorem; valued at more than forty cents per pound the duty per pound shall be three and one-half times the duty imposed by this act on a pound of unwashed wool of the first class, and in addition thereto forty per centum ad valorem.

> 280. On woolen and worsted yarns made wholly or in part of wool, worsted, the hair of the camel, goat, alpaca, or other animals [valued at not more than forty cents per pound], thirty per centum ad valorem; [valued at more than forty cents per pound, thirty-five per centum ad valorem.]

392. On woolen or worsted cloths, shawls, knit fabrics, and all fabrics made on knitting machines or frames, and all manufactures of every description made wholly or in part of wool, worsted, the hair of the camel, goat, alpaca, or other animals, not specially provided for in this act, valued at not more than thirty cents per pound, the duty per pound shall be three times the duty imposed by this act on a pound of unwashed wool of the first class, and in addition thereto forty per centum ad valorem; valued at more than thirty and not more than forty cents per pound, the duty per pound shall be three and one-half times the duty imposed by this act on a pound of unwashed wool of the first class, and in addition thereto forty per centum ad valorem; valued at above forty cents per pound, the duty per pound shall be four times the duty imposed by this act on a pound of unwashed wool of the first class, and in addition thereto fifty per centum ad valorem.

> 281. On woolen or worsted cloths, shawls, knit fabrics and all fabrics made on knitting machines or frames, and all manufactures of every description made wholly or in part of wool, worsted, the hair of the camel, goat, alpaca, or other animals, and any of the above having India rubber as a component material, not specially provided for in this act, [forty] *thirty-five* per centum ad valorem.

393. On blankets, hats of wool, and flannels for underwear composed wholly or in part of wool, the hair of the camel, goat, alpaca, or other animals, valued at not more than thirty cents per pound, the duty per pound shall be the same as the duty imposed by this act on one pound and one-half of unwashed wool of the first class, and in addition thereto thirty per centum ad valorem; valued at more than thirty and not more than forty cents per pound, the duty per pound, shall be twice the

duty imposed by this act on a pound of unwashed wool of the first class; valued at more than forty cents and not more than fifty cents per pound, the duty per pound shall be three times the duty imposed by this act on a pound of unwashed wool of the first class; and in addition thereto upon all the above-named articles thirty-five per centum ad valorem. On blankets and hats of wool composed wholly or in part of wool, the hair of the camel, goat, alpaca, or other animal, valued at more than fifty cents per pound, the duty per pound shall be three and a half times the duty imposed by this act on a pound of unwashed wool of the first-class, and in addition thereto forty per centum ad valorem. Flannels composed wholly or in part of wool, the hair of the camel, goat, alpaca, or other animals, valued at above fifty cents per pound shall be classified and pay the same duty as women's and children's dress goods, coat linings, Italian cloths, and goods of similar character and description provided by this act.

> 282. On blankets, hats of wool, and flannels for underwear and felts for paper-maker's use and printing machines, composed wholly or in part of wool, the hair of the camel, goat, alpaca, or other animals, valued at not more than thirty cents per pound, twenty-five per centum ad valorem; valued at more than thirty [and not more than forty] cents per pound, thirty per centum ad valorem; [valued at more than forty cents per pound], thirty-five per centum ad valorem:] *Provided*, That on blankets over three yards in length the same duties shall be paid as on woolen and worsted cloths, and on flannels weighing over four ounces per square yard, the same duties as on dress goods.

394. On women's and children's dress goods, coat linings, Italian cloths, and goods of similar character or description of which the warp consists wholly of cotton or other vegetable material, with the remainder of the fabric composed wholly or in part of wool, worsted, the hair of the camel, goat, alpaca, or other animals, valued at not exceeding fifteen cents per square yard, seven cents per square yard, and in addition thereto forty per centum ad valorem; valued at above fifteen cents per square yard, eight cents per square yard, and in addition thereto fifty per centum ad valorem: *Provided*, That on all such goods weighing over four ounces per square yard the duty per pound shall be four times the duty imposed by this act on a pound of unwashed wool of the first class, and in addition thereto fifty per centum ad valorem.

395. On women's and children's dress goods, coat linings, Italian cloth, bunting, and goods of similar description or character composed wholly or in part of wool, worsted, the hair of the camel, goat, alpaca, or other animals, and not specially provided for in this act, the duty shall be twelve cents per square yard, and in addition thereto fifty per centum ad valorem: *Provided*, That on all such goods weighing over four ounces per square yard the duty per pound shall be four times the duty imposed by this act on a pound of unwashed wool of the first class, and in addition thereto fifty per centum ad valorem.

> 283. On women's and children's dress goods, coat linings, Italian cloth, bunting, and goods of similar description or character composed wholly or in part of wool, worsted, the hair of the camel, goat, alpaca, or other animals, and not specially provided for in this act, [forty] *thirty-five* per centum ad valorem.
>
> NOTE.—This covers Pars. 394 and 395.

396. On clothing, ready made, and articles of wearing apparel of every description, made up or manufactured wholly or in part not specially provided for in this act, felt not woven, and not specially provided for in this act, and plushes and other pile fabrics, all the foregoing, composed wholly or in part of wool, worsted, the hair of the camel, goat, alpaca, or other animals the duty per pound shall be

four and one-half times the duty imposed by this act on a pound of unwashed wool of the first class, and in addition thereto sixty per centum ad valorem.

> 284. On clothing, ready made, and articles of wearing apparel of every description, made up or manufactured wholly or in part not specially provided for in this act, felts not woven, and not specially provided for in this act, and plushes and other pile fabrics, *and imitations of fur*, all the foregoing, composed wholly or in part of wool, worsted, the hair of the camel, goat, alpaca, or other animals, including those having India rubber as a component material, [forty-five] *forty* per centum ad valorem.

397. On cloaks, dolmans, jackets, talmas, ulsters, or other outside garments for ladies and children's apparel and goods of similar description, or used for like purposes, composed wholly or in part of wool, worsted, the hair of the camel, goat, alpaca, or other animals, made up or manufactured wholly or in part, the duty per pound shall be four and one-half times the duty imposed by this act on a pound of unwashed wool of the first class, and in addition thereto sixty per centum ad valorem.

> 285. [On cloaks, dolmans, jackets, talmas, ulsters, or other outside garments for ladies and children's apparel and goods of similar description, or used for like purposes, composed wholly or in part of wool, worsted, the hair of the camel, goat, alpaca, or other animals, made up or manufactured wholly or in part, forty-five per centum ad valorem.]

398. On webbings, gorings, suspenders, braces, beltings, bindings, braids, galloons, fringes, gimps, cords, cords and tassels, dress trimmings, laces and embroideries, head nets, buttons, or barrel buttons, or buttons of other forms, for tassels or ornaments, wrought by hand or braided by machinery any of the foregoing which are elastic or non-elastic, made of wool, worsted, the hair of the camel, goat, alpaca, or other animals, or of which wool, worsted, the hair of the camel, goat, alpaca, or other animals is a component material, the duty shall be sixty cents per pound, and in addition thereto sixty per centum ad valorem.

> 286. On webbings, gorings, suspenders, braces, beltings, bindings, braids, galloons, fringes, gimps, cords, cords and tassels, dress trimmings, laces and embroideries, head nets, buttons, or barrel buttons, or buttons of other forms, for tassels or ornaments, any of the foregoing which are elastic or non-elastic, made of wool, worsted, the hair of the camel, goat, alpaca, or other animals, or of which wool, worsted, the hair of the camel, goat, alpaca, or other animals is a component material, [forty] *thirty-five* per centum ad valorem.

399. Aubusson, Axminster, Moquette, and Chenille carpets, figured or plain, carpets woven whole for rooms, and all carpets or carpeting of like character or description, and oriental, Berlin, and other similar rugs, sixty cents per square yard, and in addition thereto forty per centum ad valorem.

> 287. Aubusson, Axminster, Moquette, and Chenille carpets, figured or plain, carpets woven whole for rooms, and all carpets or carpeting of like character or description, and oriental, Berlin, and other similar rugs, thirty-five per centum ad valorem.

400. Saxony, Wilton, and Tournay velvet carpets, figured or plain, and all carpets or carpeting of like character or description, sixty cents per square yard, and in addition thereto forty per centum ad valorem.

> 288. Saxony, Wilton, and Tournay velvet carpets, figured or plain, and all carpets or carpeting of like character or description, thirty-five per centum ad valorem.

401. Brussels carpets, figured or plain, and all carpets or carpeting of like character or description, forty-four cents per square yard, and in addition thereto forty per centum ad valorem.
> 289. Brussels carpets, figured or plain, and all carpets or carpeting of like character or description, thirty per centum ad valorem.

402. Velvet and tapestry velvet carpets, figured or plain, printed on the warp or otherwise, and all carpets or carpeting of like character or description, forty cents per square yard, and in addition thereto forty per centum ad valorem.
> 290. Velvet and tapestry velvet carpets, figured or plain, printed on the warp or otherwise, and all carpets or carpeting of like character or description, thirty per centum ad valorem.

403. Tapestry Brussels carpets, figured or plain, and all carpets or carpeting of like character or description, printed on the warp or otherwise, twenty-eight cents per square yard, and in addition thereto forty per centum ad valorem.
> 291. Tapestry Brussels carpets, figured or plain, and all carpets or carpeting of like character or description, printed on the warp or otherwise, thirty per centum ad valorem.

404. Treble ingrain, three-ply and all chain Venetian carpets, nineteen cents per square yard, and in addition thereto forty per centum ad valorem.
> 292. Treble ingrain, three-ply and all chain Venetian carpets, thirty per centum ad valorem.

405. Wool Dutch and two-ply ingrain carpets, fourteen cents per square yard, and in addition thereto forty per centum ad valorem.
> 293. Wool Dutch, and two-ply ingrain carpets, twenty-five per centum ad valorem.

406. Druggets and bockings, printed, colored, or otherwise, twenty-two cents per square yard, and in addition thereto forty per centum ad valorem. Felt carpeting, figured or plain, eleven cents per square yard, and in addition thereto forty per centum ad valorem.
> 294. Druggets and bockings, printed, colored, or otherwise, felt carpeting, figured or plain, twenty-five per centum ad valorem.

· 407. Carpets and carpeting of wool, flax or cotton, or composed in part of either, not specially provided for in this act, fifty per centum ad valorem.
> 295. Carpets and carpeting of wool, flax or cotton, or composed in part of either, not specially provided for in this act, twenty-five per centum ad valorem.

408. Mats, rugs, screens, covers, hassocks, bed sides, art squares, and other portions of carpets or carpeting made wholly or in part of wool, and not specially provided for in this act, shall be subjected to the rate of duty herein imposed on carpets or carpetings of like character or description.
> 296. Mats, rugs *for floors*, screens, covers, hassocks, bed sides, art squares, and other portions of carpets or carpeting made wholly or in part of wool, and not specially provided for in this act, shall be subjected to the rate of duty herein imposed on carpets or carpetings of like character or description.
>
> 297. The reduction of the rates of duty herein provided for manufactures of wool shall take effect December second, eighteen hundred and ninety-four; [and on all rates of duty in the woolen schedule, except on carpets, there shall be a reduction of one per centum ad valorem to take effect on the first day of July, eighteen hundred and ninety-six, and thereafter of a like amount on the first day of July, eighteen hundred and ninety-seven, eighteen hundred and ninety-eight, eighteen hundred and ninety-nine, and nineteen hundred, respectively].

Schedule L.—Silk and Silk Goods.

409. Silk partially manufactured from cocoons or from waste-silk, and not further advanced or manufactured than carded or combed silk, fifty cents per pound.

410. Thrown silk, not more advanced than singles, tram, organzine, sewing silk, twist, floss, and silk threads or yarns of every description, except spun silk, thirty per centum ad valorem; spun silk in skeins or cops or on beams, thirty-five per centum ad valorem.

> 298. Silk partially manufactured from cocoons or from waste-silk, and not further advanced or manufactured than carded or combed silk, [twenty-five cents per pound] *twenty per centum ad valorem*. Thrown silk, not more advanced than singles, tram, organzine, sewing silk, twist, floss, and silk threads or yarns of every description, [except spun silk, twenty per centum ad valorem;] *and* spun silk in skeins, cops, warps or on beams, [twenty] *twenty-five* per centum ad valorem.

NOTE.—Paragraphs 409 and 410 consolidated.

411. Velvets, plushes, or other pile fabrics, containing, exclusive of selvedges, less than seventy-five per centum in weight of silk, one dollar and fifty cents per pound and fifteen per centum ad valorem; containing, exclusive of selvedges, seventy-five per centum or more in weight of silk, three dollars and fifty cents per pound, and fifteen per centum ad valorem ; but in no case shall any of the foregoing articles pay a less rate of duty than fifty per centum ad valorem.

> 299. Velvets, plushes, chenilles, or other pile fabrics, forty-five per centum ad valorem.

412. Webbings, gorings, suspenders, braces, beltings, bindings, braids, galloons, fringes, cords and tassels, any of the foregoing which are elastic or non-elastic, buttons, and ornaments, made of silk, or of which silk is the component material of chief value, fifty per centum ad valorem.

> 300. Webbings, gorings, suspenders, braces, beltings, bindings, braids, galloons, fringes, cords and tassels, any of the foregoing which are elastic or non-elastic, buttons, and ornaments, made of silk, or of which silk is the component material of chief value, forty per centum ad valorem.

413. Laces and embroideries, handkerchiefs, neck rufflings and ruchings, clothing ready-made, and articles of wearing apparel of every description, including knit goods, made up or manufactured wholly or in part by the tailor, seamstress, or manufacturer, composed of silk, or of which silk is the component material of chief value, not specially provided for in this act, sixty per centum ad valorem: *Provided*, That all such clothing ready-made and articles of wearing apparel when composed in part of India rubber (not including gloves or elastic articles that are specially provided for in this act), shall be subject to a duty of eight cents per ounce, and in addition thereto sixty per centum ad valorem.

> 301. Laces and articles made wholly or in part of lace, and embroideries, including articles or fabrics embroidered by hand or machinery, handkerchiefs, neck rufflings and ruchings, clothing ready-made, and articles of wearing apparel of every description, including knit goods, made up or manufactured wholly or in part by the tailor, seamstress, or manufacturer, composed of silk, or of which silk is the component material of chief value, and beaded silk goods not specially provided for in this act, [fifty] *forty-five* per centum ad valorem.

414. All manufactures of silk, or of which silk is the component material of chief value, not specially provided for in this act, fifty per centum ad valorem: *Provided,* That all such manufactures of which

wool, or the hair of the camel, goat, or other like animals is a component material, shall be classified as manufactures of wool.

> 302. All manufactures of silk, or of which silk is the component material of chief value, including those having India rubber as a component material, not specially provided for in this act, forty-five per centum ad valorem.

Schedule M.—Pulp, Papers, and Books.

Pulp and Paper.—

415. Mechanically ground wood pulp, two dollars and fifty cents per ton dry weight; chemical wood pulp unbleached, six dollars per ton dry weight; bleached, seven dollars per ton dry weight.

> Pulp and Paper:
> 303. Mechanically ground wood pulp and chemical wood pulp unbleached or bleached, ten per centum ad valorem.

416. Sheathing paper, ten per centum ad valorem.

> 304. Sheathing paper and roofing felt, ten per centum ad valorem.

417. Printing paper unsized, suitable only for books and newspapers, fifteen per centum ad valorem.

> 305. [Printing paper unsized, suitable only for books and newspapers, twelve per centum ad valorem.]
> Note.—For Senate provision see paragraph 306.

418. Printing paper sized or glued, suitable only for books and newspapers, twenty per centum ad valorem.

> 306. Printing paper, *unsized*, sized or glued, suitable only for books and newspapers, [fifteen] *ten* per centum ad valorem.

419. Papers known commercially as copying paper, filtering paper, silver paper, and all tissue paper, white or colored, made up in copying books, reams, or in any other form, eight cents per pound, and in addition thereto fifteen per centum ad valorem; albumenized or sensitized paper, thirty-five per centum ad valorem.

> 307. Papers known commercially as copying paper, filtering paper, silver paper, and [all] tissue paper, white, printed, or colored, made up in copying books, reams, or in any other form, and albumenized or sensitized paper, [twenty-five] *thirty* per centum ad valorem.

420. Papers known commercially as surface-coated papers, and manufactures thereof, card-boards, lithographic prints from either stone or zinc, bound or unbound (except illustrations when forming a part of a periodical, newspaper, or in printed books accompanying the same), and all articles produced either in whole or in part by lithographic process, and photograph, autograph, and scrap albums, wholly or partially manufactured, thirty-five per centum ad valorem.

> 308. Parchment papers, surface-coated papers, and manufactures thereof, cardboards, lithographic prints from either stone or zinc, bound or unbound (except illustrations when forming a part of a periodical, newspaper, or in printed books accompanying the same), and all articles produced either in whole or in part by lithographic process, and photograph, autograph, and scrap albums, wholly or partially manufactured, [twenty-five] *thirty* per centum ad valorem.

Manufactures of Paper.

421. Paper envelopes, twenty-five cents per thousand.

> Manufactures of Paper:
> 309. Paper envelopes, twenty per centum ad valorem.

422. Paper hangings and paper for screens or fire-boards, writing-paper, drawing-paper, and all other paper not especially provided for in this act, twenty-five per centum ad valorem.

> 310. Paper hangings and paper for screens or fireboards, writing paper, drawing paper, and all other paper not specially provided for in this act, twenty per centum ad valorem.

423. Books, including blank books of all kinds, pamphlets, and engravings, bound or unbound, photographs, etchings, maps, charts, and all printed matter not especially provided for in this act, twenty-five per centum ad valorem.

> 311. Blank books of all kinds twenty per centum ad valorem. Books, including pamphlets, and engravings, bound or unbound, photographs, etchings, maps, charts, and all printed matter not specially provided for in this act, twenty-five per centum ad valorem.

424. Playing cards, fifty cents per pack.

> 312. Playing cards, in packs not exceeding fifty-four cards and at a like rate for any number in excess, ten cents per pack and fifty per centum ad valorem.

425. Manufactures of paper, or of which paper is the component material of chief value, not specially provided for in this act, twenty-five per centum ad valorem.

> 313. Manufactures of paper, or of which paper is the component material of chief value, not specially provided for in this act, twenty per centum ad valorem.

SCHEDULE N.—SUNDRIES.

426. Bristles, ten cents per pound.

> NOTE.—Placed upon free list. Par. 420.

427. Brushes, and brooms of all kinds, including feather dusters and hair pencils in quills, forty per centum ad valorem.

> 314. Hair pencils, brushes and feather dusters, thirty per centum ad valorem. Brooms, twenty per centum ad valorem.

BUTTONS AND BUTTON FORMS.—

428. Button forms: Lastings, mohair, cloth, silk, or other manufactures of cloth, woven or made in patterns of such size, shape, or form, or cut in such manner as to be fit for buttons exclusively, ten per centum ad valorem.

> BUTTONS AND BUTTON FORMS:
> 315. Button forms: Lastings, mohair, cloth, silk, or other manufactures of cloth, woven or made in patterns of such size, shape, or form, or cut in such manner as to be fit for buttons exclusively, ten per centum ad valorem.

429. Buttons commercially known as Agate buttons, twenty-five per centum ad valorem. Pearl and shell buttons, two and one-half cents per line button measure of one-fortieth of one inch per gross, and in addition thereto twenty-five per centum ad valorem.

> 316. Buttons commercially known as agate buttons, twenty-five per centum ad valorem. Pearl and shell buttons, wholly or partially manufactured, one cent per line per gross and fifteen per centum ad valorem.

430. Ivory, vegetable ivory, bone or horn buttons, fifty per centum ad valorem.

> 317. [Ivory,] *Buttons of ivory*, vegetable ivory, glass, bone, or horn [buttons,] wholly or partially manufactured, twenty-five per centum ad valorem.

431. Shoe-buttons, made of paper, board, papier maché, pulp, or other similar material not specially provided for in this act, valued at not exceeding three cents per gross, one cent per gross.

> 318. Shoe-buttons, made of paper, board, papier maché, pulp, or other similar material not specially provided for in this act, twenty-five per centum ad valorem.

432. Coal, bituminous, and shale, seventy-five cents per ton of twenty-eight bushels, eighty pounds to the bushel; coal slack or culm, such as will pass through a half-inch screen, thirty cents per ton of twenty-eight bushels, eighty pounds to the bushel.

> NOTE.—Placed upon free list by House. Par. 441.
> 318¼. *Coal, bituminous and shale, forty cents per ton; coal slack or culm, fifteen cents per ton.*

433. Coke, twenty per centum ad valorem.

> NOTE.—Placed upon free list by House. Par. 442.
> 318½. *Coke, fifteen per centum ad valorem.*

434. Cork bark, cut into squares or cubes, ten cents per pound; manufactured corks, fifteen cents per pound.

> 319. [Manufactured corks], *Corks, manufactured* [twenty per centum ad valorem], *ten cents per pound.*
> NOTE.—Cork bark, cut into squares or cubes. See free list. Par. 457.

435. Dice, draughts, chess-men, chess-balls, and billiards, pool, and bagatelle balls, of ivory, bone, or other materials, fifty per centum ad valorem.

> 320. Dice, draughts, chess-men, chess-balls, and billiard, pool, and bagatelle balls, of ivory, bone, or other materials, [fifty] *thirty* per centum ad valorem.

436. Dolls, doll-heads, toy marbles of whatever material composed, and all other toys not composed of rubber, china, porcelain, parian, bisque, earthen or stoneware, and not specially provided for in this act, thirty-five per centum ad valorem.

> 321. Dolls, doll-heads, toy marbles of whatever material composed, and all other toys not composed of rubber, china, porcelain, parian, bisque, earthen or stoneware, and not specially provided for in this act, twenty-five per centum ad valorem. [This paragraph shall not take effect until October first, eighteen hundred and ninety-four.]

437. Emery grains, and emery manufactured, ground, pulverized, or refined, one cent per pound.

> 322. Emery grains, and emery manufactured, ground, pulverized, or refined, [one cent per pound] *twenty per centum ad valorem.*

EXPLOSIVE SUBSTANCES.—

438. Fire-crackers of all kinds, eight cents per pound, but no allowance shall be made for tare or damage thereon.

> EXPLOSIVE SUBSTANCES:
> 323. Fire-crackers of all kinds, [eight cents per pound,] *fifty per centum ad valorem,* but no allowance shall be made for tare or damage thereon.

439. Fulminates, fulminating powders, and like articles, not specially provided for in this act, thirty per centum ad valorem.

> 324. Fulminates, fulminating powders, and like articles, not specially provided for in this act, thirty per centum ad valorem.

440. Gunpowder, and all explosive substances used for mining, blasting, artillery, or sporting purposes, when valued at twenty

cents or less per pound, five cents per pound; valued above twenty cents per pound, eight cents per pound.

<blockquote>325. Gunpowder, and all explosive substances used for mining, blasting, artillery, or sporting purposes, [when valued at twenty cents or less per pound, five cents per pound; valued above twenty cents per pound, eight cents per pound] ten per centum ad valorem.</blockquote>

441. Matches, friction or lucifer, of all descriptions, per gross of one hundred and forty-four boxes, containing not more than one hundred matches per box, ten cents per gross; when imported otherwise than in boxes containing not more than one hundred matches each, one cent per one thousand matches.

<blockquote>326. Matches, friction or lucifer, of all descriptions, [twenty] ten per centum ad valorem.</blockquote>

442. Percussion-caps, forty per centum ad valorem.

<blockquote>327. Percussion caps, thirty per centum ad valorem; blasting caps, thirty-five per centum ad valorem.</blockquote>

443. Feathers and downs of all kinds, crude or not dressed, colored, or manufactured, not specially provided for in this act, ten per centum ad valorem; when dressed, colored, or manufactured, including quilts of down and other manufactures of down, and also including dressed and finished birds suitable for millinery ornaments, and artificial and ornamental feathers and flowers, or parts thereof, of whatever material composed, not specially provided for in this act, fifty per centum ad valorem.

<blockquote>328. Feathers and downs of all kinds, crude or not dressed, colored, or manufactured, not specially provided for in this act, free; when dressed, colored, or manufactured, including quilts of down and other manufactures of down, and also including dressed and finished birds suitable for millinery ornaments, and artificial and ornamental feathers, fruits, grains, leaves, flowers, and stems, or parts thereof, of whatever material composed, suitable for millinery use, not specially provided for in this act, thirty-five per centum ad valorem.</blockquote>

444. Furs, dressed on the skin but not made up into articles, and furs not on the skin, prepared for hatters' use, twenty per centum ad valorem.

<blockquote>329. Furs, dressed on the skin but not made up into articles, twenty per centum ad valorem [and] furs not on the skin, prepared for hatters' use, ten per centum ad valorem.
330. Fans of all kinds, except common palm leaf fans, forty per centum ad valorem.</blockquote>

445. Glass beads, loose, unthreaded or unstrung, ten per centum ad valorem.

<blockquote>NOTE.—This paragraph transferred to glass schedule. See paragraph 99.</blockquote>

446. Gun-wads of all descriptions, thirty-five per centum ad valorem.

<blockquote>331. Gun wads of all descriptions, [twenty-five] ten per centum advalorem.</blockquote>

447. Hair, human, if clean or drawn but not manufactured, twenty per centum ad valorem.

<blockquote>332. Hair, human, if clean or drawn but not manufactured, twenty per centum ad valorem.</blockquote>

448. Hair-cloth, known as "crinoline-cloth," eight cents per square yard.

<blockquote>333. Hair-cloth, known as "crinoline cloth," [thirty per centum ad valorem] and</blockquote>

449. Hair-cloth, known as "hair seating," thirty cents per square yard.

> 334. Hair-cloth, known as "hair seating," twenty-five per centum ad valorem.

450. Hair, curled, suitable for beds or mattresses, fifteen per centum ad valorem.

> NOTE.—Placed upon free list. Par. 504.

451. Hats, for men's, women's, and children's wear, composed of the fur of the rabbit, beaver, or other animals, or of which such fur is the component material of chief value, wholly or partially manufactured, including fur hat bodies, fifty-five per centum ad valorem.

> 335. Hats for men's, women's, and children's wear, composed of the fur of the rabbit, beaver, or other animals, or of which such fur is the component material of chief value, wholly or partially manufactured, including fur hat bodies, [thirty] *thirty-five* per centum ad valorem.

JEWELRY AND PRECIOUS STONES—

452. Jewelry: All articles, not elsewhere specially provided for in this act, composed of precious metals or imitations thereof, whether set with coral, jet, or pearls, or with diamonds, rubies, cameos, or other precious stones, or imitations thereof, or otherwise, and which shall be known commercially as "jewelry," and cameos in frames, fifty per centum ad valorem.

> JEWELRY AND PRECIOUS STONES:
> 336. Jewelry: All articles, not specially provided for in this act, commercially known as "jewelry," and cameos in frames, thirty-five per centum ad valorem.

453. Pearls, ten per centum ad valorem.

> 337. Pearls, [fifteen] *ten* per centum ad valorem.

454. Precious stones of all kinds, cut but not set, ten per centum ad valorem; if set, and not specially provided for in this act, twenty-five per centum ad valorem. Imitations of precious stones composed of paste or glass not exceeding one inch in dimensions, not set, ten per centum ad valorem.

> 338. Precious stones of all kinds, cut but not set, [thirty] *fifteen* per centum ad valorem; if set, and not specially provided for in this act, including pearls set or strung, [thirty-five] *thirty* per centum ad valorem; *imitations of precious stones, composed of paste or glass, not exceeding an inch in dimensions, not set, ten per centum ad valorem* [and on uncut precious stones, of all kinds, fifteen per centum ad valorem].

LEATHER AND MANUFACTURES OF—

455. Bend or belting leather and sole leather, and leather not specially provided for in this act, ten per centum ad valorem.

> LEATHER AND MANUFACTURES OF:
> 339. Sole leather [five] *ten* per centum ad valorem.
> 340. Bend or belting leather, and leather not specially provided for in this act, ten per centum ad valorem.

456. Calf-skins, tanned, or tanned and dressed, dressed upper leather, including patent, enameled, and japanned leather, dressed or undressed, and finished; chamois or other skins not specially enumerated or provided for in this act, twenty per centum ad valorem; book-binders' calf-skins, kangaroo, sheep and goat skins, including lamb and kid skins, dressed and finished, twenty per centum ad valorem; skins for morocco, tanned but unfinished, ten per centum ad valorem; piano forte leather and piano forte action leather, thirty-five per centum ad valorem;

japanned calf-skins, thirty per centum ad valorem; boots and shoes, made of leather, twenty-five per centum ad valorem.

341. Calf-skins, tanned, or tanned and dressed, dressed upper leather, including patent, enameled, and japanned leather, dressed or undressed, and finished; chamois or other skins not specially enumerated or provided for in this act, [fifteen] *twenty* per centum ad valorem; book binders' calf-skins, kangaroo, sheep and goat skins, including lamb and kid skins, dressed and finished, [fifteen] *twenty* per centum ad valorem; skins for morocco, tanned but unfinished, ten per centum ad valorem; piano forte leather and piano forte action leather, [twenty-five] *twenty* per centum ad valorem; boots and shoes made of leather, twenty per centum ad valorem.

457. But leather cut into shoe uppers or vamps, or other forms, suitable for conversion into manufactured articles, shall be classified as manufactures of leather, and pay duty accordingly.

342. Leather cut into shoe uppers or vamps, or other forms, suitable for conversion into manufactured articles, twenty per centum ad valorem.

458. Gloves of all descriptions, composed wholly or in part of kid or other leather, and whether wholly or partly manufactured shall pay duty at the rates fixed in connection with the following specified kinds thereof, fourteen inches in extreme length when stretched to the full extent, being in each case hereby fixed as the standard, and one dozen pairs as the basis, namely: Ladies' and children's schmaschen of said length or under, one dollar and seventy-five cents per dozen; ladies' and children's lamb of said length or under, two dollars and twenty-five cents per dozen; ladies' and children's kid of said length or under, three dollars and twenty-five cents per dozen; ladies' and children's suedes of said length or under, fifty per centum ad valorem; all other ladies' and children's leather gloves, and all men's leather gloves of said length or under, fifty per centum ad valorem; all leather gloves over fourteen inches in length, fifty per centum ad valorem; and in addition to the above rates there shall be paid on all men's gloves one dollar per dozen; on all lined gloves one dollar per dozen; on all pique or prick seam gloves, fifty cents per dozen; on all embroidered gloves, with more than three single strands or cords, fifty cents per dozen pairs. *Provided*, That all gloves represented to be of a kind or grade below their actual kind or grade shall pay an additional duty of five dollars per dozen pairs: *Provided further*, That none of the articles named in this paragraph shall pay a less rate of duty than fifty per centum ad valorem.

343. Gloves made wholly or in part of leather, whether wholly or partly manufactured, shall pay duty at the following rates, the lengths stated in each case being the extreme length when stretched to their full extent, namely:

344. Ladies' or children's "glace" finish, Schmaschen (of sheep origin), not over fourteen inches in length, one dollar per dozen pairs; over fourteen inches and not over seventeen inches in length, one dollar and fifty cents per dozen pairs; over seventeen inches in length, two dollars per dozen pairs; men's "glace" finish, Schmaschen (sheep), two dollars per dozen pairs.

345. Ladies' or children's "glace" finish, lamb, or sheep, not over fourteen inches in length, one dollar and seventy-five cents per dozen pairs; over fourteen and not over seventeen inches in length, two dollars and seventy-five cents per dozen pairs; over seventeen inches in length, three dollars and seventy-five cents per dozen pairs. Men's "glace" finish, lamb, or sheep, three dollars per dozen pairs.

346. Ladies' or children's "glace" finish, goat, kid, or other leather than of sheep origin, not over fourteen inches in length, two dollars and twenty-

five cents per dozen pairs; over fourteen and not over seventeen inches in length, three dollars per dozen pairs; over seventeen inches in length, four dollars per dozen pairs; men's "glace" finish, kid, goat, or other leather than of sheep origin, three dollars per dozen pairs.

347. Ladies' or children's, of sheep origin, with exterior grain surface removed, by whatever name known, not over fourteen inches in length, one dollar and seventy-five cents per dozen pairs; over fourteen and not over seventeen inches in length, two dollars and seventy-five cents per dozen pairs; over seventeen inches in length, three dollars and seventy-five cents per dozen pairs; men's, of sheep origin, with exterior surface removed, by whatever name known, three dollars per dozen pairs.

348. Ladies or children's kid, goat, or other leather than of sheep origin, with exterior grain surface removed, by whatever name known, not over fourteen inches in length, two dollars and twenty-five cents per dozen pairs; over fourteen inches and not over seventeen inches in length, three dollars per dozen pairs; over seventeen inches in length, four dollars per dozen pairs; men's goat, kid, or other leather than of sheep origin, with exterior grain surface removed, by whatever name known, three dollars per dozen pairs.

349. In addition to the foregoing rates, there shall be paid on all leather gloves, when lined, sixty cents per dozen pairs.

350. Glove tranks, with or without the usual accompanying pieces, shall pay seventy-five per centum of the duty provided for the gloves in the fabrication of which they are suitable.

MISCELLANEOUS MANUFACTURES.—

459. Manufactures of alabaster, amber, asbestos, bladders, coral, cat-gut or whip-gut or worm-gut, jet, paste, spar, wax, or of which these substances or either of them is the component material of chief value, not specially provided for in this act, twenty-five per centum ad valorem; osier or willow prepared for basketmakers' use, thirty per centum ad valorem; manufactures of osier or willow, forty per centum ad valorem.

MISCELLANEOUS MANUFACTURES:
351. Manufactures of amber, asbestus, bladders, coral, cat-gut or whip-gut or worm-gut, jet, paste, spar, wax, or of which these substances or either of them is the component material of chief value, not specially provided for in this act, twenty-five per centum ad valorem; osier or willow prepared for basketmakers' use, twenty per centum ad valorem; manufactures of osier or willow, twenty-five per centum ad valorem.

460. Manufactures of bone, chip, grass, horn, India-rubber, palm leaf, straw, weeds, or whalebone, or of which these substances or either of them is the component material of chief value, not specially provided for in this act, thirty per centum ad valorem.

352. Manufactures of bone, chip, grass, horn, India-rubber, palm leaf, straw, weeds, or whalebone, or of which these substances or either of them is the component material of chief value, not specially provided for in this act, twenty-five per centum ad valorem. But the terms grass and straw shall be understood to mean these substances in their natural form and structure and not the separated fiber thereof.

461. Manufactures of leather, fur, gutta-percha, vulcanized India rubber, known as hard rubber, human hair, papier-mache, indurated fiber wares and other manufactures composed of wood or other pulp, or of which these substances or either of them is the component material of chief value, all of the above not specially provided for in this act, thirty-five per centum ad valorem.

353. Manufactures of leather, fur, gutta-percha, vulcanized India rubber, known as hard rubber, human hair, papier-mache, plaster of Paris, indurated fiber wares and other manufactures composed of wood or other pulp, or of which these substances or either of them is the component material of chief value, all of the above not specially provided for in this act, thirty per centum ad valorem.

TA——5

462. Manufactures of ivory, vegetable ivory, mother-of-pearl, and shell, or of which these substances or either of them is the component material of chief value, not specially provided for in this act, forty per centum ad valorem.

> 354. Manufactures of ivory, vegetable ivory, mother-of-pearl, gelatine, and shell, or of which these substances or either of them is the component material of chief value, not specially provided for in this act, and manufactures known commercially as bead or beaded trimmings or ornaments, thirty-five per centum ad valorem.

463. Masks, composed of paper or pulp, thirty-five per centum ad valorem.

> 355. Masks, composed of paper or pulp, twenty-five per centum ad valorem.

464. Matting made of cocoa fiber or rattan, twelve cents per square yard; mats made of cocoa-fiber or rattan, eight cents per square foot.

> 356. Matting and mats, made of cocoa fiber or rattan, *and floor matting manufactured from round or split straw, including what is commonly known as Chinese matting,* twenty per centum ad valorem.

465. Paintings, in oil or water colors, and statuary, not otherwise provided for in this act, fifteen per centum ad valorem; but the term "statuary" as herein used shall be understood to include only such statuary as is cut, carved, or otherwise wrought by hand from a solid block or mass of marble, stone, or alabaster, or from metal, and as is the professional production of a statuary or sculptor only.

> NOTE.—Placed upon the free list. Par. 575.

466. Pencils of wood filled with lead or other material, and pencils of lead, fifty cents per gross and thirty per centum ad valorem; slate pencils, four cents per gross.

> 357. Pencils of wood filled with lead or other material, [thirty-five] *forty* per centum ad valorem; slate pencils, [twenty-five] *thirty* per centum ad valorem.

467. Pencil-leads not in wood, ten per centum ad valorem.

> 358. Pencil leads not in wood, ten per centum ad valorem.

PIPES AND SMOKERS' ARTICLES.—

468. Pipes, pipe bowls, of all materials, and all smokers' articles whatsoever, not specially provided for in this act, including cigarette books, cigarette-book covers, pouches for smoking or chewing tobacco, and cigarette paper in all forms, seventy per centum ad valorem; all common tobacco pipes of clay, fifteen cents per gross.

> PIPES AND SMOKERS' ARTICLES:
> 359. Pipes, pipe bowls, of all materials, and all smokers' articles whatsoever, not specially provided for in this act, including cigarette books, cigarette-book covers, pouches for smoking or chewing tobacco, and cigarette paper in all forms, fifty per centum ad valorem; all [common] tobacco pipes *and pipe bowls* of clay, [valued at not more than fifty cents per gross, ten cents per gross] *ten per centum ad valorem.*

469. Plush, black, known commercially as hatters' plush, composed of silk, or of silk and cotton, and used exclusively for making men's hats, ten per centum ad valorem.

> NOTE.—Placed upon free list. Par. 593.

470. Umbrellas, parasols, and sun-shades, covered with silk, or alpaca, fifty-five per centum ad valorem; if covered with other material, forty-five per centum ad valorem.

> 360. Umbrellas, parasols, and sunshades, covered with material composed wholly or in part of silk, wool or goat hair, forty-five per centum ad valorem; if covered with paper or other material, [thirty-five] *thirty* per centum ad valorem.

471. Umbrellas, parasols, and sunshades, sticks for, if plain, finished or unfinished, thirty-five per centum ad valorem; if carved, fifty per centum ad valorem.

> 361. Umbrellas, parasols, and sunshades, sticks for, if plain or carved, finished or unfinished, thirty per centum ad valorem.

472. Waste, not specially provided for in this act, ten per centum ad valorem.

> 362. Waste, not specially provided for in this act, ten per centum ad valorem.

Free List.

Sec. 2. On and after the sixth day of October, eighteen hundred and ninety, unless otherwise specially provided for in this act, the following articles when imported shall be exempt from duty:

> Sec. 2. [On and after] *After* the [first] *thirtieth* day of June, eighteen hundred and ninety-four, unless otherwise provided for in this act, the following articles, when imported, shall be exempt from duty:

473. Acids used for medicinal, chemical, or manufacturing purposes, not specially provided for in this act.

> 363. Acids used for medicinal, chemical, or manufacturing purposes, not specially provided for in this act.

474. Aconite.

> 364. Aconite.

475. Acorns, raw, dried or undried, but unground.

> 365. Acorns, raw, dried or undried, but unground.

476. Agates, unmanufactured.

> 366. Agates, unmanufactured.

477. Albumen.

> 367. Albumen.

478. Alizarine, natural or artificial, and dyes commercially known as Alizarine yellow, Alizarine orange, Alizarine green, Alizarine blue, Alizarine brown, Alizarine black.

> 368. Alizarin, and alizarin colors or dyes, natural or artificial.

479. Amber, unmanufactured, or crude gum.

> 369. Amber, unmanufactured, or crude gum.

480. Ambergris.

> 370. Ambergris.
> 371. Ammonia, carbonate of, muriate of, or sal ammoniac and sulphate of.

481. Aniline salts.

> 372. Aniline salts.

482. Any animal imported specially for breeding purposes shall be admitted free: *Provided*, That no such animal shall be admitted free unless pure bred of a recognized breed, and duly registered in the book of record established for that breed: *And provided further*, That certificate of such record and of the pedigree of such animal shall be produced and submitted to the customs officer, duly authenticated by the proper custodian of such book of record, together with the affidavit of the owner, agent, or importer that such animal is the identical animal described in said certificate of record and pedigree. The Secretary of the Treasury may prescribe such additional regulations as may be required for the strict enforcement of this provision.

> 373. Any animal imported specially for breeding purposes shall be admitted free: *Provided*, That no such animal shall be admitted free unless pure bred of a recognized breed, and duly registered in the book of record established for that breed, and the Secretary of the Treasury may prescribe such additional regulations as may be required for the strict enforcement of this provision.
>
> *Any cattle, horses, sheep, or other domestic animals which have strayed across the boundary line into any foreign country, or where such domestic animals have been or may be driven across such boundary line by the owner for pasturage purposes, the same may be brought back to the United States free of duty under regulations to be prescribed by the Secretary of the Treasury.*

483. Animals brought into the United States temporarily for a period not exceeding six months, for the purpose of exhibition or competition for prizes offered by any agricultural or racing association; but a bond shall be given in accordance with regulations prescribed by the Secretary of the Treasury; also, teams of animals, including their harness and tackle and the wagons or other vehicles actually owned by persons emigrating from foreign countries to the United States with their families, and in actual use for the purpose of such emigration under such regulations as the Secretary of the Treasury may prescribe; and wild animals intended for exhibition in zoölogical collections for scientific and educational purposes, and not for sale or profit.

> 374. Animals brought into the United States temporarily for a period not exceeding six months, for the purpose of exhibition or competition for prizes offered by any agricultural [or racing] association; but a bond shall be given in accordance with regulations prescribed by the Secretary of the Treasury; also, teams of animals, including their harness and tackle and the wagons or other vehicles actually owned by persons emigrating from foreign countries to the United States with their families, and in actual use for the purpose of such emigration under such regulations as the Secretary of the Treasury may prescribe; and wild animals intended for exhibition in zoological collections for scientific and educational purposes, and not for sale or profit.

484. Annatto, roucou, rocoa, or orleans, and all extracts of.

> 375. Annatto, roucou, rocoa, or orleans, and all extracts of.

485. Antimony ore, crude sulphite of.

> 376. Antimony ore, crude sulphite of, and antimony, as regulus or metal.

486. Apatite.

> 377. Apatite.
> 378. [Apples, green or ripe.]
> 379. [Apples, dried, desiccated, evaporated or prepared in any manner, and not otherwise provided for in this act.]

487. Argal, or argol, or crude tartar.

> 380. Argal, or argol, or crude tartar.

488. Arrow root, raw or unmanufactured.
> 381. Arrow root, raw or unmanufactured.

489. Arsenic and sulphide of, or orpiment.
> 382. Arsenic and sulphide of, or orpiment

490. Arseniate of aniline.
> 383. Arseniate of aniline.

491. Art educational stops, composed of glass and metal and valued at not more than six cents per gross.
> 384. Art educational stops, composed of glass and metal, and valued at not more than six cents per gross.
> 385. Articles imported by the United States.

492. Articles in a crude state used in dyeing or tanning not specially provided for in this act.
> 386. Articles in a crude state used in dyeing or tanning not specially provided for in this act.

493. Articles the growth, produce, and manufacture of the United States, when returned after having been exported, without having been advanced in value or improved in condition by any process of manufacture or other means; casks, barrels, carboys, bags, and other vessels of American manufacture exported filled with American products, or exported empty and returned filled with foreign products, including shooks when returned as barrels or boxes; also quicksilver flasks or bottles, of either domestic or foreign manufacture, which shall have been actually exported from the United States; but proof of the identity of such articles shall be made, under general regulations to be prescribed by the Secretary of the Treasury; and if any such articles are subject to internal tax at the time of exportation such tax shall be proved to have been paid before exportation and not refunded: *Provided,* That this paragraph shall not apply to any article upon which an allowance of drawback has been made, the re-importation of which is hereby prohibited except upon payment of duties equal to the drawbacks allowed; or to any article manufactured in bonded-warehouse and exported under any provision of law: *And provided further,* That when manufactured tobacco which has been exported without payment of internal-revenue tax shall be re-imported it shall be retained in the custody of the collector of customs until internal-revenue stamps in payment of the legal duties shall be placed thereon.

> 387. Articles the growth, produce, and manufacture of the United States, when returned after having been exported, without having been advanced in value or improved in condition by any process of manufacture or other means; casks, barrels, carboys, bags, and other vessels of American manufacture exported filled with American products, or exported empty and returned filled with foreign products, including shooks when returned as barrels or boxes; also quicksilver flasks or bottles, of either domestic or foreign manufacture, which shall have been actually exported from the United States; but proof of the identity of such articles shall be made, under general regulations to be prescribed by the Secretary of the Treasury; but the exemption of bags from duty shall apply only to such domestic bags as may be imported by the exporter thereof; and if any such articles are subject to internal tax at the time of exportation such tax shall be proved to have been paid before exportation and not refunded: *Provided,* That this paragraph shall not apply to any article upon which an allowance of drawback has been made, the re-importation of which is hereby prohibited except upon payment of duties equal to the drawbacks allowed; or to any article manufactured in bonded-warehouse and exported under any provision of law: *And provided further,* That when manufactured tobacco which has been exported without payment of internal-rev-

cuuo tax shall be re-imported it shall be retained in the custody of the collector of customs until internal-revenue stamps in payment of the legal duties shall be placed thereon.

494. Asbestos, unmanufactured.
   388. Asbestos, unmanufactured.
495. Ashes, wood and lye of, and beet-root ashes.
   389. Ashes, wood and lye of, and beet-root ashes.
496. Asphaltum and bitumen, crude.
   390. Asphaltum and bitumen, crude or dried, but not otherwise manipulated or treated.
497. Asafetida.
   391. Asafetida.
   392. Bacon and hams [beef, mutton, and pork] [see Par. 224½], and meats of all kinds, prepared or preserved, not specially provided for in this act.
498. Balm of Gilead.
   393. Balm of Gilead.
499. Barks, cinchona or other from which quinine may be extracted.
   394. Barks, cinchona or other, from which quinine may be extracted.
500. Baryta, carbonate of, or witherite.
   395. Baryta, carbonate of, or witherite, and baryta, sulphate of, er barytes, unmanufactured, including barytes earth.
501. Bauxite, or beauxite.
   396. Bauxite, or beauxite.
502. Beeswax.
   397. Beeswax.
503. Bells, broken, and bell metal broken and fit only to be remanufactured.
   398. Bells, broken, and bell metal broken fit only to be remanufactured.
   399. All binding twine manufactured in whole or in part from New Zealand hemp, istle or Tampico fiber, manila, sisal grass, or sunn, of single ply and measuring not exceeding six hundred feet to the pound.
504. Birds, stuffed, not suitable for millinery ornaments, and bird skins, prepared for preservation, but not further advanced in manufacture.
   400. Birds, stuffed, not suitable for millinery ornaments, and bird skins, prepared for preservation, but not further advanced in manufacture.
505. Birds and land and water fowls.
   401. Birds and land and water fowls.
506. Bismuth.
   402. Bismuth.
507. Bladders, including fish-bladders or fish-sounds, crude, and all integuments of animals not specially provided for in this act.
   403. Bladders, and all integuments of animals, crude, salted for preservation, and unmanufactured, not specially provided for in this act.
508. Blood, dried.
   404. Blood, dried.
   405. Blue vitriol, or sulphate of copper.
509. Bologna sausages.
   406. Bologna sausages.

510. Bolting-cloths, especially for milling purposes, but not suitable for the manufacture of wearing apparel.
>407. Bolting-cloths, especially for milling purposes, but not suitable for the manufacture of wearing apparel.

511. Bones, crude, or not burned, calcined, ground, steamed, or otherwise manufactured, and bone-dust or animal carbon, and bone ash, fit only for fertilizing purposes.
>408. Bones, crude, or not burned, calcined, ground, steamed, or otherwise manufactured, and bone dust or animal carbon, and bone ash, fit only for fertilizing purposes.
>409. [Bone char, suitable for use in decolorizing sugars.]

512. Books, engravings, photographs, bound or unbound etchings, maps, and charts, which shall have been printed and bound or manufactured more than twenty years at the date of importation.
>410. Books, engravings, photographs, bound or unbound, etchings, maps, and charts, which shall have been printed more than twenty years at the date of importation, and all hydrographic charts, and books and periodicals devoted exclusively to original scientific research, and publications issued for their subscribers by scientific and literary associations or academies, or publications of individuals for private circulation.

513. Books and pamphlets printed exclusively in languages other than English; also books and music, in raised print, used exclusively by the blind.
>411. Books and pamphlets printed exclusively in languages other than English; also books and music, in raised print, used exclusively by the blind.

514. Books, engravings, photographs, etchings, bound or unbound, maps and charts imported by authority or for the use of the United States or for the use of the Library of Congress.
>412. Books, engravings, photographs, etchings, bound or unbound, maps and charts imported by authority or for the use of the United States or for the use of the Library of Congress.

515. Books, maps, lithographic prints, and charts, specially imported, not more than two copies in any one invoice, in good faith, for the use of any society incorporated or established for educational, philosophical, literary, or religious purposes, or for the encouragement of the fine arts, or for the use or by order of any college, academy, school, or seminary of learning in the United States, subject to such regulations as the Secretary of the Treasury shall prescribe.
>413. Books, maps, lithographic prints, and charts, specially imported, not more than two copies in any one invoice, in good faith, for the use of any society incorporated or established for educational, philosophical, literary, or religious purposes, or for the encouragement of the fine arts, or for the use or by order of any college, academy, school, or seminary of learning in the United States, subject to such regulations as the Secretary of the Treasury shall prescribe.

516. Books, or libraries, or parts of libraries, and other household effects of persons or families from foreign countries, if actually used abroad by them not less than one year, and not intended for any other person or persons, nor for sale.
>414. Books, libraries, usual furniture, and similar household effects of persons or families from foreign countries, if actually used abroad by them not less than one year, and not intended for any other person or persons, nor for sale.
>415. Borax, crude, or borate of soda, or borate of lime.

517. Brazil paste.
>416. Brazil paste.

518. Braids, plaits, laces, and similar manufactures composed of straw, chip, grass, palm-leaf, willow, osier, or rattan, suitable for making or ornamenting hats, bonnets, and hoods.

> 417. [Braids, plaits, laces, and similar manufactures composed of straw, chip, grass, palm leaf, willow, osier, or rattan, and sweat leathers, bindings, bands, and tips, when cut to length for trimming felt or wool hats, suitable for making or ornamenting hats, bonnets, and hoods.]
> *Straw, chip, grass, palm leaf, willow, osier, or rattan, in the form of braids, plaits, laces, suitable for making or ornamenting hats, bonnets, and hoods; also when imported for trimming men's and boys' hats only, hat bands not exceeding two and one-half inches in width and when cut in lengths not exceeding thirty-seven inches; hat bindings not exceeding one and one-quarter inches in width and when cut in lengths not exceeding fifty-four inches; and hat linings composed in whole or in part of silk, satin, or cotton, when cut in pieces not exceeding twelve by sixteen inches, or five by thirty inches.*

519. Brazilian pebble, unwrought or unmanufactured.
> 418. Brazilian pebble, unwrought or unmanufactured.

520. Breccia, in block or slabs.
> 419. Breccia, in block or slabs.
> 420. Bristles.

521. Bromine.
> 421. Bromine.
> 422. Broom corn.

522. Bullion, gold or silver.
> 423. Bullion, gold or silver.

523. Burgundy pitch.
> 424. Burgundy pitch.
> 425. Cabbages.

524. Cabinets of old coins and medals, and other collections of antiquities, but the term "antiquities" as used in this act shall include only such articles as are suitable for souvenirs or cabinet collections, and which shall have been produced at any period prior to the year seventeen hundred.

> 426. Old coins and medals, and other antiquities, but the term "antiquities" as used in this act shall include only such articles as are suitable for souvenirs or cabinet collections, and which shall have been produced at any period prior to the year seventeen hundred.

525. Cadmium.
> 427. Cadmium.

526. Calamine.
> 428. Calamine.

527. Camphor, crude.
> 429. Camphor.

528. Castor or castoreum.
> 430. Castor or castorum.

529. Catgut, whip-gut, or worm-gut, unmanufactured, or not further manufactured than in strings or cords.
> 431. Catgut, whipgut, or wormgut, unmanufactured, or not further manufactured than in strings or cords.

530. Cerium.
> 432. Cerium.

531. Chalk, unmanufactured.
> 433. Chalk, unmanufactured.

532. Charcoal.
>434. Charcoal.

533. Chicory-root, raw, dried, or undried, but unground.
>435. Chicory root, raw, dried, or undried, but unground.
>436. Cider.

534. Civet, crude.
>437. Civet, crude.
>438. Chromate of iron or chromic ore.

535. Clay—Common blue clay in casks suitable for the manufacture of crucibles.
>439. Clay—Common blue clay in casks suitable for the manufacture of crucibles.
>440. Clays or earths, unwrought or unmanufactured, not specially provided for in this act.

536. Coal, anthracite.
>441. Coal, anthracite, [bituminous, and shale, and coal slack or culm.]
>442. [Coke.]

537. Coal stores of American vessels; but none shall be unloaded.
>NOTE.—This paragraph omitted from new bill.

538. Coal tar, crude.
>443. Coal tar, crude, and all preparations and products of coal tar, not colors or dyes, not specially provided for in this act.

539. Cobalt and cobalt ore.
>444. Cobalt and cobalt ore, and oxide of cobalt.

540. Cocculus indicus.
>445. Cocculus, indicus.

541. Cochineal.
>446. Cochineal.

542. Cocoa, or cacao, crude, and fiber, leaves, and shells of.
>447. Cocoa, or cacao, crude, [and fiber] leaves, and shells of.

543. Coffee.
>448. Coffee.

544. Coins, gold, silver, and copper.
>449. Coins, gold, silver, and copper.

545. Coir, and coir yarn.
>450. Coir, and coir yarn.

546. Copper, old, taken from the bottom of American vessels compelled by marine disaster to repair in foreign ports.
>451. Copper imported in the form of ores.
>452. Old copper, fit only for manufacture, clipping from new copper, and all composition metal of which copper is a component material of chief value not specially provided for in this act.
>453. Copper, regulus of, and black or coarse copper, and copper cement.
>454. Copper in plates, bars, ingots, or pigs, and other forms, not manufactured, not specially provided for in this act.
>455. Copperas, or sulphate of iron.

547. Coral, marine, uncut, and unmanufactured.
>456. Coral, marine, uncut, and unmanufactured.

548. Cork wood, or cork bark, unmanufactured.
>457. Cork-wood or cork-bark, unmanufactured, or cut into squares or cubes.

549. Cotton, and cotton waste or flocks.
    458. Cotton, and cotton waste or flocks.
    459. Cotton ties of iron or steel cut to lengths, punched or not punched, with or without buckles, for baling cotton.

550. Cryolite, or kryolith.
    460. Cryolite, or kryolith.

551. Cudbear.
    461. Cudbear.

552. Curling-stones, or quoits, and curling-stone handles.
    462. Curling stones, or quoits, and curling-stone handles.

553. Curry, and curry-powder.
    463. Curry, and curry powder.

554. Cutch.
    464. Cutch.

555. Cuttle-fish bone.
    465. Cuttlefish bone.

556. Dandelion roots, raw, dried, or undried, but unground.
    466. Dandelion roots, raw, dried, or undried, but unground.

557. Diamonds and other precious stones, rough or uncut, including glaziers' and engravers' diamonds not set, and diamond dust or bort, and jewels to be used in the manufacture of watches.
    467. [Glaziers'] *Diamonds and other precious stones, rough or uncut, including miners', glaziers',* and engravers' diamonds not set, and diamond dust or bort, and jewels to be used in the manufacture of watches or clocks.

558. Divi-divi.
    468. Divi-divi.

559. Dragon's blood.
    469. Dragon's blood.

560. Drugs, such as barks, beans, berries, balsams, buds, bulbs, and bulbous roots, excrescences such as nut-galls, fruits, flowers, dried fibers, and dried insects, grains, gums, and gum-resin, herbs, leaves, lichens, mosses, nuts, roots, and stems, spices, vegetables, seeds aromatic, and seeds of morbid growth, weeds, and woods used expressly for dyeing; any of the foregoing which are not edible and are in a crude state, and not advanced in value or condition by refining or grinding, or by other process of manufacture, and not specially provided for in this act.
    470. Drugs, such as barks, beans, berries, balsams, buds, bulbs, bulbous roots, excrescences, fruits, flowers, dried fibers, dried insects, grains, gums, and gum-resin, herbs, leaves, lichens, mosses, nuts, roots, and stems, spices, vegetables, seeds aromatic, seeds of morbid growth, weeds, and woods used expressly for dyeing; any of the foregoing which are not edible, whether crude or advanced in value or condition by refining or grinding, or by other process of manufacture, and not specially provided for in this act.

561. Eggs of birds, fish, and insects.
    471. Eggs and yolks of, and eggs of birds, fish, and insects.

562. Emery ore.
    472. Emery ore.

563. Ergot.
    473. Ergot.

564. Fans, common palm-leaf and palm-leaf unmanufactured.
> 474. Common palm leaf fans, and palm leaf unmanufactured.

565. Farina.
> 475. Farina.

566. Fashion-plates, engraved on steel or copper or on wood, colored or plain.
> 476. Fashionplates, engraved on steel or copper or on wood, colored or plain.

567. Feathers and downs for beds.
> 477. Feathers and downs for beds, and feathers and downs of all kinds, crude or not dressed, colored, or manufactured, not specially provided for in this act.

568. Feldspar.
> 478. Feldspar.

569. Felt, adhesive, for sheathing vessels.
> 479. Felt, adhesive, for sheathing vessels.

570. Fibrin, in all forms.
> 480. Fibrin, in all forms.

571. Fish, the product of American fisheries, and fresh or frozen fish (except salmon) caught in fresh waters by American vessels, or with nets or other devices owned by citizens of the United States.
> 481. Fish, frozen or packed in ice, fresh.

572. Fish for bait.
> 482. Fish for bait.

573. Fish skins.
> 483. Fish skins.

574. Flint, flints, and ground flint stones.
> 484. Flint, flints, and ground flint stones.

575. Floor matting manufactured from round or split straw, including what is commonly known as Chinese matting.
> 485. [Floor matting manufactured from round or split straw, including what is commonly known as Chinese matting]. See also Par. 464.

576. Fossils.
> 486. Fossils.

577. Fruit-plants, tropical and semitropical, for the purpose of propagation or cultivation.
> 487. Fruit plants, tropical and semitropical, for the purpose of propagation or cultivation.

FRUITS AND NUTS—
578. Currants, Zante or other.
> NOTE.—See paragraphs 213 and 217.

579. Dates.
> 488. [Dates.] NOTE.—For Senate action see paragraph 213b.

580. Fruits, green, ripe, or dried, not specially provided for in this act.
> 489. Fruits, green, ripe, or dried not specially provided for in this Act.

581. Tamarinds.
> 490. Tamarinds.

582. Cocoanuts.

583. Brazil nuts.
> 491. Cocoanuts, [Brazil nuts,] cream nuts, palm nuts, and palm nut kernels.

584. Cream nuts.
> NOTE.—See paragraph 491.

585. Palm nuts.
> NOTE.—See paragraph 491.

586. Palm-nut kernels.
> NOTE.—See paragraph 491.

587. Furs, undressed.
> 492. Furs, undressed.

588. Fur-skins of all kinds not dressed in any manner.
> 493. Fur skins of all kinds not dressed in any manner.

589. Gambier.
> 494. [Gambier.]

590. Glass, broken, and old glass, which can not be cut for use, and fit only to be remanufactured.
> 495. Glass, broken, and old glass, which can not be cut for use, and fit only to be remanufactured.

591. Glass plates or disks, rough-cut or unwrought, for use in the manufacture of optical instruments, spectacles, and eye-glasses, and suitable only for such use: *Provided, however,* That such disks exceeding eight inches in diameter may be polished sufficiently to enable the character of the glass to be determined.
> 496. Glass plates or disks, rough-cut or unwrought, for use in the manufacture of optical instruments, spectacles, and eyeglasses, and suitable only for such use: *Provided, however,* That such disks exceeding eight inches in diameter may be polished sufficiently to enable the character of the glass to be determined.

GRASSES AND FIBERS—

592. Istle or Tampico fiber.
> NOTE.—See paragraph 497.

593. Jute.
> NOTE.—See paragraph 497.

594. Jute butts.
> NOTE.—See paragraph 497.

595. Manilla.
> NOTE.—See paragraph 497.

596. Sisal-grass.
> NOTE.—See paragraph 497.

597. Sunn.
> NOTE.—See paragraph 497.

And all other textile grasses or fibrous vegetable substances, unmanufactured or undressed, not specially provided for in this act.
> GRASSES AND FIBERS:
> 497. Istle or Tampico fiber, jute, jute butts, manila, sisal grass, sunn, flax straw, flax not hackled, tow of flax or hemp, hemp not hackled, hemp, flax, jute, and tow wastes, and all other textile grasses or fibrous vegetable substances, unmanufactured or undressed, not specially provided for in this Act.

598. Gold beaters' molds and gold beaters' skins.
> 498. Gold-beaters' molds and gold-beaters' skins.

599. Grease, and oils, such as are commonly used in soap-making or in wire-drawing, or for stuffing or dressing leather, and which are fit only for such uses, not specially provided for in this act.

> 499. Grease and oils, such as are commonly used in soap-making or in wire-drawing, or for stuffing or dressing leather, and which are fit only for such uses, *and cod oil*, not specially provided for in this Act.

600. Guano, manures, and all substances expressly used for manure.

> 500. Guano, manures, and all substances expressly used for manure.

601. Gunny bags and gunny cloths, old or refuse, fit only for remanufacture.

> 501. Gunny bags and gunny cloths, old or refuse, fit only for remanufacture.

602. Guts, salted.

> 502. [Guts, salted.]

603. Gutta-percha, crude.

> 503. Gutta-percha, crude.

604. Hair of horse, cattle, and other animals, cleaned or uncleaned, drawn or undrawn, but unmanufactured, not specially provided for in this act; and human hair, raw, uncleaned, and not drawn.

> 504. Hair of horse, cattle, and other animals, cleaned or uncleaned, drawn or undrawn, and curled hair suitable for beds or mattresses, not specially provided for in this act; and human hair, raw, uncleaned, and not drawn.

605. Hides, raw or uncured, whether dry, salted, or pickled, Angora goat-skins, raw, without the wool, unmanufactured, asses' skins, raw or unmanufactured, and skins, except sheep-skins with the wool on.

> 505. Hides and skins, raw or uncured, whether dry, salted or pickled.

606. Hide-cuttings, raw, with or without hair, and all other glue stock.

> 506. Hide cuttings, raw, with or without hair, and all other glue stock.

607. Hide rope.

> 507. Hide rope.

608. Hones and whetstones.

> 508. Hones and whetstones.

609. Hoofs, unmanufactured.

> 509. Hoofs, unmanufactured.

610. Hop roots for cultivation.

> 510. Hop roots for cultivation.

611. Horns and parts of, unmanufactured, including horn strips and tips.

> 511. Horns, and parts of, unmanufactured, including horn strips and tips.

612. Ice.

> 512. Ice.

613. India rubber, crude, and milk of, and old scrap or refuse India rubber which has been worn out by use and is fit only for remanufacture.

> 513. India rubber, crude, and milk of, and old scrap or refuse India rubber, which has been worn out by use and is fit only for remanufacture.

614. Indigo.

> 514. Indigo, and extracts or pastes of, and carmines.

615. Iodine, crude.

> 515. Iodine, crude, and resublimed.

616. Ipecac.
>516. Ipecac.

617. Iridium.
>517. Iridium.
>[518. Iron ore, including manganiferous iron ore, also the dross or residuum from burnt pyrites, and sulphur ore, as pyrites or sulphuret of iron in its natural state.]

618. Ivory and vegetable ivory, not sawed, cut or otherwise manufactured.
>519. Ivory sawed or cut into logs, but not otherwise manufactured, and vegetable ivory.

619. Jalap.
>520. Jalap.

620. Jet, unmanufactured.
>521. Jet, unmanufactured.

621. Joss-stick, or Joss-light.
>522. Joss stick, or Joss light.

622. Junk, old.
>523. Junk, old.

623. Kelp.
>524. Kelp.

624. Kieserite.
>525. Kieserite.

625. Kyanite, or cyanite, and kainite.
>526. Kyanite, or cyanite, and kainite.

626. Lac-dye, crude, seed, button, stick, and shell.
>527. Lac-dye, crude, seed, button, stick, and shell.

627. Lac spirits.
>528. Lac spirits.

628. Lactarine.
>529. Lactarine.
>530. Lard.

629. Lava, unmanufactured.
>531. Lava, unmanufactured.

630. Leeches.
>532. Leeches.

631. Lemon juice, lime juice, and sour-orange juice.
>533. Lemon juice, lime juice, and sour-orange juice.

632. Licorice-root, unground.
>534. Licorice root, unground.

633. Life-boats and life-saving apparatus specially imported by societies incorporated or established to encourage the saving of human life.
>535. Lifeboats and life-saving apparatus specially imported by societies incorporated or established to encourage the saving of human life.

634. Lime, citrate of.
>536. Lime, citrate of.

635. Lime, chloride of, or bleaching-powder.
>537. Lime, chloride of, or bleaching powder.

636. Lithographic stones not engraved.
538. Lithographic stones not engraved.

637. Litmus, prepared or not prepared.
539. Litmus, prepared or not prepared.

638. Loadstones.
540. Loadstones.

639. Madder and munjeet, or Indian madder, ground or prepared, and all extracts of.
541. Madder and munjeet, or Indian madder, ground or prepared, and all extracts of.
542. Magnesia, sulphate of, or Epsom salts.

640. Magnesite, or native mineral carbonate of magnesia.
543. Magnesite, or native mineral carbonate of magnesia.

641. Magnesium.
544. Magnesium.

642. Magnets.
545. Magnets.

643. Manganese, oxide and ore of.
546. Manganese, oxide and ore of.

644. Manna.
547. Manna.

645. Manuscripts.
548. Manuscripts.

646. Marrow, crude.
549. Marrow, crude.

647. Marsh mallows.
550. Marsh mallows.

648. Medals of gold, silver, or copper, such as trophies or prizes.
551. Medals of gold, silver, or copper, and other metallic articles manufactured as trophies or prizes, and actually received *or bestowed and accepted* as honorary distinctions.
552. Mica, and metallic mineral substances in a crude state and metals unwrought, not specially provided for in this act.

649. Meerschaum, crude or unmanufactured.
553. Meerschaum, crude or unmanufactured.
554. Milk, fresh.

650. Mineral waters, all not artificial.
555. Mineral waters, all not artificial, and mineral salts of the same, obtained by evaporation, when accompanied by duly authenticated certificate, showing that they are in no way artificially prepared, and are the product of a designated mineral spring; lemonade, soda water, and all similar waters.

651. Minerals, crude, or not advanced in value or condition by refining or grinding, or by other process of manufacture, not specially provided for in this act.
556. Minerals, crude, or not advanced in value or condition by refining or grinding, or by other process of manufacture, not specially provided for in this Act.

652. Models of inventions and of other improvements in the arts, including patterns for machinery, but no article shall be deemed a model or pattern which can be fitted for use otherwise.

> 557. Models of inventions and of other improvements in the arts. including patterns for machinery, but no article shall be deemed a model or pattern which can be fitted for use otherwise.

653. Moss, sea-weeds, and vegetable substances, crude or unmanufactured, not otherwise specially provided for in this act.

> 558. Moss, seaweeds, and vegetable substances, crude or unmanufactured, not otherwise specially provided for in this Act.

654. Musk, crude, in natural pods.

> 559. Musk, crude, in natural pods.

655. Myrobolan.

> 560. Myrobolan.

656. Needles, hand sewing, and darning.

> 561. Needles, hand-sewing and darning.

657. Newspapers and periodicals; but the term "periodicals" as herein used shall be understood to embrace only unbound or paper-covered publications, containing current literature of the day and issued regularly at stated periods, as weekly, monthly, or quarterly.

> 562. Newspapers and periodicals; but the term "periodicals" as herein used shall be understood to embrace only unbound or paper covered publications, containing current literature of the day and issued regularly at stated periods, as weekly, monthly, or quarterly.
> 563. Nickel, nickel oxide, alloy of any kind in which nickel is the component material of chief value.

658. Nux vomica.

> 564. Nux vomica.

659. Oakum.

> 565. Oakum.
> 566. Ocher and ochery earths, sienna and sienna earths, umber and umber earths, not specially provided for in this act, dry.

660. Oil cake.

> 567. Oil cake.

661. OILS: Almond, amber, crude and rectified ambergris, anise or anise-seed, aniline, aspic or spike lavender, bergamot, cajeput, caraway, cassia, cinnamon, cedrat, chamomile, citronella or lemon grass, civet, fennel, Jasmine or Jasimine, Juglandium, Juniper, lavender, lemon, limes, mace, neroli or orange flower, nut oil or oil of nuts not otherwise specially provided for in this act, orange oil, olive oil for manufacturing or mechanical purposes unfit for eating and not otherwise provided for in this act, ottar of roses, palm and cocoanut, rosemary or anthoss, sesame or sesamum-seed or bean, thyme, origanum red or white, valerian; and also spermaceti, whale, and other fish oils of American fisheries, and all other articles the produce of such fisheries.

> 568. OILS: Almond, amber, crude and rectified ambergris, anise or anise-seed, aniline, aspic or spike lavender, bergamot, cajeput, caraway, cassia, cinnamon, cedrat, chamomile, citronella or lemon grass, civet, cotton seed, croton, fennel, Jasmine or Jasimine, Juglandium, Juniper, lavender, lemon, lime, mace, neroli or orange flower, nut oil or oil of nuts not otherwise specially provided for in this act, orange oil, olive oil for manufacturing or mechanical purposes unfit for eating and not otherwise provided for in this act, ottar of roses, palm and cocoanut, rosemary or anthoss, sesame or sesamum-seed or bean, thyme, origanum red or white, valerian; and also spermaceti, whale, and other fish oils of American fisheries, and all [other articles the produce] *fish and other products* of such fisheries; petroleum, crude or refined.

662. Olives, green or prepared.
> 569. [Olives, green or prepared.]

663. Opium, crude, or unmanufactured, and not adulterated, containing nine per centum and over of morphia.
> NOTE.—See paragraph 36.

664. Orange and lemon peel, not preserved, candied, or otherwise prepared.
> 570. Orange and lemon peel, not preserved, candied, or otherwise prepared.

665. Orchil, or orchil liquid.
> 571. Orchil, or orchil liquid.

666. Orchids, lily of the valley, azaleas, palms, and other plants used for forcing under glass for cut flowers or decorative purposes.
> [572. Orchids, lilly of the valley, azaleas, palms, and other plants used for forcing under glass for cut flowers or decorative purposes.]

667. Ores, of gold, silver, and nickel, and nickel matte: *Provided*, That ores of nickel, and nickel matte, containing more than two per centum of copper, shall pay a duty of one-half of one cent per pound on the copper contained therein.
> 573. Ores, of gold, silver, and nickel, and nickel matte.

668. Osmium.
> 574. Osmium.
> 575. Paintings, in oil or water colors, original drawings and sketches, and artists' proofs of etchings and engravings, and statuary, not otherwise provided for in this act, but the term "statuary" as herein used shall be understood to include only [such] professional productions in marble, stone, alabaster, wood, or metal, of a statuary or sculptor [only], *and the word "painting," as used in this act, shall not be understood to include such as are made wholly or in part by stenciling or other mechanical process.*

669. Palladium.
> 576. Palladium.

670. Paper stock, crude, of every description, including all grasses, fibers, rags (other than wool), waste, shavings, clippings, old paper, rope ends, waste rope, waste bagging, old or refuse gunny bags or gunny cloth, and poplar or other woods, fit only to be converted into paper.
> 577. Paper stock, crude, of every description, including all grasses, fibers, rags, waste, shavings, clippings, old paper, rope ends, waste rope, waste bagging, old or refuse gunny bags or gunny cloth, and poplar or other woods, fit only to be converted into paper.

671. Paraffine.
> 578. Paraffine.

672. Parchment and vellum.
> 579. Parchment and vellum.

673. Pearl, mother of, not sawed, cut, polished, or otherwise manufactured.
> 580. Pearl, mother of, not sawed or cut, or otherwise manufactured.
> 581. Pease, green, in bulk or in barrels, sacks, or similar packages.

674. Peltries and other usual goods and effects of Indians passing or repassing the boundary line of the United States, under such regulations as the Secretary of the Treasury may prescribe: *Provided*, That this exemption shall not apply to goods in bales or other packages unusual among Indians.
> 582. Peltries and other usual goods and effects of Indians passing or repassing the boundary line of the United States, under such regulations

as the Secretary of the Treasury may prescribe: *Provided,* That this exemption shall not apply to goods in bales or other packages unusual among Indians.

675. Personal and household effects not merchandise of citizens of the United States dying in foreign countries.
>583. Personal and household effects not merchandise of citizens of the United States dying in foreign countries.

676. Pewter and britannia metal, old, and fit only to be remanufactured.
>584. Pewter and britannia metal, old, and fit only to be re-manufactured.

677. Philosophical and scientific apparatus, instruments, and preparations; statuary, casts of marble, bronze, alabaster, or plaster of Paris; paintings, drawings, and etchings, specially imported in good faith for the use of any society or institution incorporated or established for religious, philosophical, educational, scientific, or literary purposes, or for encouragement of the fine arts, and not intended for sale.
>585. Philosophical and scientific apparatus, *utensils,* instruments and preparations, *including bottles and boxes containing the same;* statuary, casts of marble, bronze, alabaster, or plaster of Paris; paintings, drawings, and etchings, *including stained or painted window glass or stained or painted glass windows,* specially imported in good faith for the use of any society or institution incorporated or established for religious, philosophical, educational, scientific, or literary purposes, or for encouragement of the fine arts, and not intended for sale.

678. Phosphates, crude or native.
>586. Phosphates, crude or native.

679. Plants, trees, shrubs, roots, seed-cane, and seeds, all of the foregoing imported by the Department of Agriculture or the United States Botanic Garden.
>587. Plants, trees, shrubs, and vines of all kinds commonly known as nursery stock, not specially provided for in this act.

680. Plaster of Paris and sulphate of lime, unground.
>588. Plaster of Paris and sulphate of lime, unground.

681. Platina, in ingots, bars, sheets, and wire.
>589. Platina, in ingots, bars, sheets, and wire.

682. Platinum, unmanufactured, and vases, retorts, and other apparatus, vessels, and parts thereof composed of platinum, for chemical uses.
>590. Platinum, unmanufactured, and vases, retorts, and other apparatus, vessels, and parts thereof composed of platinum, adapted for chemical uses.
>591. Plows, tooth and disk harrows, harvesters, reapers, agricultural drills and planters, mowers, horserakes, cultivators, threshing machines and cotton gins: *Provided, That all the articles mentioned in paragraph five hundred and ninety-one, when imported from any country which lays an import duty on like articles coming from the United States, shall be subject to the duties existing prior to the passage of this act.*

683. Plumbago.
>592. Plumbago.
>593. Plush, black, known commercially as hatters' plush, composed of silk, or of silk and cotton, and used exclusively for making men's hats.

684. Polishing-stones.
>594. Polishing-stones and burnishing-stones.

685. Potash, crude, carbonate of, or "black salts." Caustic potash, or hydrate of, not including refined in sticks or rolls. Nitrate of pot-

ash, or saltpeter, crude. Sulphate of potash, crude or refined. Chlorate of potash. Muriate of potash.

> 595. Potash, crude, carbonate of, or " black salts." Caustic potash, or hydrate of, including refined in sticks or rolls. Nitrate of potash, or saltpeter, crude. Sulphate of potash, crude or refined. Chlorate of potash. Muriate of potash.

686. Professional books, implements, instruments, and tools of trade, occupation, or employment, in the actual possession at the time of persons arriving in the United States; but this exemption shall not be construed to include machinery or other articles imported for use in any manufacturing establishment, or for any other person or persons, or for sale.

> 596. Professional books, implements, instruments, and tools of trade, occupation, or employment, in the actual possession at the time of persons arriving in the United States; but this exemption shall not be construed to include machinery or other articles imported for use in any manufacturing establishment, or for any other person or persons, or for sale, *nor shall it be construed to include theatrical scenery, properties, and apparel, but such articles brought by proprietors or managers of theatrical exhibitions arriving from abroad for temporary use by them in such exhibitions and not for any other person and not for sale shall be admitted free of duty under such regulations as the Secretary of the Treasury may prescribe; but bonds shall be given for the payment to the United States of such duties as may be imposed by law upon any and all such articles as shall not be exported within six months after such importation: Provided, That the Secretary of the Treasury may in his discretion extend such period for a further term of six months in case application shall be made therefor.*

687. Pulu.
> 597. Pulu.

688. Pumice.
> 598. Pumice.
> 599. Quicksilver.

689. Quills, prepared or unprepared, but not made up into complete articles.
> 600. Quills, prepared or unprepared, but not made up into complete articles.

690. Quinia, sulphate of, and all alkaloids or salts of cinchona bark.
> 601. Quinia, sulphate of, and all alkaloids or salts of cinchona bark.

691. Rags, not otherwise specially provided for in this act.
> 602. Rags, not otherwise specially provided for in this Act.

692. Regalia and gems, statues, statuary and specimens of sculpture, where specially imported in good faith for the use of any society incorporated or established solely for educational, philosophical, literary, or religious purposes, or for the encouragement of fine arts, or for the use or by order of any college, academy, school, seminary of learning, or public library in the United States; but the term "regalia" as herein used shall be held to embrace only such insignia of rank or office or emblems as may be worn upon the person or borne in the hand during public exercises of the society or institution, and shall not include articles of furniture or fixtures, or of regular wearing apparel, nor personal property of individuals.

> 603. Regalia and gems, statues, statuary, and specimens of sculpture where specially imported in good faith for the use of any society incorporated or established solely for educational, philosophical, literary, or religious purposes, or for the encouragement of fine arts, or for the use or by order of any college, academy, school seminary of learning, or public library in the United States; but the term "regalia" as herein used shall be held to embrace only such insignia of rank or office or emblems, as may

be worn upon the person or borne in the hand during public exercises of the society or institution, and shall not include articles of furniture or fixtures, or of regular wearing apparel, nor personal property of individuals.

693. Rennets, raw or prepared.
>604. Rennets, raw or prepared.

694. Saffron and safflower, and extract of, and saffron cake.
>605. Saffron and safflower, and extract of, and saffron cake.

695. Sago, crude, and sago flour.
>606. Sago, crude, and sago flour.

696. Salacine.
>607. Salacine.
>608. Salt in bulk, and salt in bags, sacks, barrels, or other packages, but the coverings shall pay the same rate of duty as if imported separately: *Provided,* That if salt is imported from any country which imposes a duty upon salt exported from the United States, then there shall be levied, paid, and collected upon such salt the rate of duty existing prior to the passage of this act.

697. Sauer-krout.
>609. Sauerkraut.

698. Sausage skins.
>610. [Sausage skins.]

699. Seeds; anise, canary, caraway, cardamon, coriander, cotton, cummin, fennel, fenugreek, hemp, hoarhound, mustard, rape, Saint John's bread or bene, sugar-beet, mangel-wurzel, sorghum or sugar cane for seed, and all flower and grass seeds; bulbs and bulbous roots, not edible; all the foregoing not specially provided for in this act.
>611. Seeds [anise, canary, caraway, cardamom, coriander, cotton, croton cummin, fennel, fenugreek, hemp, hoarhound, mustard, rape, Saint John's bread or bene, sugar-beet, mangel-wurzel, sorghum or sugar cane for seed, and all flower and grass seeds] *of all kinds,* bulbs and bulbous roots, not edible; all the foregoing not specially provided for in this act.

700. Selep or saloup.
>612. Selep, or saloup.

701. Shells of all kinds, not cut, ground, or otherwise manufactured.
>613. Shells of all kinds, not cut, ground, or otherwise manufactured.

702. Shotgun barrels, forged, rough bored.
>614. Shotgun barrels, forged, rough bored.

703. Shrimps, and other shell fish.
>615. Shrimps, and other shellfish.

704. Silk, raw, or as reeled from the cocoon, but not doubled, twisted, or advanced in manufacture in any way.
>616. Silk, raw, or as reeled from the cocoon, *but not doubled, twisted, nor advanced in manufacture in any way.*

705. Silk cocoons and silk-waste.
>617. Silk cocoons and silk waste.

706. Silk worm's eggs.
>618. Silk worm's eggs.

707. Skeletons and other preparations of anatomy.
>619. Skeletons and other preparations of anatomy.

708. Snails.
>620. Snails.

709. Soda, nitrate of, or cubic nitrate, and chlorate of.
> 621. Soda, nitrate of, or cubic nitrate, and chlorate of.
> 622. Sulphate of soda, or salt cake, or niter cake.

710. Sodium.
> 623. Sodium.

711. Sparterré, suitable for making or ornamenting hats.
> 624. Sparterre, suitable for making or ornamenting hats.

712. Specimens of natural history, botany, and mineralogy, when imported for cabinets or as objects of science, and not for sale.
> 625. Specimens of natural history, botany, and mineralogy, when imported for cabinets or as objects of science, and not for sale.

SPICES—

713. Cassia, cassia vera, and cassia buds, unground.
> 626. Cassia, cassia vera, and cassia buds, unground.

714. Cinnamon, and chips of, unground.
> 627. Cinnamon, and chips of, unground.

715. Cloves and clove stems, unground.
> 628. Cloves and clove stems, unground.

716. Ginger-root, unground and not preserved or candied.
> 629. Ginger-root, unground and not preserved or candied.

717. Mace.
> 630. Mace.

718. Nutmegs.
> 631. Nutmegs.

719. Pepper, black or white, unground.
> 632. Pepper, black or white, unground.

720. Pimento, unground.
> 633. Pimento, unground.
> 634. [Seeds of all kinds not specially provided for in this act.]

721. Spunk.
> 635. Spunk.

722. Spurs and stilts used in the manufacture of earthen, porcelain, and stone ware.
> 636. Spurs and stilts used in the manufacture of earthen, porcelain, and stone ware.
> 637. Straw.

723. Stone and sand: Burr-stone in blocks, rough or manufactured, and not bound up into mill-stones; cliff-stone, unmanufactured, pumice-stone, rotten-stone, and sand, crude or manufactured.
> 638. Stone and sand: Burr-stone and blocks, rough or manufactured, or bound up into mill-stones; cliff-stone, unmanufactured; free-stone, granite, sandstone, limestone, and other building or monumental stone, except marble, unmanufactured or undressed, not specially provided for in this act; pumice stone, rotten-stone, and sand, crude or manufactured.

724. Storax, or styrax.
> 639. Storax, or styrax.

725. Strontia, oxide of, and protoxide of strontian, and strontianite, or mineral carbonate of strontia.
> 640. Strontia, oxide of, and protoxide of strontian, and strontianite, or mineral carbonate of strontia.

726. Sugars, all not above number sixteen Dutch standard in color, all tank bottoms, all sugar drainings and sugar sweepings, sirups of cane juice, melada, concentrated melada, and concrete and concentrated molasses, and molasses.
>641. [Sugars all: All tank bottoms, all sugar drainings and sugar sweepings, sirups of cane juice, melada, concentrated melada, and concrete and concentrated molasses, and molasses.] See also Par. 182¼.

727. Sulphur, lac or precipitated, and sulphur or brimstone, crude, in bulk, sulphur ore, as pyrites, or sulphuret of iron in its natural state, containing in excess of twenty-five per centum of sulphur (except on the copper contained therein) and sulphur not otherwise provided for.
>642. Sulphur, refined, lac or precipitated, and sulphur or brimstone, crude, in bulk, sulphur ore, as pyrites, or sulphuret of iron in its natural state, containing in excess of twenty-five per centum of sulphur, and sulphur not otherwise provided for.

728. Sulphuric acid which at the temperature of sixty degrees Fahrenheit does not exceed the specific gravity of one and three hundred and eighty thousandths, for use in manufacturing superphosphate of lime or artificial manures of any kind, or for any agricultural purposes.
>643. Sulphuric acid.

729. Sweepings of silver and gold.
>644. Sweepings of silver and gold.
>645. Tallow and wool grease, including that known commercially as degras or brown wool grease.

730. Tapioca, cassava or cassady.
>646. Tapioca, cassava or cassady.

731. Tar and pitch of wood, and pitch of coal-tar.
>647. Tar and pitch of wood, and pitch of coal tar.

732. Tea and tea-plants.
>648. Tea and tea plants.
>649. Teazles.

733. Teeth, natural, or unmanufactured.
>650. Teeth, natural, or unmanufactured.

734. Terra alba.
>651. Terra alba.

735. Terra japonica.
>652. Terra japonica.

736. Tin ore, cassiterite or black oxide of tin, and tin in bars, blocks, pigs, or grain or granulated, until July the first, eighteen hundred and ninety-three, and thereafter as otherwise provided for in this act.
>653. Tin ore, cassiterite or black oxide of tin, and tin in bars, blocks, pigs, or grain or granulated.

737. Tinsel wire, lame, or lahn.
>654. Tinsel wire, lame, or lahn.

738. Tobacco stems.
>655. Tobacco stems.

739. Tonquin, tonqua, or tonka beans.
>656. Tonquin, tonqua, or tonka beans.

740. Tripoli.
>657. Tripoli.

741. Turmeric.
   658. Turmeric.
742. Turpentine, Venice.
   659. Turpentine, Venice.
743. Turpentine, spirits of.
   660. Turpentine, spirits of.
744. Turtles.
   661. Turtles.
745. Types, old, and fit only to be remanufactured.
   662. Types, old, and fit only to be remanufactured.
746. Uranium, oxide and salts of.
   663. Uranium, oxide and salts of.
747. Vaccine virus.
   664. Vaccine virus.
748. Valonia.
   665. Valonia.
749. Verdigris, or subacetate of copper.
   666. Verdigris, or subacetate of copper.
750. Wafers, unmedicated.
   667. Wafers, unmedicated.
751. Wax, vegetable or mineral.
   668. Wax, vegetable or mineral.
752. Wearing apparel and other personal effects (not merchandise) of persons arriving in the United States, but this exemption shall not be held to include articles not actually in use and necessary and appropriate for the use of such persons for the purposes of their journey and present comfort and convenience, or which are intended for any other person or persons, or for sale: *Provided, however,* That all such wearing apparel and other personal effects as may have been once imported into the United States and subjected to the payment of duty, and which may have been actually used and taken or exported to foreign countries by the persons returning therewith to the United States, shall, if not advanced in value or improved in condition by any means since their exportation from the United States, be entitled to exemption from duty, upon their identity being established, under such rules and regulations as may be prescribed by the Secretary of the Treasury.

   669. Wearing apparel and other personal effects (not merchandise) of persons arriving in the United States, not residents thereof, but this exemption shall not be held to include articles not actually in use and necessary and appropriate for the use of such persons for the purposes of their journey and present comfort and convenience, or which are intended for any other person or persons, or for sale.
   670. Wearing apparel and other personal effects (not merchandise) in actual use of residents of the United States, returning thereto from foreign countries, not exceeding two hundred and fifty dollars in value and not intended for use of other persons nor for sale: *Provided, however,* That all the wearing apparel and other personal effects of such persons so returning as may have been by them taken out of the United States to foreign countries, and which have not been advanced in value nor improved in condition by any process of labor, or manufacture in such countries, shall be admitted free of duty without regard to their value upon their identity being established under such rules and regulations as the Secretary of the Treasury may prescribe.

753. Whalebone, unmanufactured.
    671. Whalebone, unmanufactured.

754. WOOD.—Logs, and round unmanufactured timber not specially enumerated or provided for in this act.
    WOOD:
        672. Logs, and round unmanufactured timber not specially enumerated or provided for in this Act.

755. Fire wood, handle-bolts, heading-bolts, stave-bolts, and shingle-bolts, hop-poles, fence-posts, railroad ties, ship timber, and ship-planking, not specially provided for in this act.
    673. Firewood, handle bolts, heading bolts, stave bolts, and shingle bolts, hop poles, fence posts, railroad ties, ship timber, and ship planking, not specially provided for in this Act.
    674. Timber, hewn and sawed, and timber used for spars and in building wharves.
    675. Timber, squared or sided.
    676. Sawed boards, plank, deals, and other lumber.
    677. Pine clapboards.
    678. Spruce clapboards.
    679. Hubs for wheels, posts, last blocks, wagon blocks, oar blocks, gun blocks, heading, and all like blocks or sticks, rough hewn or sawed only.
    680. Laths.
    681. Pickets and palings.
    682. Shingles.
    683. Staves of wood of all kinds, wood unmanufactured: *Provided*, That [any] all of the articles mentioned in [paragraph] *paragraphs* six hundred and seventy-two to six hundred and eighty-three, inclusive, when imported from any country which lays an export duty on [the same or] any of them, shall be subject to the duties existing prior to the passage of this act.

756. Woods, namely, cedar, lignum-vitæ, lancewood, ebony, box, granadilla, mahogany, rosewood, satinwood, and all forms of cabinet woods, in the log, rough or hewn; bamboo and rattan unmanufactured; briar-root or briar-wood, and similar wood unmanufactured, or not further manufactured than cut into blocks suitable for the articles into which they are intended to be converted; bamboo, reeds, and sticks of partridge, hair-wood, pimento, orange, myrtle, and other woods not otherwise specially provided for in this act, in the rough, or not further manufactured than cut into lengths suitable for sticks for umbrellas, parasols, sun-shades, whips, or walking-canes; and India malacca joints, not further manufactured than cut into suitable lengths for the manufactures into which they are intended to be converted.
    684. Woods, namely, cedar, lignum-vitæ, lancewood, ebony, box, granadilla, mahogany, rosewood, satinwood, and all forms of cabinet woods, in the log, rough or hewn; bamboo and rattan unmanufactured; briar root or briar wood, and similar wood unmanufactured, or not further manufactured than cut into blocks suitable for the articles into which they are intended to be converted; bamboo, reeds, and sticks of partridge, hair wood, pimento, orange, myrtle, and other woods, not otherwise specially provided for in this Act, in the rough, or not further manufactured than cut into lengths suitable for sticks for umbrellas, parasols, sunshades, whips, or walking canes; and India malacca joints, not further manufactured than cut into suitable lengths for the manufactures into which they are intended to be converted.
    685. All wool of the sheep, hair of the camel, goat, alpaca, and other like animals, and all wool and hair on the skin, noils, yarn waste, card waste, bur waste, rags and flocks, including all waste, or rags composed wholly or in part of wool: *Provided*, That this paragraph shall take effect on and after August second, eighteen hundred and ninety-four.

757. Works of art, the production of American artists residing temporarily abroad, or other works of art, including pictorial paintings on glass, imported expressly for presentation to a national institution, or

to any State or municipal corporation, or incorporated religious society, college, or other public institution, except stained or painted window-glass or stained or painted glass windows; but such exemption shall be subject to such regulations as the Secretary of the Treasury may prescribe.

> 686. Works of art, the production of American artists residing temporarily abroad, or other works of art, including pictorial paintings on glass, imported expressly for presentation to a national institution, or to any State or municipal corporation, or incorporated religious society, college, or other public institution [including stained or painted window-glass or stained or painted glass windows]; but such exemption shall be subject to such regulations as the Secretary of the Treasury may prescribe.

758. Works of art, drawings, engravings, photographic pictures, and philosophical and scientific apparatus brought by professional artists, lecturers, or scientists arriving from abroad for use by them temporarily for exhibition and in illustration, promotion, and encouragement of art, science, or industry in the United States, and not for sale, and photographic pictures, paintings, and statuary, imported for exhibition by any association established in good faith and duly authorized under the laws of the United States, or of any State, expressly and solely for the promotion and encouragement of science, art, or industry, and not intended for sale, shall be admitted free of duty, under such regulations as the Secretary of the Treasury shall prescribe; but bonds shall be given for the payment to the United States of such duties as may be imposed by law upon any and all of such articles as shall not be exported within six months after such importation: *Provided*, That the Secretary of the Treasury may, in his discretion, extend such period for a further term of six months in cases where applications therefor shall be made.

> 687. Works of art, drawings, engravings, photographic pictures, and philosophical and scientific apparatus brought by professional artists, lecturers, or scientists arriving from abroad for use by them temporarily for exhibition and in illustration, promotion, and encouragement of art, science, or industry in the United States, and not for sale, and photographic pictures, [paintings, and statuary] imported for exhibition by any association established in good faith and duly authorized under the laws of the United States, or of any State, expressly and solely for the promotion and encouragement of science, art, or industry, and not intended for sale, shall be admitted free of duty, under such regulations as the Secretary of the Treasury shall prescribe; but bonds shall be given for the payment to the United States of such duties as may be imposed by law upon any and all such articles as shall not be exported within six months after such importation: *Provided*, That the Secretary of the Treasury may, in his discretion, extend such period for a further term of six months in cases where applications therefor shall be made.

759. Works of art, collections in illustration of the progress of the arts, science, or manufactures, photographs, works in terra-cotta, parian, pottery, or porcelain, and artistic copies of antiquities in metal or other material hereafter imported in good faith for permanent exhibition at a fixed place by any society or institution established for the encouragement of the arts or of science, and all like articles imported in good faith by any society or association for the purpose of erecting a public monument, and not intended for sale, nor for any other purpose than herein expressed; but bonds shall be given under such rules and regulations as the Secretary of the Treasury may prescribe, for the payment of lawful duties which may accrue should any of the articles aforesaid be sold, transferred, or used contrary to this provision, and such articles shall be subject, at any time, to examination and inspection by the proper officers of the customs: *Provided*, That the privileges of this

and the preceding section shall not be allowed to associations or corporations engaged in or connected with business of a private or commercial character.

688. Works of art, collections in illustration of the progress of the arts, science, or manufactures, photographs, works in terra cotta, parian, pottery, or porcelain, and artistic copies of antiquities in metal or other material, hereafter imported in good faith for permanent exhibition at a fixed place by any society or institution established for the encouragement of the arts or of science, and all like articles imported in good faith by any society or association for the purpose of erecting a public monument, and not intended for sale, nor for any other purpose than herein expressed; but bonds shall be given under such rules and regulations as the Secretary of the Treasury may prescribe, for the payment of lawful duties which may accrue should any of the articles aforesaid be sold, transferred, or used contrary to this provision, and such articles shall be subject, at any time, to examination and inspection by the proper officers of the customs: *Provided*, That the privileges of this and the preceding section shall not be allowed to associations or corporations engaged in or connected with business of a private or commercial character.

760. Yams.
    689. Yams.
761. Zaffer.
    690. Zaffer.

SEC. 3. That with a view to secure reciprocal trade with countries producing the following articles, and for this purpose, on and after the first day of January, eighteen hundred and ninety-two, whenever, and so often as the President shall be satisfied that the Government of any country producing and exporting sugars, molasses, coffee, tea, and hides, raw and uncured, or any of such articles, imposes duties or other exactions upon the agricultural or other products of the United States, which, in view of the free introduction of such sugar, molasses, coffee, tea, and hides into the United States, he may deem to be reciprocally unequal and unreasonable, he shall have the power and it shall be his duty to suspend, by proclamation to that effect, the provisions of this act relating to the free introduction of such sugar, molasses, coffee, tea, and hides, the production of such country, for such time as he shall deem just, and in such case and during such suspension duties shall be levied, collected, and paid upon sugar, molasses, coffee, tea, and hides, the product of or exported from such designated country, as follows, namely:

All sugars not above number thirteen Dutch standard in color shall pay duty on their polariscopic tests as follows, namely:

All sugars not above number thirteen Dutch standard in color, all tank bottoms, sirups of cane juice or of beet juice, meluda, concentrated melada, concrete and concentrated molasses, testing by the polariscope not above seventy-five degrees, seven-tenths of one cent per pound; and for every additional degree or fraction of a degree shown by the polariscopic test, two hundredths of one cent per pound additional.

All sugars above number thirteen Dutch standard in color shall be classified by the Dutch standard of color, and pay duty as follows, namely: All sugar above number thirteen and not above number sixteen Dutch standard of color, one and three-eighths cents per pound.

All sugar above number sixteen and not above number twenty Dutch standard of color, one and five-eighths cents per pound.

All sugars above number twenty Dutch standard of color, two cents per pound.

Molasses testing above fifty-six degrees, four cents per gallon.

Sugar drainings and sugar sweepings shall be subject to duty either as molasses or sugar, as the case may be, according to polariscopic test.

On coffee, three cents per pound.

On tea, ten cents per pound.

Hides, raw or uncured, whether dry, salted, or pickled, Angora goat-skins, raw, without the wool, unmanufactured, asses' skins, raw or unmanufactured, and skins, except sheep-skins, with the wool on, one and one-half cents per pound.

NOTE.—Above Section 3 repealed by section 104 of this act.

SEC. 4. That there shall be levied, collected, and paid on the importation of all raw or unmanufactured articles, not enumerated or provided for in this act, a duty of ten per centum ad valorem, and on all articles manufactured, in whole or in part, not provided for in this act, a duty of twenty per centum ad valorem.

> SEC. 3. That there shall be levied, collected, and paid on the importation of all raw or unmanufactured articles, not enumerated or provided for in this act, a duty of ten per centum ad valorem; and on all articles manufactured, in whole or in part, not provided for in this act, a duty of twenty per centum ad valorem.

SEC. 5. That each and every imported article, not enumerated in this act, which is similar, either in material, quality, texture, or the use to which it may be applied, to any article enumerated in this act as chargeable with duty shall pay the same rate of duty which is levied on the enumerated article which it most resembles in any of the particulars before mentioned; and if any nonenumerated article equally resembles two or more enumerated articles on which different rates of duty are chargeable there shall be levied on such nonenumerated article the same rate of duty as is chargeable on the article which it resembles paying the highest rate of duty; and on articles not enumerated, manufactured of two or more materials, the duty shall be assessed at the highest rate at which the same would be chargeable if composed wholly of the component material thereof of chief value; and the words "component material of chief value," wherever used in this act, shall be held to mean that component material which shall exceed in value any other single component material of the article; and the value of each component material shall be determined by the ascertained value of such material in its condition as found in the article. If two or more rates of duty shall be applicable to any imported article it shall pay duty at the highest of such rates.

> SEC. 4. That each and every imported article, not enumerated in this act, which is similar, either in material, quality, texture, or the use to which it may be applied, to any article enumerated in this act as chargeable with duty shall pay the same rate of duty which is levied on the enumerated article which it most resembles in any of the particulars before mentioned; and if any nonenumerated article equally resembles two or more enumerated articles on which different rates of duty are chargeable there shall be levied on such nonenumerated article the same rate of duty as is chargeable on the article which it resembles paying the highest rate of duty; and on articles not enumerated, manufactured of two or more materials, the duty shall be assessed at the highest rate at which the same would be chargeable if composed wholly of the component material thereof of chief value; and the words "component material of chief value," wherever used in this act, shall be held to mean that component material which shall exceed in value any other single component material of the article; and the value of each component material shall be determined by the ascertained value of such material in its condition as found in the article. If two or more rates of duty shall be applicable to any imported article it shall pay duty at the highest of such rates.

SEC. 6. That on and after the first day of March, eighteen hundred and ninety-one, all articles of foreign manufacture, such as are usually or ordinarily marked, stamped, branded, or labeled, and all packages containing such or other imported articles, shall, respectively, be plainly marked, stamped, branded, or labeled in legible English words, so as to indicate the country of their origin; and unless so marked, stamped, branded, or labeled they shall not be admitted to entry.

> SEC. 5. That all articles of foreign manufacture, such as are usually or ordinarily marked, stamped, branded, or labeled, and all packages containing such or other imported articles, shall, respectively, be plainly marked, stamped, branded, or labeled in legible English words, so as to indicate the country of their origin; and [unless] *until* so marked, stamped, branded, or labeled they shall not be delivered to the importer [except under such regulations as the Secretary of the Treasury may prescribe.]

SEC. 7. That on and after March first, eighteen hundred and ninety-one, no article of imported merchandise which shall copy or simulate the name or trade-mark of any domestic manufacture or manufacturer, shall be admitted to entry at any custom-house of the United States. And in order to aid the officers of the customs in enforcing this prohibition any domestic manufacturer who has adopted trade-marks may require his name and residence and a description of his trade-marks to be recorded in books which shall be kept for that purpose in the Department of the Treasury under such regulations as the Secretary of the Treasury shall prescribe, and may furnish to the Department facsimiles of such trade-marks; and thereupon the Secretary of the Treasury shall cause one or more copies of the same to be transmitted to each collector or other proper officer of the customs.

> SEC. 6. That no article of imported merchandise which shall copy or simulate the name or trade-mark of any domestic manufacture or manufacturer, shall be admitted to entry at any custom-house of the United States. And in order to aid the officers of the customs in enforcing this prohibition any domestic manufacturer who has adopted trade-marks may require his name and residence and a description of his trade-marks to be recorded in books which shall be kept for that purpose in the Department of the Treasury under such regulations as the Secretary of the Treasury shall prescribe, and may furnish to the Department facsimiles of such trade-marks; and thereupon the Secretary of the Treasury shall cause one or more copies of the same to be transmitted to each collector or other proper officer of the customs.

SEC. 8. That all lumber, timber, hemp, manilla, wire rope, and iron and steel rods, bars, spikes, nails, plates, tees, angles, beams, and bolts and copper and composition metal which may be necessary for the construction and equipment of vessels built in the United States for foreign account and ownership or for the purpose of being employed in the foreign trade, including the trade between the Atlantic and Pacific ports of the United States, after the passage of this act, may be imported in bond, under such regulations as the Secretary of the Treasury may prescribe; and upon proof that such materials have been used for such purpose no duties shall be paid thereon. But vessels receiving the benefit of this section shall not be allowed to engage in the coastwise trade of the United States more than two months in any one year, except upon the payment to the United States of the duties on which a rebate is herein allowed: *Provided*, That vessels built in the United States for foreign account and ownership shall not be allowed to engage in the coastwise trade of the United States.

> SEC. 7. That all articles of foreign production which may be necessary for the construction of vessels, including machinery and equipment, built in

the United States for foreign account and ownership or for the purpose of being employed in the foreign trade, including the trade between the Atlantic and Pacific ports of the United States, after the passage of this act, may be imported in bond, under such regulations as the Secretary of the Treasury may prescribe; and upon proof that such materials have been used for such purpose no duties shall be paid thereon. But vessels receiving the benefit of this section shall not be allowed to engage in the coastwise trade of the United States more than two months in any one year, except upon the payment to the United States of the duties on which a rebate is herein allowed: *Provided*, That vessels built in the United States for foreign account and ownership shall not be allowed to engage in the coastwise trade of the United States.

SEC. 9. That all articles of foreign production needed for the repair of American vessels engaged in foreign trade, including the trade between the Atlantic and Pacific ports of the United States, may be withdrawn from bonded warehouses free of duty, under such regulations as the Secretary of the Treasury may prescribe.

SEC. 8. That all articles of foreign production needed for the repair of American vessels engaged in foreign trade, including the trade between the Atlantic and Pacific ports of the United States, may be withdrawn from bonded warehouses free of duty, under such regulations as the Secretary of the Treasury may prescribe.

SEC. 10. That all medicines, preparations, compositions, perfumery, cosmetics, cordials, and other liquors manufactured wholly or in part of domestic spirits, intended for exportation, as provided by law, in order to be manufactured and sold or removed, without being charged with duty and without having a stamp affixed thereto, shall, under such regulations as the Secretary of the Treasury may prescribe, be made and manufactured in warehouses similarly constructed to those known and designated in Treasury regulations as bonded warehouses, class two: *Provided*, That such manufacturer shall first give satisfactory bonds to the collector of internal revenue for the faithful observance of all the provisions of law and the regulations as aforesaid, in amount not less than half of that required by the regulations of the Secretary of the Treasury from persons allowed bonded warehouses. Such goods, when manufactured in such warehouses, may be removed for exportation under the direction of the proper officer having charge thereof, who shall be designated by the Secretary of the Treasury without being charged with duty, and without having a stamp affixed thereto. Any manufacturer of the articles aforesaid, or any of them, having such bonded warehouse as aforesaid, shall be at liberty, under such regulations as the Secretary of the Treasury may prescribe, to convey therein any materials to be used in such manufacture which are allowed by the provisions of law to be exported free from tax or duty, as well as the necessary materials, implements, packages, vessels, brands, and labels for the preparation, putting up, and export of the said manufactured articles; and every article so used shall be exempt from the payment of stamp and excise duty by such manufacturer. Articles and materials so to be used may be transferred from any bonded warehouse in which the same may be, under such regulation as the Secretary of the Treasury may prescribe, into any bonded warehouse in which such manufacture may be conducted, and may be used in such manufacture, and when so used shall be exempt from stamp and excise duty; and the receipt of the officer in charge as aforesaid shall be received as a voucher for the manufacture of such articles. Any materials imported into the United States may, under such rules as the Secretary of the Treasury may prescribe, and under the direction of the proper officer, be removed in original packages from on shipboard, or from the bonded warehouse in which the same may be, into the bonded warehouse in which such manufacture may be carried on, for the purpose of being used in such manufacture, without payment of duties thereon, and may there be used in such manufacture. No article so removed, nor any article manufactured in said bonded warehouse, shall be taken therefrom except for exportation, under the direction of the proper officer having charge thereof as aforesaid, whose certificate, describing the articles by their mark or otherwise, the quantity, the date of importation, and name of vessel, with such additional particulars as may from time to time be required, shall be received by the collector of customs in cancellation of the bond or return of the amount of foreign import duties. All labor performed and services rendered under these regulations shall be under the supervision of an officer of the customs, and at the expense of the manufacturer.

SEC. 9. That all articles manufactured in whole or in part of imported materials, *or of materials subject to internal-revenue tax*, and intended for exportation without being charged with duty and without having an internal-revenue stamp affixed thereto shall, under such regulations as the Secretary of the Treasury may prescribe, in order to be so manufactured and exported be made and manufactured in bonded warehouses similar to those known and designated in Treasury Regulations as bonded warehouses, class two: *Provided*, That the manufacturer of such articles shall first give satisfactory bonds for the faithful observance of all the provisions of law and of such regulations as shall be prescribed by the Secretary of the Treasury.

Whenever goods manufactured in any bonded warehouse established under the provisions of the preceding paragraph shall be exported directly therefrom or shall be duly laden for transportation and immediate exportation under the supervision of the proper officer who shall be duly designated for that purpose, such goods shall be exempt from duty and from the requirements relating to revenue stamps.

Any materials used in the manufacture of such goods, and any packages, coverings, vessels, brands, and labels used in putting up the same may, under the regulations of the Secretary of the Treasury, be conveyed without the payment of revenue tax or duty into any bonded manufacturing warehouse, and imported goods may, under the aforesaid regulations, be transferred without the exaction of duty from any bonded warehouse into any bonded manufacturing warehouse; but this privilege shall not be held to apply to implements, machinery, or apparatus to be used in the construction or repair of any bonded manufacturing warehouse or for the prosecution of the business carried on therein.

No articles or materials received into such bonded manufacturing warehouse shall be withdrawn or removed therefrom except for direct shipment and exportation or for transportation and immediate exportation in bond under the supervision of the officer duly designated therefor by the collector of the port, who shall certify to such shipment and exportation, or ladening for transportation, as the case may be, describing the articles by their mark or otherwise, the quantity, the date of exportation, and the name of the vessel. All labor performed and services rendered under these provisions shall be under the supervision of a duly designated officer of the customs and at the expense of the manufacturer.

A careful account shall be kept by the collector of all merchandise delivered by him to any bonded manufacturing warehouse, and a sworn monthly return, verified by the customs officers in charge, shall be made by the manufacturers containing a detailed statement of all imported merchandise used by him in the manufacture of exported articles.

Before commencing business the proprietor of any manufacturing warehouse shall file with the Secretary of the Treasury a list of all the articles intended to be manufactured in such warehouse and state the formula of manufacture and the names and quantities of the ingredients to be used therein.

Articles manufactured under these provisions may be withdrawn under such regulations as the Secretary of the Treasury may prescribe for transportation and delivery into any bonded warehouse at an exterior port for the sole purpose of immediate export therefrom.

The provisions of Revised Statutes thirty-four hundred and thirty-three shall, so far as may be practicable, apply to any bonded manufacturing warehouse established under this act and to the merchandise conveyed therein.

SEC. 11. All persons are prohibited from importing into the United States from any foreign country any obscene book, pamphlet, paper, writing, advertisement, circular, print, picture, drawing, or other representation, figure, or image on or of paper or other material, or any cast, instrument, or other article of an immoral nature, or any drug or medicine, or any article whatever, for the prevention of conception, or for causing unlawful abortion. No such articles, whether imported separately or contained in packages with other goods entitled to entry, shall be admitted to entry; and all such articles shall be proceeded against, seized, and forfeited by due course of law. All such prohibited articles and the package in which they are contained in the course of importation shall be detained by the officer of customs, and proceedings taken against the same as prescribed in the following section, unless it appears to the satisfaction of the collector of customs that the obscene articles contained in the package were inclosed therein without the knowledge or consent of the importer, owner, agent, or consignee: *Provided*, That the drugs hereinbefore mentioned, when imported in bulk and not put up for any of the purposes hereinbefore specified, are excepted from the operation of this section.

SEC. 10. That all persons are prohibited from importing into the United States from any foreign country any obscene book, pamphlet, paper, writing, advertisement, circular, print, picture, drawing, or other representation, figure, or image on or of paper or other material, or any cast, instrument, or other article of an immoral nature, or any drug or medicine, or any article whatever, for the prevention of conception, or for causing unlawful abortion. No such articles, whether imported separately or contained in packages with other goods entitled to entry, shall be admitted to entry; and all such articles shall be proceeded against, seized, and forfeited by due course of law. All such prohibited articles and the package in which they are contained in the course of importation shall be detained by the officer of customs, and proceedings taken against the same as hereinafter prescribed, unless it appears to the satisfaction of the collector of customs that the obscene articles contained in the package were inclosed therein without the knowledge or consent of the importer, owner, agent, or consignee: *Provided*, That the drugs hereinbefore mentioned, when imported in bulk and not put up for any of the purposes hereinbefore specified, are excepted from the operation of this section.

SEC. 12. That whoever, being an officer, agent, or employee of the Government of the United States, shall knowingly aid or abet any person engaged in any violation of any of the provisions of law prohibiting importing, advertising, dealing in, exhibiting, or sending or receiving by mail obscene or indecent publications or representations, or means for preventing conception or procuring abortion, or other articles of indecent or immoral use or tendency, shall be deemed guilty of a misdemeanor, and shall for every offense be punishable by a fine of not more than five thousand dollars, or by imprisonment at hard labor for not more than ten years, or both.

SEC. 11. That whoever, being an officer, agent, or employee of the Government of the United States, shall knowingly aid or abet any person engaged in any violation of any of the provisions of law prohibiting importing, advertising, dealing in, exhibiting, or sending or receiving by mail obscene or indecent publications or representations, or means for preventing conception or procuring abortion, or other articles of indecent or immoral use or tendency, shall be deemed guilty of a misdemeanor, and shall for every offense be punishable by a fine of not more than five thousand dollars, or by imprisonment at hard labor for not more than ten years, or both.

SEC. 13. That any judge of any district or circuit court of the United States, within the proper district, before whom complaint in writing of any violation of the two preceding sections is made, to the satisfaction of such judge, and founded on knowledge or belief, and if upon belief, setting forth the grounds of such belief, and supported by oath or affirmation of the complainant may issue, conformably to the Constitution, a warrant directed to the marshal or any deputy marshal, in the proper district, directing him to search for, seize, and take possession of any such article or thing mentioned in the two preceding sections, and to make due and immediate return thereof to the end that the same may be condemned and destroyed by proceedings, which shall be conducted in the same manner as other proceedings in the case of municipal seizure, and with the same right of appeal or writ of error.

SEC. 12. That any judge of any district or circuit court of the United States, within the proper district, before whom complaint in writing of any violation of the two preceding sections is made, to the satisfaction of such judge, and founded on knowledge or belief, and if upon belief, setting forth the grounds of such belief, and supported by oath or affirmation of the complainant, may issue, conformably to the Constitution, a warrant directed to the marshal or any deputy marshal in the proper district, directing him to search for, seize, and take possession of any such article or thing mentioned in the two preceding sections, and to make due and immediate return thereof to the end that the same may be condemned and destroyed by proceedings, which shall be conducted in the same manner as other proceedings in the case of municipal seizure, and with the same right of appeal or writ of error.

SEC. 14. That machinery for repair may be imported into the United States without payment of duty, under bond, to be given in double the appraised value thereof, to be withdrawn and exported after said machinery shall have been repaired; and the Secretary of the Treasury is authorized and directed to prescribe such rules and regulations as may be necessary to protect the revenue against fraud, and secure the identity and character of all such importations when again withdrawn and exported, restricting and limiting the export and withdrawal to the same port of entry where imported, and also limiting all bonds to a period of time of not more than six months from the date of the importation.

SEC. 13. That machinery for repair may be imported into the United States without payment of duty, under bond, to be given in double the appraised value thereof, to be withdrawn and exported after said machinery shall have been repaired; and the Secretary of the Treasury is authorized and directed to prescribe such rules and regulations as may be necessary to protect the revenue against fraud and secure the identity and character of all such importations when again withdrawn and exported, restricting and limiting the export and withdrawal to the same port of entry where imported, and also limiting all bonds to a period of time of not more than six months from the date of the importation.

SEC. 15. That the produce of the forests of the State of Maine upon the Saint John River and its tributaries, owned by American citizens, and sawed or hewed in the Province of New Brunswick by American citizens, the same being unmanufactured in whole or in part, which is now admitted into the ports of the United States free of duty, shall continue to be so admitted under such regulations as the Secretary of the Treasury shall, from time to time, prescribe.

SEC. 16. That the produce of the forests of the State of Maine upon the Saint Croix River and its tributaries owned by American citizens, and sawed in the Province of New Brunswick by American citizens, the same being unmanufactured in whole or in part, shall be admitted

into the ports of the United States free of duty, under such regulations as the Secretary of the Treasury shall, from time to time, prescribe.
NOTE.—Sections 15 and 16 omitted in new bill.

SEC. 17. That a discriminating duty of ten per centum ad valorem, in addition to the duties imposed by law, shall be levied, collected, and paid on all goods, wares, or merchandise which shall be imported in vessels not of the United States; but this discriminating duty shall not apply to goods, wares, and merchandise which shall be imported in vessels not of the United States, entitled, by treaty or any act of Congress, to be entered in the ports of the United States on payment of the same duties as shall then be paid on goods, wares, and merchandise imported in vessels of the United States.

> SEC. 14. That a discriminating duty of ten per centum ad valorem, in addition to the duties imposed by law, shall be levied, collected, and paid on all goods, wares, or merchandise which shall be imported in vessels not of the United States; but this discriminating duty shall not apply to goods, wares, and merchandise which shall be imported in vessels not of the United States, entitled, by treaty or any act of Congress, to be entered in the ports of the United States on payment of the same duties as shall then be paid on goods, wares, and merchandise imported in vessels of the United States.

SEC. 18. That no goods, wares, or merchandise, unless in cases provided for by treaty, shall be imported into the United States from any foreign port or place, except in vessels of the United States, or in such foreign vessels as truly and wholly belong to the citizens or subjects of that country of which the goods are the growth, production, or manufacture, or from which such goods, wares, or merchandise can only be, or most usually are, first shipped for transportation. All goods, wares, or merchandise imported contrary to this section, and the vessel wherein the same shall be imported, together with her cargo, tackle, apparel, and furniture, shall be forfeited to the United States; and such goods, wares, or merchandise, ship, or vessel, and cargo shall be liable to be seized, prosecuted, and condemned, in like manner, and under the same regulations, restrictions, and provisions as have been heretofore established for the recovery, collection, distribution, and remission of forfeitures to the United States by the several revenue laws.

> SEC. 15. That no goods, wares, or merchandise, unless in cases provided for by treaty, shall be imported into the United States from any foreign port or place, except in vessels of the United States, or in such foreign vessels as truly and wholly belong to the citizens or subjects of that country of which the goods are the growth, production, or manufacture, or from which such goods, wares, or merchandise can only be, or most usually are, first shipped for transportation. All goods, wares, or merchandise imported contrary to this section, and the vessel wherein the same shall be imported, together with her cargo, tackle, apparel, and furniture, shall be forfeited to the United States; and such goods, wares, or merchandise, ship, or vessel, and cargo, shall be liable to be seized, prosecuted, and condemned in like manner, and under the same regulations, restrictions, and provisions as have been heretofore established for the recovery, collection, distribution, and remission of forfeitures to the United States by the several revenue laws.

SEC. 19. That the preceding section shall not apply to vessels or goods, wares, or merchandise imported in vessels of a foreign nation which does not maintain a similar regulation against vessels of the United States.

> SEC. 16. That the preceding section shall not apply to vessels or goods, wares, or merchandise imported in vessels of a foreign nation which does not maintain a similar regulation against vessels of the United States.

SEC. 20. That the importation of neat cattle and the hides of neat cattle from any foreign country into the United States is prohibited: *Provided*, That the operation of this section shall be suspended as to any foreign country or countries, or any parts of such country or countries, whenever the Secretary of the Treasury shall officially determine, and give public notice thereof that such importation will not tend to the introduction or spread of contagious or infectious diseases among the cattle of the United States; and the Secretary of the Treasury is hereby authorized and empowered, and it shall be his duty, to make all necessary orders and regulations to carry this section into effect, or to suspend the same as therein provided, and to send copies thereof to the proper officers in the United States, and to such officers or agents of the United States in foreign countries as he shall judge necessary.

> SEC. 17. That the importation of neat cattle and the hides of neat cattle from any foreign country into the United States is prohibited: *Provided*, That the operation of this section shall be suspended as to any foreign country or countries, or any parts of such country or countries, whenever the Secretary of the Treasury shall officially determine, and give public notice thereof that such importation will not tend to the introduction or spread of contagious or infectious diseases among the cattle of the United States; and the Secretary of the Treasury is hereby authorized and empowered, and it shall be his duty, to make all necessary orders and regulations to carry this section into effect, or to suspend the same as herein provided, and to send copies thereof to the proper officers in the United States, and to such officers or agents of the United States in foreign countries as he shall judge necessary.

SEC. 21. That any person convicted of a willful violation of any of the provisions of the preceding section shall be fined not exceeding five hundred dollars, or imprisoned not exceeding one year, or both, in the discretion of the court.

> SEC. 18. That any person convicted of a willful violation of any of the provisions of the preceding section shall be fined not exceeding five hundred dollars, or imprisoned not exceeding one year, or both, in the discretion of the court.

SEC. 22. That upon the reimportation of articles once exported of the growth, product, or manufacture of the United States upon which no internal tax has been assessed or paid, or upon which such tax has been paid and refunded by allowance or drawback, there shall be levied, collected, and paid a duty equal to the tax imposed by the internal-revenue laws upon such articles, except articles manufactured in bonded warehouses and exported pursuant to law, which shall be subject to the same rate of duty as if originally imported.

> SEC. 19. That upon the reimportation of articles once exported of the growth, product, or manufacture of the United States, upon which no internal tax has been assessed or paid, or upon which such tax has been paid and refunded by allowance or drawback, there shall be levied, collected, and paid a duty equal to the tax imposed by the internal-revenue laws upon such articles, except articles manufactured in bonded warehouses and exported pursuant to law, which shall be subject to the same rate of duty as if originally imported.

SEC. 23. That whenever any vessel laden with merchandise in whole or in part subject to duty has been sunk in any river, harbor, bay, or waters subject to the jurisdiction of the United States, and within its limits, for the period of two years, and is abandoned by the owner thereof, any person who may raise such vessel shall be permitted to bring any merchandise recovered therefrom into the port nearest to the place where such vessel was so raised, free from the payment of any duty thereupon, and without being obliged to enter the same at the custom-house; but under such regulations as the Secretary of the Treasury may prescribe.

SEC. 20. That whenever any vessel laden with merchandise in whole or in part subject to duty has been sunk in any river, harbor, bay, or waters subject to the jurisdiction of the United States, and within its limits, for the period of two years, and is abandoned by the owner thereof, any person who may raise such vessel shall be permitted to bring any merchandise recovered therefrom into the port nearest to the place where such vessel was so raised, free from the payment of any duty thereupon, [and without being obliged to enter the same at the custom-house,] but under such regulations as the Secretary of the Treasury may prescribe.

SEC. 24. That the works of manufacturers engaged in smelting or refining metals in the United States may be designated as bonded warehouses under such regulations as the Secretary of the Treasury may prescribe: *Provided,* That such manufacturers shall first give satisfactory bonds to the Secretary of Treasury. Metals in any crude form requiring smelting or refining to make them readily available in the arts, imported into the United States to be smelted or refined and intended to be exported in a refined but unmanufactured state, shall, under such rules as the Secretary of the Treasury may prescribe and under the direction of the proper officer, be removed in original packages or in bulk from the vessel or other vehicle on which it has been imported, or from the bonded warehouse in which the same may be into the bonded warehouse in which such smelting and refining may be carried on, for the purpose of being smelted and refined without payment of duties thereon, and may there be smelted and refined, together with other metals of home or foreign production: *Provided,* That each day a quantity of refined metal equal to the amount of imported metal refined that day shall be set aside, and such metal so set aside shall not be taken from said works except for exportation, under the direction of the proper officer having charge thereof as aforesaid, whose certificate, describing the articles by their marks or otherwise, the quantity, the date of importation, and the name of vessel or other vehicle by which it was imported, with such additional particulars as may from time to time be required, shall be received by the collector of customs as sufficient evidence of the exportation of the metal, or it may be removed, under such regulations as the Secretary of the Treasury may prescribe, to any other bonded warehouse, or upon entry for, and payment of duties, for domestic consumption. All labor performed and services rendered under these regulations shall be under the supervision of an officer of the customs, to be appointed by the Secretary of the Treasury, and at the expense of the manufacturer.

SEC. 21. That the works of manufacturers engaged in smelting or refining metals, or both smelting and refining, in the United States may be designated as bonded warehouses under such regulations as the Secretary of the Treasury may prescribe: *Provided,* That such manufacturers shall first give satisfactory bonds to the Secretary of the Treasury. Ores or metals in any crude form requiring smelting or refining to make them readily available in the arts, imported into the United States to be smelted or refined and intended to be exported in a refined but unmanufactured state, shall, under such rules as the Secretary of the Treasury may prescribe, and under the direction of the proper officer, be removed in original packages or in bulk from the vessel or other vehicle on which they have been imported, or from the bonded warehouse in which the same may be, into the bonded warehouse in which such smelting or refining, or both, may be carried on, for the purpose of being smelted or refined, or both, without payment of duties thereon, and may there be smelted or refined, together with other metals of home or foreign production: *Provided,* That each day a quantity of refined metal equal to the amount of imported metal smelted or refined that day shall be set aside, and such metal so set aside shall not be taken from said works except for transportation to another bonded warehouse or for exportation, under the direction of the proper officer having charge thereof as aforesaid, whose certificate, describing the articles by their marks or otherwise, the quantity, the date of importation, and the name of vessel or other vehicle by which it was imported, with such additional particulars as may from time to time be required, shall be received by the collector of customs as sufficient evidence of the exportation of the metal, or it may be removed under such regulations as the Secretary of the Treasury may prescribe, upon entry and payment of duties, for domestic consumption. All labor performed and services rendered under these regulations shall be under the supervision of an officer of the customs, to be appointed by the Secretary of the Treasury, and at the expense of the manufacturer.

SEC. 25. That where imported materials on which duties have been paid are used in the manufacture of articles manufactured or produced in the United States, there shall be allowed on the exportation of such articles a drawback equal in amount to the duties paid on the materials used, less one per centum of such duties: *Provided*, That when the articles exported are made in part from domestic materials, the imported materials, or the parts of the articles made from such materials shall so appear in the completed articles that the quantity or measure thereof may be ascertained: *And provided further*, That the drawback on any article allowed under existing law shall be continued at the rate herein provided. That the imported materials used in the manufacture or production of articles entitled to drawback of customs duties when exported shall in all cases where drawback of duties paid on such materials is claimed, be identified, the quantity of such materials used and the amount of duties paid thereon shall be ascertained, the facts of the manufacture or production of such articles in the United States and their exportation therefrom shall be determined, and the drawback due thereon shall be paid to the manufacturer, producer, or exporter, to the agent of either or to the person to whom such manufacturer, producer, exporter or agent shall in writing order such drawback paid, under such regulations as the Secretary of the Treasury shall prescribe.

SEC. 22. That where imported materials on which duties have been paid are used in the manufacture of articles manufactured or produced in the United States there shall be allowed on the exportation of such articles a drawback equal in amount to the duties paid on the materials used, less one per centum of such duties: *Provided*, That when the articles exported are made in part from domestic materials the imported materials, or the parts of the articles made from such materials, shall so appear in the completed articles that the quantity or measure thereof may be ascertained: *And provided further*, That the drawback on any article allowed under existing law shall be continued at the rate herein provided. That the imported materials used in the manufacture or production of articles entitled to drawback of customs duties when exported shall, in all cases where drawback of duties paid on such materials is claimed, be identified, the quantity of such materials used and the amount of duties paid thereon shall be ascertained, the facts of the manufacture or production of such articles in the United States and their exportation therefrom shall be determined, and the drawback due thereon shall be paid to the manufacturer, producer, or exporter, to the agent of either or to the person to whom such manufacturer, producer, exporter, or agent shall in writing order such drawback paid, under such regulations as the Secretary of the Treasury shall prescribe: [*Provided further*, That a drawback shall be allowed equal to the duty paid, less one per centum, upon any imported bagging made of jute butts, which shall have been used exclusively as outside covering for lint cotton when exported, the rate and amount of such drawback to be ascertained under such regulations as the Secretary of the Treasury may prescribe.]

Note.—The preceding sections of existing law are reproduced from the act of October 1, 1890.

[PUBLIC—No. 145.]

NOTE.—The following sections of existing law, Nos. 1 to 30, are reproduced from the act of June 10, 1890:

Be it enacted by the Senate and House of Representatives of the United States of America in Congress assembled, That all merchandise imported into the United States shall, for the purpose of this act, be deemed and held to be the property of the person to whom the merchandise may be consigned; but the holder of any bill of lading consigned to order and indorsed by the consignor shall be deemed the consignee thereof; and in case of the abandonment of any merchandise to the underwriters the latter may be recognized as the consignee.

SEC. 23. That all merchandise imported into the United States shall, for the purpose of this act, be deemed and held to be the property of the person to whom the merchandise may be consigned; but the holder of any bill of lading consigned to order and indorsed by the consignor shall be deemed the consignee thereof; and in case of the abandonment of any merchandise to the underwriters the latter may be recognized as the consignee.

SEC. 2. That all invoices of imported merchandise shall be made out in the currency of the place or country from whence the importations shall be made or if purchased in the currency actually paid therefor, shall contain a correct description of such merchandise, and shall be made in triplicate or in quadruplicate in case of merchandise intended for immediate transportation without appraisement, and signed by the person owning or shipping the same, if the merchandise has been actually purchased, or by the manufacturer or owner thereof, if the same has been procured otherwise than by purchase, or by the duly authorized agent of such purchaser, manufacturer, or owner.

SEC. 24. That all invoices of imported merchandise shall be made out in the currency of the place or country from whence the importations shall be made, or if purchased, in the currency actually paid therefor to the vendor or vendors of the merchandise, shall contain a correct description of such merchandise, and shall be made in triplicate or in quadruplicate in case of merchandise intended for immediate transportation without appraisement, and signed by the person owning or shipping the same, if the merchandise has been actually purchased, or by the manufacturer or owner thereof, if the same has been procured otherwise than by purchase, or by the duly authorized agent of such purchaser, manufacturer, or owner.

SEC. 3. That all such invoices shall, at or before the shipment of the merchandise, be produced to the consul, vice-consul, or commercial agent of the United States, of the consular district in which the merchandise was manufactured or purchased as the case may be, for export to the United States, and shall have indorsed thereon, when so produced, a declaration signed by the purchaser, manufacturer, owner, or agent, setting forth that the invoice is in all respects correct and true, and was made at the place from which the merchandise is to be exported to the United States; that it contains, if the merchandise was obtained by purchase, a true and full statement of the time when, the place where, the person from whom the same was purchased, and the actual cost thereof, and of all charges thereon, as provided by this act; and that no discounts, bounties, or drawbacks are contained in the invoice but such as have been actually allowed thereon; and when obtained in any other manner than by purchase, the actual market value or wholesale price thereof at the time of exportation to the United States in the principal markets of the country from whence exported; that such actual market value is the price at which the merchandise described in the invoice is freely offered for sale to all purchasers in said markets, and that it is the price which the manufacturer or owner making the declaration would have received, and was willing to receive, for such merchandise sold in the ordinary course of trade, in the usual wholesale quantities, and that it includes all charges thereon as provided by this act; and the actual quantity thereof; and that no different invoice of the merchandise mentioned in the invoice so produced has been or will be furnished to anyone. If the merchandise was actually purchased, the declaration shall also contain a statement that the currency in which such invoice is made out is that which was actually paid for the merchandise by the purchaser.

SEC. 25. That all such invoices shall, at or before the shipment of the merchandise, be produced to the consul, vice-consul, or commercial agent of the United States of the consular district, or the adjoining district in cases where the Secretary of the Treasury shall so direct, in which the merchandise was manufactured or purchased, as the case may be, for export to the United States, and shall have indorsed thereon, when so produced, a declaration signed by the purchaser, manufacturer, [shipper,] owner, or agent, setting forth that the invoice is in all respects correct and true, and was made at the place from which the merchandise is to be exported to the United States; that it contains, if the merchandise was obtained by purchase, a true and full statement of the time when, the place where, the person from whom the same was purchased, and the actual cost thereof, and of all charges thereon as provided by this act; and that no discounts, bounties, or drawbacks are contained in the invoice but such as have been actually allowed thereon; and when obtained in any other manner than by purchase the actual market value or wholesale price thereof at the time of exportation to the United States in the principal markets of the country from whence exported; that such actual market value is the price at which the merchandise described in the invoice is freely offered for sale to all purchasers in said markets, and that it is the price which the manufacturer or owner making the declaration would have received, and was willing to receive, for such merchandise sold in the ordinary course of trade, in the usual wholesale quantities, and that it includes *and specifies in detail* all charges thereon as provided by this act, and the actual quantity thereof; and that no different invoice of the merchandise mentioned in the invoice so produced has been or will be furnished to any one. If the merchandise was actually purchased the declaration shall also contain a statement that the currency in which such invoice is made out is that which was actually paid for the merchandise by the purchaser. Consuls shall refuse certification of any invoice not made in accordance with the provisions herein set forth.

SEC. 4. That, except in case of personal effects accompanying the passenger, no importation of any merchandise exceeding one hundred dollars in dutiable value shall be admitted to entry without the production of a duly certified invoice thereof as required by law, or of an affidavit made by the owner, importer, or consignee, before the collector or his deputy, showing why it is impracticable to produce such invoice; and no entry shall be made in the absence of a certified invoice, upon affidavit as aforesaid, unless such affidavit be accompanied by a statement in the form of an invoice, or otherwise, showing the actual cost of such merchandise, if purchased, or if obtained otherwise than by purchase, the actual market value or wholesale price thereof at the time of exportation to the United States, in the principal markets of the country from which the same has been imported; which statement shall be verified by the oath of the owner, importer, consignee, or agent desiring to make entry of the merchandise, to be administered by the collector or his deputy, and it shall be lawful for the collector or his deputy to examine the deponent under oath touching the sources of his knowledge, information, or belief in the premises, and to require him to produce any letter, paper, or statement of account, in his possession, or under his control, which may assist the officers of customs in ascertaining the actual value of the importation or any part thereof; and in default of such production when so requested, such owner, importer, consignee, or agent shall be thereafter debarred from producing any such letter, paper, or statement for the purpose of avoiding any additional duty, penalty, or forfeiture incurred under this act, unless he shall show to the satisfaction of the court or the officers of the customs, as the case may be, that it was not in his power to produce the same when so demanded; and no merchandise shall be admitted to entry under the provisions of this section unless the collector shall be satisfied that the failure to produce a duly certified invoice is due to causes beyond the control of the owner, consignee, or agent thereof: *Provided*, That the Secretary of the Treasury may make regulations by which books, magazines, and other periodicals published and imported in successive parts, numbers, or volumes, and entitled to be imported free of duty, shall require but one declaration for the entire series. And when entry of merchandise exceeding one hundred dollars in value is made by a statement in the form of an invoice the collector shall require a bond for the production of a duly certified invoice.

SEC. 26. That, except in case of personal effects accompanying the passenger, *and personal and household effects specially enumerated in the free list of this act*, no importation of any merchandise exceeding one hundred dollars in dutiable value shall be admitted to entry without the production of a duly certified invoice thereof, as required by law, or of an affidavit made by the owner, importer, or consignee before the collector or his deputy, showing why it is impracticable to produce such invoice; and no entry shall be made in the absence of a certified invoice, upon affidavit as aforesaid, unless such affidavit be accompanied by a statement in the form of an invoice, or otherwise, showing the actual cost of such merchandise, if purchased, or if obtained otherwise than by purchase, the actual market value or wholesale price thereof at the time of exportation to the United States in the principal markets of the country from which the same has been imported, the name of the consular district, and the name of the [port or] place from which the merchandise was procured; which statement shall be verified by the oath of the owner, importer, consignee, or agent desiring to make entry of the merchandise, to be administered by the collector or his deputy, and it shall be the duty of the collector or his deputy to examine the [respondent] *deponent* under oath touching the sources of his knowledge, information, or belief in the premises, and to require him to produce any letter, paper, or statement of account in his possession, or under his control, which may assist the officers of customs in ascertaining the actual value of the importation or any part thereof; and in default of such production when so requested, such owner, importer, consignee, or agent shall be thereafter debarred from producing any such letter, paper, or statement for the purpose of avoiding any additional duty, penalty, or forfeiture incurred under this act, unless he shall show to the satisfaction of the court or the officers of the customs, as the case may be, that it was not in his power to produce the same when so demanded; and no merchandise shall be admitted to entry under the provisions of this section unless the collector shall be satisfied that the failure to produce a duly certified invoice is due to causes beyond the control of the owner, consignee, or agent thereof: *Provided*, That the Secretary of the Treasury may make regulations by which books, magazines, and other periodicals published and imported in successive parts, numbers, or volumes, and entitled to be imported free of duty, shall require but one declaration for the entire series. And when entry of merchandise exceeding one hundred dollars in value is made by a statement in the form of an invoice, the collector shall require a bond for the production of a duly certified invoice in a penal sum which shall be double the amount of the estimated duties, and in the sum of one hundred dollars if the merchandise be free of duty, and when in the case of merchandise exempt from duty or subject to a specific duty it shall be found, on liquidation of the entry thereof, that the amount of duty assessable thereon is not dependent upon the price or value thereof, the bond given for production of a duly certified invoice may be cancelled without requiring production of such invoice.

SEC. 5. That whenever merchandise imported into the United States is entered by invoice, one of the following declarations, according to the nature of the case, shall be filed with the collector of the port, at the time of entry by the owner, importer, consignee, or agent, which declaration so filed shall be duly signed by the owner, importer, consignee, or agent, before the collector, or before a notary public or other officer duly authorized by law to administer oaths and take acknowledgments, who may be designated by the Secretary of the Treasury to receive such declarations and to certify to the identity of the persons making them, under regulations to be prescribed by the Secretary of the Treasury; and every officer so designated shall file with the collector of the port a copy of his official signature and seal: *Provided*, That if any of the invoices or bills of lading of any merchandise imported in any one vessel, which should otherwise be embraced in said entry, have not been received at the date of the entry, the declaration may state the fact, and thereupon such merchandise of which the invoices or bills of lading are not produced shall not be included in such entry, but may be entered subsequently.

DECLARATION OF CONSIGNEE, IMPORTER, OR AGENT.

I, ——— ———, do solemnly and truly declare that I am the consignee [importer or agent] of the merchandise described in the annexed entry and invoice; that the invoice and bill of lading now presented by me to the collector of ——— ——— are the true and only invoice and bill of lading by me received of all the goods, wares, and merchandise imported in the ———, whereof ——— ——— is master, from ——— ———, for account of any person whomsoever for whom I am authorized to enter the same; that the said invoice and bill of lading are in the state in which they were actually received by me, and that I do not know or believe in the existence of any other invoice or bill of lading of the said goods, wares, and merchandise; that the entry now delivered to the collector contains a just and true account of the said goods, wares, and merchandise, according to the said invoice and bill of lading; that nothing has been, on my part, nor to my knowledge on the part of any other person, concealed or suppressed, whereby the United States may be defrauded of any part of the duty lawfully due on the said goods, wares, and merchandise; that the said invoice and the declaration therein are in all respects true, and were made by the person by whom the same purports to have been made; and that if at any time hereafter I discover any error in the said invoice, or in the account now rendered of the said goods, wares, and merchandise, or receive any other invoice of the same, I will immediately make the same known to the collector of this district. And I do further solemnly and truly declare that to the best of my knowledge and belief [insert the name and residence of the owner or owners] is [or are] the owner (or owners) of the goods, wares, and merchandise mentioned in the annexed entry; that the invoice now produced by me exhibits the actual cost (if purchased) or the actual market value or wholesale price (if otherwise obtained) at the time of exportation to the United States in the principal markets of the country from whence imported of the said goods, wares, and merchandise, and includes and specifies the value of all cartons, cases, crates, boxes, sacks, and coverings of any kind, and all other costs, charges, and expenses incident to placing said goods, wares, and merchandise in condition, packed ready for shipment to the United States, and no other or different discount, bounty, or drawback but such as has been actually allowed on the same.

DECLARATION OF OWNER IN CASES WHERE MERCHANDISE HAS BEEN ACTUALLY PURCHASED.

I, —— ——, do solemnly and truly declare that I am the owner of the merchandise described in the annexed entry and invoice; that the entry now delivered by me to the collector of —— contains a just and true account of all the goods, wares, and merchandise imported by or consigned to me, in the —— ——, whereof —— —— is master, from ——; that the invoice and entry which I now produce contain a just and faithful account of the actual cost of the said goods, wares, and merchandise and include and specifies the value of all cartons, cases, crates, boxes, sacks, and coverings of any kind, and all other costs, charges, and expenses incident to placing said goods, wares, and merchandise in condition, packed ready for shipment to the United States, and no other discount, drawback, or bounty but such as has been actually allowed on the same; that I do not know nor believe in the existence of any invoice or bill of lading other than those now produced by me, and that they are in the state in which I actually received them. And I further solemnly and truly declare that I have not in the said entry or invoice concealed or suppressed anything whereby the United States may be defrauded of any part of the duty lawfully due on the said goods, wares, and merchandise; that to the best of my knowledge and belief the said invoice and the declaration thereon are in all respects true, and were made by the person by whom the same purports to have been made; and that if at any time hereafter I discover any error in the said invoice or in the account now produced of the said goods, wares, and merchandise, or receive any other invoice of the same, I will immediately make the same known to the collector of this district.

DECLARATION OF MANUFACTURER OR OWNER IN CASES WHERE MERCHANDISE HAS NOT BEEN ACTUALLY PURCHASED.

I, —— ——, do solemnly and truly declare that I am the owner (or manufacturer) of the merchandise described in the annexed entry and invoice; that the entry now delivered by me to the collector of —— contains a just and true account of all the goods, wares, and merchandise imported by or consigned to me in the ——, whereof —— —— is master, from ——; that the said goods, wares, and merchandise were not actually bought by me, or by my agent, in the ordinary mode of bargain and sale, but that nevertheless the invoice which I now produce contains a just and faithful valuation of the same, at their actual market value or wholesale price, at the time of exportation to the United States, in the principal markets of the country from whence imported for my account (or for account of myself and partners); that such actual market value is the price at which the merchandise described in the invoice is freely offered for sale to all purchasers in said markets, and is the price which I would have received and was willing to receive for such merchandise sold in the ordinary course of trade in the usual wholesale quantities; that the said invoice contains also a just and faithful account of all the cost of finishing said goods, wares, and merchandise to their present condition, and includes and specifies the value of all cartons, cases, crates, boxes, sacks, and coverings of any kind, and all other costs and charges incident to placing said goods, wares, and merchandise in condition packed ready for shipment to the United States, and no other discount, drawback, or bounty but such as has been actually allowed on the said goods, wares, and merchandise; that the said invoice and the declaration thereon are in all respects true, and were made by the person by whom the same purports to have been made; that I do not know nor believe in the existence of any invoice or bill of lading other than those now produced by me, and that they are in the state in which I actually received them. And I do further solemnly and truly declare that I have not in the said entry or invoice concealed or suppressed anything whereby the United States may be defrauded of any part of the duty lawfully due on the said goods, wares, and merchandise; and that if at any time hereafter I discover any error in the said invoice, or in the account now produced of the said goods, wares, and merchandise, or receive any other invoice of the same, I will immediately make the same known to the collector of this district.

SEC. 27. That whenever merchandise imported into the United States is entered by invoice one of the following declarations, according to the nature of the case, shall be filed with the collector of the port at the time of [the] entry by the owner, importer, consignee, or agent, which declaration so filed shall be duly signed by the owner, importer, consignee, or agent, before the collector or before a notary public or other officer duly authorized by law to administer oaths and take acknowledgements, who may be designated by the Secretary of the Treasury to receive such declarations and to certify to the identity of the persons making them, under regulations to be prescribed by the Secretary of the Treasury; and every officer so designated shall file with the collector of the port a copy of his official signature and seal: *Provided*, That if any of the invoices or bills of lading of any merchandise imported in any one vessel, which should otherwise be embraced in said entry, have not been received at the date of the entry the declaration may state the fact, and thereupon such merchandise, of which the invoices or bills of lading are not produced, shall not be included in such entry, but may be entered subsequently.

DECLARATION OF CONSIGNEE, IMPORTER, OR AGENT.

I, ———, do solemnly and truly declare that I am the consignee (importer or agent) of the merchandise described in the annexed entry and invoice; that the invoice and bill of lading now presented by me to the collector of ——— are the true and only invoice and bill of lading by me received of all the goods, wares, and merchandise imported in the ———, whereof ——— is master, from ———, for [the] account of any person whomsoever for whom I am authorized to enter the same; that the [same] *said* invoice and bill of lading are in the state in which they were actually received by me, and that I do not know or believe in the existence of any other invoice or bill of lading of the said goods, wares, and merchandise; that the entry now delivered to the collector contains a just and true account of the said goods, wares, and merchandise, according to the said invoice and bill of lading; that nothing has been, on my part, nor to my knowledge on the part of any other person, concealed or suppressed whereby the United States may be defrauded of any part of the duty lawfully due on the said goods, wares, and merchandise; that the said invoice and the declaration therein are in all respects true, and were made by the person by whom the same purports to have been made; and that if at any time hereafter I discover any error in the said invoice or in the account now rendered of the said goods, wares, and merchandise, or receive any other invoice of the same, I will immediately make the same known to the collector of this district. And I do further solemnly and truly declare that to the best of my knowledge and belief [insert the name and residence of the owner or owners] is (or are) the owner (or owners) of the goods, wares, and merchandise mentioned in the annexed entry; that the invoice now produced by me exhibits the actual cost (if purchased) or the actual market value or wholesale price (if otherwise obtained) at the time of exportation to the United States in the principal markets of the country from whence imported, of the said goods, wares, and merchandise, and includes and specifies in detail the value of all cartons, cases, crates, boxes, sacks, and coverings of any kind, including the value of the usual and necessary outside sacks, crates, packing boxes, and other outside coverings and straw or necessary packing materials, as hereinafter referred to, and all other costs, charges, and expenses incident to placing said goods, wares, and merchandise in condition, packed ready for shipment to the United States, and no other or different discount, bounty, or drawback but such as has been actually allowed on the same.

DECLARATION OF OWNER IN CASES WHERE MERCHANDISE HAS BEEN ACTUALLY PURCHASED.

I, ———— ————, do solemnly and truly declare that I am the owner of the merchandise described in the annexed entry and invoice; that the entry now delivered by me to the collector of ———— contains a just and true account of all the goods, wares, and merchandise imported by or consigned to me in the ————, whereof ———— is master, from ————; that the invoice and entry which I now produce contain a just and faithful account of the actual cost of the said goods, wares, and merchandise, and include and specify in detail the value of all cartons, cases, crates, boxes, sacks, and coverings of any kind, including the value of the usual and necessary outside sacks, crates, packing boxes, and other outside coverings and straw or necessary packing materials, as hereinafter referred to; and all other costs, charges, and expenses incident to placing said goods, wares, and merchandise in condition, packed ready for shipment to the United States, and no other discount, drawback, or bounty but such as has been actually allowed on the same; that I do not know nor believe in the existence of any invoice or bill of lading other than those now produced by me, and that they are in the state in which I actually received them. And I further solemnly and truly declare that I have not in the said entry or invoice concealed or suppressed anything whereby the United States may be defrauded of any part of the duty lawfully due on the said goods, wares, and merchandise; that to the best of my knowledge and belief the said invoice and the declaration thereon are in all respects true, and were made by the person by whom the same purports to have been made; and that if at any time hereafter I discover any error in the said invoice or in the account now produced of the said goods, wares, and merchandise, or receive any other invoice of the same, I will immediately make the same known to the collector of this district.

DECLARATION OF MANUFACTURER OR OWNER IN CASES WHERE MERCHANDISE HAS NOT BEEN ACTUALLY PURCHASED.

I, ———— ————, do solemnly and truly declare that I am the owner (or manufacturer) of the merchandise described in the annexed entry and invoice; that the entry now delivered by me to the collector of ———— contains a just and true account of all the goods, wares, and merchandise imported by or consigned to me in the ————, whereof ———— is master, from ————; that the said goods, wares, and merchandise were not actually bought by me, or by my agent, in the ordinary mode of bargain and sale, but that nevertheless the invoice which I now produce contains a just and faithful valuation of the same, at their actual market value or wholesale price, at the time of exportation to the United States, in the principal markets of the country from whence imported for my account (or for account of myself or partners); that such actual market value is the price at which the merchandise described in the invoice is freely offered for sale to all purchasers in said markets, and is the price which I would have received, and was willing to receive, for such merchandise sold in the ordinary course of trade in the usual wholesale quantities; that the said invoice contains also a just and faithful account of all the cost of finishing such goods, wares, and merchandise to their present condition, and includes and specifies, in detail, the value of all cartons, cases, crates, boxes, sacks, and coverings of any kind, including the value of the usual and necessary outside sacks, crates, packing boxes, and other outside coverings and straw or necessary packing materials, as hereinafter referred to, and all other costs and charges incident to placing said goods, wares, and merchandise in condition, packed ready for shipment to the United States, and no other discount, drawback, or bounty but such as has been actually allowed on the said goods, wares, and merchandise; that the said invoice and the declaration thereon are in all respects true, and were made by the person by whom the same purports to have been made; that I do not know nor believe in the existence of any invoice or bill of lading other than those now produced by me, and that they are in the state in which I actually received them. And I do further solemnly and truly declare that I have not in the said entry or invoice concealed or suppressed anything whereby the United States may be defrauded of any part of the duty lawfully due on the said goods, wares, and merchandise; and that if at any time hereafter I discover any error in the said invoice, or in the account now produced of the said goods, wares, and merchandise, or receive any other invoice of the same, I will immediately make the same known to the collector of this district.

SEC. 6. That any person who shall knowingly make any false statement in the declarations provided for in the preceding section, or shall aid or procure the making of any such false statement as to any matter material thereto, shall, on conviction thereof, be punished by a fine not exceeding five thousand dollars, or by imprisonment at hard labor not more than two years, or both, in the discretion of the court: *Provided*, That nothing in this section shall be construed to relieve imported merchandise from forfeiture by reason of such false statement or for any cause elsewhere provided by law.

> SEC. 28. That any person who shall knowingly make any false statement in the declarations provided for in the preceding section, or shall aid or procure the making of any such false statement, as to any matter material thereto, shall, on conviction thereof, be punished by a fine not exceeding five thousand dollars, or by imprisonment at hard labor not more than two years, or both, in the discretion of the court: *Provided*, That nothing in this section shall be construed to relieve imported merchandise from forfeiture by reason of such false statements, or for any cause elsewhere provided by law.

SEC. 7. That the owner, consignee, or agent of any imported merchandise which has been actually purchased, may, at the time when he shall make and verify his written entry of such merchandise, but not afterwards, make such addition in the entry to the cost or value given in the invoice, or pro forma invoice, or statement in form of an invoice, which he shall produce with his entry, as in his opinion may raise the same to the actual market value or wholesale price of such merchandise at the time of exportation to the United States, in the principal markets of the country from which the same has been imported; but no such addition shall be made upon entry to the invoice value of any imported merchandise obtained otherwise than by actual purchase; and the collector within whose district any merchandise may be imported or entered, whether the same has been actually purchased or procured otherwise than by purchase, shall cause the actual market value or wholesale price of such merchandise to be appraised; and if the appraised value of any article of imported merchandise shall exceed by more than ten per centum the value declared in the entry, there shall be levied, collected, and paid, in addition to the duties imposed by law on such merchandise, a further sum equal to two per centum of the total appraised value for each one per centum that such appraised value exceeds the value declared in the entry; and the additional duties shall only apply to the particular article or articles in each invoice which are undervalued; and if such appraised value shall exceed the value declared in the entry more than forty per centum, such entry may be held to be presumptively fraudulent, and the collector of customs may seize such merchandise and proceed as in cases of forfeiture for violations of the customs laws; and in any legal proceedings which may result from such seizure the fact of such undervaluation shall be presumptive evidence of fraud, and the burden of proof shall be on the claimant to rebut the same, and forfeiture shall be adjudged unless he shall rebut said presumption of fraudulent intent by sufficient evidence: *Provided*, That the forfeitures provided for in this section shall apply to the whole of the merchandise or the value thereof in the case or package containing the particular article or articles in each invoice which are undervalued: *And provided further*, That all additional duties, penalties, or forfeitures, applicable to merchandise entered by a duly certified invoice shall be alike applicable to goods entered by a pro forma invoice or statement in form of an invoice. The duty shall not, however, be assessed upon an amount less than the invoice or entered value.

SEC. 29. That the owner, consignee, or agent of any imported merchandise which has been actually purchased may, at the time when he shall make and verify his written entry of such merchandise, but not afterward, make such addition in the entry to the cost or value given in the invoice, or pro forma invoice, or statement in form of an invoice, which he shall produce with his entry, as in his opinion may raise the same to the actual market value or wholesale price of such merchandise, at the time of exportation to the United States, in the principal markets of the country from which the same has been imported; but no such addition shall be made upon entry to the invoice value of any imported merchandise obtained otherwise than by actual purchase; and the collector within whose district any merchandise may be imported or entered, whether the same has been actually purchased or procured otherwise than by purchase, shall cause the actual market value or wholesale price of such merchandise to be appraised, and if the appraised value of any article of imported merchandise subject to ad valorem duty or duty based upon value, shall exceed the value declared in the entry, there shall be levied, collected, and paid, in addition to the duties imposed by law on such merchandise at its appraised value, an additional duty [equal to the amount of the lawful rate of duty upon the sum which the appraising officer, in order to make market value, adds to the value declared in the entry; that is to say, the lawful rate of duty upon the merchandise in question shall be doubled upon the amount added by the appraising officer to make market value, and such] *of one per centum of the total appraised value for each one per centum that such appraised value exceeds the value declared in the entry, but the* additional duties shall only apply to the [particular] article or articles in each invoice which are [advanced by the appraising officer to make market value] *undervalued, and shall not exceed forty per centum of the appraised value of such article or articles*. Such additional duties shall not be construed to be penal, and shall not be remitted [and] *nor* shall [not] *they* be refunded [on] *in case of the* exportation of the merchandise, and shall not be subject to the benefit of drawback: *Provided*, That nothing herein contained shall restrict the powers of the general appraisers to review according to law the valuations made by local appraisers, and if such appraised value *of any merchandise* shall exceed the value declared in the entry more than forty per centum, such entry shall be held to be presumptively fraudulent, and the collector of customs shall seize such merchandise and proceed as in cases of forfeiture for violations of the customs law; and in any legal proceedings which may result from such seizure the fact of such undervaluation shall be presumptive evidence of fraud, and the burden of proof shall be on the claimant to rebut the same, and forfeiture shall be adjudged unless he shall rebut said presumption of fraudulent intent by sufficient evidence: *Provided*, That the forfeitures provided for in this section shall apply to the whole of the merchandise or the value thereof in the case or package containing the particular article or articles in each invoice which are undervalued: *And provided further*, That all additional duties, penalties, or forfeitures, applicable to merchandise entered by a duly certified invoice shall be alike applicable to goods entered by a pro forma invoice or statement in form of an invoice. The duty shall not, however, be assessed upon an amount less than the invoice or entered value.

SEC. 8. That when merchandise entered for customs duty has been consigned for sale by or on account of the manufacturer thereof to a person, agent, partner, or consignee in the United States, such person, agent, partner, or consignee shall, at the time of the entry of such merchandise, present to the collector of customs at the port where such entry is made, as a part of such entry, and in addition to the certified invoice or statement in the form of an invoice required by law, a statement signed by such manufacturer, declaring the cost of production of such merchandise, such cost to include all the elements of cost as stated in section eleven of this act. When merchandise entered for customs duty has been consigned for sale by or on account of a person other than the manufacturer of such merchandise to a person, agent, partner, or consignee in the United States, such person, agent, partner, or consignee shall, at the time of the entry of such merchandise, present to the collector of customs at the port where such entry is made, as a part of such entry, a statement signed by the consignor thereof, declaring that the merchandise was actually purchased by him or for his account, and showing the time when, the place where, and from whom he purchased the merchandise, and in detail the price he paid for the same: *Provided*, That the statements required by this section shall be made in triplicate, and shall bear the attestation of the consular officer of the United States resident within the consular district wherein the merchandise was manufactured, if consigned by the manufacturer or for his account, or from whence it was imported when consigned by a person other than the manufacturer, one copy thereof to be delivered to the person making the statement, one copy to be transmitted with the triplicate invoice of the merchandise to the collector of the port in the United States to which the merchandise is consigned, and the remaining copy to be filed in the consulate.

SEC. 9. That if any owner, importer, consignee, agent, or other person shall make or attempt to make any entry of imported merchandise by means of any fraudulent or false invoice, affidavit, letter, paper, or by means of any false statement, written or verbal, or by means of any false or fraudulent practice or appliance whatsoever, or shall be guilty of any willful act or omission by means whereof the United States shall be deprived of the lawful duties, or any portion thereof, accruing upon the merchandise, or any portion thereof, embraced or referred to in such invoice, affidavit, letter, paper, or statement, or affected by such act or omission, such merchandise, or the value thereof, to be recovered from the person making the entry, shall be forfeited, which forfeiture shall only apply to the whole of the merchandise or the value thereof in the case or package containing the particular article or articles of merchandise to which such fraud or false paper or statement relates; and such person shall, upon conviction, be fined for each offense a sum not exceeding five thousand dollars, or be imprisoned for a time not exceeding two years, or both, in the discretion of the court.

SEC. 30. That if any owner, importer, consignee, agent, or other person shall make or attempt to make any entry of imported merchandise by means of any fraudulent or false invoice, affidavit, letter, paper, or by means of any false statement, written or verbal, or by means of any false or fraudulent practice or appliance whatsoever, or shall be guilty of any willful act or omission by means whereof the United States [might] may or shall be deprived of the lawful duties, or any portion thereof, accruing upon the merchandise, or any portion thereof, embraced or referred to in such invoice, affidavit, letter, paper, or statement, or affected by such act or omission, such merchandise, or the value thereof, to be recovered from the person making the entry, shall be forfeited, which forfeiture shall only apply to the whole of the merchandise or the value thereof, in the case or package containing the particular article or articles of merchandise to which such fraud or false paper or statement relates; and such person shall, upon conviction, be fined for each offense a sum not exceeding five thousand dollars, or be imprisoned for a time not exceeding two years, or both, in the discretion of the court.

SEC. 10. That it shall be the duty of the appraisers of the United States, and every of them, and every person who shall act as such appraiser, or of the collector, as the case may be, by all reasonable ways and means in his or their power to ascertain, estimate, and appraise (any invoice or affidavit thereto or statement of cost, or of cost of production to the contrary notwithstanding) the actual market value and wholesale price of the merchandise at the time of exportation to the United States, in the principal markets of the country whence the same has been imported, and the number of yards, parcels, or quantities, and actual market value or wholesale price of every of them, as the case may require.

SEC. 31. That it shall be the duty of the appraisers of the United States, the general appraisers, and every of them, and every person who shall act as appraiser, or of the collector, as the case may be, by all reasonable ways and means in his or their power to ascertain, estimate, and appraise (any invoice or affidavit thereto or statement of cost, or of cost of production to the contrary notwithstanding) the actual market value and wholesale price of the merchandise at the time of exportation to the United States, in the principal markets of the country whence the same has been imported, and the number of yards, parcels, or quantities, and actual market value or wholesale price of every [one] of them, as the case may require, and to state for the information of the collector, *when required by him*, the character and component materials of the merchandise.

SEC. 11. That when the actual market value, as herein defined, of any article of imported merchandise wholly or partially manufactured and subject to ad valorem duty, or to duty based in whole or in part on value, can not be ascertained to the satisfaction of the appraising officer, the appraiser or appraisers shall use all available means to ascertain the cost of production of such merchandise at the time of exportation to the United States, and at the place of manufacture; such cost of production to include cost of materials and of fabrication, all general expenses covering each and every outlay of whatsoever nature incident to such production, together with the expense of preparing and putting up such merchandise ready for shipment, and an addition of eight per cent upon the total cost as thus ascertained; and in no such case shall such merchandise be appraised upon original appraisal or reappraisement at less than the total cost of production as thus ascertained.

SEC. 32. That when the actual market value, as herein defined, of any article of imported merchandise wholly or partially manufactured and subject to ad valorem duty, or to duty based in whole or in part on value, can not be ascertained to the satisfaction of the appraising officer, the appraiser or appraisers shall use all available means to ascertain the cost of production of such merchandise at the time of exportation to the United States and at the place of manufacture, such cost of production to include cost of materials and fabrication; all general expenses covering each and every outlay of whatsoever nature incident to such production, together with the expense of preparing and putting up such merchandise ready for shipment, and an addition of not [more] *less* than eight per centum upon the total cost as thus ascertained; and in no case shall such merchandise be appraised upon original appraisal or reappraisement at less than the total cost as thus ascertained.

SEC. 12. That there shall be appointed by the President, by and with the advice and consent of the Senate, nine general appraisers of merchandise, each of whom shall receive a salary of seven thousand dollars a year. Not more than five of such general appraisers shall be appointed from the same political party. They shall not be engaged in any other business, avocation, or employment, and may be removed from office at any time by the President for inefficiency, neglect of duty, or malfeasance in office. They shall be employed at such ports and within such territorial limits as the Secretary of the Treasury may from time to time prescribe, and are hereby authorized to exercise the powers and duties devolved upon them by this act, and to exercise, under the general direction of the Secretary of the Treasury, such other supervision over appraisements and classifications for duty of imported merchandise as may be needful to secure lawful and uniform appraisements and classifications at the several ports. Three of the general appraisers shall be on duty as a board of general appraisers daily (except Sunday and legal holidays) at the port of New York, during the business hours prescribed by the Secretary of the Treasury, at which port a place for samples shall be provided, under such rules and regulations as the Secretary of the Treasury may from time to time prescribe, which shall include rules as to the classes of articles to be deposited, the time of their retention, and as to their disposition, which place of samples shall be under the immediate control and direction of the board of general appraisers on duty at said port.

> SEC. 33. That section eight of the act entitled "An act to simplify the laws in relation to the collection of the revenues," approved June tenth, eighteen hundred and ninety, be, and the same is hereby, repealed, and section twelve of the said last mentioned act is hereby continued in force, [but said section twelve of said act shall, after the provision " that they shall not be engaged in any other business, avocation, or employment, and may be removed from office at any time by the President for inefficiency, neglect of duty, or malfeasance in office," be amended so as to read "They shall be employed as boards of three or otherwise at such ports and within such territorial limits as the Secretary of the Treasury may from time to time prescribe, and are hereby authorized to exercise the powers and duties devolved upon them by this act and to exercise, under the direction of the Secretary of the Treasury, such other supervision over appraisements and classifications for duty of imported merchandise as he, the Secretary, may deem needful to secure lawful and uniform appraisements and classifications at the several ports. At least one board of three of the general appraisers shall be on duty as a board of general appraisers daily (except Sundays and legal holidays) at the port of New York, during the business hours prescribed by the Secretary of the Treasury, at which port a place for samples shall be provided, under such rules and regulations as the Secretary of the Treasury may from time to time prescribe, which shall include rules as to the classes of articles to be deposited, the time of their retention, and as to their disposition, which place of samples shall be under the control and direction of the board or boards of general appraisers on duty at said port. Said board of general appraisers shall elect a president and vice-president from among their number, and by a majority vote of the full board adopt rules and regulations for the conduct of business, subject to the approval of the Secretary of the Treasury.]

SEC. 13. That the appraiser shall revise and correct the reports of the assistant appraisers as he may judge proper, and the appraiser or, at ports where there is no appraiser, the person acting as such shall report to the collector his decision as to the value of the merchandise appraised. At ports where there is no appraiser, the certificate of the customs officer to whom is committed the estimating and collection of duties, of the dutiable value of any merchandise required to be appraised, shall be deemed and taken to be the appraisement of such merchandise. If the collector shall deem the appraisement of any imported merchandise too low he may order a reappraisement, which shall be made by one of the general appraisers, or, if the importer, owner, agent, or consignee of such merchandise shall be dissatisfied with the appraisement thereof, and shall have complied with the requirements of law with respect to the entry and appraisement of merchandise, he may, within two days thereafter give notice to the collector, in writing, of such dissatisfaction, on the receipt of which the collector shall at once direct a reappraisement of such merchandise by one of the general appraisers. The decision of the appraiser or the person acting as such (in cases where no objection is made thereto, either by the collector or by the importer, owner, consignee, or agent), or of the general appraiser in cases of reappraisement, shall be final and conclusive as to the dutiable value of such merchandise against all parties interested therein, unless the importer, owner, consignee, or agent of the merchandise shall be dissatisfied with such decision, and shall, within two days thereafter, give notice to the collector in writing of such dissatisfaction, or unless the collector shall deem the appraisement of the merchandise too low, in either case the collector shall transmit the invoice and all the papers appertaining thereto to the board of three general appraisers, which shall be on duty at the port of New York, or to a board of three general appraisers who may be designated by the Secretary of the Treasury for such duty at that port or at any other port, which board shall examine and decide the case thus submitted, and their decision, or that of a majority of them, shall be final and conclusive as to the dutiable value of such merchandise against all parties interested therein, and the collector or the person acting as such shall ascertain, fix, and liquidate the rate and amount of duties to be paid on such merchandise, and the dutiable costs and charges thereon, according law.

SEC. 34. That the appraiser shall revise and correct the reports of the assistant appraisers as he may judge proper, and the appraiser, or at ports where there is no appraiser, the person acting as such, shall report to the collector his decision as to the value of the merchandise appraised. At ports where there is no appraiser the certificate of the customs officer, to whom is committed the estimating and collection of duties, of the dutiable value of any merchandise required to be appraised, shall be deemed and taken to be the appraisement of such merchandise. If the collector shall deem the appraisement of any imported merchandise too low he may order a reappraisement, which shall be made by one of the general appraisers, in the manner prescribed in sections thirty-one and thirty-two of this act, or if the importer, owner, agent, or consignee of such merchandise shall be dissatisfied with the appraisement thereof, and shall have complied with the requirements of law with respect to the entry and appraisement of merchandise, he may, within five days thereafter, give notice to the collector, in writing, of such dissatisfaction, on the receipt of which the collector shall at once direct a reappraisement of such merchandise by one of the general appraisers. The decision of the appraiser or the person acting as such (in cases where no objection is made thereto, either by the collector or by the importer, owner, consignee, or agent), or of the general appraiser in cases of reappraisement, shall be final and conclusive as to the dutiable value of such merchandise against all parties interested therein, unless the importer, owner, consignee, or agent of the merchandise shall be dissatisfied with such decision, and shall, within five days thereafter, give notice to the collector, in writing, of such dissatisfaction, or unless the collector shall deem the appraisement of the merchandise too low, in either case the collector shall transmit the invoice and all the papers appertaining thereto to the board of three general appraisers, which shall be on duty at the port of New York, or to a board of three general appraisers who may be designated by the Secretary of the Treasury for such duty at that port or at any other port, which board shall examine, and decide the case thus submitted, and their decision, or that of a majority of them, shall be final and conclusive as to the dutiable

TA——8

value of such merchandise against all parties interested therein, and the collector or the person acting as such shall ascertain, fix, and liquidate the rate and amount of duties to be paid on such merchandise, and the dutiable costs and charges thereon, according to law.

SEC. 14. That the decision of the collector as to the rate and amount of duties chargeable upon imported merchandise, including all dutiable costs and charges, and as to all fees and exactions of whatever character (except duties on tonnage), shall be final and conclusive against all persons interested therein, unless the owner, importer, consignee, or agent of such merchandise, or the person paying such fees, charges, and exactions other than duties, shall, within ten days after "but not before" such ascertainment and liquidation of duties, as well in cases of merchandise entered in bond as for consumption, or within ten days after the payment of such fees, charges, and exactions, if dissatisfied with such decision, give notice in writing to the collector, setting forth therein distinctly and specifically, and in respect to each entry or payment, the reasons for his objections thereto, and if the merchandise is entered for consumption shall pay the full amount of the duties and charges ascertained to be due thereon. Upon such notice and payment the collector shall transmit the invoice and all the papers and exhibits connected therewith to the board of three general appraisers, which shall be on duty at the port of New York, or to a board of three general appraisers who may be designated by the Secretary of the Treasury for such duty at that port or at any other port, which board shall examine and decide the case thus submitted, and their decision, or that of a majority of them, shall be final and conclusive upon all persons interested therein, and the record shall be transmitted to the proper collector or person acting as such who shall liquidate the entry accordingly, except in cases where an application shall be filed in the circuit court within the time and in the manner provided for in section fifteen of this act.

SEC. 35. That the decision of the collector as to the rate and amount of duties chargeable upon imported merchandise, including all dutiable costs and charges, and as to all fees and exactions of whatever character (except duties on tonnage), shall be final and conclusive against all persons interested therein, unless the owner, importer, consignee, or agent of such merchandise, or the person paying such fees, charges, and exactions other than duties, shall, within ten days after, [exclusive of Sundays and State holidays,] but not before such ascertainment and liquidation of duties, as well in cases of merchandise entered in bond as for consumption, or within [a like period,] *ten days* after the payment of such fees, charges, and exactions, if dissatisfied with such decision, give notice in writing to the collector, setting forth therein distinctly and specifically and, in respect to each entry or payment, the reasons for his objections thereto, and if the merchandise is entered for consumption shall pay [within ten days, exclusive of Sundays and State holidays, after said ascertainment and liquidation of duties,] the full amount of the duties and charges ascertained to be due thereon. Upon such notice and payment the collector shall transmit the invoice and all the papers and exhibits connected therewith to the board of three general appraisers, which shall be on duty at the port of New York, or to a board of three general appraisers who may be designated by the Secretary of the Treasury for such duty at that port or at any other port, which board shall examine and decide the case thus submitted, and their decision, or that of a majority of them, shall be final and conclusive upon all persons interested therein, and the record shall be transmitted to the proper collector or person acting as such who shall liquidate the entry accordingly, except in cases where an application shall be filed in the circuit court of appeals for a review of any question of law arising in the case within the time and in the manner hereinafter provided within the time and in the manner provided for in section thirty-six of this act.

SEC. 15. That if the owner, importer, consignee, or agent of any imported merchandise, or the collector, or the Secretary of the Treasury, shall be dissatisfied with the decision of the board of general appraisers, as provided for in section fourteen of this act, as to the construction of the law and the facts respecting the classification of such merchandise and the rate of duty imposed thereon under such classification, they, or either of them, may, within thirty days next after such decision, and not afterwards, apply to the circuit court of the United States within the district in which the matter arises for a review of the questions of law and fact involved in such decision. Such application shall be made by filing in the office of the clerk of said circuit court a concise statement of the errors of law and fact complained of, and a copy of such statement shall be served on the collector, or on the importer, owner, consignee, or agent, as the case may be. Thereupon the court shall order the board of appraisers to return to said circuit court the record and the evidence taken by them, together with a certified statement of the facts involved in the case, and their decisions thereon; and all the evidence taken by and before said appraisers shall be competent evidence before said circuit court; and within twenty days after the aforesaid return is made the court may, upon the application of the Secretary of the Treasury, the collector of the port, or the importer, owner, consignee, or agent, as the case may be, refer it to one of said general appraisers, as an officer of the court, to take and return to the court such further evidence as may be offered by the Secretary of the Treasury, collector, importer, owner, consignee, or agent, within sixty days thereafter, in such order and under such rules as the court may prescribe; and such further evidence with the aforesaid returns shall constitute the record upon which said circuit court shall give priority to and proceed to hear and determine the questions of law and fact involved in such decision, respecting the classification of such merchandise and the rate of duty imposed thereon under such classification, and the decision of such court shall be final, and the proper collector, or person acting as such, shall liquidate the entry accordingly, unless such court shall be of opinion that the question involved is of such importance as to require a review of such decision by the Supreme Court of the United States, in which case said circuit court, or the judge making the decision may, within thirty days thereafter, allow an appeal to said Supreme Court; but an appeal shall be allowed on the part of the United States whenever the Attorney-General shall apply for it within thirty days after the rendition of such decision. On such original application, and on any such appeal, security for damages and costs shall be given as in the case of other appeals in cases in which the United States is a party. Said Supreme Court shall have jurisdiction and power to review such decision, and shall give priority to such cases, and may affirm, modify, or reverse such decision of such circuit court, and remand the case with such orders as may seem to it proper in the premises, which shall be executed accordingly. All final judgments, when in favor of the importer, shall be satisfied and paid by the Secretary of the Treasury from the permanent indefinite appropriation provided for in section twenty-three of this act. For the purposes of this section the circuit courts of the United States shall be deemed always open, and said circuit courts, respectively, may establish, and from time to time alter, rules and regulations not inconsistent herewith for the procedure in such cases as they shall deem proper.

SEC. 36. That if the owner, importer, consignee, or agent of any imported merchandise, *or the collector with the approval of the Secretary of the Treasury*, or the Secretary of the Treasury, shall be dissatisfied with the decision of the board of general appraisers as hereinbefore provided, as to the construction of the law respecting the classification of such merchandise and the rate of duty imposed thereon under such classification [they or either of them], *the owner, importer, consignee, or agent, or the collector with the approval of the Secretary of the Treasury* may, within thirty days next after such decision, and not afterwards, apply to the circuit court of appeals of the United States within the district in which the matter arises for a review of the questions of law only involved in such decision. Such application shall be made by filing in the office of the clerk of said circuit court of appeals a concise statement of the errors of law complained of, and [a copy] *two copies* of such statement shall be served on the collector, who shall forthwith transmit [the same] *one of them* to the Secretary of the Treasury, or on the importer, owner, consignee, or agent, as the case may be. Thereupon said circuit court of appeals, or any judge thereof, shall order the board of appraisers to return to said circuit court the record consisting of the invoice and the papers and exhibits connected therewith originally transmitted by the collector to the said board, together with a certified statement of the facts found by them in the case, with their decision thereon. The board of appraisers shall not return to said circuit court of appeals any of the evidence taken by or before them in the case. The certified statement or findings of fact returned as aforesaid shall be conclusive as to all questions of fact arising in the case upon all parties and upon said circuit court of appeals; but said circuit court of appeals, if it deems the statement of facts returned by the board of appraisers insufficient to enable the said court to determine the correctness of the decision of the said board of appraisers in respect to classification and rate of duty may submit such question or questions as it deems advisable to said board of appraisers and require a further finding or findings of fact thereon, and the said board of appraisers shall forthwith, on receiving an order from the said court for further findings of fact on questions submitted to them by the said court as hereinbefore provided, proceed to determine such questions and return their findings of fact thereon to the said circuit court of appeals. The aforesaid returns shall constitute the record and case upon which said circuit court of appeals shall give priority to and proceed to hear and determine the questions of law only involved in such decisions of the said board of appraisers respecting the classification of such merchandise and the rate of duty imposed thereon under such classification. The decision of said court shall be final and the proper collector or person acting as such shall liquidate the entry accordingly: *Provided, however*, That in such cases the said circuit courts of appeals shall have the same power to certify questions of law to the Supreme Court of the United States, and the said Supreme Court of the United States shall have the same powers to take control of such cases by certiorari or otherwise after they have been brought into the said circuit courts of appeals that are now conferred by law upon said courts or any of them in respect to subjects within the appellate jurisdiction of said circuit court of appeals. All final judgments when in favor of the importer shall be satisfied and paid by the Secretary of the Treasury from the permanent indefinite appropriation provided for in section forty-five of this act. For the purpose of this section the circuit courts of appeals of the United States shall be deemed always open, and said courts, respectively, may establish and from time to time alter rules and regulations not inconsistent herewith for the procedure in such cases as they shall deem proper.

[All hearings before said board of general appraisers upon questions of fact arising out of classification of imported merchandise shall be public, and the proper officer of the United States and the importer, owner, consignee, agent, or person aggrieved by the decision undergoing investigation may be present and offer evidence.]

[The person or his attorney making the protest in this act provided for, shall have the right to amend said protest at any time prior to ten days before hearing upon said protest.]

SEC. 16. That the general appraisers, or any of them, are hereby authorized to administer oaths, and said general appraisers, the boards of general appraisers, the local appraisers, or the collectors, as the case may be, may cite to appear before them, and examine upon oath, any owner, importer, agent, consignee, or other person touching any matter or thing which they, or either of them, may deem material respecting any imported merchandise, in ascertaining the dutiable value or classification thereof; and they, or either of them, may require the production of any letters, accounts, or invoices relating to said merchandise, and may require such testimony to be reduced to writing, and when so taken it shall be filed in the office of the collector, and preserved for use or reference until the final decision of the collector or said board of appraisers shall be made respecting the valuation or classification of said merchandise, as the case may be.

SEC. 37. That the general appraisers, or any of them, are hereby authorized to administer oaths, and said general appraisers, the boards of general appraisers, the local appraisers, or the collectors, as the case may be, may cite to appear before them and examine upon oath any owner, importer, agent, consignee, or other person touching any matter or thing which they, or either of them, may deem material respecting any imported merchandise in ascertaining the dutiable value or classification thereof; and they, or either of them, may require the production of any letters, accounts, or invoices relating to said merchandise, and may require such testimony to be reduced to writing, and when so taken it shall be filed and preserved for use or reference until the final decision of the collector or said board of appraisers shall be made respecting the valuation or classification of said merchandise, as the case may be.

SEC. 17. That if any person so cited to appear shall neglect or refuse to attend, or shall decline to answer, or shall refuse to answer in writing any interrogatories, and subscribe his name to his deposition, or to produce such papers, when so required by a general appraiser, or a board of general appraisers, or a local appraiser, or a collector, he shall be liable to a penalty of one hundred dollars; and if such person be the owner, importer, or consignee, the appraisement which the general appraiser, or board of general appraisers, or local appraiser, or collector, where there is no appraiser, may make of the merchandise, shall be final and conclusive; and any person who shall willfully and corruptly swear falsely on an examination before any general appraiser, or board of general appraisers, or local appraiser, or collector, shall be deemed guilty of perjury; and if he is the owner, importer, or consignee, the merchandise shall be forfeited.

SEC. 38. That if any person so cited to appear shall neglect or refuse to attend, or shall decline to answer, or shall refuse to answer in writing any interrogatories, and subscribe his name to his deposition, or to produce such papers, when so required by a general appraiser, or a board of general appraisers, or a local appraiser, or a collector, he shall be liable to a penalty of one hundred dollars; and if such person be the owner, importer, or consignee the appraisement which the general appraiser, or board of general appraisers, or local appraiser, or collector, where there is no appraiser, may make of the merchandise shall be final and conclusive; and any person who shall wilfully and corruptly swear falsely on an examination before any general appraiser, or board of general appraisers, or local appraiser, or collector, shall be deemed guilty of perjury; and if he is the owner, importer, or consignee the merchandise shall be forfeited.

SEC. 18. That all decisions of the general appraisers and of the boards of general appraisers, respecting values and rates of duty, shall be preserved and filed, and shall be open to inspection under proper regulations to be prescribed by the Secretary of the Treasury. All decisions of the general appraisers shall be reported forthwith to the Secretary of the Treasury and to the Board of General Appraisers on duty at the port of New York, and the report to the Board shall be accompanied, whenever practicable, by samples of the merchandise in question, and it shall be the duty of the said Board, under the direction of the Secretary of the Treasury, to cause an abstract to be made and published of such decisions of the appraisers as they may deem important, and of the decisions of each of the general appraisers and boards of general appraisers, which abstract shall contain a general description of the merchandise in question, and of the value and rate of duty fixed in each case, with reference, whenever practicable, by number or other designation, to samples deposited in the place of samples at New York, and such abstract shall be issued from time to time, at least once in each week, for the information of customs officers and the public.

SEC. 39. That all decisions of the general appraisers and of the boards of general appraisers respecting values and rates of duty shall be preserved and filed, and shall be open to inspection under proper regulations to be prescribed by the Secretary of the Treasury. All decisions of the general appraisers shall be reported forthwith to the Secretary of the Treasury and to the Board of General Appraisers on duty at the port of New York, and the report to the Board shall be accompanied, whenever practicable, by samples of the merchandise in question, and it shall be the duty of the said Board, under the direction of the Secretary of the Treasury, to cause an abstract to be made and published of such decisions of the appraisers as they may deem important, and of the decisions of each of the general appraisers and boards of general appraisers, which abstract shall contain a general description of the merchandise in question and of the value and rate of duty fixed in each case, with reference, whenever practicable, by number or other designation, to samples deposited in the place of samples at New York; and such abstract shall be issued from time to time, at least once in each week, for the information of customs officers and the public.

SEC. 19. That whenever imported merchandise is subject to an ad valorem rate of duty, or to a duty based upon or regulated in any manner by the value thereof, the duty shall be assessed upon the actual market value or wholesale price of such merchandise as bought and sold in usual wholesale quantities, at the time of exportation to the United States, in the principal market of the country from whence imported, and in the condition in which such merchandise is there bought and sold for exportation to the United States, or consigned to the United States for sale, including the value of all cartons, cases, crates, boxes, sacks, and coverings of any kind, and all other costs, charges, and expenses incident to placing the merchandise in condition, packed ready for shipment to the United States, and if there be used for covering or holding imported merchandise, whether dutiable or free, any unusual article or form designed for use otherwise than in the bona fide transportation of such merchandise to the United States, additional duty shall be levied and collected upon such material or article at the rate to which the same would be subject if separately imported. That the words "value" or "actual market value" whenever used in this act or in any law relating to the appraisement of imported merchandise shall be construed to mean the actual market value or wholesale price as defined in this section.

SEC. 40. That whenever imported merchandise is subject to an ad valorem rate of duty, or to a duty based upon or regulated in any manner by the value thereof, the duty shall be assessed upon the actual market value or wholesale price of such merchandise as bought and sold in usual wholesale quantities at the time of exportation to the United States in the principal markets of the country from whence imported and in the condition in which such merchandise is there bought and sold in wholesale quantities, including the value of all cartons, inside wrappings, coverings, bands and labels, but the value of the usual and necessary outside sacks, crates, packing boxes, or other outside coverings and straw or necessary packing material shall not be estimated as part of the value of said merchandise in determining the amount of duties for which it is liable: *Provided*, That if any packages, sacks, crates, boxes, coverings, or packing materials of any kind used for covering, holding, or packing imported merchandise, whether dutiable or free, shall be of any unusual material, or are salable as merchandise, or designed for use otherwise than in the bona fide transportation of such merchandise to the United States, then duty shall be levied and collected on said sacks, crates, boxes, coverings, or packing materials at the rate to which the same would be subject if separately imported. *That the word "value" or "actual market value," whenever used in this Act or in any law relating to the appraisement of imported merchandise shall be construed to mean the actual market value or wholesale price as defined in this section.*

SEC. 20. Any merchandise deposited in any public or private bonded warehouse may be withdrawn for consumption within three years from the date of original importation on payment of the duties and charges to which it may be subject by law at the time of such withdrawal: *Provided*, That nothing herein shall affect or impair existing provisions of law in regard to the disposal of perishable or explosive articles.

SEC. 41. That when duties are based upon the weight of merchandise deposited in any public or private bonded warehouse said duties shall be levied and collected upon the weight of such merchandise at the time of its withdrawal and any merchandise deposited in bond in any public or private bonded warehouse may be withdrawn for consumption within three years from the date of original importation on payment of the duties and charges to which it may be subject by law at the time of such withdrawal: *Provided*, That nothing herein shall affect or impair existing provisions of law in regard to the disposal of perishable or explosive articles.

SEC. 21. That in all suits or informations brought, where any seizure has been made pursuant to any act providing for or regulating the collection of duties on imports or tonnage, if the property is claimed by any person, the burden of proof shall lie upon such claimant: *Provided*, That probable cause is shown for such prosecution, to be judged of by the court.

SEC. 42. That in all suits or informations brought, where any seizure has been made pursuant to any act providing for or regulating the collection of duties on imports or tonnage, if the property is claimed by any person, the burden of proof shall lie upon such claimant: *Provided*, That probable cause is shown for such prosecution, to be judged of by the court.

SEC. 22. That all fees exacted and oaths administered by officers of the customs, except as provided in this act, under or by virtue of existing laws of the United States, upon the entry of imported goods and the passing thereof through the customs, and also upon all entries of domestic goods, wares, and merchandise for exportation, be, and the same are hereby, abolished; and in case of entry of merchandise for exportation, a declaration, in lieu of an oath, shall be filed, in such form and under such regulations as may be prescribed by the Secretary of the Treasury; and the penalties provided in the sixth section of this act for false statements in such declaration shall be applicable to declarations made under this section: *Provided*, That where such fees, under existing laws, constitute, in whole or in part, the compensation of any officer, such officer shall receive, from and after the passage of this act, a fixed sum for each year equal to the amount which he would have been entitled to receive as fees for such services during said year.

SEC. 43. That all fees exacted and oaths administered by officers of the customs, except as provided in this act, under or by virtue of existing laws of the United States, upon the passing of merchandise through the customs, or for the customs weighing and gauging of the same, *and upon the transportation of merchandise in bond and all fees exacted upon the filing of bonds and of special outward manifests and upon the issuance of permits for the landing or delivery of merchandise* be, and the same are hereby, abolished; and in case of entry of merchandise for exportation a declaration, in lieu of an oath, shall be filed, in such form and under such regulations as may be prescribed by the Secretary of the Treasury; and the penalties provided in the thirtieth section of this act for false statements in such declaration shall be applicable to declarations made under this section: *Provided,* That where such fees, under existing laws, constitute in whole or in part the compensation of any officer, such officer shall receive, from and after the passage of this act, a fixed sum for each year equal to the amount which he would have been entitled to receive as fees for such services during said year.

SEC. 23. That no allowance for damage to goods, wares, and merchandise imported into the United States shall hereafter be made in the estimation and liquidation of duties thereon; but the importer thereof may, within ten days after entry, abandon to the United States all or any portion of goods, wares, and merchandise included in any invoice, and be relieved from the payment of the duties on the portion so abandoned: *Provided,* That the portion so abandoned shall amount to ten per centum or over of the total value or quantity of the invoice; and the property so abandoned shall be sold by public auction or otherwise disposed of for the account and credit of the United States under such regulations as the Secretary of the Treasury may prescribe.

[SEC. 44. That no allowance for damage to goods, wares, and merchandise imported into the United States shall hereafter be made in the estimation and liquidation of duties thereon save as provided in Revised Statutes, section twenty-nine hundred and eighty-four, as amended in section eighty-seven of this act; but the importer thereof may, within ten days after the date of the appraiser's return on the invoice, abandon to the United States all or any portion of goods, wares, and merchandise included in any invoice, and be relieved from the payment of the duties on the portion so abandoned: *Provided,* That the portions so abandoned shall amount to ten per centum or over of the total value or quantity of the invoice; and the property so abandoned shall be sold by public auction or otherwise disposed of for the account and credit of the United States, under such regulations as the Secretary of the Treasury may prescribe.]

SEC. 24. That whenever it shall be shown to the satisfaction of the Secretary of the Treasury that, in any case of unascertained or estimated duties, or payments made upon appeal, more money has been paid to or deposited with a collector of customs than, as has been ascertained by final liquidation thereof, the law required to be paid or deposited, the Secretary of the Treasury shall direct the Treasurer to refund and pay the same out of any money in the Treasury not otherwise appropriated. The necessary moneys therefor are hereby appropriated, and this appropriation shall be deemed a permanent indefinite appropriation; and the Secretary of the Treasury is hereby authorized to correct manifest clerical errors in any entry or liquidation, for or against the United States, at any time within one year of the date of such entry, but not afterwards: *Provided,* That the Secretary of the Treasury shall, in his annual report to Congress, give a detailed statement of the various sums of money refunded under the provisions of this act or of any other act of Congress relating to the revenue, together with copies of the rulings under which repayments were made.

SEC. 45. That whenever it shall be shown to the satisfaction of the Secretary of the Treasury that, in any case of unascertained or estimated duties or payments made upon appeal, more money has been paid to or deposited with a collector of customs than, as has been ascertained by final liquidation thereof, the law required to be paid or deposited, the Secretary of the Treasury shall direct the Treasurer to refund and pay the same out of any money in the Treasury not otherwise appropriated. The necessary moneys therefor are hereby appropriated, and this appropriation shall be deemed a permanent indefinite appropriation; and the Secretary of the Treasury is hereby authorized to correct manifest *clerical* errors in any entry or liquidation, for or against the United States, at any time within [three years] *one year* of the date of such entry, but not afterward: *Provided*, That the Secretary of the Treasury shall, in his annual report to Congress, give a detailed statement of the various sums of money refunded under the provisions of this act or of any other act of Congress relating to the revenue, together with copies of the rulings under which repayments were made.

SEC. 25. That from and after the taking effect of this act no collector or other officer of the customs shall be in any way liable to any owner, importer, consignee, or agent of any merchandise, or any other person, for or on account of any rulings or decisions as to the classification of said merchandise or the duties charged thereon, or the collection of any dues, charges, or duties on or on account of said merchandise, or any other matter or thing as to which said owner, importer, consignee, or agent of such merchandise might, under this act, be entitled to appeal from the decision of said collector or other officer, or from any board of appraisers provided for in this act.

> SEC. 46. That from and after the taking effect of this act no collector or other officer of the customs shall be in anyway liable to any owner, importer, consignee, or agent of any merchandise, or any other person, for or on account of any rulings or decisions as to the classification of said merchandise or the duties charged thereon, or the collection of any dues, charges, or duties on or on account of said merchandise, or any other matter or thing as to which said owner, importer, consignee, or agent of such merchandise might, under this act, be entitled to appeal from the decision of said collector or other officer, or from any board of appraisers provided for in this act.

SEC. 26. That any person who shall give or offer to give or promise to give any money or thing of value, directly or indirectly, to any officer or employee of the United States in consideration of or for any act or omission contrary to law in connection with or pertaining to the importation, appraisement, entry, examination, or inspection of goods, wares, or merchandise, including herein any baggage, or of the liquidation of the entry thereof, or shall by threats or demands, or promises of any character, attempt to improperly influence or control any such officer or employee of the United States as to the performance of his official duties shall, on conviction thereof, be fined not exceeding two thousand dollars, or be imprisoned at hard labor not more than one year, or both, in the discretion of the court; and evidence of such giving or offering, or promising to give, satisfactory to the court in which such trial is had, shall be regarded as prima facie evidence that such giving or offering or promising was contrary to law, and shall put upon the accused the burden of proving that such act was innocent, and not done with an unlawful intention.

> SEC. 47. That any person who shall give, or offer to give or promise to give, any money or thing of value, directly or indirectly, to any officer or any employee of the United States, in consideration of or for any act or omission contrary to law in connection with or pertaining to the importation, appraisement, entry, examination, or inspection of goods, wares, or merchandise, including herein any baggage, or of the liquidation of the entry thereof, or shall by threats or demands, or promises of any character, attempt to improperly influence or control any such officer or employee of the United States as to the performance of his official duties, shall, on conviction thereof, be fined not exceeding two thousand dollars, or be imprisoned at hard labor not more than one year, or both, in the discretion of the court; and evidence of such giving, or offering or promising to give, satisfactory to the court in which such trial is had shall be regarded as prima facie evidence that such giving or offering or promising was contrary to law, and shall put upon the accused the burden of proving that such act was innocent and not done with an unlawful intention.

SEC. 27. That any officer or employee of the United States who shall, excepting for lawful duties or fees, solicit, demand, exact, or receive from any person, directly or indirectly, any money or thing of value, in connection with or pertaining to the importation, appraisement, entry, examination, or inspection of goods, wares, or merchandise, including herein any baggage, or liquidation of the entry thereof, on conviction thereof, shall be fined not exceeding five thousand dollars, or be imprisoned at hard labor not more than two years, or both, in the discretion of the court. And evidence of such soliciting, demanding, exacting, or receiving, satisfactory to the court in which such trial is had, shall be regarded as prima facie evidence that such soliciting, demanding, exacting, or receiving was contrary to law, and shall put upon the accused the burden of proving that such act was innocent and not with an unlawful intention.

SEC. 48. That any officer or employee of the United States who shall, excepting for lawful duties or fees, solicit, demand, exact, or receive from any person, directly or indirectly, any money or thing of value in connection with or pertaining to the importation, appraisement, entry, examination, or inspection of goods, wares, or merchandise, including herein any baggage, or liquidation of the entry thereof, on conviction thereof shall be fined not exceeding five thousand dollars, or be imprisoned at hard labor not more than two years, or both, in the discretion of the court. And evidence of such soliciting, demanding, exacting, or receiving satisfactory to the court in which such trial is had shall be regarded as prima-facie evidence that such soliciting, demanding, exacting, or receiving was contrary to law, and shall put upon the accused the burden of proving that such act was innocent and not with an unlawful intention.

SEC. 28. That any baggage or personal effects arriving in the United States in transit to any foreign country may be delivered by the parties having it in charge to the collector of the proper district, to be by him retained, without the payment or exaction of any import duty, or to be forwarded by such collector to the collector of the port of departure and to be delivered to such parties on their departure for their foreign destination, under such rules and regulations as the Secretary of the Treasury may prescribe.

SEC. 49. That any baggage or personal effects arriving in the United States in transit to any foreign country may be delivered by the parties having it in charge to the collector of the proper district, to be by him retained without the payment or exaction of any import duty, or to be forwarded by such collector to the collector of the port of departure, and to be delivered to such parties on their departure for their foreign destination, under such rules and regulations as the Secretary of the Treasury may prescribe.

SEC. 29. That sections twenty-six hundred and eight, twenty-eight hundred and thirty-eight, twenty-eight hundred and thirty-nine, twenty-eight hundred and forty-one, twenty-eight hundred and forty-three, twenty-eight hundred and forty-five, twenty-eight hundred and fifty-three, twenty-eight hundred and fifty-four, twenty-eight hundred and fifty-six, twenty-eight hundred and fifty-eight, twenty-eight hundred and sixty, twenty-nine hundred, and twenty-nine hundred and two, twenty-nine hundred and five, twenty-nine hundred and seven, twenty-nine hundred and eight, twenty-nine hundred and nine, twenty-nine hundred and twenty-two, twenty-nine hundred and twenty-three, twenty-nine hundred and twenty-four, twenty-nine hundred and twenty-seven, twenty-nine hundred and twenty-nine, twenty-nine hundred and thirty, twenty-nine hundred and thirty-one, twenty-nine hundred and thirty-two, twenty-nine hundred and forty-three, twenty-nine hundred and forty-five, twenty-nine hundred and fifty-two, three thousand and eleven, three thousand and twelve, three thousand and twelve and one-half, three thousand and thirteen of the Revised Statutes of the United States be, and the same are hereby, repealed, and sections nine, ten, eleven, twelve, fourteen, and sixteen of an act entitled "An act to amend the customs-revenue laws and to repeal moieties," approved June twenty-second, eighteen hundred and seventy-four, and sections seven, eight, and nine of the act entitled "An act to reduce internal-revenue taxation, and for other purposes," approved March third, eighteen hundred and eighty-three, and all other acts and parts of acts inconsistent with the provisions of this act, are hereby repealed, but the repeal of existing laws or modifications thereof embraced in this act shall not affect any act done, or any right accruing or accrued, or any suit or proceeding had or commenced in any civil cause before the said repeal or modifications; but all rights and liabilities under said laws shall continue and may be enforced in the same manner as if said repeal or modifications had not been made. Any offenses committed, and all penalties or forfeitures or liabilities incurred prior to the passage of this act under any statute embraced in or changed, modified, or repealed by this act may be prosecuted and punished in the same manner and with the same effect as if this act had not been passed. All acts of limitation, whether applicable to civil causes and proceedings or to the prosecution of offenses or for the recovery of penalties or forfeitures embraced in or modified, changed, or repealed by this act, shall not be affected thereby; and all suits, proceedings, or prosecutions, whether civil or criminal, for causes arising or acts done or committed prior to the passage of this act, may be commenced and prosecuted within the same time and with the same effect as if this act had not been passed. *And provided further*, That nothing in this act shall be construed to repeal the provisions of section three thousand and fifty-eight of the Revised Statutes as amended by the act approved February twenty-third, eighteen hundred and eighty-seven, in respect to the abandonment of merchandise to underwriters or the salvors of property, and the ascertainment of duties thereon.

SEC. 50. That the collector or chief officer of the customs at any port of entry or delivery may issue a license to any person desiring to transact business as a custom-house broker. Such license shall be granted for a period of one year, and may be revoked for cause at any time by the Secretary of the Treasury. From and after the first day of June, eighteen hundred and ninety-four, no person shall transact business as a custom-house broker without a license granted in accordance with this provision. But this act shall not be so construed as to prohibit any importer from transacting business at a custom-house pertaining to his own importations.

SEC. 30. That this act shall take effect on the first day of August, eighteen hundred and ninety, except so much of section twelve as provides for the appointment of nine general appraisers, which shall take effect immediately.

SEC. 51. That all goods, wares, articles, and merchandise manufactured wholly or in part in any foreign country by convict labor shall not be entitled to entry at any of the ports of the United States, and the importation thereof is hereby prohibited, and the Secretary of the Treasury is authorized to prescribe such regulations as may be necessary for the enforcement of this provision.

SEC. 52. That the value of foreign coin as expressed in the money of account of the United States shall be that of the pure metal of such coin of standard value; and the values of the standard coins in circulation of the various nations of the world shall be estimated quarterly by the Director of the Mint, and be proclaimed by the Secretary of the Treasury, immediately after the passage of this act and thereafter quarterly on the first day of January, April, July, and October in each year. *And the values so proclaimed shall be followed in estimating the value of all foreign merchandise exported to the United States during the quarter for which the value is pro-*

claimed, and the date of the consular certification of any invoice shall, for the purposes of this section, be considered the date of exportation: Provided, That the Secretary of the Treasury may order the reliquidation of any entry at a different value, whenever satisfactory evidence shall be produced to him showing that the value in United States currency of the foreign money specified in the invoice was, at the date of certification, at least ten per centum more or less than the value proclaimed during the quarter in which the consular certification occurred.

SEC. 53. That section twenty-eight hundred and four of the Revised Statutes be amended so as to read:

"SEC. 2804. No cigars shall be imported unless the same are packed in boxes of not more than five hundred cigars in each box; and no entry of any imported cigars shall be allowed of less quantity than three thousand in a single package; and all cigars on importation shall be placed in public store or bonded warehouse, and shall not be removed therefrom until the same shall have been inspected and a stamp affixed to each box indicating such inspection, and also a serial number to be recorded in the custom-house. And the Secretary of the Treasury is hereby authorized to provide the requisite stamps, and to make all necessary regulations for carrying the above provisions of law into effect." [From and after the first day of July, eighteen hundred and ninety-four, there shall be collected an internal-revenue tax on all cigarettes wrapped in paper weighing not more than three pounds a thousand, manufactured for sale or offered for sale in the United States, of one dollar per thousand.]

SEC. 54. That from and after the first day of January, eighteen hundred and ninety-five, there shall be levied, collected, and paid annually upon the gains, profits, and income [of every person residing in the United States, or any citizen of the United States residing abroad, derived in each preceding calendar year,] *received in the preceding calendar year by every citizen of the United States and every person residing therein,* whether said *gains, profits, or income be* derived from any kind of property, rents, interest, dividends, or salaries, or from any profession, trade, employment, or vocation carried on in the United States or elsewhere, *or from any other source whatever,* a tax of two per centum on the amount so derived over and above four thousand dollars, and a like tax shall be levied, collected, and paid annually upon the gains, profits, and income from all property *owned* and of every business, trade, or profession carried on in the United States by persons residing without the United States, [and not citizens thereof]. And the tax herein provided for shall be assessed, collected, and paid upon the gains, profits, and income for the year ending the thirty-first day of December next preceding the time for levying, collecting, and paying said tax.

SEC. 55. That in estimating the gains, profits, and income of any person there shall be included all income derived from interest upon notes, bonds, and other securities, except such bonds of the United States as are by the law of their issuance exempt from all Federal taxation; profits realized within the year from sales of *real estate purchased [within the year or] within two years previous to the year for which income is estimated; interest received or accrued upon all notes, bonds, mortgages, or other forms of indebtedness bearing interest, whether paid or not, if good and collectible, less the interest which has become due from said person *or which has been paid by him* during the year; the amount of all premium on bonds, notes, or coupons; the amount of sales of live stock, sugar, *cotton,* wool, butter, cheese, pork, beef, mutton, or other meats, hay, and grain, or other vegetable, or other productions, being the growth or produce of the estate of such person, less the amount expended in the purchase or production of said stock or produce, and not including any part thereof consumed directly by the family; [the amount of money, notes, bonds, choses in action] *money* and the value of [any] *all* personal property [received] *acquired* by gift, [devise,] or inheritance; all other gains, profits, and income derived from any source whatever and the share of any person [of] *in* the gains or profits of all companies, whether incorporated or partnership, who would be entitled to the same if divided, whether divided or otherwise, except the amount of income received from institutions or corporations whose officers, as required by law, withhold a per centum of the dividends, interest, gains, profits, and income made by such institutions *or corporations,* and pay the same to the officer authorized to receive the same; and except that portion of the salary, *compensation,* or pay received for services in the civil, military, naval, or other service of the United States, including Senators, Representatives, and Delegates in

Congress, from which the tax has been deducted, and except that portion of any salary upon which the employer is required by law to *withhold*, and does[,] withhold, the tax and pays the same to the officer authorized to receive it. In computing incomes the necessary expenses actually incurred in carrying on any business, occupation, or profession [may] *shall* be deducted and also all interest [actually] due [and] *or paid within* the year by such person on existing indebtedness. And [in addition to four thousand dollars exempt from income tax, as hereinbefore provided,] all national, State, county, school, and municipal taxes, not including those assessed against local benefits, paid within the year shall be deducted from the gains, profits, or income of the person who has actually paid the same, whether such person be owner, tenant, or mortgagor; *also* losses actually sustained during the year, *incurred in trade or* arising from fires, *storms*, or shipwreck, [or incurred in trade,] and not [covered] *compensated for* by insurance or otherwise, [and compensated for,] and debts ascertained to be worthless, but excluding all estimated depreciation of values and losses within the year on sales of real estate purchased *within* two years previous to the year for which income is estimated: *Provided*, That no deduction shall be made for any amount paid out for new buildings, permanent improvements, or betterments, made to increase the value of any property or estate: *Provided further*, That only one deduction of four thousand dollars shall be made from the aggregate income of all the members of any family, composed of one or both parents, and one or more minor children, or husband and wife; that guardians shall be allowed to make a deduction in favor of each and every ward, except that in case where two or more wards are comprised in one family, and have joint property [interest] *interests*, the aggregate deduction in their favor shall not exceed four thousand dollars: *And provided further*, That in cases where the salary or other compensation paid to any person in the employment or service of the United States shall not exceed the rate of four thousand dollars per annum, or shall be by fees, or uncertain or irregular in the amount or in the time during which the same shall have accrued or been earned, such salary or other compensation shall be included in estimating the annual gains, profits, or income of the person to whom the same shall have been paid, and shall include that portion of any income or salary upon which a tax has not been paid by the employer, where the employer is required by law to pay on the excess over four thousand dollars.

SEC. 56. That it shall be the duty of all persons of lawful age having an income of more than three thousand five hundred dollars for the taxable year, computed on the basis herein prescribed, to make and render a list or return, on or before the day [prescribed] *provided* by law, in such form and manner as may be [prescribed] *directed* by the Commissioner of Internal Revenue, with the approval of the Secretary of the Treasury, to the *collector or a* deputy collector of the district in which they reside, or to such officer or agent as the Commissioner of Internal Revenue may designate, of the amount of their income, gains, and profits, as aforesaid; and all guardians and trustees, executors, administrators, agents, receivers, and all persons *or corporations* acting in any [other] fiduciary capacity, shall make and render a list or return, as aforesaid, to the *collector or a* deputy collector of the district in which such person *or corporation* acting in a fiduciary capacity resides *or does business*, or to such officer or agent as the Commissioner of Internal Revenue may designate, of the amount of income, gains, and profits of any minor or person for whom they act, but persons having less than three thousand five hundred dollars income are not required to make such report; and the *collector*, deputy collector, or officer or agent designated by the Commissioner of Internal Revenue, shall require every list or return to be verified by the oath or affirmation of the party rendering it and may increase the amount of any list or return if he has reason to believe that the same is understated; and in case any such person having a taxable income shall neglect or refuse to make and render such list and return, or shall render a false or fraudulent list or return, it shall be the duty of the *collector*, deputy collector, or officer or agent designated by the Commissioner of Internal Revenue, to make such list, according to the best information he can obtain, by the examination of such person, or his books or accounts, or any other evidence, and to add fifty per centum as a penalty to the amount of the tax due on such list in all cases of willful neglect or refusal to make and render a list or return; and in all cases of a false or fraudulent list or return having been rendered to add one hundred per centum as a penalty to the amount of tax ascertained to be due, the tax and the additions thereto a a penalty to be assessed and collected in the manner provided for in other cases of willful neglect or refusal to render a list or return, or of rendering a false or fraudulent return: *Provided*, That any [party] *person, or corporation* in his, [or] her, *or its* own behalf, or as such fiduciary, shall be permitted to declare, under oath or affirmation, the form and manner of which shall be prescribed by the Commissioner of Internal Revenue, with the approval of the Secretary of the Treasury, that he, [or] she, or his or her *or its* ward or beneficiary, was not possessed of an income of four thousand dollars, liable to be assessed according to the provisions of this Act; or may declare that he, [or] she, *or it, or his, her, or its ward or beneficiary* has been assessed and *has* paid an income tax elsewhere in the same year, under authority of the United States, upon *all* his, [or] her, *or its* income, gains, or profits, *and upon all the income, gains, or profits for which he, she, or it is liable as such fiduciary*, as prescribed by law; and if the *collector*, deputy collector, or other designated officer or agent, shall be satisfied of the truth of the declaration, *such person or corporation* shall thereupon be exempt from income tax in the said district for that year; or if the list or return of any [party] *person* shall have been increased by the *collector*, deputy collector, or other designated officer or agent, such [party] *person* may [exhibit his books and accounts, and] be permitted to prove [and declare, under oath or affirmation,] the amount of income liable to be assessed; but such [oaths and evidence] *proof* shall not be considered as conclusive of the facts, and no deductions claimed in such cases shall be made or allowed until approved by the *collector*, deputy collector, or other designated officer or agent. Any person feeling aggrieved by the decision of the deputy collector, or [other designated] *any* officer or agent *other than the collector*, in such cases may appeal to the collector of the district, and his decision thereon, unless reversed by the Commissioner of Internal Revenue, shall be final. If [the person is] dissatisfied with the decision of the collector [he may] *such person may* submit [his] *the* case, with all the papers, to the Commissioner of Internal Revenue for his decision, and [if he desires to] *may* furnish the testimony of witnesses to prove any relevant facts [he will also serve] *having served* notice to that effect upon the Commissioner of Internal Revenue, as herein prescribed.

Such notice [must] *shall* state the time and place at which, and the officer before whom, the testimony will be taken; the name, age, residence, and business of the proposed witness, with the questions to be propounded to the witness, or a brief statement of the substance of the testimony he is expected to give.

The notice shall be delivered or mailed to the Commissioner *of Internal Revenue* a sufficient number of days previous to the day fixed for taking the testimony, to allow him, after its receipt, at least five days, exclusive of the period required for mail communication with the place at which the testimony is to be taken, in which to give, should he so desire, instructions as to the cross-examination of the proposed witness.

Whenever practicable, the affidavit or deposition shall be taken before a collector or deputy collector of internal revenue, in which case reasonable notice shall be given to the collector or deputy collector of the time fixed for taking the deposition or affidavit:

Provided further, That no penalty shall be assessed upon any person for such neglect or refusal or for making or rendering a false or fraudulent return, except after reasonable notice of the time and place of hearing, to be [regulated] *prescribed* by the Commissioner of Internal Revenue [, with the approval of the Secretary of the Treasury, so as to give the person charged an opportunity to be heard].

SEC. 57. The taxes on incomes herein imposed shall be due and payable on or before the first day of July in each year; and to any sum or sums annually due and unpaid after the first day of July as aforesaid, and for ten days after notice and demand thereof by the collector, there shall be levied, in addition thereto, the sum of five per centum on the amount of taxes unpaid, and interest at the rate of one per centum per month upon said tax from the time the same [became] *becomes* due, as a penalty, except from the estates of deceased, insane, or insolvent persons.

SEC. 58. [That every nonresident person owning property in the United States or receiving income from the United States shall pay a tax on the income received as if resident in the United States.] Any [such] nonresident may [also] receive the benefit of the [exemption] *exemptions hereinbefore provided for* by filing with the deputy collector of any district a true list of all his property [in the United States, or] *and* sources of income in *the United States* [, in the same manner as] *and complying with the provisions of section fifty-six of this Act as if a* resident [is required to do]. In computing income [for purpose of exemptions] he shall include all income from every source, but shall only pay on that part of the income which is derived from any source in the United States. In case such nonresident fails to file such statement, [then] the [deputy] *collector* of each district shall collect the tax on the income derived from *property situated in* his district, *subject to income tax*, making no allowance for exemptions, and all property belonging to such nonresident shall be liable to distraint for tax: *Provided*, That nonresident corporations shall be subject to *the* same laws as to tax as resident corporations, and the collection of the tax shall be made in *the* same manner as provided for collections of taxes against nonresident persons.

Sec. 59. That there shall be levied and collected a tax of two per centum on all dividends in script or money [thereafter declared due,] wherever and whenever the same be payable to stockholders, policy-holders, or depositors or [parties whatsoever,] *to any persons,* including nonresidents, whether citizens or aliens, as part of the earnings, income, or gains of any bank, *banking institutions*, trust company, saving institution, and of any fire, marine, life, [inland] *or other* insurance company, either stock or mutual, under whatever name or style known or called *and doing business* in the United States [or Territories,] whether specially incorporated or existing under general laws, and on all undistributed sums, or sums made or added during the year to their surplus or contingent funds; [on all dividends, annuities, or interest paid by corporations or associations organized for profit by virtue of the laws of the United States or of any State or Territory, by means of which the liability of the individual stockholders is in anywise limited, in cash, script, or otherwise; and the net income of all such corporations in excess of such dividends, annuities, and interest, or from any other sources whatever;] and said banks, *banking institutions*, trust companies, saving institutions, and insurance companies, [and other companies, and all other corporations,] shall pay the said tax, and are hereby authorized and required to deduct and withhold from all payments made on account of any dividends or sums of money that may be due and payable as aforesaid, the said tax of two per centum. And a list or return shall be made and rendered to the *collector*, deputy collector, or other officer or agent designated by the Commissioner of Internal Revenue, [within thirty days after any dividends or sums of money become due or payable as aforesaid] *on or before the tenth day of the month following that in which such dividends become due and payable* ; and said list or return shall contain a true and faithful account of the amount of taxes as aforesaid; and there shall be annexed thereto a declaration of the president, cashier, [or] treasurer, or the principal accounting officer of the bank, *banking institution*, trust company, savings institution, or insurance company, [or other corporation,] under oath or affirmation, in form and manner as may be prescribed by the Commissioner of Internal Revenue, with the approval of the Secretary of the Treasury, that the same contains a true and faithful account of the taxes as aforesaid. And for any default in the making or rendering of such list or return, with such declaration annexed, the bank, *banking institution*, trust company, savings institution, or insurance company [, or other corporation] making such default, shall forfeit as a penalty the sum of one thousand dollars; and in case of any default in making or rendering said list or return, or of any default in the payment of the tax as required, or any part thereof, the assessment and collection of the tax and penalty shall be in accordance with the general provisions of law in other cases of neglect and refusal: *Provided*, That the tax upon the dividends of life insurance companies shall not be deemed due until such dividends are payable; nor shall the portion of premiums returned by mutual life insurance companies to their policy-holders, nor the interest allowed or paid to the depositors in savings banks or savings institutions, be considered as dividends: *And provided further*, That this act shall not apply to the income or dividends received or paid by such building and loan associations as are organized under the laws of any State, [or] Territory *or the District of Columbia*, and which do not make loans except to shareholders *for the purpose only of enabling such shareholders to provide for themselves homes* [within the State where such associations have been organized]. For the purposes of this Act "dividend" shall include every payment in the way of division among the owners of the stock or capital of a corporation, or persons entitled to a share of its profits or income, whether such dividends are paid out of profits or not, or are paid in cash or otherwise.

SEC. 60. That any bank, [building association, or other] banking institution, *trust company, savings institution, or insurance company* which shall neglect or omit to make dividends or additions to its surplus or contingent fund as often as once in six months shall make a list or return in duplicate, under oath or affirmation of the president, or cashier, or principal accounting officer, to the *collector or* deputy collector of the district in which it is located, or to the officer or agent designated by the Commissioner of Internal Revenue, on the first day of January and July in each year, or within thirty days thereafter, of the amount of profits which have accrued or been earned or received by said bank, *banking institution, trust company, savings institution, or insurance* company during the six months next preceding said first days of January and July *respectively*; and shall present one of said lists or returns and pay to the collector of the district a [duty] *tax* of two per centum on such profits, and in case of default to make such list or return and payment within the thirty days, as aforesaid, shall be subject to the provisions of the foregoing [section] *sections* of this act: *Provided,* That when any dividend is made which includes any part of the surplus or contingent fund of any bank, *banking institution,* trust company, savings institution, *or* insurance [or railroad] company, which has been assessed and the [duty] *tax* paid thereon, the amount of [duty] *tax* so paid on that portion of the surplus or contingent fund may be deducted from the [duty] *tax* on such dividend.

SEC. 61. That any railroad, canal, turnpike, canal navigation or slackwater company, and any telephone, telegraph, electric light *company,* [and] gas company, water company, and any street railway company, or other corporation, *or association doing business in the United States and* indebted for any money for which bonds or other evidence of indebtedness have been issued, payable in one or more years after date, upon which interest is stipulated to be paid, [or coupons representing the interest,] or any such company, [or other] corporation, *or association* that may have declared any dividend in scrip or money due or payable to its stockholders, including nonresidents, whether citizens or aliens, as part of [the] *its* earnings, profits, income, or gains [of such company], and [all] *when* profits of such company, [or] corporation, *or association are* carried to the account of any fund, or used for construction, shall be subject to and pay a tax of two per centum on the amount of all such interest, [or coupons,] dividends, or profits, whenever and wherever the same shall be payable, and to whatsoever [party or] person the same may be payable, including nonresidents, whether citizens or aliens; and said companies, *corporations, or associations* are [hereby] *required to pay said tax and are* authorized to deduct and withhold from all payments on account of any interest [,or coupons,] and dividends, due and payable as aforesaid, the tax of two per centum; and the payment of the amount of said tax so deducted from the interest [or coupons] or dividends, and certified by the president or treasurer or other principal accounting officer of said company, [or] corporation, *or association* shall discharge said company, [or] corporation, *or association* from that amount of the dividend, or interest, [or coupon] on the bonds or other evidences of their indebtedness [so] held by any person or party whatever, except where said companies, [or] corporations, *or associations* may have contracted otherwise. And a list or return shall be made and rendered to the *collector,* deputy collector, or other officer or agent designated by the Commissioner of Internal Revenue, on or before the tenth day of the month following that in which said interest [,coupons,] or dividends become due and payable, and as often as every six months; and said list or return shall contain a true and faithful account of the amount of tax, and there shall be annexed thereto a declaration of the president, [or] treasurer, *cashier,* or other principal accounting officer of the company, [or] corporation, *or association,* under oath or affirmation, in form or manner as may be prescribed by the Commissioner of Internal Revenue, that the same contains a true and faithful account of [said tax] *the amount so due and payable, with the tax due thereon.* And for any default in making or rendering such list or return, with the declaration annexed, or of the payment of the tax as aforesaid, the company, [or] corporation, *or association* making such default shall forfeit as a penalty the sum of five hundred dollars and double the amount of the tax; and in case of any default in making or rendering said list or return, or of the payment of the tax or any part thereof, as aforesaid, the assessment and collection of the tax and penalty shall be made according to the provisions of law in other cases of neglect or refusal: *Provided, That whenever any* [of the companies or] *company,* [corporations] *corporation, or association* [mentioned in this section] shall be unable to pay all [of] the interest on [their] *its* indebtedness, [and shall in fact fail to pay all of such interest, that in such cases] the tax levied by this section shall be paid to the United States [only] on the amount of interest *only* which the company pays or is able to pay *: Provided further, That dividends or interest accruing to States, counties, or municipalities, and dividends, interest, or annuities accruing to corporations or associations organized and conducted solely for charitable, religious, or educational purposes, or to any trustee or other fiduciary, on stocks, shares, funds, or securities held solely for charitable, religious, or educational purposes, or salaries due to State, county, or municipal officers, shall not be subject to such tax or deduction.*

SEC. 62. That there shall be levied, collected, and paid on all salaries of officers, or payments for services to persons in the civil, military, naval, or other employment or service of the United States, including Senators and Representatives and Delegates in Congress, when exceeding the rate of four thousand dollars per annum, a tax of two per centum on the excess above the said four thousand dollars; and it shall be the duty of all paymasters and all disbursing officers under the Government of the United States, or persons in the employ thereof, when making any payment to any officers or persons as aforesaid, whose compensation is determined by a fixed salary, or upon settling or adjusting the accounts of such officers or persons, to deduct and withhold the aforesaid tax of two per centum; and the pay roll, receipts, or account of officers or persons paying such tax as aforesaid shall be made to exhibit the fact of such payment. And it shall be the duty of the accounting officers of the Treasury Department, when auditing the accounts of any paymaster or disbursing officer, or any officer withholding his salary from moneys received by him, or when settling or adjusting the accounts of any such officer, to require evidence that the taxes mentioned in this section have been deducted and paid over to the Treasurer of the United States, or other officer authorized to receive the same. Every corporation which pays to any employee a salary or compensation exceeding four thousand dollars per annum shall report the same to the *collector or* deputy collector of his district and [pay the tax hereinbefore provided to the deputy collector of his district, and such payment shall be charged against the amount due such employee. And the same rules and penalties prescribed for the individual making his own return shall apply to such corporation employee: *Provided,* That payments of prize money shall be regarded as income from salaries, and the tax thereon shall be adjusted and collected in like manner: *And provided further,* That in case it should become necessary for showing the true receipts of the Government under the operations of this section upon the books of the Treasury Department, the requisite amount may be carried from unappropriated moneys in the Treasury to the credit of said account] *said employee shall pay thereon, subject to the exemptions herein provided for, the tax of two per centum on the excess of his salary over four thousand dollars.*

SEC. 63. That sections thirty-one hundred and sixty-seven, thirty-one hundred and seventy-two, thirty-one hundred and seventy-three, and thirty-one hundred and seventy-six of the Revised Statutes of the United States as amended are hereby amended so as to read as follows:

"SEC. 3167. That if any collector or deputy collector, or other officer or internal-revenue agent acting under the authority of any revenue law of the United States, divulges to any party, or makes known in any other manner than may be provided by law, the operations, style of work, or apparatus of any manufacturer or producer visited by him in the discharge of his official duties, or the amount or source of income, profits, losses, expenditures, or any information obtained by him in the discharge of such duties, he shall be subject to a fine of not exceeding one thousand dollars, or to be imprisoned for not exceeding one year, or both, at the discretion of the court, and shall be dismissed from office and be forever thereafter incapable of holding any office under the Government."

"SEC. 3172. That every collector shall, from time to time, cause his deputies to proceed through every part of his district and inquire after and concerning all persons therein who are liable to pay any internal revenue tax, and all persons owning or having the care and management of any objects liable to pay any tax, and to make a list of such persons and enumerate said objects.

"SEC. 3173. That it shall be the duty of any person, partnership, firm, association, or corporation, made liable to any duty, special tax, or other tax imposed by law, when not otherwise provided for, in case of a special tax, on or before the thirty-first day of July in each year, in case of income tax on or before the first [day] *Monday* of March in each year, and in other cases before the day on which the taxes accrue, to make a list or return, verified by oath or affirmation, to the *collector or a* deputy collector of the district where located, of the articles or objects, including the amount of annual income, charged with a duty or tax, the quantity of goods, wares, and merchandise made or sold, and charged with a tax, the several rates and aggregate amount, according to the forms and regulations to be prescribed by the Commissioner of Internal Revenue, with the approval of the Secretary of the Treasury, for which such person, partnership, firm, association, or corporation is liable: *Provided*, That if any person liable to pay any duty or tax, or owning, possessing, or having the care or management of property, goods, wares, and merchandise, articles or objects liable to pay any duty, tax, or license, shall fail to make and exhibit a list or return required by law, but shall consent to disclose the particulars of any and all the property, goods, wares, and merchandise, articles and objects liable to pay any duty or tax, or any business or occupation liable to pay any tax as aforesaid, then, and in that case, it shall be the duty of the *collector or* deputy collector to make such list or return, which, being distinctly read, consented to, and signed and verified by oath or affirmation by the person so owning, possessing, or having the care and management as aforesaid, may be received as the list of such person: *Provided further*, That in case no annual list or return has been rendered by such person to the *collector or* deputy collector as required by law, and the person shall be absent from his or her residence or place of business at the time *the collector or a* deputy collector shall call for the annual list or return, it shall be the duty of such *collector or* deputy collector to leave at such place of residence or business, with some one of suitable age and discretion, if such be present, otherwise to deposit in the nearest post-office a note or memorandum addressed to such person, requiring him or her to render to such *collector or* deputy collector the list or return required by law, within ten days from the date of such note or memorandum, verified by oath or affirmation. And if any person on being notified or required as aforesaid shall refuse or neglect to render such list or return within the time required as aforesaid or whenever any person who is required to deliver a monthly or other return of objects subject to tax fails to do so at the time required, or delivers any return which, in the opinion of the collector, is false or fraudulent, or contains any undervaluation or understatement, it shall be lawful for the collector to summon such person, or any other person having possession, custody, or care of books of account containing entries relating to the business of such person, or any other person he may deem proper, to appear before him and produce such books, at a time and place named in the summons, and to give testimony or answer interrogatories, under oath, respecting any objects liable to tax or the returns thereof. The collector may summon any person residing or found within the State in which his district lies; and when the person intended to be summoned does not reside and can not be found within such State, he may enter any collection district where such person may be found, and there make the examination herein authorized. And to this end he may there exercise all the authority which he might lawfully exercise in the district for which he was commissioned.

"SEC. 3176. That the collector or any deputy collector in every district shall enter into and upon the premises, if it be necessary, of every person therein who has taxable property and who refuses or neglects to render any return or list required by law, or who renders a false or fraudulent return or list, and make, according to the best information which he can obtain, including that derived from the evidence elicited by the examination of the collector, and on his own view and information, such list or return, according to the form prescribed, of the income, property, and objects liable to tax owned or possessed or under the care or management of such person, and the Commissioner of Internal Revenue shall assess the tax thereon, including the amount, if any, due for special *tax*, income or other tax, and in case of any return of a false or fraudulent list or valuation intentionally he shall add one hundred per centum to such tax; and in case of a refusal or neglect, except in cases of sickness or absence, to make a list or return, or to verify the same as aforesaid, he shall add fifty per centum to such tax. In case of neglect occasioned by sickness or absence as aforesaid the collector may allow such further time for making and delivering such list or return as he may deem necessary, not exceeding thirty days. The amount so added to the tax shall be collected at the same time and in the same manner as the tax unless the neglect or falsity is discovered after the tax has been paid, in which case the amount so added shall be collected in the same manner as the tax; and the list or return so made and subscribed by such collector or deputy collector shall be held *prima facie* good and sufficient for all legal purposes."

SEC. 64. [That every corporation doing business for profit shall make and render to the collector of its collection district, on or before the tenth day of the month after that in which any dividends or shares of profits, annuities, interest, or coupons become due and payable, a full return thereof, containing a true and faithful account of the amount so due or payable and of the amount of the tax thereon; and to such return there shall be annexed a declaration of the president, treasurer, cashier, or other principal officer of such corporation, under oath or affirmation, to the effect that the same contains a true and faithful account of all the amounts so due or payable and of the tax thereon, as aforesaid, such return and declaration thereto annexed to be made in such form and manner as may be prescribed by the Commissioner of Internal Revenue.]

SEC. 65. That ever corporation doing business for profit shall make and render to the collector of its collection district, *in its return as to income tax required by section thirty-one hundred and seventy-three of the Revised Statutes of the United States as amended by this Act,* on or before the first Monday of [February] *March* in every year, beginning with the year eighteen hundred and ninety-five, a full return, verified by oath or affirmation, [as provided in the last section,] in such form as the Commissioner of Internal Revenue may prescribe, of all the following matters for the whole calendar year last preceding the date of such return:

First. The gross profits of such corporation, from all kinds of business of every name and nature.

Second. The expenses of such corporation, exclusive of interest, annuities, and dividends.

Third. The net profits of such corporation, without allowance for interest, annuities, or dividends.

Fourth. The amount paid on account of interest, annuities and dividends stated separately.

Fifth. The amount paid in salaries of four thousand dollars or less to each person employed.

Sixth. The amount paid in salaries of more than four thousand dollars to each person employed.

SEC. 66. That it shall be the duty of every corporation doing business for profit to keep full, regular, and accurate books of account, upon which all its transactions shall be entered from day to day, in regular order, which books shall, at all reasonable times, be open to the inspection of [the assessors and inspectors appointed in pursuance to this Act; but such inspection shall only be had for the purpose of verifying the returns made by such corporations, as in this Act provided for] *any internal-revenue officer or agent.*

SEC. 67. [That the taxes imposed by this Act upon dividends, interest, coupons and annuities shall be levied upon and collected from all such dividends, coupons, interest and annuities whenever and wherever the same may be payable to all parties whatsoever, including nonresidents, whether citizens or aliens, except as hereinafter provided; and every corporation paying any tax on such dividends, coupons, interest or annuities may deduct and retain from all payments made on account thereof a proportionate amount of the tax so paid: *Provided,* That dividends, interest or annuities accruing to corporations not doing business for profit or to States, counties and municipalities, or to individuals on funds or securities held for charitable or educational purposes shall not be subject to such deduction.]

SEC. 68. That it shall be the duty of every collector of internal revenue, to whom any payment is made under the provisions of this Act, to give to the person making such payment a full written or printed receipt, expressing the amount paid and the particular account for which such payment was made; and whenever such payment is made [otherwise than by a corporation,] such collector shall, if required, give a separate receipt for each tax paid by any debtor, on account of payments made to or to be made by him to separate creditors in such form that such debtor can conviently produce the same separately to his several creditors in satisfaction of their respective demands to the amounts specified in such receipts; and such receipts shall be sufficient evidence in favor of such debtor, to justify him in withholding the amount therein expressed from his next payment to his creditor; but such creditor may, upon giving to his debtor a full written receipt, acknowledging the payment to him of whatever sum may be actually paid, and accepting the amount of tax paid as aforesaid (specifying the same) as a further satisfaction of the debt to that amount, require the surrender to him of such collector's receipt.

SEC. 69. [That no rule or regulation established by the Commissioner of Internal Revenue under this Act shall be valid without the approval of the Secretary of the Treasury in writing; nor shall the same be binding upon any corporation, or upon any person not an internal-revenue officer, until it has been printed and conspicuously posted in the offices of the commissioner and the collector of the collection district in which such person or corporation has an office or residence.]

SEC. 70. [That if any person, in any case, matter, hearing, or other proceeding in which an oath or affirmation shall be required to be taken or administered, under or by virtue of this Act, shall, upon the taking of such oath or affirmation, knowingly and willfully swear or affirm falsely, every person so offending shall be deemed guilty of perjury, and shall, on conviction thereof, be subject to the like punishment and penalties now provided by the laws of the United States for the crime of perjury.]

SEC. 71. That the Secretary of the Treasury shall have power to relieve and release from all forfeitures and penalties imposed by this Act, in such cases as he may deem proper; but this shall not apply to any penalties imposed by law as the punishment of a misdemeanor or other crime.

SEC. 72. That on and after the first day of July, eighteen hundred and ninety-four, there shall be levied, collected, and paid, by adhesive stamps, a tax of two cents for and upon every pack of playing cards *containing not more than fifty-four cards,* manufactured and sold or removed, and also upon every pack in the stock of any dealer on and after that date; and the Commissioner of Internal Revenue, with the approval of the Secretary of the Treasury, shall make regulations as to dies and adhesive stamps.

SEC. 73. That in all cases where an adhesive stamp is used for denoting the tax imposed by this Act upon playing cards, except as hereinafter provided, the person using or affixing the same shall write thereon the initials of his name and the date on which such stamp is attached or used, so that it may not again be used. And every person who fraudulently makes use of an adhesive stamp to denote any tax imposed by this Act without so effectually canceling and obliterating such stamp shall forfeit the sum of fifty dollars. The Commissioner of Internal Revenue is authorized to prescribe such method for the cancellation of stamps as substitute for, or in addition to the method prescribed in this section as he may deem expedient and effectual. And he is authorized, in his discretion, to make the application of such method imperative upon the manufacturers of playing cards.

SEC. 74. That every manufacturer of playing cards shall register with the collector of the district his name or style, place of residence, trade, or business, and the place where such business is to be carried on, and a failure to register as herein provided and required shall subject such person to a penalty of fifty dollars.

SEC. 75. That the Commissioner of Internal Revenue shall cause to be prepared, for payment of the tax upon playing cards, suitable stamps denoting the tax thereon. Such stamps shall be furnished to collectors requiring them, and collectors shall, if there be any manufacturers of playing cards within their respective districts, keep on hand at all times a supply equal in amount to two months' sales thereof, and shall sell the same only to such manufacturers as have registered as required by law and to importers of playing cards, who are required to affix the same to imported playing cards, and to persons who are required by law to affix the same to stocks of playing cards on hand when the tax thereon imposed first takes effect. Every collector shall keep an account of the number and denominate values of the stamps sold by him to each manufacturer and to other persons above described.

SEC. 76. That if any person shall forge or counterfeit, or cause or procure to be forged or counterfeited, any stamp, die, plate, or other instrument, or any part of any stamp, die, plate, or other instrument which shall have been provided or may hereafter be provided, made, or used in pursuance of the provisions of this Act or of any previous provisions of law on the same subjects, or shall forge, counterfeit, or resemble, or cause or procure to be forged, counterfeited, or resembled the impression or any part of the impression of any such stamp, die, plate, or other instrument, as aforesaid, upon any paper, or shall stamp or mark or cause or procure to be stamped or marked any paper with any such forged or counterfeited stamp, die, plate, or other instrument or part of any stamp, die, plate, or other instrument, as aforesaid, with intent to defraud the United States of any of the taxes hereby imposed or any part thereof; or if any person shall utter, or sell, or expose to sale any paper, article, or thing having thereupon the impression of any such counterfeited stamp, die, plate, or other instrument, or any part of any stamp, die, plate, or other instrument, or any such forged, counterfeited, or resembled impression, or part of impression, as aforesaid, knowing the same to be forged, counterfeited, or resembled; or if any person shall knowingly use or permit the use of any stamp, die, plate, or other instrument which shall have been so provided, made, or used, as aforesaid, with intent to defraud the United States; or if any person shall fraudulently cut, tear, or remove, or cause or procure to be cut, torn, or removed, the impression of any stamp, die, plate, or other instrument, which shall have been provided, made, or used in pursuance of this act, or of any previous provisions of law on the same subjects, from any paper, or any instrument or writing charged or chargeable with any of the taxes imposed by law; or if any person shall fraudulently use, join, fix, or place, or cause to be used, joined, fixed, or placed, to, with, or upon any paper, or any instrument or writing charged or chargeable with any of the taxes hereby imposed, any adhesive stamp, or the impression of any stamp, die, plate, or other instrument, which shall have been provided, made, or used in pursuance of law, and which shall have been cut, torn, or removed from any other paper or any instrument or writing charged or chargeable with any of the taxes imposed by law; or if any person shall willfully remove or cause to be removed, alter or cause to be altered, the canceling or defacing marks on any adhesive stamp, with intent to use the same, or to cause the use of the same, after it shall have been once used, or shall knowingly or willfully sell or buy such washed or restored stamps or offer the same for sale, or give or expose the same to any person for use, or knowingly use the same, or prepare the same with intent for the further use thereof; or if any person shall knowingly and without lawful excuse (the proof whereof shall lie on the person accused) have in his possession any washed, restored, or altered stamps, which have been removed from any article, paper, instrument, or writing, then, and in every such case, every person so offending, and every person knowingly and willfully aiding, abetting, or assisting in committing any such offense as aforesaid, shall, on conviction thereof, forfeit the said counterfeit, washed, restored, or altered stamps and the articles upon which they are placed and be punished by fine not exceeding one thousand dollars, or by imprisonment and confinement to hard labor not exceeding five years, or both, at the discretion of the court. And the fact that any adhesive stamp so bought, sold, offered for sale, used, or had in possession as aforesaid, has been washed or restored by removing or altering the canceling or defacing marks thereon, shall be prima-facie proof that such stamp has been once used and removed by the possessor thereof from some paper, instrument, or writing charged with taxes imposed by law, in violation of the provisions of this section.

Sec. 77. That whenever any person makes, prepares, and sells or removes for consumption or sale, playing cards, whether of domestic manufacture or imported, upon which a tax is imposed by law, without affixing thereto an adhesive stamp denoting the tax before mentioned, he shall incur a penalty of fifty dollars for every omission to affix such stamp: *Provided*, That playing cards may be removed from the place of manufacture for export to a foreign country, without payment of tax, or affixing stamps thereto, under such regulations and the filing of such bonds as the Commissioner of Internal Revenue, with the approval of the Secretary of the Treasury, may prescribe.

Sec. 78. That every manufacturer or maker of playing cards who, after the same are so made, and the particulars hereinbefore required as to stamps have been complied with, takes off, removes, or detaches, or causes, or permits, or suffers to be taken off, or removed, or detached, any stamp, or who uses any stamp, or any wrapper or cover to which any stamp is affixed, to cover any other article or commodity than that originally contained in such wrapper or cover, with such stamp when first used, with the intent to evade the stamp duties, shall, for every such article, respectively, in respect of which any such offense is committed, be subject to a penalty of fifty dollars, to be recovered together with the costs thereupon accruing; and every such article or commodity as aforesaid shall also be forfeited.

SEC. 79. That every maker or manufacturer of playing cards who, to evade the tax or duty chargeable thereon, or any part thereof, sells, exposes for sale, sends out, removes, or delivers any playing cards before the duty thereon has been fully paid, by affixing thereon the proper stamp, as provided by law, or who, to evade as aforesaid, hides or conceals, or causes to be hidden or concealed, or removes or conveys away, or deposits, or causes to be removed or conveyed away from or deposited in any place, any such article or commodity, shall be subject to a penalty of fifty dollars, together with the forfeiture of any such article or commodity.

SEC. 80. That the tax on playing cards shall be paid by the manufacturer thereof. Every person who offers or exposes for sale playing cards, whether the articles so offered or exposed are of foreign manufacture and imported or are of domestic manufacture, shall be deemed the manufacturer thereof, and subject to all the duties, liabilities, and penalties imposed by law in regard to the sale of domestic articles without the use of the proper stamps denoting the tax paid thereon, and all such articles of foreign manufacture shall, in addition to the import duties imposed on the same, be subject to the stamp tax prescribed in this Act.

SEC. 81. That whenever any article upon which a tax is required to be paid by means of a stamp is sold or removed for sale by the manufacturer thereof, without the use of the proper stamp, in addition to the penalties imposed by law for such sale or removal, it shall be the duty of the Commissioner of Internal Revenue, within a period of not more than two years after such removal or sale, upon such information as he can obtain, to estimate the amount of the tax which has been omitted to be paid, and to make an assessment therefor upon the manufacturer or producer of such article. He shall certify such assessment to the collector, who shall immediately demand payment of such tax, and upon the neglect or refusal of payment by such manufacturer or producer, shall proceed to collect the same in the manner provided for the collection of other assessed taxes.

[SEC. 82. That on and after the first day of the second calendar month after the passage of this Act there shall be levied and collected on all distilled spirits in bond at that time, or that may be produced in the United States, on which the tax is not paid before that day, a tax of one dollar on each proof gallon, or wine gallon when below proof, to be paid by the distiller, owner, or person having possession thereof, on or before removal from the warehouse, and within three years from the date of the original entry for deposit in any distillery or special bonded warehouse, except in cases of withdrawals therefrom without payment of tax as now authorized by law; warehousing bonds, covering the taxes on all distilled spirits entered for deposit into distillery or special bonded warehouse on and after the date named in this section and remaining therein on the fifth day of the following month, shall be given by the distiller or owner of said spirits as required by existing laws, conditioned, however, for payment of taxes at the rate imposed by this Act and before removal from warehouse and within three years, as to fruit brandy, from the date of the original gauge, and as to all other spirits from the date of the original entry for deposit.]

[SEC. 83. That warehousing bonds or transportation and warehousing bonds covering the taxes on distilled spirits entered for deposit into distillery or special bonded warehouses prior to the date named in the eighty-second section of this Act, and on which taxes have not been paid prior to that date, shall continue in full force and effect for the time named in said bonds. Whenever the tax is paid on or after the aforesaid date, pursuant to the provisions of the warehousing, or transportation and warehousing bonds aforesaid, there shall be added to the ninety cents per taxable gallon an additional tax sufficient to make the tax paid equal to that imposed by section eighty-two of this Act. The Commissioner of Internal Revenue may require the distillers or owners of the spirits to give bonds for the additional tax, and before the expiration of the original bonds shall prescribe rules and regulations for reentry for deposit and for new bonds as provided in the eighty-second section of this Act and conditioned for payment of tax at the rate imposed by this Act and before removal of spirits from warehouse, and within three years, as to fruit brandy, from the date of the original gauge, and as to all other spirits from the date of the original entry for deposit. The distiller or owner of the spirits may request regauge of same prior to the expiration of three years from the date of the original entry or original gauge. If the distiller or owner of the spirits fails or refuses to give the bonds for the additional tax or to reenter and rebond the same the Commissioner of Internal Revenue may proceed as now provided by law for failure or refusal to give warehousing bonds or original entry into distillery or special bonded warehouse.]

[SEC. 81. That whenever the owner of any distilled spirits shall desire to withdraw the same from the distillery warehouse, or from a special bonded warehouse, he may file with the collector a notice giving a description of the packages to be withdrawn and request that the distilled spirits be regauged; and thereupon the collector shall direct the gauger to regauge the same, and mark upon the package so regauged the number of gauge or wine gallons and proof gallons therein contained. If upon such regauging it shall appear that there has been a loss of distilled spirits from any cask or package, without the fault or negligence of the distiller or owner thereof, taxes shall be collected only on the quantity of distilled spirits contained in such cask or package at the time of the withdrawal thereof from the distillery warehouse or special bonded warehouse: *Provided, however,* That the allowance which shall be made for such loss of spirits as aforesaid shall not exceed one proof gallon for two months, or part thereof; one and one-half gallons for three and four months; two gallons for five and six months; two and one-half gallons for seven and eight months; three gallons for nine and ten months; three and one-half gallons for eleven and twelve months; four gallons for thirteen, fourteen, and fifteen months; four and one-half gallons for sixteen, seventeen, and eighteen months; five gallons for nineteen, twenty, and twenty-one months; five and one-half gallons for twenty-two, twenty-three, and twenty-four months; six gallons for twenty-five, twenty-six, and twenty-seven months; six and one-half gallons for twenty-eight, twenty-nine, and thirty months; seven gallons for thirty-one, thirty-two, and thirty-three months; seven and one-half gallons for thirty-four, thirty-five, and thirty six months; and no further allowance shall be made: *And provided further,* That taxes may be collected on the quantity contained in each cask or package as shown by the original entry for deposit into the warehouse, or, as to fruit brandy, by the original gauge for which the owner or distiller does not request a regauge before the expiration of three years from the date of original entry or gauge: *Provided, also,* That the foregoing allowance of loss shall apply only to casks or packages of a capacity of forty or more wine gallons, and that the allowance for loss on casks or packages of less capacity than forty gallons shall not exceed one-half the amount allowed on said forty-gallon cask or package; but no allowance shall be made on casks or packages of less capacity than twenty gallons: *And provided further,* That the proof of such distilled spirits shall not in any case be computed at the time of withdrawal at less than one hundred per centum.]

SEC. 82. *That on and after the first day of the second calendar month after the passage of this Act there shall be levied and collected on all distilled spirits in bond at that time, or that have been or that may be then or thereafter produced in the United States, on which the tax is not paid before that day, a tax of one dollar and ten cents on each proof gallon, or wine gallon when below proof, and a proportionate tax at a like rate on all fractional parts of such proof or wine gallon: Provided, That in computing the tax on any package of spirits all fractional parts of a gallon, less than one-tenth, shall be excluded.*

The Commissioner of Internal Rerenue, with the approval of the Secretary of the Treasury, shall prescribe and furnish suitable stamps denoting the payment of the internal-revenue tax imposed by this section; and until such stamps are prepared and furnished, the stamps now used to denote the payment of the internal-revenue tax on distilled spirits shall be affixed to all packages containing distilled spirits on which the tax imposed by this section is paid; and the Commissioner of Internal Rerenue shall, by assessment or otherwise, cause to be collected the tax on any fractional gallon contained in each of such packages as ascertained by the original gauge, or regauge when made, before or at the time of removal of such packages from warehouse or other place of storage; and all provisions of existing laws relating to stamps denoting the payment of internal-revenue tax on distilled spirits, so far as applicable, are hereby extended to the stamps provided for in this section.

That the tax herein imposed shall be paid by the distiller of the spirits, on or before their removal from the distillery or place of storage, except in case the removal therefrom without payment of tax is authorized by law; and (upon spirits lawfully deposited in any distillery warehouse, or other bonded warehouse, established under internal-revenue laws) within eight years from the date o° the original entry for deposit in any distillery warehouse, or from the date of original gauge of fruit brandy deposited in special-bonded warehouse, except in case of withdrawal therefrom without payment of tax as authorized by law.

SEC. 83. That warehousing bonds and transportation and warehousing bonds, conditioned for the payment of the taxes on all distilled spirits entered for deposit into distillery or special bonded warehouses on and after the date named in the last preceding section, shall be given by the distiller of said spirits as required by existing laws, conditioned, however, for payment of taxes at the rate imposed by this Act and before removal from warehouse and within eight years; as to fruit brandy, from the date of the original gauge, and as to all other spirits from the date of the original entry for deposit, and all warehousing bonds or transportation and warehousing bonds conditioned for the payment of the taxes on distilled spirits entered for deposit into distillery or special bonded warehouses prior to that date shall continue in full force and effect for the time named in said bonds, except where new or additional bonds are required under existing law. Whenever the tax is paid on or after the aforesaid date, pursuant to the provisions of the warehousing or transportation and warehousing bonds aforesaid, there shall be added to the ninety cents per taxable gallon an additional tax sufficient to make the tax paid on said spirits equal to that imposed by this Act. The Commissioner of Internal Revenue may require the distillers of the spirits to give bonds for the additional tax, and before the expiration of the original bonds shall prescribe rules and regulations for re-entry for deposit and for new bonds as provided for spirits originally entered for deposit under this Act, and conditioned for payment of tax at the rate imposed by this Act and before removal of the spirits from warehouse, and within eight years; as to fruit brandy, from the date of the original gauge, and as to all other spirits from the date of original entry for deposit. If the distiller of the spirits fails or refuses to give the bond for the additional tax, or to re-enter and rebond the spirits, the Commissioner of Internal Revenue may proceed to collect the tax as now provided by law for failure or refusal to give warehousing bonds on original entry into distillery warehouse or special-bonded warehouse, and the provisions of section four of the Act of May twenty-eighth, eighteen hundred and eighty (twenty-first Statutes, one hundred and forty-five), so far as applicable, are hereby extended to bonds given under the provisions of this section: Provided, That the distiller may, at his option and under such regulations as the Commissioner of Internal Revenue, with the approval of the Secretary of the Treasury, shall prescribe, execute an annual bond for the spirits so deposited in lieu of the bonds herein provided.

SEC. 84. That the distiller of any distilled spirits deposited in any distillery warehouse, or special-bonded warehouse, or in any general-bonded warehouse established under the provisions of this Act may, prior to the expiration of four years from the date of original gauge as to fruit brandy, or original entry as to all other spirits, file with the collector a notice giving a description of the packages containing the spirits, and request a regauge of the same, and thereupon the collector shall direct a gauger to regauge the spirits, and to mark upon each such package the number of gauge or wine gallons and proof gallons therein contained. If upon such regauging it shall appear that there has been a loss of distilled spirits from any cask or package, without the fault or negligence of the distiller thereof, taxes shall be collected only on the quantity of distilled spirits contained in such cask or package at the time of the withdrawal thereof from the distillery warehouse or other bonded warehouse: Provided, however, That the allowance which shall be made for such loss of spirits as aforesaid shall not exceed one proof gallon for two months or part thereof; one and one-half gallons for three and four months; two gallons for five and six months; two and one-half gallons for seven and eight months; three gallons for nine and ten months; three and one-half gallons for eleven and twelve months; four gallons for thirteen, fourteen, and fifteen months; four and one-half gallons for sixteen, seventeen, and eighteen months; five gallons for nineteen, twenty, and twenty-one months; five and one-half gallons for twenty-two, twenty-three, and twenty-four months; six gallons for twenty-five, twenty-six, and twenty-seven months; six and one-half gallons for twenty-eight, twenty-nine, and thirty months; seven gallons for thirty-one, thirty-two, and thirty-three months; seven and one-half gallons for thirty-four, thirty-five, and thirty-six months; eight gallons for thirty-seven, thirty-eight, thirty-nine, and forty months; eight and one-half gallons for forty-one, forty-two, forty-three, and forty-four mouths; nine gallons for forty-five, forty-six, forty-seven, and forty-eight months; and no further allowance shall be made: And provided further, That in case such spirits shall remain in warehouse after the same have been regauged, the packages containing the spirits shall, at the time of withdrawal from warehouse and at such other times as the Commissioner of Internal Revenue may direct, be again regauged or inspected; and if found to contain a larger quantity than shown by the first regauge, the tax shall be collected and paid on the quantity contained in each such package as shown by the original gauge: And provided further, That taxes shall be collected on the quantity contained in each cask or package as shown by the original gauge, where the distiller does not request a regauge before the expiration of four years from the date of original entry or gauge: Provided also, That the foregoing allowance of loss shall apply only to casks or packages of a capacity of forty or more wine gallons, and that the allowance for loss on casks or packages of less capacity than forty gallons shall not exceed one-half the amount allowed on said forty-gallon cask or package; but no allowance shall be made on casks or packages of less capacity than twenty gallons: And provided further, That the proof of such distilled spirits shall not in any case be computed at the time of withdrawal at less than one hundred per centum.

SEC. 85. That the Commissioner of Internal Revenue shall be, and is hereby, authorized, in his discretion and upon the execution of such bond as he may prescribe, to establish one or more warehouses, not exceeding ten in number in any one collection district, to be known and designated as general bonded warehouses, and to be used exclusively for the storage of spirits distilled from materials other than fruit, each of which warehouses shall be in the charge of a storekeeper or storekeeper and gauger to be appointed, assigned, transferred, and paid in the same manner as such officers for distillery warehouses are now appointed, assigned, transferred, and paid. Every such warehouse shall be under the control of the collector of internal revenue of the district in which such warehouse is located, and shall be in the joint custody of the storekeeper and proprietor thereof, and kept securely locked, and shall at no time be unlocked or opened or remain open except in the presence of such storekeeper or other person who may be designated to act for him, as provided in the case of distillery warehouses; and such warehouses shall be under such further regulations as the Commissioner of Internal Revenue, with the approval of the Secretary of the Treasury, may prescribe.

SEC. 86. That any distilled spirits made from materials other than fruit, and lawfully deposited in a distillery warehouse, may, upon application of the distiller thereof, be removed from such distillery warehouse to any general bonded warehouse established under the provisions of the preceding section; and the removal of said spirits to said general bonded warehouse shall be under such regulations, and after making such entries and executing and filing with the collector of the district in which the spirits were manufactured, such bonds and bills of lading, and the giving of such other additional security, as may be prescribed by the Commissioner of Internal Revenue and approved by the Secretary of the Treasury.

SEC. 87. That all spirits intended for deposit in a general bonded warehouse, before being removed from the distillery warehouse, shall have affixed to each package an engraved stamp indicative of such intention, to be provided and furnished to the several collectors as in the case of other stamps, and to be charged to them and accounted for in the same manner.

SEC. 88. That any spirits removed in bond as aforesaid may, upon its arrival at a general bonded warehouse, be deposited therein upon making such entries, filing such bonds and other securities, and under such regulations as shall be prescribed by the Commissioner of Internal Revenue, with the approval of the Secretary of the Treasury. It shall be one of the conditions of the warehousing bond covering such spirits that the principal named in said bond shall pay the tax on the spirits as specified in the entry or cause the same to be paid within eight years from the date of the original entry of the same into the distillery warehouse, and before withdrawal, except as hereinafter provided.

SEC. 89. That any spirits may be withdrawn once and no more from one general bonded warehouse for transportation to another general bonded warehouse, and when intended to be so withdrawn, shall have affixed thereto another general bonded warehouse stamp indicative of such intention; and the withdrawal of such spirits, and their transfer to and entry into such general bonded warehouse shall be under such regulations and upon the filing of such notices, entries, bonds, and bills of lading as the Commissioner of Internal Revenue, with the approval of the Secretary of the Treasury, may, from time to time, prescribe; and the bonds covering spirits in general bonded warehouses shall be given by distillers of the spirits, and shall be renewed at such times as the Commissioner of Internal Revenue may, by regulations, require.

SEC. 90. That the provisions of existing law in regard to the withdrawal of distilled spirits from warehouses upon payment of tax, or for exportation, or for transfer to a manufacturing warehouse, and as to the gauging, marking, branding, and stamping of the spirits upon such withdrawals, and in regard to withdrawals for the use of the United States or scientific institutions or colleges of learning, including the provisions for allowance for loss by accidental fire or other unavoidable accident, are hereby extended and made applicable to spirits deposited in general bonded warehouses under this act.

SEC. 91. *Whenever distilling shall have been suspended at any distillery for a period or periods aggregating six months during any calendar year, and the quantity of spirits remaining in the distillery warehouse does not exceed five thousand proof gallons, or whenever, in the opinion of the Commissioner of Internal Revenue, any distillery warehouse or general bonded warehouse is unsafe or unfit for use, or the merchandise therein is liable to loss or great wastage, he may in either such case discontinue such warehouse and require the merchandise therein to be transferred to such other warehouse as he may designate, and within such time as he may prescribe; and all the provisions of section thirty-two hundred and seventy-two of the Revised Statutes of the United States relating to transfers of spirits from warehouses, including those imposing penalties, are hereby made applicable to transfers to or from general bonded warehouses established under this act.*

SEC. 92. *The tax upon any distilled spirits removed from a distillery warehouse for deposit in a general bonded warehouse, and in respect of which any requirement of this act is not complied with, shall, at any time when knowledge of such fact is obtained by the Commissioner of Internal Revenue, be assessed by him upon the distiller of the same, and returned to the collector, who shall immediately demand payment of such tax, and upon the neglect of payment by the distiller shall proceed to collect the same by distraint. But this provision shall not exclude any other remedy or proceeding provided by law to enforce the payment of the tax. If it shall appear at any time that there has been a loss of distilled spirits from any cask or package deposited in a general bonded warehouse or special bonded warehouse, other than the loss provided for in section thirty-two hundred and twenty-one of the Revised Statutes of the United States, which, in the opinion of the Commissioner of Internal Revenue, is excessive, he may instruct the collector of the district in which the loss has occurred to require the withdrawal from warehouse of such cask or package of distilled spirits and to collect the tax accrued upon the original quantity of distilled spirits entered into the warehouse in such cask or package, less only the allowance for loss provided by law. If the said tax is not paid on demand the collector shall report the amount due, as shown by the original gauge, upon his next monthly list, and it shall be assessed and collected as other taxes are assessed and collected.*

SEC. 93. *That in case any distilled spirits removed from a distillery warehouse for deposit in a general bonded warehouse shall fail to be deposited in such general bonded warehouse within ten days after such removal, or within the time specified in any bond given on such removal, or if any distilled spirits deposited in any general bonded warehouse shall be taken therefrom, for export or otherwise, without full compliance with the provisions of this act, and with the requirements of any regulations made thereunder, and with the terms of any bond given on such removal, or if any distilled spirits which have been deposited in a general bonded warehouse shall be found elsewhere, not having been removed therefrom according to law, any person who shall be guilty of such failure, or any person who shall in any manner violate any provision of the next preceding eleven sections of this act, shall be subject, on conviction, to a fine of not less than one hundred dollars nor more than five thousand dollars, and to imprisonment for not less than three months nor more than three years for every such failure or violation; and the spirits as to which such failure or violation, or unlawful removal shall take place shall be forfeited to the United States.*

SEC. 94. *That all assessments made under the provisions of section thirty-three hundred and nine of the Revised Statutes of the United States, and Acts amendatory thereof, shall be at the rate of tax imposed by this act on each proof gallon.*

SEC. 95. *That no distiller who has given the required bond and who sells only distilled spirits of his own production at the place of manufacture, or at the place of storage in bond, in the original packages to which the tax-paid stamps are affixed, shall be required to pay the special tax of a wholesome liquor dealer on account of such sales.*

SEC. 96. *That storekeepers, and storekeepers and gaugers, when transferred from one distillery to another, either in the same district or in different districts, shall receive compensation not exceeding four dollars per day during the time necessarily occupied in traveling from one distillery to the other, together with actual and necessary traveling expenses.*

SEC. 97. *That the officer holding the combined office of storekeeper and gauger, under the provisions of the legislative, executive, and judicial appropriation Act, approved August fifteenth, eighteen hundred and seventy-six (Nineteenth Statutes, page one hundred and fifty-two), may be assigned by the Commissioner of Internal Revenue to perform the separate duties of a storekeeper at any distillery, or at any general or special bonded warehouse, or to perform any of the duties of a gauger under the internal-revenue laws. And the said officer, before entering upon the discharge of such separate duties, shall give a bond to* be approved by the Commissioner of Internal Revenue for the faithful discharge of his duties in such form and for such amount as the Commissioner may prescribe.

SEC. 98. That internal-revenue gaugers may be assigned to duty at distilleries, rectifying houses, or wherever gauging is required to be done, and transferred from one place of duty to another, by the Commissioner of Internal Revenue, in like manner as storekeepers and storekeepers and gaugers are now assigned and transferred.

SEC. 99. That section thirty-three hundred and twenty of the Revised Statutes of the United States, as amended, be further amended by striking out all after said number and substituting the following:

"Whenever any cask or package, containing five wine gallons or more, is filled for shipment, sale, or delivery on the premises of any rectifier who has paid the special tax required by law, it shall be inspected and gauged by a United States gauger whose duty it shall be to mark and brand the same and place thereon an engraved stamp, which shall state the date when affixed and the number of proof gallons, and shall be in such form as shall be prescribed by the Commissioner of Internal Revenue with the approval of the Secretary of the Treasury: Provided, That when such cask or package is filled on the premises of a rectifier rectifying less than five hundred barrels a year, counting forty gallons of proof spirits to the barrel, it may be gauged, marked, branded, and stamped by a United States gauger, or it may be gauged, marked, branded, and stamped by the rectifier, as the Commissioner of Internal Revenue, with the approval of the Secretary of the Treasury, may by regulations prescribe.

Sec. 100. That whenever any person intending to commence or to continue the business of a distiller shall execute a bond under the provisions of section thirty-two hundred and sixty of the Revised Statutes of United States, and file the same with the collector of internal revenue for the district in which he proposes to distill, the collector may refuse to approve said bond if the person offering the same shall have been previously convicted, in a court of competent jurisdiction, of any fraudulent noncompliance with any of the provisions of law relating to the duties and business of distillers, or if the Commissioner of Internal Revenue, with the approval of the Secretary of the Treasury, shall have compromised such an offense with the person upon the payment of penalties or otherwise, and, in case of such refusal, the person so proposing to distill may appeal to the Commissioner of Internal Revenue, whose decision in the matter shall be final.

SEC. [85] 101. That section forty-three of the Act approved October first, eighteen hundred and ninety, entitled "An Act to reduce the revenue and equalize duties on imports, and for other purposes," be amended so as to read as follows:

"That the wine spirits mentioned in section forty-two of this Act is the product resulting from the distillation of fermented grape juice and shall be held to include the product commonly known as grape brandy; and the pure sweet wine which may be fortified free of tax, as provided in said section, is fermented grape juice only, and shall contain no other substance of any kind whatever introduced before, at the time of, or after fermentation and such sweet wine shall contain not less than four per centum of saccharine matter, which saccharine strength may be determined by testing with Billings saccharometer or must scale, such sweet wine, after the evaporation of the spirit contained therein, and restoring the sample tested to original volume by addition of water: Provided, That the addition of pure boiled or condensed grape must, or pure crystallized cane or beet sugar to the pure grape juice aforesaid, or the fermented product of such grape juice prior to the fortification provided for by this Act for the sole purpose of perfecting sweet wines according to commercial standard, shall not be excluded by the definition of pure, sweet wine aforesaid: Provided further, That the cane or beet sugar so used shall not be in excess of ten per cent of the weight of wines to be fortified under this Act."

SEC. [86] 102. [That all Acts and parts of Acts inconsistent herewith are hereby repealed.] Every person whose business it is to manufacture tobacco or snuff for himself, or who employs others to manufacture tobacco or snuff, whether such manufacture be by cutting, pressing, grinding, crushing, or rubbing of any raw or leaf-tobacco, or otherwise preparing raw or leaf tobacco, or manufactured or partially manufactured tobacco or snuff, or the putting up for use or consumption of scraps, waste, clippings, stems, or deposits of tobacco resulting from any process of handling tobacco, or by the working or preparation of leaf-tobacco, tobacco-stems, scraps, clippings, or waste, by sifting, twisting, screening, or any other process, shall be regarded as a manufacturer of tobacco.

Every person shall also be regarded as a manufacturer of tobacco whose business it is to sell leaf tobacco in quantities less than the original hogshead, case or bale; or who sells directly to consumers, or to persons other than duly registered dealers in leaf tobacco, or to duly registered dealers in manufactured tobacco, snuff or cigars, or to persons who purchase in original packages for export; and all tobacco so sold by such person shall be regarded as manufactured tobacco, and such manufactured tobacco shall be put up and prepared by such manufacturer in such packages only as the Commissioner of Internal Revenue with the approval of the Secretary of the Treasury shall prescribe: Provided, That farmers and growers of tobacco who sell leaf tobacco of their own growth and raising shall not be regarded as manufacturers of tobacco; and so much of section three thousand two hundred and forty-four of the Revised Statutes of the United States, and acts amendatory thereof, as are in conflict with this Act are hereby repealed.

[Sec. 87. That section twenty-nine hundred and eighty-four, of the Revised Statutes of the United States be, and the same is hereby, amended so as to read as follows:]

["Sec. 2984. The Secretary of the Treasury is hereby authorized, except as otherwise specially provided in this Act, upon production of satisfactory proof to him of the actual injury or destruction, in whole or in part, of any merchandise, from any cause whatsoever, while the same remained in the custody of the officers of the customs in any public or private warehouse under bond, or in the appraisers' stores undergoing appraisal, in pursuance of law or regulations of the Treasury Department, or while in transportation under bond from the port of entry to any other port in the United States, or while in the custody of officers of the customs and not in bond, or while within the limits of any port of entry, and before the same have been landed under the supervision of the officers of the customs, to abate or refund, as the case may be, out of any moneys in the Treasury not otherwise appropriated, the amount of impost duties paid or accruing thereupon, and likewise to cancel any warehouse bond or bonds, or enter satisfaction thereon in whole or part, as the case may be."]

SEC. [88] 103. That the Act of June twentieth, eighteen hundred and seventy-six (Nineteenth United States Statutes, page sixty), be amended by insertion after the words "imported into the United States by such firm or partnership" the following: "Or for any other purpose connected with the general transaction of business at any custom-house."

SEC. [89] 104. That [section] *sections three, fifteen and sixteen* of an Act approved October first, eighteen hundred and ninety, entitled "An Act to reduce the revenue and equalize duties on imports, and for other purposes," [is] *are* hereby repealed [,]; and [that] all *agreements or arrangements made or proclaimed between the United States and foreign governments under the provisions of said section are hereby abrogated, of which the President shall give such notice to the authorities of said foreign governments as may be required by the terms of such agreements or arrangements.*

SEC. 105. *All Acts and parts of Acts* inconsistent with the provisions of this Act are hereby repealed, but the repeal of existing laws or modifications thereof embraced in this Act shall not affect any act done, or any right accruing or accrued, or any suit or proceeding had or commenced in any civil cause before the said repeal or modifications; but all rights and liabilities under said laws shall continue and may be enforced in the same manner as if said repeal or modifications had not been made. Any offenses committed and all penalties or forfeitures or liabilities incurred prior to the passage of this Act under any statute embraced in or changed, modified, or repealed by this Act may be prosecuted or punished in the same manner and with the same effect as if this Act had not been passed. All Acts of limitation, whether applicable to civil causes and proceedings or to the prosecution of offenses or for the recovery of penalties or forfeitures embraced in or modified, changed, or repealed by this Act shall not be affected thereby; and all suits, proceedings, or prosecutions, whether civil or criminal, for causes arising or acts done or committed prior to the passage of this Act, may be commenced and prosecuted within the same time and with the same effect as if this Act had not been passed: *And provided further,* That nothing in this Act shall be construed to repeal the provisions of section three thousand and fifty-eight of the Revised Statutes as amended by the Act approved February twenty-third, eighteen hundred and eighty-seven, in respect to the abandonment of merchandise to underwriters or the salvors of property, and the ascertainment of duties thereon.

Passed the House of Representatives February 1, 1894.
Attest: JAMES KERR,
Clerk.

FIFTY-THIRD CONGRESS, SECOND SESSION.

H. R. 4864.

IMPORTED MERCHANDISE, 1893,

WITH THE

RATES AND DUTIES COLLECTED UNDER EXISTING LAW;

ALSO

THE RATES AND ESTIMATED REVENUES UNDER BILL AS PASSED BY THE HOUSE OF REPRESENTATIVES AND AS AMENDED BY THE FINANCE COMMITTEE REPORTED TO THE SENATE MARCH 20, 1894.

PREPARED UNDER DIRECTION OF THE COMMITTEE ON FINANCE, BY CHARLES H. EVANS, TREASURY DEPARTMENT.

IMPORTED MERCHANDISE, 1893, WITH THE RATES AND DUTIES COL
REVENUES UNDER BILL AS PASSED BY THE HOUSE OF REPRESENT
TO THE SENATE.

Paragraph		Importations of fiscal year, June 30, 1893.			
		Quantities.	Values.	Duties.	Unit of value.
	SCHEDULE A—CHEMICALS, OILS, AND PAINTS.				
	Acids—				
1	Acetic or pyroligneous—				
	Specific gravity not exceeding 1.047 ....lbs..	7,675	$873.00	$115.13	$0.11
	Specific gravity exceeding 1.047.lbs..	10,746	1,922.00	429.84	.18
2	Boracic ....lbs..	771,775	40,568.00	38,588.75	.053
3	Chromic ....lbs..	3,318	609.00	199.08	.18
4	Citric ....lbs..	13,815.30	4,633.79	1,831.53	.35
6	Tannic or tannin..................lbs..	1,443	597.00	1,082.25	.41
7	Tartaric ....lbs..	130	39.50	13.00	.30
8	Alcoholic perfumery, including cologne water and other toilet waters.......galls..	17,467.06	296,706.77	183,287.47	16.99
	Compounds, alcoholic, not specially provided for ....galls..	4,301.75	6,215.00	10,157.24	1.44
9	Alumina, alum, alum cake, patent alum, sulphate of alumina, and aluminous cake, and alum in crystals or ground.......lbs..	4,572,923	73,806.17	27,437.52	.016
11	Blacking of all kinds.............................		127,106.41	31,776.61	
	Bone char, suitable for use in decolorizing sugar..		17.00	4.25	
14	Borax, refined ....lbs..	11,230	1,327.00	561.50	.118
15	Chalk—				
	Prepared, precipitated, French and rod ....lbs..	474,521	14,821.46	4,745.21	.031
16	Chalk preparations, all other, not specially provided for.......................		10,591.25	2,118.25	
17	Chloral hydrate........................lbs..		(†)		
18	Chloroform ....lbs..	11	14.00	2.75	1.27
	Coal-tar colors or dyes, not specially provided for.................................		2,322,258.00	812,790.30	
21	Collodion, and all compounds of pyroxyline...................................lbs..	395	309.00	197.50	.78
	In finished or partly finished articles.lbs..	14,909.30	48,515.05	21,074.35	3.26
	Rolled or in sheets, but not made up into articles ....lbs..	13,720.50	9,452.00	8,232.30	.69
22	Coloring for brandy, wine, beer, or other liquors..		1,789.00	894.50	
	Ethers—				
25	Sulphuric ....lbs..	20	2.00	8.00	.10
25	Of all kinds, not specially provided for ....lbs..	729.63	2,033.00	720.63	2.79
26	Fruit ethers, oils, or essences.......lbs..	762.50	800.00	1,900.25	1.05
	Logwood and other dyewoods, extracts and decoctions of ....lbs..	3,757,259	287,723.00	32,876.03	.077
	Sumac—				
	Extract of............................lbs..	2,880,210	108,447.00	25,201.85	0.038
	Bark for dyeing or tanning, extracts of—				
	Other than hemlock, not specially provided for..............................lbs..	672	71.00	5.88	.11
27	Fish glue or isinglass—				
	Valued at not above 7 cents per pound, ...lbs..	5,041	301.00	75.61	.059
	Valued at above 7 cents and not above 30 cents per pound...............lbs..	17,425	2,681.15	670.29	.15
	Valued at above 30 cents per pound.lbs..	14,424	13,332.00	3,999.60	.92
	Gelatin—				
	Valued at not above 7 cents per pound, lbs..				
	Valued at above 7 cents and not above 30 cents per pound...............lbs..	267,093	48,042.00	12,010.50	.18
	Valued at above 30 cents per pound.lbs..	328,794	229,531.09	68,859.83	.70
	Glue—				
	Valued at not above 7 cents per pound, ...lbs..	1,777,547	101,932.00	26,663.24	.037
	Valued at above 7 cents and not above 30 cents per pound...............lbs..	4,154,181	449,861.64	112,465.41	.11
	Valued at above 30 cents per pound.lbs..	266	108.00	32.40	.41
28	Glycerin—				
	Crude, not purified ....lbs..	14,325,111	768,565.00	250,689.44	.054
	Refined ....lbs..	284,795.40	24,394.00	12,815.81	.086
30	Ink of all kinds and ink powders		86,930.93	26,087.09	
32	Iodoform ....lbs..	175	649.00	262.50	3.71

*No data for alumina. †No data.

141

LECTED UNDER EXISTING LAW; ALSO THE RATES AND ESTIMATED
ATIVES AND AS AMENDED BY THE FINANCE COMMITTEE AND REPORTED

Duties estimated under—		Rates of duty under—			Average ad valorem under—			Paragraph.
House bill.	Senate bill.	Present law.	House bill.	Senate bill.	Present.	House bill.	Senate bill.	
					Per ct.	Per ct.	Per ct.	
$174.60	$174.00	1½ cts. per lb..	20 per cent...	20 per cent...	13.19	20	20	1
384.40	384.40	4 cts. per lb ..			22.36			
8,113.60	8,113.60	5 cts. per lb ..	20 per cent...	20 per cent...	95.12	20	20	
60.90	60.90	6 cts. per 'b..	10 per ccut...	10 per cent...	32.09	10	10	3
926.75	926.75	10 cts. per lb.	20 per cent...	20 per cent...	28.73	20	20	4
505.05	505.05	75 cts. per lb.	35 cts. per lb.	35 cts. per lb.	181.28	84.60	84.60	6
7.90	3.95	10 cts. per lb.	20 per cent...	10 per cent...	32.91	20	10	7
109,110.81	109,110.81	$2.50 per gall. and 50 p. c.	$2 per gall. and 25 p. c.	$2 per gall. and 25 p. c.	61.77	36.77	36.77	8
10,157.24	10,157.24	$2 per gall. and 25 p. c.	....do	....do........	163.43	163.43	163.43	
(*)		⅙ cent per lb.	10 per cent...	10 per cent...		10	10	9
14,761.23	22,141.85		20 per cent...	30 per cent...	37.18	20	30	
25,421.28	25,412.28	25 per cent...	20 per cent...	20 per cent...	25	20	20	11
	3.40	25 per cent...	Free	....do........	25	Free.	20	
265.40	265.40	5 cts. per lb..	20 per cent...	....do........	42.31	20	20	14
2,964.29	2,964.29	1 cent per lb.	....do	....do........	32.02	20	20	16
2,118.25	2,118.25	20 per cent...	....do	....do........	20	20	20	16
		50 cts. per lb.	25 cts per cent...	25 cts per cent...		25	25	
2.75	2.75	25 cts. per lb.	25 cts per lb.	25 cts. per lb..	19.64	19.64	19.64	17
464,451.60	464,451.60	35 per cent...	20 per cent...	20 per cent...	35	20	20	18
158.00	158.00	50 cts. per lb.	40 cts. per lb.	40 cts. per lb.	63.91	49.13	49.13	21
21,831.72	21,831.72	60 cts. per lb. and 25 p. c.	45 per cent...	45 per cent...	43.44	45	45	
6,860.25	6,860.25	60 cts. per lb.	50 cts. per lb.	50 cts. per lb.	87.08	72.57	72.57	
894.50	536.79	50 per cent ...	50 per cent...	30 per cent...	50	50	30	22
7.00	7.00	40 cts. per lb.	35 cts. per lb.	35 cts. per lb.	400	350	350	25
729.63	729.63	$1 per pound.	$1 per pound.	$1 per pound.	35.89	35.89	35.89	25
762.50	762.50	$2.50 per lb..	$1 per pound.	$1 per pound.	238.28	95.32	95.32	26
28,772.30	28,772.30	⅜ cent per lb..	10 per cent....	10 per cent...	11.43	10	10	
10,844.70	10,844.70	⅜ cent per lb.	10 per cent...	10 per cent...	23.24	10	10	
7.10	7.10	....do	....do	....do........	8.28	10	10	
75.25	75.25	1½ cts. per lb.	25 per cent...	25 per cent...	25.12	25	25	27
670.29	670.29	25 per cent...	....do	....do........	25	25	25	
3,333.00	3,333.00	30 per cent...	....do	....do........	30	25	25	
....	....	1½ cts. per lb.	....do	....do........	....	25	25	
12,010.50	12,010.50	25 per cent...	....do	....do........	25	25	25	
57,382.77	57,382.77	30 per cent...	....do	....do........	30	25	25	
25,483.00	25,483.00	1½ cts. per lb.	....do	....do........	26.16	25	25	
112,465.41	112,465.41	25 per cent...	....do	....do........	25	25	25	
27.00	27.00	30 per cent...	....do	....do........	30	25	25	
143,251.11	143,251.11	1½ cts. per lb.	1 cent per lb.	1 ct. per lb ..	32.62	19.64	19.64	28
8,543.86	8,543.86	4½ cts. per lb.	3 cents per lb.	3 cts. per lb..	52.54	35.03	35.03	
17,391.39	17,391.39	30 per cent...	20 per cent...	20 per cent...	30	20	20	30
175.00	162.25	$1.50 per lb ..	$1 per pound.	25 per cent...	40.45	26.97	25	32

IMPORTED MERCHANDISE, 1893, WITH THE RATES AND

Paragraph.		Importations of fiscal year, June 30, 1893.			
		Quantities.	Values.	Duties.	Unit of value.
	SCHEDULE A.—CHEMICALS, OILS, AND PAINTS—Continued.				
33	Licorice, extracts of, in paste, rolls, or other form...........lbs..	904,636.40	$107,405.00	$49,755.05	$0.12
34	Magnesia—				
	Calcined...........lbs..	21,486.25	4,225.00	1,718.90	.20
	Carbonate of, medicinal...........lbs..	66,316	4,994.00	2,652.64	.075
35	Morphia, or morphine, and all salts thereof,	23,580	25,035.00	17,685.00	1.06
	Oils:				
36	Alizarine assistant, or soluble oil, or oleate of soda, or Turkey red oil—Containing 50 per cent or more of castor oil...........galls..				
	All other...........galls..	2,901	1,157.00	347.10	.40
37	Castor...........galls..	286	228.00	223.80	.80
38	Cod liver...........galls..	190,431.50	99,709.00	28,564.73	.52
41	Flaxseed or linseed, raw, boiled, or oxidized...........galls..	7,405.90	2,491.00	2,369.91	.34
	Poppy-seed oil, raw, boiled, or oxidized...........galls..	5,457.37	3,212.00	1,746.38	.59
42	Fusel oil, or amylic alcohol...........lbs..	606,243	20,017.00	2,001.70	.033
43	Hemp seed and rape seed...........galls..	265,368.25	110,020.00	26,536.83	.41
44	Olive, fit for salad purposes...........galls..	693,593.51	901,694.45	242,757.80	1.30
45	Peppermint...........lbs..	1,286.85	2,187.00	1,029.48	1.701
46	Seal...........galls..	54,820.50	18,706.00	4,385.64	.34
	Fish, not specially provided for...galls..	560,661	141,880.50	45,572.88	.25
	Whale, not specially provided for.galls..	107,193	25,297.00	8,875.44	.23
	Opium:				
47	Aqueous, extract of, for medicinal uses, and tincture of, as laudanum, and all other liquid preparations of, not specially provided for...........		716.25	286.50	
	Opium, crude or manufactured, and not adulterated, containing 9 per cent and over of morphia...........	612,510.77	1,178,305.00		1.92
48	Prepared for smoking, and opium, containing less than 9 per cent of morphia...........lbs..	66,678.75	471,058.00	800,145.00	7.07
49	Paints and colors:				
	Baryta, sulphate of, or barytes, including barytes earth—Manufactured...........tons..	1,031.38	11,698.00	6,930.90	11.34
50	Blues, such as Berlin, Prussian, Chinese, and all others containing ferrocyanide of iron—Dry, or ground in or mixed with oil...........lbs..	218,241	65,385.00	13,094.46	.30
51	Blanc fixe, or satin white or artificial sulphate of barytes...........lbs..	506,343	7,988.00	3,797.58	.016
52	Black, made from bone, ivory, or vegetable, including boneblack and lampblack, dry or ground in oil or water.lbs..	516,068	26,513.00	6,653.25	.052
53	Chrome yellow, chrome green, and all other chromium colors, in which lead and bichromate of potash or soda are component parts—Dry or ground in or mixed with oil...........lbs..	172,409	25,150.00	7,758.44	.15
54	Ocher and ochery earths—Ground in oil...........lbs..	40,674	3,106.00	510.12	.076
	Sienna and sienna earths—Ground in oil...........lbs..	24,223	1,719.00	363.35	.071
	Umber and umber earths—Ground in oil...........lbs..	16,666	969.00	250.00	.058
	Ultramarino...........lbs..	929,313	90,617.00	41,819.10	.098
56	Spirit varnishes...........galls..	1,300.53	4,967.00	3,455.16	3.82
	All other including gold size or Japan...........galls..	39,530.87	105,815.96	37,035.59	2.68
57	Vermilion red, colors containing quicksilver, dry or ground in oil or water...........lbs..	66,752	20,026.08	8,010.24	.45
	Vermilion red, not containing quicksilver, but made of lead, etc...........	(*)	(*)	(*)	(*)

* No data.

DUTIES COLLECTED UNDER EXISTING LAW, ETC.—Continued.

Duties estimated under—		Rates of duty under—			Average ad valorem under—			Paragraph.
House bill.	Senate bill.	Present law.	House bill.	Senate bill.	Present.	House bill.	Senate bill.	
					Per ct.	Per ct.	Per ct.	
$45,231.82	$36,185.45	5¼ cts. per lb.	5 cents per lb.	4 cts. per lb.	46.32	42.10	33.69	33
1,504.04	1,207.50	8 cts. per lb.	7 cents per lb.	30 per cent.	40.71	35.62	30	34
1,989.48	1,408.20	4 cts. per lb.	3 cents per lb.	....do........	53.12	39.84	30	
17,685.00	17,685.00	50 cts. per oz.	75 cts. per oz.	75 cts. per oz.	70.03	47.09	47.09	35
....	....	80 cts. per gal.	30 per cent.	30 per cent.	30	30	30	36
347.10	347.10	30 per cent.						
100.10	100.00	80 cts. per gal.	35 cts. per gal.	35 cts. per gal.	100.35	43.87	43.87	37
19,941.80	19,941.60	15 cts. per gal.	20 per cent.	20 per cent.	28.65	20	20	38
1,110.89	1,110.89	32 cts. per gal.	15 cts. per gal.	15 cts. per gal.	95.14	44.60	44.60	41
818.60	818.60	....do........			54.37	25.46	25.46	
2,001.70	2,001.70	10 per cent.	10 per cent.	10 per cent.	13	10	10	42
26,536.83	26,536.83	10 cts. per gal.	10 cts. per gal.	10 cts. per gal.	24.12	24.12	24.12	43
242,757.80	225,423.61	35 cts. per gal.	35 cts. per gal.	25 per cent.	26.92	26.92	25	44
546.75	437.40	80 cts. per lb.	25 per cent.	20 per cent.	47.07	25	25	45
4,670.50	3,741.20	8 cts. per gal.	....do........	....do........	23.45	25	20	46
35,470.12	28,276.10	....do........	....do........	....do........	32.12	25	20	
6,324.25	5,059.40	....do........	....do........	....do........	33.90	25	20	
179.06	143.25	40 per cent.	....do........	....do........	40	25	20	47
612,510.77	612,510.77	Free........	$1 per pound.	$1 per pound.	Free..	51.98	51.98	
400,072.50	400,072.50	$12 per lb.	$6 per pound.	$6 per pound.	169.65	84.82	84.82	48
3,094.14	2,924.50	$6.72 per ton.	$3 per ton.	25 per cent.	59.25	26.45	25	49
13,094.46	13,094.46	6 cts. per lb.	6 cts. per lb.	6 cts. per lb.	20.03	20.03	20.03	50
1,972.00	1,972.00	½ ct. per lb.	25 per cent.	25 per cent.	47.54	25	25	51
5,322.00	5,322.00	25 per cent.	20 per cent.	20 per cent.	25	20	20	52
3,879.22	3,879.22	4½ cts. per lb.	2¼ cts. per lb.	2¼ cts. per lb.	80.84	15.42	15.42	53
518.42	776.50	1½ cts. per lb.	1¼ cts. per lb.	25 per cent.	19.64	16.37	25	54
302.80	429.75	....do........	....do........	....do........	21.14	17.02	25	
233.32	242.25	....do........	....do........	....do........	25.80	21.50	25	
18,123.40	18,123.40	4½ cts. per lb.	20 per cent.	20 per cent.	46.15	20	20	
2,958.45	2,958.45	$1.32 per gall. and 35 p. c.	$1.32 per gall. and 25 p. c.	$1.32 per gall. and 25 p. c.	69.56	59.56	59.56	56
26,453.99	26,453.99	35 per cent.	25 per cent.	25 per cent.	35	25	25	
5,985.21	5,985.21	12 cts. per lb.	20 per cent.	20 per cent.	26.77	20	20	57
(*)	(*)	25 per cent.	6 cents per lb.	6 cents per lb.	25	....	....	

TA——10

IMPORTED MERCHANDISE, 1893, WITH THE RATES AND

Paragraph.		Importations of fiscal year, June 30, 1893.			
		Quantities.	Values.	Duties.	Unit of value.
	SCHEDULE A.—CHEMICALS, OILS, AND PAINTS— Continued.				
	Paints and colors—Continued.				
58	Wash blue containing ultramarine..lbs..	231,455	$41,538.00	$8,443.65	.15
59	Whiting and Paris white—				
	Dry......................................lbs..	281,018	988.30	1,408.11	.003
	Ground in oil (putty).............lbs..	57,608	304.00	576.08	.005
60	Zinc, oxide of, and white paint containing zinc, but not containing lead—				
	Dry......................................lbs..	3,611,934	144,817.00	45,524.23	.040
	Ground in oil......................lbs..	337,941	14,612.00	5,913.90	.043
61	All other paints and colors—				
	Dry or mixed, or ground in water or oil, including lakes, not specially provided for, and artists' colors of all kinds, in tubes or otherwise..	....	503,033.87	125,758.48	....
	Mixed or ground with water or solutions other than oil, and commercially known as artists' water-color paints...	....	50,768.00	17,030.40	....
	Crayons...	....	11,543.00	2,885.75	....
	Smalts and frostings...........................	....	1,279.00	310.75	....
	Brown—				
	Spanish, Indian red, and colcothar or oxide of iron..........................	....	141,615.00	35,403.75	....
	Vandyke, Cassel earth, or Cassel brown.......................................	....	35.00	8.75	....
62	Lead, acetate of—				
	Brown..lbs..				
	White...lbs..	2,185	154.25	120.18	.071
63	Litharge...lbs..	75,394	2,383.00	2,261.82	.032
64	Lead, nitrate of.............................lbs..	79	13.00	2.37	.16
65	Orange, mineral...........................lbs..	1,666,650	74,024.00	58,332.79	.044
66	Red..lbs..	1,013,854.75	33,361.00	30,415.64	.033
67	White, dry or in pulp, and ground or mixed in oil, and white paint containing lead.............................lbs..	815,526	41,310.50	24,465.79	.051
68	Phosphorus...................................lbs..	89,874	44,068.00	17,974.80	.49
	Potash—				
69	Chromate and bichromate of........lbs..	969,067	79,174.18	20,072.01	.028
71	Hydriodate, iodide, and iodate of...lbs..	187	475.00	93.50	2.54
72	Nitrate of, or saltpeter, refined.....lbs..	129,216	6,061.30	1,292.46	.047
73	Prussiate of—				
	Red..lbs..	16,679	5,743.00	1,667.90	.34
	Yellow..lbs..	1,047,910	206,250.00	52,395.50	.20
	Preparations, medicinal, including medicinal proprietary preparations—				
74	Of which alcohol is a component part, or in the preparation of which alcohol is used....................lbs..	170,723.88	550,363.63	85,361.90	3.22
75	Of which alcohol is not a component part..	....	617,859.20	154,464.84	....
	Calomel and other mercurial preparations..	13,495	7,941.28	2,779.43	.59
76	Preparations or products known as alkalies, and alkaloids, and all combinations of the same, and all chemical compounds and salts, by whatever name known..	....	874,706.34	218,676.50	....
	All other essential oils, and combinations of..	1,164,790	239,596.29	50,899.06	.21
	All other fixed or expressed oils, and combinations of.........................galls..	16,285	3,650.00	914.75	.22
	All other rendered oils and combinations of..galls..	1,437	688.00	159.50	.44
	Bicarbonate of potash.......................	74,983	3,903.00	975.75	.052
77	Preparations used as applications to the hair, mouth, teeth, or skin, such as cosmetics, dentifrices, pastes, pomades, powders, and tonics, including all known as toilet preparations, not specially provided for......................lbs..	....	209,777.25	104,888.07	....
78	Santonine, and all salts thereof containing 80 per cent or over of santonine..lbs..	230	352.00	575.00	1.53

DUTIES COLLECTED UNDER EXISTING LAW, ETC.—Continued.

Duties estimated under—		Rates of duty under—			Average ad valorem under—			Paragraph.
House bill.	Senate bill.	Present law.	House bill.	Senate bill.	Present.	House bill.	Senate bill.	
					Per ct.	*Per ct.*	*Per ct.*	
$8,307.60	$8,307.00	3 cents per lb.	20 per cent...	20 per cent...	20.83	20	20	58
247.08	290.49	½ cent per lb.	25 per cent...	30 per cent...	142.48	25	30	59
76.00	91.20	1 cent per lb.	....do	....do	189.50	25	30	
28,903.40	36,204.25	1½ cts. per lb..	20 per cent...	25 per cent...	31.44	20	25	60
2,022.40	3,653.00	1¾ cts. per lb..	....do	....do	40.47	20	25	
125,758.48	125,758.48	25 per cent...	25 per cent...	....do	25	25	25	61
14,192.00	14,192.00	30 per cent...	....do	....do	30	25	25	
2,885.75	2,885.75	25 per cent...	....do	....do	25	25	25	
310.75	310.75	....do	....do	....do	25	25	25	
35,408.75	35,408.75	....do	....do	....do	25	25	25	
8.75	8.75	....do	....do	....do	25	25	25	
....	....	3½ cts. per lb..	1¾ cts. per lb..	1¾ cts. per lb..	....	....	....	62
60.00	60.09	5¼ cts. per lb..	2⅝ cts. per lb..	2⅝ cts. per lb..	78.04	30.02	30.02	
1,130.01	1,130.91	3 cents per lb.	1½ cts. per lb..	1½ cts. per lb..	94.91	47.45	47.45	63
1.18	1.18	....do	....do	....do	18.23	9.11	9.11	64
29,166.39	29,166.39	3½ cts. per lb..	1¾ cts. per lb..	1¾ cts. per lb..	78.80	39.40	39.40	65
15,207.82	15,207.82	3 cents per lb.	1½ cts. per lb..	1½ cts. per lb..	91.17	45.59	45.59	66
12,232.80	12,232.80	....do	....do	....do	50.21	29.60	29.00	67
11,017.00	11,017.00	20 cts. per lb.	25 per cent...	25 per cent...	40.79	25	25	68
15,834.84	19,793.54	3 cents per lb.	20 per cent...	....do	36.72	20	25	69
46.75	47.50	50 cts. per lb.	25 cts. per lb.	10 per cent...	19.68	9.84	10	71
646.23	606.14	1 cent per lb.	½ cent per lb.	....do	21.32	10.06	10	72
1,148.60	1,148.60	10 cts. per lb.	20 per cent...	20 per cent...	20.04	20	20	73
41,251.80	41,251.80	5 cents per lb.	....do	....do	25.40	20	20	
85,301.96	85,301.96	50 cts. per lb.	50 cts. per lb.	50 cts. per lb.	15.51	15.51	15.51	74
154,464.84	154,464.84	25 per cent...	25 per cent...	25 per cent...	25	25	25	75
1,985.32	1,985.32	35 per cent...	....do	....do	35	25	25	
218,070.50	218,070.59	25 per cent...	....do	....do	25	25	25	76
59,809.06	59,809.06	....do	....do	....do	25	25	25	
914.75	914.75	....do	....do	....do	25	25	25	
159.50	159.50	....do	....do	....do	25	25	25	
975.75	975.75	....do	....do	....do	25	25	25	
83,910.90	62,933.17	50 per cent...	40 per cent...	30 per cent...	50	40	30	77
230.00	230.00	$2.50 per lb...	$1 per pound.	$1 per pound.	163.35	65.34	65.34	78

IMPORTED MERCHANDISE, 1893, WITH THE RATES AND

Paragraph.		Importations of fiscal year, June 30, 1893.			
		Quantities.	Values.	Duties.	Unit of value.
	SCHEDULE A.—CHEMICALS, OILS, AND PAINTS—Continued.				
79	Soap:				
	Castile..........................lbs..	4,235,477	$271,731.97	$52,943.53	$0.064
	Fancy, perfumed, and all descriptions of toilet..........................lbs..	831,993.33	340,457.65	124,799.02	.41
	All other, not specially provided for.....	....	64,473.00	12,894.60	......
80	Soda—				
	Bicarbonate of, or supercarbonate of, or saleratus......................lbs..	1,193,380	19,735.63	11,933.80	.017
81	Hydrate of, or caustic.............lbs..	55,531,899	1,290,082.09	555,318.90	.023
82	Bichromate and chromate of........lbs..	671,503	44,183.00	20,145.09	.066
83	Soda ash.........................lbs..	388,811,970	4,860,787.77	972,104.97	.012
	Sal, or soda crystals.............lbs..	27,777,489	238,923.45	69,443.72	.009
84	Silicate of, or other alkaline silicate.lbs..	608,228	6,901.00	3,041.16	.011
86	Sponges...........................	....	365,248.50	73,049.70	......
87	Strychnia, or strychnine, and all salts thereof.........................ounces..	16,538	7,053.00	6,615.20	.43
88	Sulphur, sublimed, or flowers of....tons..	128.78	4,493.00	1,287.83	34.89
89	Sumac, ground....................lbs..	14,363,922	280,953.00	57,455.68	.020
	Tartar—				
90	Cream of, and patent..............lbs..	1,333.75	373.00	80.02	.28
91	Tartars and lees crystals, partly refined.........................lbs..	20,145	2,593.00	805.80	.13
92	Tartrate of soda and potassa, or Rochelle salts.........................lbs..	1,209.50	220.00	36.29	.18
	Total Schedule A, chemicals, oils, and paints...........................	....	20,315,095.67	6,132,650.85	......
	SCHEDULE B.—EARTHS, EARTHENWARE, AND GLASSWARE.				
	Earthen, stone, and china ware:				
	Brick and tiles—				
93	Brick, fire—				
	Not glazed, enameled, ornamented, or decorated in any manner ....tons..	14,989.62	74,443.22	18,737.07	4.97
	Glazed enameled, ornamented or decorated...............tons..	715.74	10,379.59	4,670.82	14.51
94	Brick, other than fire—				
	Not glazed ornamented, painted, enameled, vitrified, or decorated......................M..	2,225	14,929.96	3,732.50	6.71
	Ornamented, glazed, painted, enameled, vitrified, or decorated......................M..	900.98	48,662.00	21,897.90	50.63
	Magnetic fire brick (not enumerated; no data).....................	....	....	....	......
94	Tiles—				
	Not glazed, ornamented, painted, enameled, vitrified, or decorated.M..	....	85,727.97	21,431.90	......
	Ornamented, glazed, painted. enameled, vitrified, or decorated, and all encaustic....................M..	....	141,331.51	63,600.52	......
	Cement:				
95	Roman, Portland, and other hydraulic, in barrels, sacks, or other packages..lbs..	1,133,212,485	3,763,691.17	906,509.94	.003
95	Other........................lbs..	1,087,199	18,341.00	3,668.20	.017
96	Lime..............................lbs..	58,900,226	114,418.50	34,800.13	.002
97	Plaster of Paris:				
	Calcined.......................tons..	3,626.72	25,276.00	6,346.77	6.97
	Ground.......................tons..	2,707.25	44,618.07	2,707.25	16.48
98	Clays or earths:				
	China clay, or kaolin.............tons..	52,671.35	399,474.41	158,014.06	7.58
	Wrought or manufactured, not specially provided for.................tons..	5,694.85	76,451.27	17,084.57	13.42
99	Brown earthenware, common stoneware, and crucibles not ornamented or decorated in any manner......................	....	66,276.68	18,560.16	......

NOTE.—The computations of the average ad valorem rates of duty are calculated upon the dutiable value only. The value of the articles that are free of duty by either the present law, House or Senate bills, are omitted.

DUTIES COLLECTED UNDER EXISTING LAW, ETC.—Continued.

Duties estimated under—		Rates of duty under—			Average ad valorem under—			Paragraph.
House bill.	Senate bill.	Present law.	House bill.	Senate bill.	Present.	House bill.	Senate bill.	
					Per ct.	*Per ct.*	*Per ct.*	
$54,346.39	$54,346.39	1¼ cts. per lb.	20 per cent...	20 per cent...	19.48	20	20	79
119,160.17	102,137.29	15 cts. per lb.	35 per cent...	30 per cent...	36.60	35	30	
6,447.30	6,447.30	20 per cent...	10 per cent...	10 per cent...	20	10	10	
5,966.90	5,920.69	1 cent per lb.	½ cent per lb.	30 per cent...	60.47	30.24	30	80
277,650.50	324,755.67	....do	....do	25 per cent...	42.75	21.37	25	81
8,836.60	11,045.75	3 cts. per lb..	20 per cent...	....do	45.59	20	25	82
972,104.97	972,104.97	½ ct. per lb..	¼ ct. per lb..	20 per cent...	20	20	20	83
34,721.86	47,784.69	....do	¼ ct. per lb..	....do	29.06	14.53	20	
1,520.58	1,398.20	¼ ct. per lb..	½ ct. per lb..	....do	43.50	21.75	20	84
36,524.85	36,524.85	20 per cent...	10 per cent...	10 per cent...	20	10	10	86
2,115.90	2,115.90	40 cts. per oz.	30 per cent...	30 per cent...	93.79	30	30	87
898.60	898.60	$10 per ton...	20 per cent...	20 per cent...	28.66	20	20	88
28,995.30	28,995.30	₁⁄₁₆ ct. per lb..	10 per cent...	10 per cent...	19.81	10	10	89
93.25	74.50	6 cts. per lb..	25 per cent...	20 per cent...	21.45	25	20	90
648.25	518.60	4 cts. per lb..	....do	....do	31.07	25	20	91
22.00	22.00	3 cts. per lb..	10 per cent...	10 per cent...	16.49	10	10	92
5,006,316.00	5,103,008.20	....	....	....	32.04	25.09	25.12	
14,888.64	18,610.80	$1.25 per ton.	20 per cent...	25 per cent...	25.15	20	25	93
3,113.87	3,113.87	45 per cent...	30 per cent...	30 per cent...	45	30	30	
2,985.99	3,732.49	25 per cent...	20 per cent...	25 per cent...	25	20	25	94
14,598.60	14,598.60	45 per cent...	30 per cent...	30 per cent...	45	30	30	
....	....	25 per cent...	$1 per ton....	$1 per ton....	25	....	....	
21,431.99	21,431.99	....do	25 per cent...	25 per cent...	25	25	25	94
56,533.80	56,533.80	45 per cent...	40 per cent...	40 per cent...	45	40	40	
906,560.94	906,569.94	8c. per 100 lbs	8c. per 100 lbs	8c. per 100 lbs	24.09	24.09	24.09	95
1,834.10	1,834.10	20 per cent...	10 per cent...	10 per cent...	20	10	10	95
11,441.85	17,162.77	6 c. per 100 lbs	15 per cent...	15 per cent...	30.41	10	15	96
3,791.40	4,533.40	$1.75 per ton.	$1.24 per ton.	$1.25 per ton.	25.11	15	17.97	97
4,461.80	2,707.25	$1 per ton....	$1 per ton....	$1 per ton....	6.07	10	6.07	
105,342.70	105,342.70	$3 per ton....	$2 per ton ...	$2 per ton....	39.56	26.38	26.38	98
5,694.85	5,694.85	....do	$1 per ton....	$1 per ton....	22.35	7.45	7.45	
13,255.33	13,255.33	25 per cent...	20 per cent...	20 per cent...	25	20	20	99

IMPORTED MERCHANDISE, 1893, WITH THE RATES AND

Paragraph.		Importations of fiscal year, June 30, 1893.			
		Quantities.	Values.	Duties.	Unit of value.
	SCHEDULE B.—EARTHS, EARTHENWARE, AND GLASSWARE—Continued.				
	Clays or earths—Continued. China, porcelain, parian, bisque, earthen, stone, and crockery ware, including plaques, ornaments, toys, charms, vases and statuettes—				
100	Painted, tinted, stained, enameled, printed, gilded, or otherwise decorated or ornamented in any manner		$6,821,092.67	$4,002,655.58	
101	Clocks, china, chief value		1,478.00	886.80	
	Plain white, and not ornamented or decorated in any manner		2,110,356.05	1,160,070.83	
100	Lava tips		18,004.00	9,935.20	
102	Gas retorts...No..	84	1,246.00	252.00	$14.83
103	Bottles and vials, flint and lime:				
	Empty—				
	Holding more than 1 pint......lbs..	2,243,470	36,613.70	22,434.70	.016
	Holding not more than 1 pint and not less than ¼ pint.............lbs..	1,300,364	23,901.00	19,505.48	.018
	Holding less than ¼ pint.....gross..	204.38	203.00	102.10	.09
	Other on which specific duty would be less than 40 per cent		48,548.50	19,419.40	
	Filled—				
	Holding more than 1 pint......lbs..	2,167,667	24,690.57	21,670.07	.011
	Holding not more than 1 pint and not less than ¼ pint...........lbs..	1,026,206	13,265.13	15,394.04	.013
	Holding less than ¼ pint.....gross..	35.94	15.00	17.97	.42
	Other on which specific duty would be less than 40 per cent		45,899.74	18,359.90	
	Bottles and vials, green and colored, molded or pressed:				
	Empty—				
	Holding more than 1 pint......lbs..	9,019,738	137,067.00	96,197.38	.014
	Holding not more than 1 pint and not less than ¼ pint.............lbs..	5,088,872	89,100.00	76,333.10	.018
	Holding less than ¼ pint......gross..	116.04	90.00	58.02	.78
	Other on which specific duty would be less than 40 per cent		10,057.00	4,022.80	
	Filled—				
	Holding more than 1 pint.......lbs..	8,762,603	122,593.00	87,626.03	.014
	Holding not more than 1 pint and not less than ¼ pint................lbs..	4,913,421	64,414.00	73,701.35	.013
	Holding less than ¼ pint......gross..	470.79	162.00	230.89	.34
	Other on which specific duty would be less than 40 per cent		110,799.54	44,319.82	
	Demijohns and carboys (covered or uncovered):				
	Empty—				
	Holding more than 1 pint.......lbs..	265,420	7,000.51	2,654.20	.026
	Other on which specific duty would be less than 40 per cent		3,788.00	1,515.20	
	Filled—				
	Other on which specific duty would be less than 40 per cent		1,057.90	423.16	
105	Flint and lime, pressed glassware, not cut, engraved, painted, etched, decorated, colored, printed, stained, silvered, or gilded		29,780.80	17,868.48	
106	Articles of glass, cut, engraved, painted, colored, printed, stained, decorated, silvered, or gilded, not including plate glass silvered, or looking-glass plates		618,333.56	371,000.12	
107	Chemical glassware for use in laboratory, and not otherwise specially provided for		42,821.00	19,269.45	
108	Thin-blown glass, blown with or without a mold, including glass chimneys		9,192.14	5,515.28	
	All other manufactures of glass, or of which glass shall be the component material of chief value, not specially provided for		1,733,871.02	1,040,822.61	
	Glass buttons		51,022.31	30,613.30	
109	Heavy-blown glass, blown with or without a mold, not cut or decorated, finished or unfinished		222,900.00	133,745.40	
110	Porcelain or opal glassware		2,413.00	1,447.80	

DUTIES COLLECTED UNDER EXISTING LAW, ETC.—Continued.

Duties estimated under—		Rates of duty under—			Average ad valorem under—			Paragraph.
House bill.	Senate bill.	Present law.	House bill.	Senate bill.	Present.	House bill.	Senate bill.	
					Per ct.	Per ct.	Per ct.	
$2,723,437.06	$3,069,491.70	60 per cent...	40 per cent...	45 per cent...	60	40	45	100
591.20	591.20	....do	35 per cent...	40 per cent...	60	35	40	101
738,799.61	738,799.61	55 per cent...	40 per cent...	....do	55	40	40	100
6,322.40	6,322.40		35 per cent...	35 per cent...		35	35	
249.20	249.20	$3 each	20 per cent...	20 per cent...	20.22	20	20	102
								103
10,984.11	14,645.48	1 ct. per lb ...	30 per cent...	40 per cent...	61.27	30	40	
7,197.30	9,596.40	1½ cts. per lb..	....do	....do	81.30	30	40	
60.90	81.20	50 c. per gross	....do	....do	50.34	30	40	
14,564.55	19,419.40	40 per cent ...	....do	....do	40	30	40	
7,407.17	9,876.22	1 ct. per lb...	....do	....do	87.79	30	40	
3,979.54	5,306.05	1½ cts. per lb .	....do	....do	116.05	30	40	
4.50	6.00	50 c. per gross	....do	....do	119.80	30	40	
13,700.92	18,359.90	40 per cent...	....do	....do	40	30	40	
41,126.10	54,834.80	1 cent per lb.	....do	....do	70.17	30	40	
26,730.00	35,640.00	1½ cents per lb.	....do	....do	85.67	30	40	
27.00	36.00	50c per gross.	....do	....do	64.47	30	40	
3,017.10	4,022.80	40 per cent...	....do	....do	40	30	40	
36,777.90	49,037.20	1 cent per lb..	....do	....do	71.48	30	40	
19,324.20	25,765.60	1½ cents per lb.	....do	....do	114.42	30	40	
48.00	64.80	50c per gross.	....do	....do	148.08	30	40	
33,239.86	44,319.82	40 per cent...	....do	....do	40	30	40	
2,100.15	2,800.20	1 cent per lb.	....do	....do	37.91	30	40	
1,136.40	1,515.20	40 per cent...	....do	....do	40	30	40	
317.87	423.10	....do	....do	....do	40	30	40	
10,423.28	11,912.32	60 per cent...	35 per cent...	....do	60	35	40	105
216,416.74	247,333.42	....do	....do	....do	60	35	40	106
14,987.35	17,128.40	45 per cent...	....do	....do	45	35	40	107
3,217.25	3,676.85	60 per cent...	....do	....do	60	35	40	108
606,854.86	693,548.40	....do	....do	....do	60	35	40	
17,857.90	20,408.92	....do	....do	....do	60	35	40	
78,018.15	89,163.60	....do	....do	....do	60	35	40	109
844.55	965.20	....do	....do	....do	60	35	40	110

IMPORTED MERCHANDISE, 1893, WITH THE RATES AND

Paragraph.		Importations of fiscal year, June 30, 1893.			
		Quantities.	Values.	Duties.	Unit of value.
	Schedule B.—Earths, Earthenware, and Glassware—Continued.				
112	Cylinder, crown, and common window glass, unpolished:				
	Not exceeding 10 by 15 inches square .lbs..	12,778,538	$370,140.49	$175,704.99	$0.029
	Above 10 by 15 inches, and not exceeding 16 by 24 inches ....lbs..	15,298,276	270,120.76	286,842.72	.018
	Above 16 by 24 inches, and not exceeding 24 by 30 inches ....lbs..	17,471,344	343,896.42	414,944.45	.020
	Above 24 by 30 inches, and not exceeding 24 by 36 inches ....lbs..	5,091,031	117,120.96	146,367.20	.023
	All above 24 by 36 inches ....lbs..	12,118,480	324,272.76	378,702.63	.027
113	Cylinder and crown glass, polished, unsilvered:				
	Not exceeding 16 by 24 inches square ....sq. ft..	67,073	13,368.00	2,682.92	.20
	Above 16 by 24 inches, and not exceeding 24 by 30 inches ......sq. ft..	162,710.67	35,394.00	9,762.64	.22
	Above 24 by 30 inches, and not exceeding 24 by 60 inches ......sq. ft..	130,853.50	40,992.00	26,170.70	.31
114	Plate glass, fluted, rolled, or rough (excess of 1 pound per square foot, dutiable at same rates):				
	Not exceeding 10 by 15 inches square ....sq. ft..	21,725	706.00	162.94	.032
	Above 10 by 15 inches, and not exceeding 16 by 24 inches......sq. ft..	83,210	587.00	332.10	.018
	Above 16 by 24 inches, and not exceeding 24 by 30 inches............sq. ft..	26,960	630.00	404.41	.023
	All above 24 by 30 inches..........sq. ft..	941,051	33,617.00	18,821.02	.041
	Plate glass, fluted, rolled, or rough, ground, smoothed, or otherwise obscured (excess of 1 pound per square foot, dutiable at same rates):				
	Not exceeding 16 by 24 inches square ....sq. ft..	1,860	449.00	93.00	.24
	Above 16 by 24 inches, and not exceeding 24 by 30 inches......sq. ft..	7,568	1,736.00	607.04	.23
	Above 24 by 30 inches, and not exceeding 24 by 60 inches......sq. ft..	1,977	1,029.00	494.25	.52
	All above 24 by 60 inches ....sq. ft..	3,629	1,987.00	1,814.50	.55
115	Plate glass, cast, polished, finished, or unfinished, and unsilvered:				
	Not exceeding 16 by 24 inches square ....sq. ft..	375,507.89	84,482.00	18,775.39	.23
	Above 16 by 24 inches, and not exceeding 24 by 30 inches............sq. ft..	1,638,407.92	394,526.00	131,072.64	.24
	Above 24 by 30 inches, and not exceeding 24 by 60 inches............sq. ft..	1,081,696.25	277,375.00	270,424.06	.26
	All above 24 by 60 inches.........sq. ft..	346,938.63	99,436.00	173,409.32	.29
116	Plate glass, cast, polished, silvered:				
	Not exceeding 16 by 24 inches square ....sq. ft..	52,785.15	15,530.00	3,167.11	.29
	Above 16 by 24 inches, and not exceeding 24 by 30 inches............sq. ft..	204,158.93	78,337.00	20,415.89	.38
	Above 24 by 30 inches, and not exceeding 24 by 60 inches............sq. ft..	1,507	1,015.00	527.45	.67
	All above 24 by 60 inches ....sq. ft..	326	390.00	195.60	1.21
	Cylinder and crown glass, polished, silvered, and looking-glass plates—				
	Not exceeding 16 by 24 inches ....sq. ft..	1,030,091.91	319,525.00	61,805.52	.31
	Above 16 by 24 inches, and not exceeding 24 by 30 inches ....sq. ft..	3,733,839.20	1,301,900.00	378,383.92	.35
	Above 24 by 30 inches, and not exceeding 24 by 60 inches............sq. ft..	847.50	596.00	296.63	.70
	All above 24 by 60 inches.........sq. ft..	58.50	80.00	35.10	1.37
118	Cylinder, crown, and common window glass, unpolished, when ground, obscured, frosted, sanded, enameled, beveled, etched, embossed, engraved, stained, colored, or otherwise ornamented or decorated:				
	Not exceeding 10 by 15 inches square ....lbs..	88,672	12,393.00	2,458.54	.14
	Above 10 by 15 inches, and not exceeding 16 by 24 inches................lbs..	67,324	2,895.00	1,551.85	.043

DUTIES COLLECTED UNDER EXISTING LAW, ETC.—Continued.

Duties estimated under—		Rates of duty under—			Average ad valorem under—			Paragraph.
House bill.	Senate bill.	Present law.	House bill.	Senate bill.	Present.	House bill.	Senate bill.	
					Per ct.	*Per ct.*	*Per ct.*	
$127,785.38	$143,758.55	1⅜ cts. per lb..	1 ct. per lb...	1⅛ cts. per lb .	47.47	34.48	38.79	112
152,982.76	172,105.61	1⅞ cts. per lb..	....do	....do	106.19	56.54	63.61	
196,552.02	218,201.80	2⅜ cts. per lb..	1⅛ cts. per lb..	1¼ cts. per lb..	120.66	57.15	63.51	
70,001.68	76,305.46	2⅞ cts. per lb..	1⅜ cts. per lb..	1½ cts. per lb..	124.97	50.73	65.19	
181,777.20	190,925.30	3⅜ cts. per lb..	1⅝ cts. per lb..	1⅝ cts. per lb..	116.79	56.04	60.73	
1,670.82	1,670.82	4 cts. per sq. ft.	2½ cts. per sq. foot.	2½ cts. per sq. foot.	20.07	12.50	12.50	113
6,508.42	6,508.42	6 cts. per sq. ft.	4 cts. per sq. ft.	4 cts. per sq. ft.	27.58	18.39	18.39	
19,628.03	19,628.03	20 cts. per sq. foot.	15 cts. per sq. foot.	15 cts. per sq. foot.	63.84	47.88	47.88	
162.94	162.94	¾ ct. per sq. ft.	¾ ct. per sq. ft.	¾ ct. per sq. ft.	23.08	23.08	23.08	114
249.08	249.08	1 ct. per sq. ft.	....do	....do	56.58	42.43	42.43	
209.01	209.61	1½ cts. per sq. foot.	1 ct. per sq. ft.	1 ct. per sq. ft.	64.19	42.90	42.90	
14,115.77	14,115.77	2 cts. per sq. ft.	1½ cts. per sq. foot.	1½ cts. per sq. foot.	48.74	36.51	36.51	
93.00	93.00	5 cts. per sq. ft.	5 cts. per sq. ft.	5 cts. per sq. ft.	20.76	20.76	20.76	
607.04	607.04	8 cts. per sq. ft.	8 cts. per sq. ft.	8 cts. per sq. ft.	34.97	34.97	34.97	
355.86	395.40	25 cts. per sq. foot.	18 cts. per sq. foot.	20 cts. per sq. foot.	48.03	34.56	38.50	
1,088.70	1,270.15	50 cts. per sq. foot.	30 cts. per sq. foot.	35 cts. per sq. foot.	91.32	54.78	63.91	
18,775.39	18,775.39	5 cts. per sq. ft.	5 cts. per sq. ft.	5 cts. per sq. ft.	22.22	22.22	22.22	115
131,072.64	131,072.64	8 cts. per sq. ft.	8 cts. per sq. ft.	8 cts. per sq. ft.	33.22	33.22	33.22	
194,705.33	216,330.25	25 c. per sq. ft.	18 c. per sq. ft.	20 c. per sq. ft.	97.49	70.02	77.80	
104,081.59	121,428.52	50 c. per sq. ft.	30 c. per sq. ft.	35 c. per sq. ft.	174.45	104.67	122.11	
3,107.11	3,107.11	6 c. per sq. ft.	6 c. per sq. ft.	6 c. per sq. ft.	20.39	20.39	20.39	116
20,415.89	20,415.89	10 c. per sq. ft.	10 c. per sq. ft.	10 c. per sq. ft.	26.06	26.06	26.06	
301.40	301.40	35 c. per sq. ft.	20 c. per sq. ft.	20 c. per sq. ft.	51.97	29.68	29.68	
114.10	114.10	60 c. per sq. ft.	35 c. per sq. ft.	35 c. per sq. ft.	49.39	28.80	28.80	
61,805.52	61,805.52	6 c. per sq. ft.	6 c. per sq. ft.	6 c. per sq. ft.	19.34	19.34	19.34	
373,383.92	373,383.92	10 c. per sq. ft	10 c. per sq. ft.	10 c. per sq. ft.	28.68	28.68	28.68	
169.50	169.50	35 c. per sq. ft.	20 c. per sq. ft.	20 c. per sq. ft.	49.77	28.44	28.44	
20.48	20.48	60 c. per sq. ft.	35 c. per sq. ft.	35 c. per sq. ft.	43.88	25.58	25.58	
2,126.02	2,126.02	1⅜ c. per lb. and 10 p. c.	1 cent per lb. and 10 p. c.	1 cent per lb. and 10 p. c.	19.84	17.15	17.15	118
962.74	962.74	1⅞ c. per lb. and 10 p. c.	....do	....do	53.60	33.25	33.25	

IMPORTED MERCHANDISE, 1893, WITH THE RATES AND

Paragraph.		Importations of fiscal year, June 30, 1893.			
		Quantities.	Values.	Duties.	Unit of value.
	SCHEDULE B.—EARTHS, EARTHENWARE, AND GLASSWARE—Continued.				
118	Cylinder crown and common window glass, unpolished, when ground, obscured, frosted, sanded, enameled, beveled, etched, embossed, engraved, stained, colored, or otherwise ornamented or decorated—Continued.				
	Above 16 by 24 inches, and not exceeding 24 by 30 inches..............lbs..	109,857	$2,728.00	$2,739.42	$0.026
	Above 24 by 30 inches, and not exceeding 24 by 36 inches..............lbs..	14,231	646.00	473.74	.045
	All above 24 by 36 inches..........lbs..	1,347,210	54,485.90	47,548.94	.040
	Cylinder and crown glass, polished, unsilvered, when ground, obscured, frosted, sanded, enameled, beveled, etched, embossed, engraved, stained, colored, or otherwise ornamented or decorated:				
	Not exceeding 16 by 24 inches square ....sq. ft..	1,289	344.00	85.96	.27
	Above 16 by 24 inches, and not exceeding 24 by 30 inches.............sq. ft..	1,434.83	395.00	125.59	.28
	Above 24 by 30 inches, but not exceeding 24 by 60 inches.............sq. ft..	427	166.00	102.00	.39
	Cylinder and crown glass, polished, silvered, when ground, obscured, frosted, sanded, enameled, beveled, etched, embossed, engraved, stained, colored, or otherwise ornamented or decorated:				
	Not exceeding 16 by 24 inches square ....sq. ft..	2,032.25	892.00	211.14	.44
	Above 16 by 24 inches, and not exceeding 24 by 30 inches............sq. ft..	3	5.00	.80	1.67
	Above 24 by 30 inches, and not exceeding 24 by 60 inches............sq. ft..	28	37.00	13.50	1.32
	All above 24 by 60 inches........sq. ft..	8	16.00	6.40	2.00
	Plate glass, cast, polished, silvered, when ground, obscured, frosted, sanded, enameled, beveled, etched, embossed, engraved, stained, colored, or otherwise ornamented or decorated:				
	Not exceeding 16 by 24 inches square ....sq. ft..	5,192	6,496.00	961.12	1.25
	Above 16 by 24 inches, and not exceeding 24 by 30 inches.............sq. ft..	64,350.53	32,936.48	9,728.68	.512
	Above 24 by 30 inches, and not exceeding 24 by 60 inches.............sq. ft..	39.50	131.00	26.92	3.31
	All above 24 by 60 inches........sq. ft..	57	116.00	45.80	2.04
	Plate glass, cast, polished, unsilvered, when ground, obscured, frosted, sanded, enameled, beveled, etched, embossed, engraved, stained, colored, or otherwise ornamented or decorated:				
	Not exceeding 16 by 24 inches square ....sq. ft..	22,931.25	7,896.00	1,936.17	.34
	Above 16 by 24 inches, and not exceeding 24 by 30 inches............sq. ft..	1,127.50	430.00	133.20	.38
	Above 24 by 30 inches, and not exceeding 24 by 60 inches............sq. ft..	208	94.00	61.40	.45
	All above 24 by 60 inches........sq. ft..	73	87.00	45.20	1.19
119	Spectacles and eyeglasses, or spectacles and eyeglass frames..................gross..	7,464.59	33,256.00	19,954.80	4.46
120	Lenses costing $1.50 per gross pairs, or less...................gross pairs..	350	507.00	304.20	1.45
121	Spectacle and eyeglass lenses with their edges ground or beveled to fit frames ....gross..	364	338.00	202.80	.98
122	Stained or painted window glass and stained or painted glass windows, and hand, pocket, or table mirrors not exceeding in size 144 square inches, with or without frames or cases, of whatever material composed....................	....	121,268.45	54,570.80	......
	Lenses of glass or pebble, wholly or partly manufactured, and not specially provided for, and fusible enamel.	....	88,083.48	39,637.56	......

DUTIES COLLECTED UNDER EXISTING LAW, ETC.—Continued.

Duties estimated under—		Rates of duty under—			Average ad valorem under—			Paragraph
House bill.	Senate bill.	Present law.	House bill.	Senate bill.	Present.	House bill.	Senate bill.	
					Per ct.	Per ct.	Per ct.	
$1,441.19	$1,441.19	2⅜ c. per lb. and 10 p. c.	1½ cts per lb. and 10 p. c.	1½ cts. per lb. and 10 p. c.	100.42	52.82	52.82	118
260.28	260.28	2⅝ c. per lb. and 10 p. c.	1⅜ cts. per lb. and 10 p. c.	1⅜ cts. per lb. and 10 p. c.	73.33	40.29	40.29	
25,656.74	25,656.74	3½ c. per lb. and 10 p. c.	1½ cts per lb. and 10 p. c.	1½ cts. per lb. and 10 p. c.	87.27	47.08	47.08	
66.62	66.62	4 c. per sq. ft. and 10 p. c.	2½ c. per sq. ft. and 10 p. c.	2½ cts. per sq. ft. and 10 p. c.	24.99	19.36	19.36	
96.89	96.89	6 c. per sq. ft. and 10 p. c.	4 c. per sq. ft. and 10 p. c.	4 cts per sq. ft. and 10 p. c.	31.79	24.60	24.60	
80.65	80.65	20 c. per sq. ft. and 10 p. c.	15 c. per sq. ft. and 10 p. c.	15 cts. per sq. ft. and 10 p. c.	61.45	48.58	48.58	
211.14	211.14	6 cts. p. sq. ft. and 10 p. ct.	6 cts. p. sq. ft. and 10 p. ct.	6 cts. p. sq. ft. and 10 p. ct.	23.07	23.67	23.67	
.80	.80	10 c. p. sq. ft. and 10 p. ct.	10 c. p. sq. ft. and 10 p. ct.	10 c. p. sq. ft. and 10 p. ct.	16	16	16	
9.30	9.30	35 c. p. sq. ft. and 10 p. ct.	20 c. p. sq. ft. and 10 p. ct.	20 c. p. sq. ft. and 10 p. ct.	36.40	25.13	25.13	
4.40	4.40	60 c. p. sq. ft. and 10 p. ct.	35 c. p. sq. ft. and 10 p. ct.	35 c. p. sq. ft. and 10 p. ct.	40	27.50	27.50	
961.12	961.12	6 c. p. sq. ft. and 10 p. ct.	6 c. p. sq. ft. and 10 p. ct.	6 c. p. sq. ft. and 10 p. ct.	14.80	14.80	14.80	
9,728.68	9,728.68	10 c. p. sq ft and 10 p. ct.	10 c. p. sq. ft. and 10 p. ct.	10 c. p. sq. ft. and 10 p. ct.	20.54	29.54	29.54	
21.00	21.00	35 c. p. sq. ft. and 10 p. ct.	20 c. p. sq. ft. and 10 p. ct.	20 c. p. sq. ft. and 10 p. ct.	20.55	16.03	16.03	
31.55	31.55	60 c. p. sq. ft. and 10 p. ct.	35 c. p. sq. ft. and 10 p. ct.	35 c. p. sq. ft. and 10 p. ct.	89.48	27.20	27.20	
1,936.17	1,936.17	5 c. p. sq. ft. and 10 p. ct.	5 c. p. sq. ft. and 10 p. ct.	5 c. p. sq. ft. and 10 p. ct.	24.52	24.52	24.52	
133.20	133.20	8 c. p. sq. ft. and 10 p. ct.	8 c. p. sq. ft. and 10 p. ct.	8 c. p. sq. ft. and 10 p. ct.	30.98	30.98	30.98	
46.84	46.84	25 c. p. sq. ft. and 10 p. ct.	20 c. p. sq. ft. and 10 p. ct.	20 c. p. sq. ft. and 10 p. ct.	65.32	49.83	49.83	
30.60	30.60	50 c. p sq. ft. and 10 p. ct.	30 c. p. sq. ft. and 10 p. ct.	30 c. p. sq. ft. and 10 p. ct.	51.95	35.17	35.17	
11,640.30	11,640.30	60 per cent...	35 per cent...	35 per cent...	60	35	35	119
177.45	177.45	....do	....do	....do	60	35	35	120
118.30	118.30	....do	....do	....do	60	35	35	121
42,443.96	42,443.96	45 per cent...	35 per cent...	35 per cent...	45	35	35	122
30,829.21	30,829.21	....do	....do	....do	45	35	35	

Paragraph.		Importations of fiscal year, June 30, 1893.			
		Quantities.	Values.	Duties.	Unit of value.
	SCHEDULE B.—EARTHS, EARTHENWARE, AND GLASSWARE—Continued.				
	Marble and stone, and manufactures of marble—				
123	In block, rough or squared, of all kinds, cu. ft	457,600.33	$758,749.60	$297,440.15	$1.66
124	Veined marble, sawed, dressed, or otherwise, including marble slabs and marble paving tiles ....cu. ft..	110,208.72	199,064.87	121,220.65	1.81
125	All manufactures of, not specially provided for	....	177,361.76	88,680.88	....
	Clocks, marble, chief value	....	76,603.00	38,301.50	....
127	Freestone, granite, sandstone, limestone, and other building or monumental stone, except marble, not specially provided for—				
128	Hewn, dressed, or polished	....	439,147.96	175,659.18	....
129	Grindstones, finished or unfinished..tons..	5,235.17	66,656.47	9,161.56	12.73
130	Slates, slate chimney pieces, mantels, slabs for tables, and all other manufactures of slate	....	6,671.31	2,001.39	....
131	Slates, roofing	....	1,878.00	469.50	....
	Total Schedule B, earths, earthenware, and glassware	....	23,513,506.16	12,101,061.60	....
	SCHEDULE C.—METALS AND MANUFACTURES OF.				
	Iron ores:				
133	All other ore ....tons..	677,301.57	1,189,035.75	507,976.19	1.76
134	Iron in pigs, kentledge, spiegeleisen, ferromanganese,* and ferrosilicon—				
	Ferrosilicon ....tons..	255	6,427.00	1,713.60	25.20
	Speigeleisen and ferromanganese..tons..	49,157.00	1,273,463.00	330,335.69	25.93
	All other........tons..	13,231.83	217,211.99	88,917.97	16.41
	Scrap iron and steel, waste or refuse, fit only to be remanufactured—				
	Iron, wrought and cast........tons..	14,330.80	201,348.88	96,303.00	14.05
	Steel ....tons..	5,831.33	91,134.00	39,186.51	15.63
135	Rolled or hammered, comprising—				
	Flats not less than 1 inch wide nor less than ⅜ of 1 inch thick........lbs..	322,078	7,098.50	2,576.63	.022
	Round iron not less than ¾ of 1 inch in diameter, and square iron not less than ¾ of 1 inch square........lbs..	2,160,170	79,115.00	19,441.53	.037
	Flats less than 1 inch wide or less than ⅜ of 1 inch thick; round iron less than ¾ of 1 inch and not less than 7/16 of 1 inch in diameter; and square iron less than ¾ of 1 inch square........lbs..	404,773	7,691.30	4,047.73	.019
136	Bars or shapes of rolled iron not specially provided for, and round iron, in coils or rods, less than 7/16 of 1 inch in diameter, lbs	276,274	4,918.90	3,038.56	.018
	Bars, blooms, billets, or sizes or shapes of any kind, in the manufacture of which charcoal is used as fuel........tons..	15,710.50	608,243.37	345,631.04	38.72
	All other, and slabs, blooms, or loops...lbs..	10,195	615.00	215.25	.060
137	Beams, girders, joists, angles, channels, car-truck channels, TT columns and posts, or parts or sections of columns and posts, deck and bulb beams, and building forms, together with all other structural shapes, of iron or steel ....lbs..	11,241,473	135,546.80	101,173.30	.012
138	Boiler or other plate iron or steel (except saw plates), not thinner than No. 10 wire gauge, sheared or unsheared, and skelp iron or steel sheared or rolled in grooves—				
	Valued above 1 cent and not above 1 4/10 cents per pound ....lbs..	702,854	9,229.00	4,565.30	.013
	Valued above 1 4/10 cents and not above 2 cents per pound ....lbs..	33,288	490.00	266.30	.015

* No data for ferromanganese.

DUTIES COLLECTED UNDER EXISTING LAW, ETC.—Continued.

Duties estimated under—		Rates of duty under—			Average ad valorem under—			Paragraph.
House bill.	Senate bill.	Present law.	House bill.	Senate bill.	Present.	House bill.	Senate bill.	
					Per ct.	*Per ct.*	*Per ct.*	
$183,040.13	$183,040.13	65 cents per cubic foot.	40 cents per cubic foot.	40 cents per cubic foot.	39.20	24.12	24.12	123
82,656.54	82,656.54	75 cents per cubic foot.	75 cents per cubic foot.	75 cents per cubic foot.	60.90	41.47	41.47	124
53,208.53	53,208.53	50 per cent..	30 per cent...	30 per cent...	50	30	30	125
19,150.75	19,150.75	....do	25 per cent...	25 per cent...	50	25	25	127
87,829.59	87,829.59	40 per cent ..	20 per cent...	20 per cent...	40	20	20	128
9,161.56	6,665.64	$1.75 per ton.	$1.75 per ton.	10 per cent...	13.74	13.74	10	129
1,333.12	1,333.12	30 per cent...	20 per cent...	20 per cent...	30	20	20	130
187.80	375.60	25 per cent...	10 per cent...	....do	25	10	20	131
8,078,228.11	8,731,495.09				51.46	34.37	37.13	
....	270,920.62	75 cents per ton.	Free	40 cents per ton.	42.70	Free.	22.77	133
1,285.40	1,446.07	$6.72 per ton.	20 per cent...	22½ per cent..	26.66	20	22.5	134
254,602.60	286,529.17	....do	{20 per cent.. 10 per cent...	22 per cent... 10 per cent...	} 25.54	{20 10	22.5 10	
43,442.40	48,872.70	....do	20 per cent...	22½ per cent..	40.94	20	22.5	
20,134.88	20,134.88	....do	10 per cent...	10 per cent...	47.83	10	10	
9,113.40	9,113.40	....do	....do	....do	43	10	10	
1,774.62	1,774.62	₁⁄₁₀ c. per lb...	25 per cent...	25 per cent...	36.30	25	25	135
19,778.75	19,778.75	₁⁄₁₀ c. per lb...	....do	....do	24.57	25	25	
1,922.82	1,922.82	1 cent per lb..	....do	....do	52.63	25	25	
1,377.29	1,229.72	1¹⁄₁₀ c. per lb..	....do	28 per cent...	61.77	25	28	136
152,060.84	152,060.84	$22 per ton....	....do	25 per cent...	56.82	25	25	
133.37	153.75	35 per cent...	22½ per cent..	....do	35	22½	25	
40,964.04	47,441.38	₁⁄₁₀ c. per lb. .	30 per cent...	35 per cent...	74.64	30	35	137
2,307.25	2,768.70	₁⁵⁄₁₀₀ c.per lb...	25 per cent...	30 per cent...	49.47	25	30	138
122.50	147.60	₁⁄₁₀ c. per lb...	....do	....do	54.35	25	30	

IMPORTED MERCHANDISE, 1893, WITH THE RATES AND

Paragraph.		Importations of fiscal year, June 30, 1893.			
		Quantities.	Values.	Duties.	Unit of value.
	SCHEDULE C.—METALS AND MANUFACTURES OF—Continued.				
138	Boiler or other plate iron or steel (except saw plates), not thinner than No. 10 wire gauge sheared or unsheared, and skelp iron or steel sheared or rolled in grooves—Continued.				
	Valued above 2 cents and not above 3 cents per pound..................lbs..	94,476	$2,338.00	$1,039.23	$0.025
	Valued above 3 cents and not above 4 cents per pound..................lbs..	3,517	130.00	52.76	.037
	Valued above 4 cents and not above 7 cents per pound..................lbs..	70,814.50	3,750.00	1,416.20	.053
	Valued above 7 cents and not above 10 cents per pound..................lbs..	47,932	4,326.00	1,342.10	.090
	Valued above 10 cents and not above 13 cents per pound..................lbs..	1,272	139.00	44.52	.11
	Valued above 13 cents per pound....lbs..	10,690	1,425.00	641.25	.13
139	Forgings of iron or steel, or forged iron and steel combined, not specially provided for.............................. lbs..	27,814	1,423.00	639.70	.051
140	Hoop, band, or scroll, or other iron or steel, valued at 3 cents per pound or less, 8 inches or less in width and less than ⅜ of 1 inch thick—				
	Not thinner than No. 10 wire gauge..lbs..	238,798	5,225.00	2,387.98	.022
	Thinner than No. 10 and not thinner than No. 20 wire gauge..........lbs..	241,137	6,406.00	2,652.50	.027
	Thinner than No. 20 wire gauge....lbs..	4,201,253	112,655.44	55,786.30	.026
141	Bars or rails for railways—				
	Flat rails, punched—				
	Iron or steel..................tons..	7	212.00	94.08	30.29
	T-rails and other railway bars—				
	Iron........................tons..	3.02	81.06	40.00	26.84
	Steel, or in part of steel......tons..	1,534.91	35,421.33	20,629.23	23.08
142	Sheets of iron or steel, common or black, including iron or steel known as common or black taggers iron or steel, and skelp iron or steel, valued at 3 cents per pound or less—				
	Thinner than No. 10 and not thinner than No. 20 wire gauge............lbs..	664,862	13,596.50	6,648.02	.020
	Thinner than No. 20 and not thinner than No. 25 wire gauge............lbs..	231,318	6,447.60	2,544.50	.025
	Thinner than No. 25 wire gauge......lbs..	7,909,002	159,424.00	111,985.06	.020
	Corrugated or crimped..............lbs..	82,222	4,561.00	1,151.11	.053
143	Sheets or plates of iron or steel (excepting what are commercially known as tin plates, terne plates, and taggers tin), galvanized or coated with zinc or spelter, or other metals, or any alloy of these metals—				
	Thinner than No. 10 and not thinner than No. 20 wire gauge........lbs..	9,577	414.00	167.60	.043
	Thinner than No. 20 and not thinner than No. 25 wire gauge..........lbs..	217,234	5,528.00	4,018.84	.025
	Thinner than No. 25 wire gauge......lbs..	25,274	1,109.00	543.39	.044
144	Sheets and plates pickled or cleaned by acid, or by any other material or process, and cold rolled, smoothed, not polished—				
	Thinner than No. 10 and not thinner than No 20 wire gauge............lbs..	114,255	4,112.00	1,428.19	.026
	Thinner than No. 20 and not thinner than No. 25 wire gauge..........lbs..	784,633	23,832.00	10,592.55	.030
	Thinner than No. 25 wire gauge......lbs..	5,002,025	113,387.00	82,533.43	.023
	Sheet iron or sheet steel, polished, planished, or glanced..........................lbs..	894,670	48,698.00	22,360.76	.054
145	Tin plates:* Sheets or plates of iron or steel, or taggers iron, or steel coated with tin or lead, or with a mixture of which these metals are a component part, by the dipping or any other process, and commercially known as tin plates, terne plates, and taggers tin—				
	Lighter than 63 pounds per 100 square feet..........................lbs..	595,031,588	16,091,765.10	13,090,603.75	.028
	All other.........................lbs..	18,648,452	560,453.91	410,265.91	.030

*Tin plate, the new rate to take effect on and after Oct. 1, 1894.

DUTIES COLLECTED UNDER EXISTING LAW, ETC.—Continued.

Duties estimated under—		Rates of duty under—			Average ad valorem under—			Paragraph.
House bill.	Senate bill.	Present law.	House bill.	Senate bill.	Present.	House bill.	Senate bill.	
					Per ct.	*Per ct.*	*Per ct.*	
584.50	701.40	1 7/10 cts. per lb.	25 per cent...	30 per cent...	44.45	25	30	
32.50	39.00	1 4/10 cts. per lb.	....do.........	....do.........	40.58	25	30	
937.50	1,125.00	2 cts. per lb..	....do.........	....do.........	37.77	25	30	
1,081.50	1,297.80	2 3/10 cents per pound.	25 per cent...	30 per cent...	31.02	25	30	
34.75	41.70	3 1/4 cts. per lb.	....do.........	....do.........	32.03	25	30	
356.25	427.50	45 per cent...	....do.........	....do.........	45	25	30	
355.75	426.90	2 7/10 cents per pound.	....do.........	....do.........	44.95	25	30	139
1,306.25	1,507.50	1 cent per pound.	....do.........	....do.........	45.70	25	30	140
1,001.50	1,921.80	1 1/10 cents per pound.	....do.........	....do.........	41.41	25	30	
28,163.86	33,796.63	1 7/10 cents per pound.	....do.........	....do.........	49.52	25	30	
42.40	47.70	$13.44 per ton	20 per cent...	22 1/2 per cent...	44.38	20	22.50	141
16.21	18.24	....do.........	....do.........	....do.........	50.09	20	22.50	
7,084.26	7,569.80	....do.........	....do.........	....do.........	58.24	20	22.50	
4,758.77	4,758.77	1 cent per pound.	35 per cent...	35 per cent...	48.90	35	35	142
2,256.66	2,256.66	1 7/10 cts. per lb.	....do.........	....do.........	39.46	35	35	
55,798.40	55,798.40	1 7/10 cts. per lb.	....do.........	....do.........	70.24	35	35	
1,596.35	1,596.35	....do.........	....do.........	....do.........	25.24	35	35	
144.90	144.90	1 1/2 cts. per lb.	35 per cent...	35 per cent...	40.48	35	35	143
1,934.80	1,934.80	1 70/100 c. per lb	....do.........	....do.........	72.70	35	35	
383.15	383.15	2 10/100 c. per lb	....do.........	....do.........	40	35	35	
1,439.20	1,439.20	1 1/4 cts. per lb..	35 per cent..	35 per cent...	34.73	35	35	144
8,341.20	8,341.20	1 70/100 c. per lb	....do.........	....do.........	44.46	35	35	
39,085.45	35,015.19	1 70/100 c. per lb	....do.........	1/2 cent per lb.	72.79	35.78	30.88	
17,044.30	17,044.30	2 1/2 cts. per lb..	....do.........	35 per cent...	45.98	35	35	
7,140,378.45	5,950,315.38	2 7/10 c. per lb	1 1/2 cts. per lb.	1 cent per lb.	78.44	42.32	35.65	145
223,783.42	186,484.52	....do.........	....do.........	....do.........	73.20	39.86	33.27	

158

IMPORTED MERCHANDISE, 1893, WITH THE RATES AND

Paragraph.		Importations of fiscal year, June 30, 1893.			
		Quantities.	Values.	Duties.	Unit of value.
	SCHEDULE C.—METALS AND MANUFACTURES OF—Continued.				
	Tin, manufactures of—				
	All manufactures of, not specially provided for......:	....	$35,426.55	$19,484.60	....
	Foil..	....	31,326.00	17,229.30	....
146	Steel ingots, cogged ingots, blooms, and slabs, by whatever process made; die blocks or blanks; billets and bars and tapered or beveled bars; steamer, crank, and other shafts; shafting; wrist or crank pins; connecting rods and piston rods; pressed, sheared, or stamped shapes; hammer molds or swaged steel; gun-barrel molds, not in bars; alloys used as substitutes for steel tools; all descriptions and shapes of dry-sand, loam, or iron-molded steel castings; and steel in all forms and shapes not specially provided for:				
	Valued at 1 cent per pound or less..lbs..	49,250,843	390,244.00	197,003.39	$0.008
	Valued at 1 cent and not above 1 7/10 cents per pound........................lbs..	6,544,056	83,760.00	32,723.32	.013
	Valued above 1 7/10 cents and not above 1 7/10 cents per pound ....lbs..	3,174,225	48,134.00	25,393.81	.015
	Valued above 1 7/10 cents, and not above 2 7/10 cents per pound................lbs..	267,906	4,398.00	2,411.60	.020
	Valued above 2 7/10 cents and not above 3 cents per pound ....lbs..	960,637	20,741.00	11,527.64	.028
	Valued above 3 cents and not above 4 cents per pound ....lbs..	2,870,033	110,535.00	45,920.51	.039
	Valued above 4 cents and not above 7 cents per pound ....lbs..	2,261,620	126,930.00	45,232.40	.056
	Valued above 7 cents and not above 10 cents per pound...............lbs..	7,212,737	665,258.27	201,956.37	.092
	Valued above 10 cents and not above 13 cents per pound ....lbs..	316,088	36,787.90	11,063.11	.12
	Valued above 13 cents and not above 16 cents per pound ....lbs..	184,485	26,371.00	7,748.37	.14
	Valued above 16 cents per pound ...lbs..	368,394.50	83,850.00	25,737.02	.23
	Sheets and plates and saw plates of steel, not specially provided for:				
	Valued above 1 cent and not above 1 7/10 cents per pound ....lbs..	33,129	366.00	165.64	.012
	Valued above 1 7/10 cents and not above 1 7/10 cents per pound ....lbs..	5,593	93.00	44.74	.016
	Valued above 1 7/10 cents and not above 2 7/10 cents per pound ....lbs..	31,500	684.00	283.50	.022
	Valued above 2 7/10 cents and not above 3 cents per pound................lbs..	404,249	11,194.94	4,850.97	.028
	Valued above 3 cents and not above 4 cents per pound...................lbs..	165,819	5,360.56	2,653.10	.032
	Valued above 4 cents and not above 7 cents per pound ....lbs..	172,607	10,886.00	3,452.14	.063
	Valued above 7 cents and not above 10 cents per pound...............lbs..	160,626	13,523.00	4,497.53	.084
	Valued above 10 cents and not above 13 cents per pound ....lbs..	62	7.00	2.17	.11
	Valued above 13 cents and not above 16 cents per pound ....lbs..	596	84.00	25.04	.14
	Valued above 16 cents per pound ...lbs..	15,858	4,479.00	1,110.06	.28
147	Wire rods:				
	Rivet, screw, fence, and other iron or steel wire rods, whether round, oval, flat, square, or in any other shape, in coils or otherwise, not smaller than No. 6 wire gauge, valued at 3½ cents or less per pound.........................lbs..	93,533,316	1,650,807.05	561,190.86	.018
	Flat iron or steel with longitudinal ribs, for the manufacture of fencing, valued at 3 cents or less per pound.......lbs..	1,533,286	27,026.00	9,199.72	.018
148	Wire of iron or steel:				
	Flat steel wire or sheet steel in strips of any width, whether drawn through dies or rolls, untempered or tempered, 1 8/10 of an inch thick or thinner....lbs..	317,225	39,827.00	19,913.50	.13

159

DUTIES COLLECTED UNDER EXISTING LAW, ETC.—Continued.

Duties estimated under—		Rates of duty under—			Average ad valorem under—			Paragraph.
House bill.	Senate bill.	Present law.	House bill.	Senate bill.	Present.	House bill.	Senate bill.	
					Per ct.	*Per ct.*	*Per ct.*	
$12,349.29	$12,349.29	55 per cent...	35 per cent...	35 per cent...	55	35	35	
10,964.10	10,964.10	....do	....do	....do	55	35	35	146
97,561.00	97,561.00	$\frac{7}{10}$ ct. per lb..	25 per cent...	25 per cent...	50.48	25	25	
20,942.25	20,942.35	$\frac{7}{10}$ ct. per lb..	....do	....do	39.06	25	25	
12,033.50	12,033.50	$\frac{7}{10}$ ct. per lb..	....do	....do	52.76	25	25	
1,349.50	1,349.50	$\frac{7}{10}$ ct. per lb..	....do	....do	44.68	25	25	
6,685.25	6,685.25	$1\frac{7}{10}$ cts. per lb.	....do	....do	43.11	25	25	
25,133.75	25,133.75	$1\frac{7}{10}$ cts. per lb.	....do	....do	41.54	25	25	
31,732.50	31,732.50	2 cts. per lb..	....do	....do	35.64	25	25	
106,314.57	106,314.57	$2\frac{7}{10}$ cts. per lb.	....do	....do	30.36	25	25	
9,196.97	9,196.97	$3\frac{1}{2}$ cts. per lb..	....do	....do	30.07	25	25	
6,502.75	6,502.75	$4\frac{7}{10}$ cts. per lb.	....do	....do	29.33	25	25	
20,932.50	20,902.50	7 cts. per lb..	....do	....do	30.75	25	25	
96.50	96.50	$\frac{7}{10}$ ct. per lb..	....do	....do	42.91	25	25	
23.25	23.25	$\frac{7}{10}$ ct. per lb..	....do	....do	48.11	25	25	
171.00	171.00	$\frac{7}{10}$ ct. per lb..	....do	....do	41.45	25	25	
2,798.73	2,798.73	$1\frac{7}{10}$ cts. per lb.	....do	....do	43.33	25	25	
1,340.14	1,340.14	$1\frac{7}{10}$ cts. per lb.	....do	....do	49.48	25	25	
2,721.50	2,721.50	2 cts. per lb..	....do	....do	31.71	25	25	
3,380.75	3,380.75	$2\frac{7}{10}$ cts. per lb.	....do	....do	33.26	25	25	
1.75	1.75	$3\frac{1}{2}$ cts. per lb.	....do	....do	31	25	25	
21.00	21.00	$4\frac{7}{10}$ cts. per lb.	....do	....do	29.81	25	25	
1,119.75	1,119.75	7 cts. per lb..	....do	....do	24.78	25	25	147
412,701.76	412,701.76	$\frac{7}{10}$ ct. per lb..	....do	....do	34	25	25	
6,756.50	6,756.50	....do	....do	....do	34.04	25	25	148
11,948.10	11,948.10	50 per cent...	30 per cent...	30 per cent...	50	30	30	

TA——11

IMPORTED MERCHANDISE, 1893, WITH THE RATES AND

Paragraph.		Importations of fiscal year, June 30, 1893.			
		Quantities.	Values.	Duties.	Unit of value.
	SCHEDULE C.—METALS AND MANUFACTURES OF—Continued.				
	Wire of iron or steel—Continued. Flat steel wire or sheet steel in strips of any width, whether drawn through dies or rolls, untempered or tempered, $\frac{1}{16}$ of an inch thick or thinner, cold-rolled, cold-hammered, blued, brightened, tempered, or polished by any process to such perfected surface finish or polish better than the grade of cold-rolled, smooth only, hereinbefore provided for—				
	Not smaller than No. 10 wire gauge............lbs..	2,605,644	$100,092.00	$32,570.55	$0.033
	Smaller than No. 10 and not smaller than No. 16 wire gauge.......lbs..	2,798,335	100,409.00	48,070.80	.036
	Smaller than No. 16 and not smaller than No. 26 wire gauge........lbs..	21,178	1,037.00	476.51	.049
	Smaller than No. 26 wire gauge..lbs..	5,633.50	648.00	169.01	.12
	Coated with zinc or tin or any other metal (except fence wire and iron or steel, flat, with longitudinal ribs, for the manufacture of fencing)—				
	Not smaller than No. 10 wire gauge ....lbs..	684	25.00	11.97	.037
	Smaller than No. 10 and not smaller than No. 16 wire gauge.......lbs..	8,867	199.00	199.51	.022
	Smaller than No. 26 wire gauge..lbs..	504	112.00	17.64	.22
	Wire of iron or steel, covered with cotton, silk, or other material, and wires or strip steel commonly known as crinoline, corset, and hat wire............lbs..	127,637	38,310.00	6,381.85	.30
	Wire of iron or steel, valued at more than 4 cents per pound (on which the specific duty does not amount to 45 per cent)..lbs..	1,755,084	208,446.00	93,500.70	.12
	— Do., galvanized..................lbs..	216	12.00	6.48	.031
	Wire, cord, for the manufacture of card clothing ....lbs..	350,967	63,372.00	23,930.20	.18
	Wire rope and wire strand:				
	Made of iron wire—				
	Smaller than No. 10 and not smaller than No. 16 wire gauge.......lbs..	5,700	212.00	156.76	.037
	Smaller than No. 16 and not smaller than No. 26 wire gauge........lbs..	71,440	4,034.00	2,321.79	.056
	Smaller than No. 26 wire gauge..lbs..	2,398	362.00	95.92	.15
	Do ....lbs..	16,491	985.00	603.16	.060
	Galvanized—				
	Smaller than No. 10 and not smaller than No. 16 wire gauge ....lbs..	12,467	456.00	405.17	.037
	Smaller than No. 16 and not smaller than No. 26 wire gauge..	2,220	148.00	83.32	.067
	Smaller than No. 26 wire gauge ....lbs..	47,620	2,471.00	2,142.90	.052
	Do ....lbs..	4,439	353.00	235.43	.080
	Made of steel wire—				
	Not smaller than No. 10 wire gauge ....lbs..	28,793	1,397.00	935.77	.049
	Smaller than No. 10 and not smaller than No. 16 wire gauge.......lbs..	129,035	8,485.00	4,838.80	.066
	Smaller than No. 16 and not smaller than No. 26 wire gauge........lbs..	230,467	20,551.00	9,794.81	.089
	Smaller than No. 26 wire gauge..lbs..	41	15.00	2.05	.37
	Galvanized—				
	Not smaller than No. 10 wire gauge ....lbs..	2,237	104.00	83.68	.046
	Smaller than No. 10 and not smaller than No. 16 wire gauge ....lbs..	4,010	191.00	208.67	.039
	Smaller than No. 16 and not smaller than No. 26 wire gauge ....lbs..	18,576	1,140.00	882.30	.061

DUTIES COLLECTED UNDER EXISTING LAW, ETC.—Continued.

Duties estimated under—		Rates of duty under—			Average ad valorem under—			Paragraph.
House bill.	Senate bill.	Present law.	House bill.	Senate bill.	Present.	House bill.	Senate bill.	
					Per ct.	*Per ct.*	*Per ct.*	
$30,027.60	$30,027.60	1¼ cts. per lb.	30 per cent	30 per cent	32.54	30	30	
30,122.70	30,122.70	1¾ cts. per lb.	do	do	48.77	20	30	
311.10	311.10	2¼ cts. per lb.	do	do	45.95	30	30	
194.40	194.40	3 cts. per lb.	do	do	26.08	30	30	
7.50	7.50	1¾ cts. per lb.	do	do	47.88	30	30	
59.70	59.70	2¼ cts. per lb.	do	do	98.25	30	30	
33.60	33.60	3½ cts. per lb.	do	do	15.75	30	30	
11,493.00	11,493.00	5 cts. per lb.	do	do	16.66	30	30	
62,538.80	62,538.80	45 per cent	do	do	45	30	30	
3.60	3.60	45 per cent + ½ ct. per lb.	do	do	54	30	30	
20,511.60	20,511.60	35 per cent	do	do	35	30	30	
74.20	74.20	2¾ cts. per lb.	35 per cent	35 per cent	73.94	35	35	
1,411.90	1,411.90	3¼ cts. per lb.	do	do	57.56	35	35	
126.70	126.70	4 cts. per lb.	do	do	26.50	35	35	
344.75	344.75	45 per cent + 1 ct. per lb.	do	do	61.74	35	35	
159.60	159.60	3¼ cts. per lb.	do	do	88.85	35	35	
51.80	51.80	3¾ cts. per lb.	do	do	53.60	35	35	
864.85	864.85	4½ cts. per lb.	do	do	86.72	35	35	
123.55	123.55	45 per cent + 1½ c. per lb.	do	do	63.86	35	35	
488.95	488.95	3½ cts. per lb.	do	do	66.08	35	35	
2,969.75	2,969.75	3¾ cts. per lb.	do	do	57.02	35	35	
7,192.85	7,192.85	4½ cts. per lb.	do	do	47.06	35	35	
5.25	5.25	5 cts. per lb.	do	do	13.67	35	35	
36.40	36.40	3¾ cts. per lb.	do	do	80.65	35	35	
66.85	66.85	4½ cts per lb.	do	do	109.25	35	35	
390.00	390.00	4¾ cts. per lb.	do	do	77.40	35	35	

IMPORTED MERCHANDISE, 1893, WITH THE RATES AND

Paragraph.		Importations of fiscal year, June 30, 1893.			
		Quantities.	Values.	Duties.	Unit of value.
	SCHEDULE C.—METALS AND MANUFACTURES OF—Continued.				
	Wire rope and wire strand—Continued. Made of steel wire—Continued. Smaller than No. 26 wire gauge ....lbs..	2,675	$182.00	$147.12	$0.068
	Not smaller than No. 5 wire gauge, cold-rolled, cold-hammered, or polished in addition to the ordinary process of hot-rolling or hammering.....lbs..	483,421	18,903.00	18,174.77	.039
	Wire cloths and wire nettings, made in meshes of any form, from iron or steel wire—				
	Not smaller than No. 10 wire gauge.lbs..	244	10.00	7.93	.041
	Galvanized— Smaller than No. 10 and not smaller than No. 16 wire gauge ....lbs..	606	122.00	30.30	.20
52	Steel ingots, cogged ingots, blooms, and slabs, by whatever process made; die blocks or blanks; billets and bars and tapered or beveled bars; steamer, crank, and other shafts; shafting; wrist or crank pins; connecting rods and piston rods; pressed, sheared, or stamped shapes; hammer molds or swaged steel; gun-barrel molds, not in bars; alloys used as substitutes for steel tools; all descriptions and shapes of dry-sand, loam, or iron-molded steel castings; and steel in all forms and shapes not specially provided for, cold-rolled, cold-hammered, or polished in anyway in addition to the ordinary process of hot rolling or hammering: Valued above 7 cents and not above 10 cents per pound ....lbs..	96	8.00	2.03	.83
	Valued above 13 cents and not above 16 cents per pound ....lbs..	33,464	5,063.00	1,489.16	.15
	Valued above 16 cents per pound...lbs..	47,295.25	13,205.00	3,428.90	.28
	Boiler or other plate iron or steel (except saw plates), not thinner than No. 10 wire gauge, sheared or unsheared, and skelp iron or steel, sheared or rolled in grooves, cold-rolled, cold-hammered, or polished in addition to the ordinary process of hot rolling or hammering— Valued above 2 cents and not above 3 cents per pound..............lbs..	1,116	27.00	15.07	.024
	Valued above 3 cents and not above 4 cents per pound ....lbs..	137	5.00	2.40	.036
	Sheets of iron or steel, common or black, including iron or steel known as common or black taggers' iron or steel, and skelp iron or steel, valued at 3 cents per pound or less, cold-rolled, cold-hammered, or polished in anyway in addition to the ordinary process of hot rolling or hammering— Thinner than No. 10 and not thinner than No. 20 wire gauge........lbs..	151,542	4,543.00	1,804.28	.030
	Thinner than No. 20 and not thinner than No. 25 wire gauge........lbs..	2,244,708	54,493.00	30,303.54	.025
	Thinner than No. 25 wire gauge.lbs..	54,823,318	1,138,277.58	904,584.75	.021
	Sheets and plates and saw plates of steel, not specially provided for, cold-rolled, cold-hammered, or polished in anyway in addition to the ordinary process of hot rolling or hammering— Valued above 16 cents per pound.lbs..	4,840	1,125.00	350.91	.23

DUTIES COLLECTED UNDER EXISTING LAW, ETC.—Continued.

Duties estimated under—		Rates of duty under—			Average ad valorem under—			Paragraph.
House bill.	Senate bill.	Present law.	House bill.	Senate bill.	Present.	House bill.	Senate bill.	
					Per ct.	Per ct.	Per ct.	
$63.70	$63.70	5¼ cts. per lb.	35 per cent...	35 per cent...	80.84	35	35	
6,616.05	6,616.05	45 p.c.+2 cts per pound.	....do	....do	90.15	35	35	
3.50	3.50	3¼ cts. per lb.	....do	....do	70.30	35	35	
42.70	42.70	4½ cts.+⅛ ct. per pound.	....do	....do	24.84	35	35	52
2.80	2.80	2⁸⁄₁₀ cts.+¼ ct. per pound.	....do	....do	36.03	35	35	
1,772.05	1,772.05	4⁷⁄₁₀ cts. per lb.	....do	....do	29.41	35	35	
4,642.75	4,642.75	7 cts. per lb.	....do	....do	25.85	35	35	
9.45	9.45	1⁷⁄₁₀ cts.+¼ ct. per lb.	....do	....do	55.81	35	35	
1.75	1.75	1⁷⁄₁₀ cts.+¼ ct. per lb.	....do	....do	48	35	35	
1,590.05	1,590.05	1¼ cts. per lb.	....do	....do	41.70	35	35	
19,072.55	19,072.55	1⁵⁵⁄₁₀₀ cts. per lb.	....do	....do	55.61	35	35	
396,397.15	411,174.89	1¹⁵⁄₁₀₀ cts. per lb.	....do	⅜ cent per lb..	79.47	35	35	
393.75	393.75	7 cts. + ¼ ct. per lb.	....do	35 per cent...	31.19	35	35	

IMPORTED MERCHANDISE, 1893, WITH THE RATES AND

Paragraph.		Importations of fiscal year, June 30, 1893.			
		Quantities.	Values.	Duties.	Unit of value.
	SCHEDULE C.—METALS AND MANUFACTURES OF—Continued.				
	Steel ingots, cogged ingots, etc.—Continued. Sheets and plates and saw plates of steel, not specially provided for, cold rolled, cold hammered, blued, brightened, tempered, or polished by any process to such perfected surface finish or polish better than the grade of cold rolled, smooth only, hereinbefore provided for—				
	Valued above 4 cents and not above 7 cents per pound............lbs..	1,742	$113.00	$56.02	$0.065
	Valued above 7 cents and not above 10 cents per pound............lbs..	267	21.00	10.81	.079
	Valued above 10 cents and not above 13 cents per pound............lbs..	2,077	233.00	98.60	.11
	Valued above 13 cents and not above 16 cents per pound............lbs..	19,137	2,976.00	1,042.94	.16
	Valued above 16 cents per pound.lbs..	8,152	4,386.00	672.55	.54
	Steel circular-saw plates— Valued above 4 cents and not above 7 cents per pound............lbs..	102,333	6,042.00	3,069.99	.059
	Valued above 7 cents and not above 10 cents per pound............lbs..	277,788	26,740.00	10,555.94	.096
	Valued above 10 cents and not above 13 cents per pound............lbs..	81,990.50	10,251.00	3,689.60	.12
153	Anchors or parts thereof, mill irons and mill cranks, of wrought iron, and wrought iron for ships, and forgings of iron or steel, for vessels, steam engines, and locomotives, or parts thereof, weighing each 25 pounds or more..................................lbs..	467,677	25,545.96	8,418.17	.055
154	Axles or parts thereof, axle bars, axle blanks, or forgings for axles, of iron or steel, without reference to the stage or state of manufacture........................lbs..	118,181	8,640.50	2,363.02	.073
155	Anvils...........................lbs..	1,762,449	112,855.57	44,061.24	.064
156	Hammers and sledges (blacksmiths'), track tools, wedges, and crowbars, of iron or steel...............................lbs..	3,065	189.00	68.98	.002
157	Tubes, pipes, flues, or stays, boiler or other, of wrought iron or steel.........lbs..	2,276,576	559,212.38	56,914.51	.25
158	Bolts, with or without threads or nuts, or bolt blanks, and finished hinges or hinge blanks of iron or steel...............lbs..	31,270	2,207.09	703.57	.071
	Nuts and washers of wrought iron or steel...............................lbs..	19,196	1,311.00	345.52	.003
159	Card clothing: Manufactured from tempered steel wire.........................sq. ft..	255,555.15	219,939.00	127,777.60	.86
	Other........................sq. ft..	14,924.03	14,394.00	3,731.00	.90
	Castings:				
160	Cast-iron pipe of every description..lbs..	3,764	171.00	33.87	.048
161	Cast-iron vessels, plates, stove plates, andirons, sad irons, tailors' irons, and hatters' irons, and castings of iron not specially provided for............lbs..	408,193	18,158.76	4,898.31	0.044
162	Malleable-iron castings, not specially provided for......................lbs..	209,632	11,526.00	3,668.58	.055
163	Hollow ware, coated, glazed, or tinned..........................lbs..	19,434	1,649.50	583.02	.085
164	Chain or chains of all kinds, made of iron or steel:				
	Not less than ¾ of 1 inch in diameter.lbs..	36,394	746.00	581.84	.021
	Less than ¾ of 1 inch and not less than ⅜ of 1 inch in diameter............lbs..	1,064	40.50	19.15	.038
	Less than ⅜ of 1 inch in diameter..lbs..	580,939	28,021.00	14,523.48	.048
	Other..........................lbs..	480,951	36,027.12	16,212.43	.075
165	Cutlery: Penknives or pocket knives of all kinds, or parts thereof, and erasers, or parts thereof, wholly or partly manufactured—				
	Valued at not more than 50 cents per dozen........................doz..	437,554.50	176,615.58	140,829.34	.40

DUTIES COLLECTED UNDER EXISTING LAW, ETC.—Continued.

Duties estimated under—		Rates of duty under—			Average ad valorem under—			Paragraph.
House bill.	Senate bill.	Present law.	House bill.	Senate bill.	Present.	House bill.	Senate bill.	
					Per ct.	*Per ct.*	*Per ct.*	
$39.55	$39.55	2 c. +1¼ c. per lb.	35 per cent...	35 per cent ..	50.11	35	35	
7.35	7.35	2₁₅/₁₆ c. + 1¼ c. per lb.	....do	....do	51.48	35	35	
81.55	81.55	3¼ c. + 1¼ c. per lb.	....do	....do	42.34	35	35	
1,041.60	1,041.60	4₁/₁₆ c. +1¼ c. per lb.	....do	....do	35.05	35	35	
1,535.10	1,535.10	7 c. + 1¼ c. per lb.	....do	....do	15.33	35	35	
2,114.70	2,114.70	3 c. per lb ...	....do	....do	50.81	35	35	
9,359.00	9,359.00	3₁/₁₀ c. per lb ..	....do	....do	39.48	35	35	
3,587.85	2,587.85	4½ c. per lb...	....do	....do	35.99	35	35	
6,386.49	6,386.49	1⅞ c. per lb ..	25 per cent...	25 per cent...	32.95	25	25	153
2,160.13	2,160.13	2 c. per lb...	....do	....do	27.35	25	25	154
28,213.80	28,213.89	2½ c. per lb ...	....do	....do	39.04	25	25	155
47.25	47.25	2¼ c. per lb ...	....do	....do	36.50	25	25	156
139,803.00	111,842.47	2½ c. per lb....	....do	20 per cent...	10.18	25	20	157
551.77	551.77	2¼ c. per lb ...	....do	25 per cent...	31.88	25	25	158
327.75	327.75	....do	....do	....do	26.35	25	25	
76,978.65	76,978.65	50 c. per sq. ft.	35 per cent...	35 per cent...	58.10	35	35	159
3,508.50	3,508.50	25 c. per sq. ft.	25 per cent...	25 per cent...	25.92	25	25	
42.75	38.48	₁/₁₀ c. per lb...	....do	22½ per cent...	19.81	25	22.5	160
4,539.00	4,539.00	1₇/₁₀ cts. per lb.	25 per cent...	25 per cent...	26.97	25	25	161
2,881.50	2,881.50	1¼ cts. per lb.	....do	....do	31.83	25	25	162
494.85	494.85	3 cts. per lb ..	30 per cent...	30 per cent...	35.33	30	30	163
223.80	223.80	1₁/₁₀ cts. per lb.	....do	....do	77.93	30	30	164
12.15	12.15	1₇/₁₀ cts. per lb.	....do	....do	47.28	30	30	
8,406.30	8,406.20	2¼ cts. per lb.	....do	....do	51.84	30	30	
10,808.28	10,808.28	45 cts. per lb	....do	....do	45	30	30	
79,490.51	79,490.51	12 c. per doz. and 50 p. ct.	45 per cent...	45 per cent...	79.72	45	45	165

IMPORTED MERCHANDISE, 1893, WITH THE RATES AND

Paragraph.		Importations of fiscal year, June 30, 1893.			
		Quantities.	Values.	Duties.	Unit of value.
	SCHEDULE C.—METALS AND MANUFACTURES OF—Continued. Cutlery—Continued. Penknives or pocket knives of all kinds, or parts thereof, and erasers or parts thereof, wholly or partly manufactured—Continued. Valued at more than 50 cents per dozen and not exceeding $1.50 per dozen ....doz..	363,156.65	$393,263.20	$378,209.97	$1.08
	Valued at more than $1.50 per dozen and not exceeding $3 per dozen ....doz..	81,263.33	182,728.06	172,027.37	2.25
	Valued at more than $3 per doz.doz..	29,283.12	158,509.19	137,820.86	5.41
	Razors and razor blades, finished or unfinished— Valued at less than $4 per dozen.doz..	78,888.81	212,808.64	142,729.04	2.70
	Valued at $4 or more per dozen.doz..	10,352.93	55,344.58	34,721.01	5.35
166	Swords, sword blades, and side arms		23,853.81	8,348.84	
167	Table knives, forks, steels, and all butchers', hunting, kitchen, bread, butter, vegetable, fruit, cheese, plumbers', painters', palette, and artists' knives of all sizes, finished or unfinished: Valued at not more that $1 per dozen pieces..........................doz..	43,326.52	24,561.12	11,700.95	.57
	Valued at more than $1 and not more than $2 per dozen pieces..........doz..	16,893.24	25,718.13	13,628.16	1.52
	Valued at more than $2 and not more than $3 per dozen pieces..........doz..	12,453.83	31,030.00	14,290.55	2.49
	Valued at more than $3 and not more than $8 per dozen pieces..........doz..	12,431.30	56,700.43	29,468.45	4.57
	Valued at more than $8 per dozen pieces ....doz..	891.23	9,514.76	4,637.00	10.68
	All carving and cooks' knives and forks of all sizes, finished or unfinished— Valued at not more than $4 per dozen pieces..........................doz..	8,233.73	18,518.00	13,780.15	2.25
168	Valued at more than $4 and not more than $8 per dozen pieces..........doz..	3,011	19,443.00	11,854.93	6.46
	Valued at more than $8 and not more than $12 per dozen pieces.........doz..	554.59	5,576.79	3,330.81	10.05
	Valued at more than $12 per dozen pieces ....doz..	257.73	4,517.28	2,643.89	17.51
	Files, file-blanks, rasps, and floats of all cuts and kinds: 4 inches in length and under.......doz..	46,592.66	24,310.00	16,307.44	.52
	Over 4 inches in length and under 9 inches..........................doz..	35,040.75	40,132.50	26,280.57	1.15
	9 inches in length and under 14 inches...	2,170.43	5,536.00	2,821.54	2.51
	14 inches in length and over.............	1,901.42	7,040.00	3,802.83	4.02
169	Firearms: Muskets and sporting rifles		74,375.92	18,503.98	
170	Pistols, revolving— Valued at not more than $1.50 each, ...No..	644	887.40	568.19	1.38
	Valued at more than $1.50 each..No..	350	1,074.00	734.90	2.90
	Shotguns, double-barreled, sporting, breech-loading— Valued at not more than $6 each..No..	46,842	212,971.00	144,802.85	4.55
	Valued at more than $6 and not more than $12 each................No..	920	8,124.15	6,523.45	8.83
	Valued at more than $12 each...No..	1,156	60,340.15	28,058.18	52.21
	Shotguns, single-barreled, breech-loading ....No..	13	213.00	87.55	16.38
171	Sheets and plates, wares or articles, of iron and steel: Enameled or glazed with vitreous glasses.		31,596.58	14,218.46	

DUTIES COLLECTED UNDER EXISTING LAW, ETC.—Continued.

Duties estimated under—		Rates of duty under—			Average ad valorem under—			Paragraph.
House bill.	Senate bill.	Present law.	House bill.	Senate bill.	Present.	House bill.	Senate bill.	
					Per ct.	*Per ct.*	*Per ct.*	
$176,968.44	$176,968.44	50 cts. per doz. and 50 p. ct.	45 per cent...	45 per cent...	96.17	45	45	
82,227.62	82,227.62	$1 per dozen and 50 p. ct.	....do	....do	94.47	45	45	
71,320.13	71,320.13	$2 per dozen and 50 p. ct.	....do	....do	86.95	45	45	
95,761.64	95,761.64	$1 per dozen and 30 p. ct.	....do	....do	67.07	45	45	
24,905.06	24,905.06	$1.75 per doz. and 30 p. ct.	....do	....do	62.74	45	45	
8,348.84	8,348.84	35 per cent...	35 per cent...	35 per cent...	35	35	35	166
8,596.39	8,596.39	10 cts. per doz. and 30 p. ct.	....do	....do	47.64	35	35	167
9,001.35	9,001.35	35 cts. p. doz. and 30 p. ct.	....do	....do	52.99	35	35	
10,860.50	10,860.50	40 cts. p. doz. and 30 p. ct.	....do	....do	46.05	35	35	
19,876.65	19,876.65	$1 per dozen and 30 p. ct.	....do	....do	51.89	35	35	
3,330.17	3,330.17	$2 per dozen and 30 p. ct.	....do	....do	48.73	35	35	
6,481.30	6,481.30	$1 per dozen and 30 p. ct.	....do	....do	74.46	35	35	
6,805.05	6,805.05	$2 per dozen and 30 p. ct.	....do	....do	60.97	35	35	
1,951.88	1,951.88	$3 per dozen and 30 p. ct.	....do	....do	59.83	35	35	168
1,581.05	1,581.05	$5 per dozen and 30 p. ct.	....do	....do	58.52	35	35	
8,508.00	8,508.00	35 cts. p. doz.	....do	....do	67.08	35	35	
14,046.37	14,046.37	75 cts. p. doz.	....do	....do	65.48	35	35	
1,937.60	1,937.60	$1.30 per doz.	....do	....do	50.97	35	35	
2,074.00	2,074.00	$2 per dozen	....do	....do	49.76	35	35	
18,593.98	18,593.98	25 per cent...	25 per cent...	25 per cent...	25	25	25	169 170
266.22	266.22	40 cents each and 35 p. ct.	30 per cent...	30 per cent...	64.03	30	30	
322.20	322.20	$1 each and 35 per cent.	....do.........	....do	68.43	30	30	
63,891.30	63,891.30	$1.50 each and 35 p. ct.	....do.........	....do	67.90	30	30	
2,437.24	2,437.24	$4 each and 35 per cent.	....do	....do	80.30	30	30	
18,104.74	18,104.74	$6 each and 35 per cent.	....do	....do	46.49	30	30	
63.90	63.90	$1 each and 35 per cent.	....do	....do	41.10	30	30	
11,058.80	11,058.80	45 per cent...	35 per cent...	35 per cent...	45	35	35	171

IMPORTED MERCHANDISE, 1893, WITH THE RATES AND

Paragraph.		Importations of fiscal year, June 30, 1893.			
		Quantities.	Values.	Duties.	Unit of value.
	SCHEDULE C.—METALS AND MANUFACTURERS OF—Continued.				
	Sheets and plates, etc.—Continued.				
172	Enameled or glazed with vitreous glasses with more than one color, or ornamented.		$85,488.00	$12,744.00	
	Nails, spikes, and tacks—				
173	Nails and spikes, cut, of iron or steel ....lbs..	6,804	288.50	63.04	$0.042
174	Nails, horseshoe, hob, and all other wrought iron or steel nails, not specially provided for...............lbs..	2,180	897.00	327.20	.11
175	Nails, wire, made of wrought iron or steel—				
	Shorter than 1 inch and lighter than No. 16 wire gauge..............lbs..	5,479	472.00	219.16	.086
	From 1 inch to 2 inches in length, and lighter than No. 12 and not lighter than No. 16 wire gauge.lbs..	29	2.00	.73	.069
	2 inches long and longer, not lighter than No. 12 wire gauge......lbs..	236	15.40	4.76	.065
176	Spikes of wrought iron or steel ....lbs..	4,036	67.80	72.65	.017
	Horse, mule, or ox shoes of wrought iron or steel ....lbs..	9,668	885.00	174.02	.092
177	Tacks, brads, or sprigs, cut—				
	Not exceeding 16 ounces to the M...M..				
178	Needles—				
	For knitting or sewing machines, crochet and tape needles, and bodkins of metal...		18,147.00	6,351.45	
179	Knitting, and all others not specially provided for...............................		23,054.00	5,763.50	
180	Engraved plates of steel...................		68.00	17.00	
	Stereotype plates and electrotype plates, and plates of other materials engraved or lithographed for printing...........		43,981.65	10,995.41	
181	Railway fish plates or splice bars, of iron or steel....................................lbs..	59,910	830.00	599.10	.014
182	Rivets of iron or steel ....lbs..	59,634	7,176.00	1,490.86	.12
183	Saws—				
	Circular saws...............................		159.00	47.70	
	Crosscut saws..................linear feet..	18,830.25	8,873.52	1,506.42	.47
	Hand, buck, and other saws not specially provided for		26,044.00	10,417.60	
	Mill, pit, and drag saws—				
	Not over 9 inches wide ..linear feet..	5	3.00	.50	.60
	Over 9 inches wide ......linear feet..				
184	Screws, commonly called wood screws—				
	½ inch and less in length ....lbs..	30	3.00	.04	10.00
	Over ½ inch and not more than 1 inch in length ....lbs..	25	3.00	2.50	.12
	Over 1 inch and not more than 2 inches in length...................................lbs..	20	3.00	1.40	.15
	More than 2 inches in length..........lbs..	466	21.00	23.30	.045
185	Wheels, or parts thereof, made of iron or steel, and steel-tired wheels, for railway purposes, whether wholly or partly finished, and iron or steel locomotive, car, or other railway tires, or parts thereof, wholly or partly manufactured...............lbs..	15,361,011	458,700.50	384,025.31	.030
	Ingots, cogged ingots, blooms, or blanks, for railway wheels and tires, without regard to the degree of manufacture ....lbs..	5,752	181.00	100.66	.031
186	Aluminum—				
	In crude form, and alloys of any kind in which aluminum is the component material of chief value..............lbs..	2,241	1,509.00	336.15	.68
188	Argentine, albata, or German silver, unmanufactured..............................lbs..	42,023	3,075.00	993.75	.095
	Brass:				
189	Bars or pigs ....lbs..	17,987	2,707.00	260.80	.15
	Old, and clippings from brass, or Dutch metal, and old sheathing, or yellow metal, fit only for remanufacture........lbs..	342,040	45,135.22	5,130.63	.13
190	Bronze powder...........................lbs..	1,350,928	447,062.50	162,111.36	.33
	Bronze or Dutch metal, in leaf, in packages of 100 leaves..........................pkgs..	2,248,318	175,907.50	179,865.42	.078
	Aluminum—leaves, in packages of 100 leaves ....pkgs..	23,915	2,001.00	2,313.20	.090

DUTIES COLLECTED UNDER EXISTING LAW, ETC.—Continued.

Duties estimated under—		Rates of duty under—			Average ad valorem under—			Paragraph.
House bill.	Senate bill.	Present law.	House bill.	Senate bill.	Present.	House bill.	Senate bill.	
					Per ct.	Per ct.	Per ct.	
$29,920.80	$29,920.80	50 per cent...	35 per cent...	35 per cent...	50	35	35	172
72.13	64.91	1 cent per lb.	25 per cent...	22½ per cent..	23.58	25	22.5	173
209.10	209.10	4 cents per lb.	30 per cent...	30 per cent...	36.48	30	30	174
								175
118.00	118.00	....do	25 per cent...	25 per cent...	46.43	25	25	
.50	.50	2½ cts. per lb.	....do	....do	36.50	25	25	
3.85	3.85	2 cents per lb.	....do	....do	30.01	25	25	
16.05	16.05	1⁷⁄₁₀ cts. p. lb.	....do	....do	107.15	25	25	176
221.25	221.25	....do	....do	....do	19.66	25	25	
								177
....	....	2¼ cts. per M.	....do	....do		25	25	178
4,536.75	4,536.75	35 per cent...	....do	....do	35	25	25	
								179
5,763.50	5,768.50	25 per cent...	....do	....do	25	25	25	
17.00	17.00	....do	....do	....do	25	25	25	180
10,095.41	10,095.41	....do	....do	....do	25	25	25	
								181
207.50	207.50	1 cent per lb.	....do	....do	72.18	25	25	
2,152.80	1,794.00	2½ cts. per lb.	30 per cent...	....do	20.78	30	25	182
								183
39.75	39.75	30 per cent...	25 per cent...	....do	30	25	25	
2,213.38	1,331.03	8 c. p. lin. ft.	....do	15 per cent...	16.98	25	15	
6,511.00	6,511.00	40 per cent...	....do	25 per cent...	40	25	25	
.75	.45	10 c. p. lin. ft.	....do	15 per cent...	16.67	25	15	
....	....	15 c. p. lin. ft.	....do	....do	....	25	15	184
1.05	.90	14 cts. per lb..	35 per cent...	30 per cent...	1.33	35	30	
1.05	.90	10 cts. per lb..	....do	....do	83.33	35	30	
1.05	.90	7 cts. per lb...	....do	....do	46.67	35	30	
7.35	6.30	5 cts. per lb...	....do	....do	110.95	35	30	
137,610.15	137,610.15	2½ cts. per lb..	30 per cent...	....do	83.72	30	30	185
54.30	54.30	1¾ cts. per lb..	....do	....do	55.01	30	30	
377.25	226.35	15 cts. per lb..	25 per cent...	15 per cent...	22.28	25	15	186
596.25	596.25	25 per cent...	15 per cent...	....do	25	15	15	188
270.70	270.70	1¼ cts. per lb..	10 per cent...	10 per cent...	9.97	10	10	189
4,513.52	4,513.52	....do	....do	....do	11.37	10	10	
134,118.75	134,118.75	12 cts. per lb..	30 per cent...	30 per cent...	36.26	30	30	190
61,567.62	61,567.62	8 cts. p. pack.	....do	....do	102.25	30	30	
520.20	520.20	....do	....do	....do	88.93	30	30	

IMPORTED MERCHANDISE, 1893, WITH THE RATES AND

Paragraph.		Importations of fiscal year, June 30, 1893.			
		Quantities.	Values.	Duties.	Unit of value.
	SCHEDULE C,—METALS AND MANUFACTURES OF—Continued.				
195	Plates, rolled, called brazier's copper, sheets, rods, pipes, and copper bottoms......lbs..	6,159	$1,050.00	$367.50	$0.17
	Sheathing or yellow metal, of which copper is the component material of chief value, and not composed wholly or in part of iron ungalvanized......................lbs..	3,326	337.00	117.95	.10
196	Gold and silver, manufactures of: Bullions and metal thread of gold, silver, or other metals not specially provided for..............................	....	132,390.00	39,717.00	......
197	Gold leaf, in packages of 500 leaves ....pkgs..	560	2,496.00	1,120.00	4.46
198	Silver leaf, in packages of 500 leaves ....pkgs..	28	27.00	21.00	.96
199	Lead, and manufactures of: Lead contained in silver ore........lbs..	59,809,044	1,190,462.31	897,135.61	.019
	Lead contained in other ore and dross ....lbs..	3,327	177.00	49.91	.053
200	Pigs and bars, molten and old refuse lead, run into blocks and bars, and old scrap lead fit only to be remanufactured.............................lbs..	3,975,521.50	161,833.00	79,510.43	.041
201	Sheets, pipes, shot, glaziers' lead, and lead wire........................lbs..	91,392	6,233.50	2,284.79	.068
204	Pens, metallic, except of gold....gross..	603,963.25	162,999.50	72,475.59	.27
205	Gold pens................................	....	155.00	46.50	......
	Penholder tips and penholders, or parts thereof...........................	....	18,559.00	5,567.70	......
206	Pins, solid head or other, including hair, safety, hat, bonnet, shawl, and belt pins..	....	358,054.48	107,416.34	......
208	Type metal.........................lbs..	909,272	28,619.00	13,639.07	.031
210	Types, new............................	....	5,779.00	1,444.75	......
211	Chronometers, box or ship's, and parts thereof...........................	....	2,043.73	204.67	......
	Watches, and parts of : Watches..............................	....	1,423,938.07	355,984.52	......
	Watch cases, movements, glasses, and parts of watches....................	....	319,023.00	79,755.75	......
	Zinc or spelter, and manufactures of :				
212	In blocks or pigs.....................lbs..	459,683	24,803.00	8,044.47	.054
213	In sheets...........................lbs..	29,378	2,516.00	734.47	.086
214	Old and worn out, fit only to be remanufactured.........................lbs..	115,097	6,543.00	1,438.72	.057
215	Manufactures, articles or wares not specially provided for :				
	Brass...............................	....	199,795.58	80,908.01	......
	Buttons, metal......................	....	195,696.00	83,063.20	......
	Carriages, etc.......................	....	515,522.82	231,985.27	......
	Clocks.............................	....	122,611.00	55,174.95	......
	Copper.............................	....	51,623.18	23,230.44	......
	Gold and silver......................	....	161,481.65	72,666.74	......
	Machinery.........................	....	3,221,025.16	1,449,731.32	......
	Iron and steel......................	....	1,135,116.80	510,802.58	......
	Lead...............................	....	2,054.84	924.68	......
	Aluminum..........................	....	1,594.00	717.30	......
	Bronze.............................	....	106,862.10	48,087.95	......
	Metals, n. e. s......................	....	5,025,203.73	2,261,341.66	......
	Musical instruments................	....	380,100.58	171,045.25	......
	Nickel.............................	....	907.00	408.15	......
	Platinum...........................	....	272.00	122.40	......
	Zinc................................	....	24,465.00	11,009.25	......
	Total Schedule C, Metals...........	....	46,173,495.23	27,003,587.41	......
	SCHEDULE D.—WOOD AND MANUFACTURES OF.				
218	Boards, planks, deal, and other sawed lumber: Of hemlock, white wood, sycamore, white pine, and bass wood—				
	Planed or finished on one side..M ft..	14,118.30	97,776.72	21,177.48	6.93
	Planed or finished on two sides..M ft..	97.79	1,281.96	195.59	13.11
	Planed on one side and tongued and grooved....................M ft..	72.08	1,040.59	144.16	14.45

DUTIES COLLECTED UNDER EXISTING LAW, ETC.—Continued.

Duties estimated under—		Rates of duty under—			Average ad valorem under—			Paragraph.
House bill.	Senate bill.	Present law.	House bill.	Senate bill.	Present.	House bill.	Senate bill.	
					Per ct.	*Per ct.*	*Per ct.*	
$210.00	$210.00	35 per cent...	20 per cent...	20 per cent...	35	20	20	195
67.40	67.40	....do	....do	....do	35	20	20	196
33,097.50	33,097.50	30 per cent...	25 per cent...	25 per cent ..	30	25	25	
873.60	748.80	$2 per pack ..	35 per cent...	30 per cent...	44.87	35	30	197
9.45	8.10	75 cts. per p..	35 per cent...	30 per cent...	77.78	35	30	198
178,569.34	448,567.30	1½ cts. per lb..	15 per cent...	¾ cent per lb.	75.36	15	37.68	199
26.55	24.95	....do	....do	....do	28.20	15	14.10	
39,755.21	39,755.21	2 cts. per lb..	1 cent per lb.	1 cent per lb.	49.13	24.56	24.56	200
1,142.39	1,558.38	2½ cts. per lb..	1¼ cts. per lb.	1¼ cts. per lb..	36.65	18.33	18.33	201
57,049.82	48,890.85	12 c. per gross.	35 per cent...	30 per cent...	44.47	35	30	204
38.75	38.75	30 per cent...	25 per cent...	25 per cent...	30	25	25	205
4,639.75	4,639.75	....do	....do	....do	30	25	25	
107,416.34	107,416.34	....do	20 per cent...	20 per cent...	30	20	20	206
4,202.85	4,202.85	1⅓ cts. per lb.	15 per cent...	15 per cent...	47.66	15	15	208
866.85	866.85	25 per cent...	....do	....do	25	15	15	
204.87	204.87	10 per cent...	10 per cent...	10 per cent...	10	10	10	210
355,984.52	355,984.52	25 per cent...	25 per cent...	25 per cent...	25	25	25	211
79,755.75	79,755.75	....do	....do	....do	25	25	25	
4,978.60	4,978.60	1⅝ cts. per lb.	20 per cent...	20 per cent...	32.32	20	20	212
629.00	629.00	2⅝ cts. per lb.	25 per cent...	25 per cent...	29.19	25	25	213
981.45	981.45	1½ cts. per lb.	15 per cent...	15 per cent...	21.99	15	15	214 215
69,928.45	59,938.67	45 per cent...	35 per cent...	30 per cent...	45	35	30	
68,493.60	58,708.80	....do	....do	....do	45	35	30	
180,432.98	154,656.84	....do	....do	....do	45	35	30	
30,652.75	30,652.75	....do	25 per cent...	25 per cent...	45	25	25	
18,068.11	15,486.95	....do	35 per cent...	30 per cent...	45	35	30	
56,518.57	48,444.49	....do	....do	....do	45	35	30	
1,127,568.80	966,487.54	....do	....do	....do	45	35	30	
397,290.91	340,535.06	....do	....do	....do	45	35	30	
719.19	616.45	....do	....do	....do	45	35	30	
557.90	478.20	....do	....do	....do	45	35	30	
37,401.73	32,058.63	....do	....do	....do	45	35	30	
1,758,820.30	1,507,561.12	....do	....do	....do	45	35	30	
133,035.20	114,030.17	....do	....do	....do	45	35	30	
317.45	272.10	....do	....do	....do	45	35	30	
95.20	81.60	....do	....do	....do	45	35	30	
8,562.75	7,339.50	....do	....do	....do	45	35	30	
15,769,653.89	14,555,313.28	....	....	....	58.48	35.06	31.52	
								218
7,059.15	7,059.15	$1.50 per M ft.	50 cts. per M ft	50 cts. per M ft	21.66	7.26	7.26	
97.79	97.79	$2 per M ft...	$1 per M ft...	$1 per M ft...	15.26	7.63	7.63	
72.08	72.08	....do	....do	....do	13.85	6.92	6.92	

IMPORTED MERCHANDISE, 1893, WITH THE RATES AND

Paragraph.		Importations of fiscal year, June 30, 1893.			
		Quantities.	Values.	Duties.	Unit of value.
	SCHEDULE D.—WOOD AND MANUFACTURES OF—Continued.				
	Boards, planks, deals, and other sawed lumber—Continued. Of hemlock, whitewood, sycamore, white pine, and bass wood—Continued. Planed on two sides and tongued and grooved ....M ft..	35.64	$675.00	$80.11	$18.94
	All sawed lumber not specially provided for: Planed on one side and tongued and grooved ....M ft..	4,899.54	46,477.00	12,248.86	9.49
	Planed or finished on one side ..M ft..	598.33	6,840.92	1,794.98	11.43
	Planed or finished on two sides.M ft..	1,745.08	21,668.07	5,235.24	12.42
	Planed on two sides and tongued and grooved ....M ft..	1,601.04	18,085.00	5,603.64	11.30
228	Shooks, sugar box, and packing boxes and packing-box shooks............		45,745.54	13,723.66	
	Casks and barrels, empty............		530.61	150.18	
	Chair cane, or reeds wrought or manufactured from rattans or reeds............		173,967.00	17,396.70	
230	Furniture, cabinet or house, wholly or partly finished		382,198.98	133,760.65	
	All other manufactures of wood, or of which wood is the component material of chief value, not especially provided for........		1,397,154.75	489,004.15	
	Musical instruments, wood, chief value.....		641,411.57	224,494.05	
	Clocks, wood, chief value............		15,095.03	5,283.48	
	Carriages and parts of, wood, chief value....		14,463.00	5,062.05	
	Total Schedule D, wood............		2,864,412.36	935,381.98	
	SCHEDULE E.—SUGAR.				
	Sugar and molasses: Molasses.................galls..	15,490,757	1,992,352.43	....	0.13
	Sugars, all not above No. 16, Dutch standard in color, tank bottoms, sugar drainings, and sugar sweepings, sirups of cane juice, melada, concentrated melada, and concrete and concentrated molasses—				
	Beet sugar...................lbs..	436,287,435	12,844,966.00	....	.029
	Cane sugar ....lbs..	3,292,496,348	101,951,431.12	....	.031
	Maple sugar ....lbs..	2,435,584	163,473.00	....	.067
	Total sugar..................lbs..	3,731,219,367	114,959,870.12	....	.031
237	Sugar, not elsewhere specified, and confectionery: Sugar, above No. 16 Dutch standard in color— Beet, cane, and other, except maple..................lbs..	82,100,010	1,248,273.75	$160,500.10	.029

173

DUTIES COLLECTED UNDER EXISTING LAW, ETC.—Continued.

Duties estimated under—		Rates of duty under—			Average ad valorem under—			Paragraph.
House bill.	Senate bill.	Present law.	House bill.	Senate bill.	Present.	House bill.	Senate bill.	
					Per ct.	Per ct.	Per ct.	
$53.46	$53.46	$2.50 per M ft.	$1.50 per M ft.	$1.50 per M ft.	13.20	7.92	7.92	
2,449.77	2,449.77	....do........	50 cts. per M ft	50 cts. per M ft	26.35	5.27	5.27	
598.33	598.33	$3 per M ft...	$1 per M ft...	$1 per M ft...	26.24	8.75	8.75	
1,745.08	1,745.08	....do........	....do........	....do........	24.16	8.05	8.05	
2,401.56	2,401.56	$3.50 per M ft.	$1.50 per M ft.	$1.50 per M ft.	30.90	13.26	13.26	
9,149.11	9,149.11	30 per cent...	20 per cent...	29 per cent...	30	20	20	228
106.12	106.12	....do........	....do........	....do........	30	20	20	
12,137.70	17,390.70	10 per cent...	7 per cent....	10 per cent...	10	7	10	
95,549.74	95,549.74	35 per cent...	25 per cent...	25 per cent...	35	25	25	230
349,288.69	349,288.69	....do........	....do........	....do........	35	25	25	
160,352.89	160,352.89	....do........	....do........	....do........	35	25	25	
3,773.91	3,773.91	....do........	....do........	....do........	35	25	25	
3,615.75	3,615.75	....do........	....do........	....do........	35	25	25	
648,451.23	653,710.13				32.66	22.64	22.82	
....	309,815.14	Free........	Free........	Not above 56°, 2 cts per gal.; above 60°, 4 cents per gal.	Free..	Free.	15.55	
....	41,043,413.03	Free........	Free........	All sugar not above 80° 1 cent per lb., and ₁/₁₀ of a cent for each additional degree up to 90°. Above 90°, and not above 98°, ₁/₁₀ cent per lb. for each additional degree. Above 98° or Dutch standard in color of 1 cent per lb., in addition to the duties imposed upon sugar testing above 98°. (Duty estimated 1₁/₁₀ cents per lb.	Free..	Free.	35.70	
....	444,585.26	₁/₁₀ cts. per lb.	Free........	Duty estimated 1₁/₁₀ cts per lb.	12.86	Free.	24.94	237

174

IMPORTED MERCHANDISE, 1893, WITH THE RATES AND

Paragraph.		Importations of fiscal year, June 30, 1893.			
		Quantities.	Values.	Duties.	Unit of value.
	SCHEDULE E.—SUGAR—Continued.				
	Sugar, not elsewhere specified, and confectionery—Continued.				
	Sugar, above No. 16 Dutch standard in color—Continued.				
	Beet, cane, and other, except maple (if export bounty is in excess of that paid on sugar of a lower grade)............lbs..	575,917	$21,431.00	$3,455.49	$0.037
	Maple.....................lbs..	115	9.20	.57	.080
238	Sugar candy and confectionery, including chocolate confectionery, made wholly or in part of sugar—				
	Valued at 12 cents or less per pound, and refined sugar, when tinctured, colored, or in any way adulterated...............lbs..	46,809.50	1,952.06	2,340.47	.042
239	Other, not specially provided for....		51,067.58	25,533.79	
240	Glucose or grape sugar............lbs..	195,194	6,175.00	1,463.97	.032
	Total Schedule E, sugar...........		118,281,131.14	193,294.48	
	NOTE.—Hawaiian molasses and sugar, now free of duty, is included in the estimate. There was imported of the same during the fiscal year 1893, from Hawaii, 67,324 gallons of molasses and 288,517,929 pounds of sugar.				
	SCHEDULE F.—TOBACCO, AND MANUFACTURES OF.				
	Tobacco, and manufactures of:				
242	Leaf tobacco, suitable for cigar wrappers—				
	Not stemmed..............lbs..	2,362,531.29	1,079,657.48	4,725,062.57	.84
	Stemmed................lbs..	6.50	19.88	17.88	3.06
243	Loaf, other, unmanufactured and not stemmed.................lbs..	16,322,179.48	6,072,330.01	5,712,762.83	.43
	Leaf, other, stemmed.........lbs..	1,461,192.80	765,541.41	730,596.40	.52
244	All other..................lbs..	346,420.84	69,777.16	138,568.34	.20
245	Snuff and snuff flour, manufactured of tobacco, ground dry, or damp, and pickled, scented or otherwise....lbs..	24,280.74	8,562.02	12,140.36	.35
246	Cigars and cheroots of all kinds....lbs..	614,018.90	2,752,928.16	3,451,317.18	4.48
	Cigarettes and paper cigars, including wrappers...................lbs..	11,473.10	39,582.00	61,524.43	3.45
	Total Schedule F, tobacco.........		12,588,407.12	14,831,989.99	
	SCHEDULE G.—AGRICULTURAL PRODUCTS AND PROVISIONS.				
	Animals, not elsewhere specified:				
247	Horses—				
	Valued at less than $150 each...No..	12,248	1,164,483.50	367,440.00	95 07
	Valued at $150 and over........No..	382	87,702.85	26,310.80	220.59
247	Mules......................No..	6	193.00	180.00	32.16
248	Cattle—				
	One year old or less............No..	2,272	10,438.00	4,544.00	4.59
	More than 1 year old..........No..	826	13,065.00	8,260.00	15.81
249	Hogs.......................No..	16,947	211,241.25	25,420.50	12.46
250	Sheep—				
	Less than 1 year old ....No..	445,813	1,519,176.25	334,359.75	3.40
	One year old or more..........No..	8,839	52,300.50	13,258.50	5.92
251	All other......................		39,045.60	7,809.12	
	Breadstuffs:				
252	Barley....................bush..	1,780,808.92	820,000.05	534,242.68	0.46
253	Barley malt...............bush..	3,558.53	4,411.00	1,601.34	1.24
254	Barley, pearled, patent, or hulled...lbs..	102,493	12,652.77	2,049.86	.13
*255	Buckwheat...............bush..	342.75	139.37	51.43	.41
*256	Corn or maize............bush..	1,885.65	1,273.63	282.87	.68
*257	Corn meal.................bush..	202.75	164.95	40.55	.81
258	Macaroni, vermicelli, and similar preparations.................lbs..	12,804,395	652,157.29	256,087.90	.051
*259	Oats.....................bush..	21,451.75	8,941.62	3,217.79	.42
*260	Oatmeal..................lbs..	439,574	24,665.05	4,305.74	.056

* Each of the above products shall be admitted free of duty from any country which

DUTIES COLLECTED UNDER EXISTING LAW, ETC.—Continued.

Duties estimated under—		Rates of duty under—			Average ad valorem under—			Paragraph
House bill.	Senate bill.	Present law.	House bill.	Senate bill.	Present.	House bill.	Senate bill.	
				Duty estimated 1¼ c. per lb	Per ct.	Per ct.	Per ct.	
....	7,976.45	₄⁄₁₀ cent per lb.	Free	per lb......	16.12	Free .	20.07	
....	1.59	₇⁄₁₀ cent per lb.	....do	....do	6.20	Free .	12.17	
$585.02	$585.62	5 cents per lb.	30 per cent..	30 per cent...	119.90	30	30	238
15,320.27	15,320.27	50 per cent...	....do	....do	50	30	30	239
926.25	926.25	¾ cent per lb .	15 per cent...	15 per cent...	23.71	15	15	240
16,832.14	41,822,623.61	....	....	....	14.55	28.43	35.36	
2,362,531.57	2,362,531.57	$2 per lb.....	$1 per lb.....	$1 per lb.....	288.68	119.34	119.34	242
8.13	8.13	$2.75 per lb...	$1.25 per lb...	$1.25 per lb...	89.03	40.87	40.87	
5,712,762.83	5,712,762.83	35 cts. per lb.	35 cts. per lb..	35 cts. per lb.	81.93	81.93	81.33	243
730,506.40	730,506.40	50 cts. per lb.	50 cts. per lb.	50 cts. per lb.	95.44	95.44	95.44	
138,568.34	138,568.34	40 cts. per lb.	40 cts. per lb.	40 cts. per lb.	198.50	198.50	198.50	244
9,712.30	9,712.30	50 cts. per lb.	....do	....do	141.78	113.32	113.32	245
2,530,288.74	2,530,288.74	$4.50 per lb. and 25 p. ct.	$3 per lb. and 25 per cent.	$3 per lb. and 25 per cent.	125.36	91.01	91.01	246
44,314.80	44,314.80	....do	....do	....do	155.44	111.95	111.95	
11,528,783.11	11,528,783.11	....	....	....	117.82	91.58	91.58	
232,896.70	232,896.70	$30 per head .	20 per cent...	20 per cent...	31.55	20	20	247
17,540.53	17,540.53	30 per cent...	....do	....do	30	20	20	
38.60	38.60	$30 per head	....do	....do	93.26	20	20	247
2,087.60	2,087.60	$2 per head ..	....do	....do	43.53	20	20	248
2,613.00	2,613.00	$10 per head	....do	....do	63.22	20	20	
42,248.25	42,248.25	$1.50 per head	....do	....do	12.03	20	20	249
303,835.25	303,835.25	75 cts. per head	....do	....do	22.01	20	20	250
10,460.10	10,460.10	$1.50 per head	....do	....do	25.35	20	20	
7,809.12	7,809.12	20 per cent...	....do	....do	20	20	20	251
206,500.00	247,800.01	30 cts. per bu.	25 per cent...	30 per cent...	64.68	25	30	252
1,543.85	1,764.40	45 cts. per bu.	35 per cent...	40 per cent...	36.30	35	40	253
3,213.19	3,856.83	2 cts. per lb ..	25 per cent...	30 per cent...	15.95	25	30	254
27.87	27.87	15 cts. per bu.	20 per cent...	20 per cent...	37	20	20	255
254.73	254.73	....do	....do	....do	23.20	20	20	256
32.00	33.90	20 cts. per bu.	....do	....do	24.58	20	20	257
163,030.32	130,431.46	2 cts. per lb ..	25 per cent...	20 per cent...	39.26	25	20	258
1,788.32	1,788.32	15 cts. per bu.	20 per cent...	....do	35.90	20	20	259
4,033.13	3,090.84	1 ct. per lb....	....do	15 per cent...	17.82	20	15	260

imposes no import duty on the like product when exported from the United States.

TA——12

IMPORTED MERCHANDISE, 1893, WITH THE RATES AND

Paragraph.		Importations of fiscal year, June 30, 1893.			
		Quantities.	Values.	Duties.	Unit of value.
	SCHEDULE G.—AGRICULTURAL PRODUCTS AND PROVISIONS—Continued.				
261	Rice:				
	Cleaned..........................lbs..	39,073,485	$698,679.97	$781,469.71	$0.018
	Uncleaned........................lbs..	17,342,405	337,732.77	216,780.00	.019
	Paddy............................lbs..	117,118	1,720.50	878.39	.015
	Rice flour, rice meal, and broken rice which will pass through a wire sieve known commercially as No. 12....lbs..	74,180,512	1,316,453.22	185,326.31	.018
*262	Rye..............................bush..	144.75	293.00	14.48	2.02
*263	Rye flour.........................lbs..				
*264	Wheat............................bush..	7,893.30	9,061.06	1,973.37	1.22
*265	Wheat flour......................bbls..	295.13	1,362.84	340.71	4.62
	Dairy products:				
266	Butter, and substitutes therefor....lbs..	72,765.75	13,280.27	4,305.95	.18
267	Cheese...........................lbs..	10,107,500.85	1,411,649.04	606,450.45	.14
268	Milk, preserved or condensed, including weight of package................lbs..	1,179,967	194,366.00	35,399.01	.088
	Milk, sugar of....................lbs..	98,785	12,089.00	7,902.80	.12
	Vegetables:				
270	Beans............................bush..	1,225,607.58	1,206,689.46	490,243.01	.98
271	Prepared or preserved—				
	Beans, pease, and mushrooms, in tins, jars, bottles, or otherwise		517,865.79	206,826.32	
277	Hay..............................tons..	104,181.21	962,221.51	416,724.86	9.24
278	Honey............................galls..	97,700.29	43,590.85	19,541.27	.45
279	Hops.............................lbs..	2,057,305.63	1,100,873.02	398,604.87	.41
280	Onions...........................bush..	542,538.75	421,538.04	217,015.48	.78
281	Pease:				
	Dried...........................bush..	326,224.39	362,549.74	65,644.87	1.10
	Split...........................bush..	278.80	880.00	139.40	3.16
	Other, in carton, papers, or small packages.............................lbs..				
283	Potatoes.........................bush..	4,295,046	2,066,763.31	1,073,960.50	.48
	Seeds, not elsewhere specified:				
284	Castor beans or seeds............bush..	147,061	148,904.00	73,530.50	1.01
285	Linseed or flaxseed ....bush..	145,935	187,826.00	43,780.50	1.29
	Poppy and other oil seeds .....bush..	12,728.25	40,582.00	3,818.47	3.19
287	Pickles and sauces		461,642.45	207,739.14	
	All other, not specially provided for.....		137,890.00	62,054.56	
288	Vegetables, other in their natural state		268,932.97	67,293.28	
	Fish:				
291	Anchovies and sardines, packed in oil or otherwise:				
	In tin boxes—				
	Whole boxes, measuring not more than 5 by 4 by 3½ inches..boxes..	6,353	2,109.29	695.30	.33
	Half boxes, measuring not more than 5 by 4 by 1⅝ inches..boxes..	509,607	126,981.00	28,480.35	.22
	Quarter boxes, measuring not more than 4⅞ by 3½ by 1¼ inches..boxes..	13,454,536	1,083,824.18	336,303.42	.081
	In any other form		45,244.06	18,097.63	
292	Cod, haddock, hake, etc., pickled, in barrels............................bbls..	20.45	158.00	40.90	7.73
	Mackerel, pickled or salted............bbls..	84,217.14	960,588.00	108,434.28	11.41
	Salmon, pickled or salted............lbs..	908,113	63,722.00	9,081.13	.070
	Other fish:				
	Pickled or salted, in barrels.......bbls..	2,726.96	20,645.73	5,453.93	7.60
293	Cod, haddock, hake, and pollock:	*			
	Dried, smoked, salted, or pickled, otherwise than in barrels...............lbs..	7,433,163	291,531.34	55,748.70	.039
	Herring, dried or smoked..........lbs..	1,710,634	33,814.57	12,829.80	.020
	Other fish, dried or smoked.........lbs..	1,334,007	55,910.06	10,005.14	.042
	Pickled or salted, not in barrels or half barrels.............................lbs..	458,951	20,043.30	3,442.17	.044
294	Herring, pickled or salted.........barrels..	163,050.01	1,151,111.65	163,050.01	7.06
295	In cans or packages made of tin or other material, except anchovies and sardines and fish packed in any other manner, not specially provided for—				
	Herring		14,285.69	4,285.71	
	Mackerel		1,008.00	302.40	
	Salmon		46.00	16.80	
	Other...........................		71,167.48	21,350.24	
296	Cans or packages, made of tin or other material, containing shell fish admitted free of duty, not exceeding 1 quart in contents..............................doz..	354,743.92	....	28,379.51	....

* Each of the above products shall be admitted free of duty from any country which

DUTIES COLLECTED UNDER EXISTING LAW, ETC.—Continued.

Duties estimated under—		Rates of duty under—			Average ad valorem under—			Paragraph.
House bill.	Senate bill.	Present law.	House bill.	Senate bill.	Present.	House bill.	Senate bill.	
					Per ct.	*Per ct.*	*Per ct.*	
$580,102.28	$586,102.28	2 cts. per lb	1½ cts. per lb	1½ cts per lb	111.85	83.80	83.80	261
173,424.05	173,424.05	1¼ cts. per lb	1 ct. per lb	1 cent per lb	64.19	40.35	40.35	
878.89	878.39	¾ ct. per lb	¾ ct. per lb	¾ cent per lb	51.04	51.04	51.04	
185,326.31	185,326.31	¼ ct. per lb	¼ ct. per lb	¼ cent per lb	14.08	14.08	14.08	
58.00	58.00	10 cts. per bu.	20 per cent	20 per cent	4.94	20	20	262
....	....	¼ ct. per lb	....do	....do	....	20	20	263
1,932.21	1,932.21	25 cts. per bu.	....do	....do	20.42	20	20	264
272.50	272.56	25 per cent	....do	....do	25	20	20	265
2,910.03	2,656.05	6 cts. per lb	4 cts. per lb	....do	32.88	21.92	20	266
352,912.26	352,912.26	....do	25 per cent	25 per cent	42.06	25	25	267
23,590.34	23,590.34	3 cts. per lb	2 cts. per lb	2 cts. per lb	33.92	22.62	22.62	269
2,417.80	4,939.25	8 cts. per lb	20 per cent	5 cts. per lb.	65.37	20	40.85	
241,337.80	241,337.80	40 cts. per bu.	....do	....do	40.63	20	20	270
153,119.73	153,119.73	40 per cent	30 per cent	30 per cent	40	30	30	271
208,362.43	192,444.30	$4 per ton	$2 per ton	20 per cent	43.31	21.65	20	277
9,770.64	8,718.17	20 cts. per gal.	10 cts. per gal.	....do	44.83	22.42	20	278
212,580.25	220,175.60	15 cts. per lb	8 cts. per lb	....do	36.21	19.28	20	279
108,607.74	84,307.00	40 cts. per bu.	20 cts. per bu.	....do	51.48	25.74	20	280
65,644.87	72,500.94	20 cts. per bu.	....do	....do	18.10	18.10	20	281
130.40	176.00	50 cts. per bu.	50 cts. per bu.	....do	15.84	15.84	20	
....	....	1 ct. per lb	1 ct. per lb	....do	....	....	20	
429,504.60	020,034.90	25 cts. per bu.	10 cts. per bu.	30 per cent	51.96	20.73	30	283
36,765.25	36,765.25	50 cts. per bu.	25 cts. per bu.	25 cts. per bu.	49.38	24.69	24.69	284
29,187.00	29,187.00	30 cts. per bu.	20 cts. per bu.	20 cts. per bu.	23.31	15.54	15.54	285
2,545.65	2,545.65	....do	....do	....do	9.41	6.28	6.28	285
138,492.74	138,492.74	45 per cent	30 per cent	30 per cent	45	30	30	287
41,369.70	41,369.70	....do	....do	....do	45	30	30	
26,893.29	26,893.29	25 per cent	10 per cent	10 per cent	25	10	10	288
								291
620.76	527.30	10 c. per box	30 per cent	25 per cent	30.12	30	25	
38,094.30	31,745.25	5 c. per box	....do	....do	23.43	30	25	
325,147.25	270,956.04	2½ c. per box	....do	....do	31.03	30	25	
13,573.22	11,311.02	40 per cent	....do	....do	40	30	25	
30.68	23.70	1 c. per pound	¾ c. per pound	15 per cent	25.80	19.42	15	292
126,323.71	144,088.20	....do	....do	....do	17.53	13.15	15	
6,810.85	9,558.30	....do	....do	....do	14.25	10.69	15	
4,090.45	3,006.86	....do	....do	....do	26.42	19.82	15	
55,748.70	44,729.70	¾ c. per ponnd	....do	....do	19.12	19.12	15	293
12,829.80	5,072.18	....do	....do	....do	37.94	37.94	15	
10,005.14	8,386.50	....do	....do	....do	17.90	17.90	15	
3,442.17	3,006.49	....do	....do	....do	17.17	17.17	15	294
163,050.01	172,066.74	½ c. per pound	½ c. per ponnd	....do	14.16	14.16	15	295
3,571.42	3,571.42	30 per cent	25 per cent	25 per cent	30	25	25	
252.00	252.00	....do	....do	....do	30	25	25	
14.00	14.00	....do	....do	....do	30	25	25	
17,791.87	17,791.87	....do	....do	....do	30	25	25	
28,370.51	....	8 cts. per doz.	8 cts. per doz.	....	....	....	....	296

imposes no import duty on the product when exported from the United States.

IMPORTED MERCHANDISE, 1893, WITH THE RATES AND

Paragraph.		Importations of fiscal year, June 30, 1893.			
		Quantities.	Values.	Duties.	Unit of value.
	SCHEDULE G.—AGRICULTURAL PRODUCTS AND PROVISIONS--Continued.				
290	Grapes..................................bbls..	158,669.57	$485,763.50	$95,321.75	$3.00
	Plums and prunes......................lbs..	23,225,821	1,040,896.48	464,516.43	.045
300	Figs......................................lbs..	10,061,092	549,488.22	251,502.31	.055
301	Oranges:				
	In packages of capacity of 1¼ cubic feet or less............................pkgs..	549,942	450,719.17	71,492.46	.82
	In packages of capacity exceeding 1¼ cubic feet and not exceeding 2½ cubic feet.............................pkgs..	783,717	1,021,044.00	105,920.25	1.30
	In packages of capacity exceeding 2½ cubic feet and not exceeding 5 cubic feet.............................pkgs..	103,264.40	211,504.53	51,632.20	2.05
	In packages of capacity exceeding 5 cubic feet....................cu. ft..	7,551	4,137.00	755.10	.55
	In bulk..............................M..	1,717.92	8,272.54	2,576.88	4.82
	Lemons:				
	In packages of capacity of 1¼ cubic feet or less............................pkgs..	4,816	4,984.00	626.08	1.03
	In packages of capacity exceeding 1¼ cubic feet and not exceeding 2½ cubic feet.............................pkgs..	2,605,217	4,948,970.00	651,304.25	1.90
	In packages of capacity exceeding 2½ cubic feet and not exceeding 5 cubic feet.............................pkgs..	14,870	39,730.87	7,435.00	2.67
	In packages of capacity exceeding 5 cubic feet.......✠..............cu. ft..	168	88.00	16.80	.52
	In bulk..............................M..	4.80	57.00	7.20	11.88
	Limes—				
	In packages of capacity of 1¼ cubic feet or less............................pkgs..	108	34.20	14.04	.32
	In packages of capacity exceeding 1¼ cubic feet and not exceeding 2½ cubic feet.............................pkgs..	33,608	44,217.10	8,402.00	1.32
	In packages of capacity exceeding 2½ cubic feet and not exceeding 5 cubic feet.............................pkgs..	1,337.50	2,650.56	668.75	1.00
	In packages of capacity exceeding 5 cubic feet....................cu. ft..	42	20.00	4.20	.48
	In bulk..............................M..	47.60	268.50	71.40	5.64
	Barrels or boxes containing oranges, lemons, or limes, exclusive of contents............	....	555,986.93	166,796.10	....
302	Raisins..................................lbs..	23,508,985	1,125,522.60	589,074.03	.48
303	Preserved—				
	Comfits, sweetmeats, and fruits preserved in sugar, sirup, molasses, or spirits, not specially provided for, and jellies of all kinds........................	....	780,352.44	273,123.36	....
	Ginger, preserved or pickled	....	11,316.00	3,900.00	....
304	Fruits preserved in their own juices	....	84,394.00	25,318.47	....
305	Orange and lemon peel, preserved or candied................................lbs..	471,821	31,538.00	9,436.42	.067
	Nuts:				
306	Almonds:				
	Not shelled........................lbs..	2,780,011	270,742.00	130,000.55	.97
	Shelled...........................lbs..	3,758,500	664,562.27	281,887.51	.017
307	Filberts and walnuts:				
	Not shelled........................lbs..	11,900,846	673,705.00	357,025.38	.057
	Shelled...........................lbs..	1,380,070	168,867.00	82,804.20	.122
308	Peanuts or ground beans:				
	Unshelled.........................lbs..	73,344	1,006.72	733.44	.014
	Shelled...........................lbs..	25	2.20	.37	.088
309	All other shelled or unshelled, not specially provided for................lbs..	1,891,970	72,350.63	28,370.77	.038
	Apples:				
	Green or ripe......................bush..	858,151.20	632,276.00	214,537.90	.74
	Dried, desiccated, evaporated ......lbs..	10,724	788.00	334.48	.047
	Currants, Zante.......................lbs..	33,166,364	1,185,532.00	....	.036
	Dates..................................lbs..	16,248,515	494,628.51	....	.03
	Olives, green or prepared................	....	510,534.88	....	....
	Nuts:				
	Cream or Brazil.......................	....	424,893.00	....	....
	Orchids, lily of the valley, azaleas, palms, and other plants used for forcing under glass for cut flowers or decorative purposes....................................	....	362,043.46	....	....

DUTIES COLLECTED UNDER EXISTING LAW, ETC.—Continued.

Duties estimated under—		Rates of duty under—			Average ad valorem under—			Paragraph.
House bill.	Senate bill.	Present law.	House bill.	Senate bill.	Present.	House bill.	Senate bill.	
					Per ct.	*Per ct.*	*Per ct.*	
$97,152.70	$97,152.70	60c. per bbl..	20 per cent...	20 per cent...	19.62	20	20	299
209,979.30	314,968.94	2 c. per pound	....do	30 per cent...	44.24	20	30	
100,897.64	164,840.46	2½ cts. per lb.	....do	....do	45.77	20	30	300
								301
54,904.20	54,904.20	13 cents per package.	8c. per cubic foot.	8 c. per cubic foot.	15.86	12.20	12.20	
156,743.40	156,743.40	25 cents per package.	....do	....do	19.18	15.34	15.34	
41,305.76	41,305.76	50 cents per package.	....do	....do	24.41	19.53	19.53	
604.08	604.08	10c. per cu. ft.	....do	....do	18.25	14.60	14.60	
2,576.88	2,576.88	$1.50 per M ..	$1.50 per M ..	$1.50 per M ..	31.15	31.15	31.15	
481.00	481.00	13 cents per package.	8c. per cubic foot.	8 c. per cubic foot.	12.50	9.66	9.66	
521,043.40	521,043.40	25 cents per package.	....do	....do	13.16	10.53	10.53	
5,948.00	5,948.00	50 cents per package.	....do	....do	18.71	14.97	14.97	
13.44	13.44	10c. per cu. ft.	....do	....do	19.00	15.27	15.27	
7.20	7.20	$1.50 per M ..	$1.50 per M ..	$1.50 per M ..	11.63	11.63	11.63	
10.80	10.80	13 cents per package.	8c. per cu. ft.	8 c. per cu. ft.	41.05	31.57	31.57	
6,721.60	6,721.60	25 cents per package.	....do	....do	19	15.25	15.25	
535.00	535.00	50 cents per package.	....do	....do	25.17	20.14	20.14	
3.36	3.36	10c. per cu. ft.	....do	....do	21	17.75	17.75	
71.40	71.40	$1.50 per M ..	$1.50 per M ..	$1.50 per M ..	26.59	26.59	26.59	
166,796.10	166,796.10	30 per cent...	30 per cent...	30 per cent ..	30	30	30	
353,984.77	337,656.78	2½ cts per lb..	1¼ cts. per lb.	....do	52.42	31.44	30	302
234,105.73	234,105.73	35 per cent...	30 per cent...	....do	'35	30	30	303
3,394.80	3,394.80	....do	....do	....do	65	30	30	304
16,878.98	16,878.98	30 per cent...	20 per cent...	20 per cent...	30	20	20	
9,461.40	9,461.40	2 cents per lb.	30 per cent...	30 per cent...	29.92	30	30	305
								306
83,400.33	67,685.50	5 cents per lb.	3 cts. per lb ..	25 per cent...	51.34	30.80	25	
187,925.00	106,140.57	7½ cts per lb..	5 cts. per lb ..	....do	42.20	28.28	25	307
238,016.92	233,790.70	3 cents per lb.	2 cts. per lb ..	35 per cent...	52.99	35.32	35	
45,202.80	59,103.45	6 cents per lb.	4 cts. per lb ..	....do	49.04	32.08	35	308
733.44	201.34	1 cent per lb .	1 ct. per lb ...	20 per cent...	72.86	72.86	20	
.37	.44	1½ cts. per lb..	1¼ cts. per lb..	....do	16.82	16.82	20	
28,379.77	14,471.96	....do	1 ct. per lb ...	....do	39.22	26.15	20	309
....	126,455.21	25cts. per bu.	Free	....do	33.93	Free.	20	
....	157.72	2 cents per lb.	....do	....do	42.41	Free.	20	
118,553.20	355,659.60	Free	10 per cent...	30 per cent...	Free.	10	30	
....	98,925.70	....do	Free	20 per cent...	Free.	Free.	20	
....	102,106.97	....do	....do	....do	Free.	Fre .	20	
....	84,978.60	....do	....do	....do	Free.	Free.	20	
....	36,204.34	....do	....do	10 per cent...	Free.	Free.	10	

IMPORTED MERCHANDISE, 1893, WITH THE RATES AND

Paragraph.		Importations of fiscal year, June 30, 1893.			
		Quantities.	Values.	Duties.	Unit of value.
	SCHEDULE G.—AGRICULTURAL PRODUCTS AND PROVISIONS—Continued.				
311	Fresh { Beef..................................lbs..	175, 180.50	$12, 492.36	$3, 503.79	$.071
	Mutton...............................lbs..	80, 011	9, 338.53	1, 600.22	.12
	Pork.................................lbs..	12, 822	1, 053.67	256.44	.082
313	Extract of meat:				
	Fluid extract.........................lbs..	37, 134.75	30, 932.00	5, 570.22	.83
	All other, not specially provided for..lbs..	150, 872	294, 127.88	52, 805.20	1.95
315	Poultry, live..............................lbs..	317, 489.25	20, 296.88	9, 524 "0	.092
	Poultry, dressed..........................lbs..	180, 062	16, 693.00	9, 003.13	.093
317	Chicory root, burnt or roasted, ground or granulated, or in rolls, or otherwise prepared..............................lbs..	1, 000, 408	69, 864.00	38, 008.16	.036
318	Chocolate, other than confectionery and sweetened chocolate................lbs..	542, 214.50	117, 716.38	10, 844.29	.22
319	Cocoa, prepared or manufactured, not specially provided for...............lbs..	1, 427, 145	492, 102.43	28, 542.91	.34
320	Cocoa butter or butterine.................lbs..	1, 540, 413.50	392, 143.00	53, 014.52	.25
321	Dandelion root and acorns, prepared, and other articles used as coffee, or as substitutes for coffee, not specially provided for..............................lbs..	1, 482, 262	56, 373.00	22, 233.94	0.037
323	Starch, and all preparations for use as starch..............................lbs..	3, 765, 596	89, 249.61	75, 311.02	.024
324	Dextrin, burnt starch, gum substitute or British gum.........................lbs..	4, 050, 215	161, 430.00	69, 753.25	.035
325	Mustard, ground or preserved, in bottles or otherwise.........................lbs..	790, 129.50	207, 412.45	79, 012.96	.26
326	Spices not elsewhere specified:				
	Cayenne pepper, unground..........lbs..	903, 581	64, 855.39	22, 589.57	.071
	Sago..............................lbs..	362, 324	6, 353.19	10, 669.72	.018
	All other, ground or powdered, not specially provided for................lbs..	119, 031.50	8, 217.05	4, 761.26	.069
327	Vinegar..............................stand. galls..	72, 851	19, 941.43	5, 463.84	.27
	Total Schedule G, agricultural products, etc..............................		39, 357, 409.55	12, 122, 493, 61	
	SCHEDULE H.—SPIRITS, WINES, ETC.				
329	Spirits distilled—				
	Brandy..........................prf. galls..	306, 693.38	836, 429.74	766, 733.44	2.73
	Other, not specially provided for, manufactured or distilled—				
	From grain.....................prf. galls..	655, 689.58	558, 975.24	1, 639, 224.08	.85
	From other materials..........prf. galls..	108, 897.08	74, 198.42	272, 242.84	.63
331	Compounds or preparations of which distilled spirits are a component part of chief value, not specially provided for..............................prf. galls..	1, 469.50	3, 763.00	3, 673.75	2.56
332	Cordials, liquors, arracks, absinthe, kirschwasser, ratafia, and other spirituous beverages, or bitters containing spirits and not specially provided for..............................prf. galls..	190, 638.55	427, 279.84	401, 506.44	2.17
334	Bay rum or bay water, whether distilled or compounded......................prf. galls..	29, 022.75	19, 562.90	44, 434.14	.66
	Wines, containing not more than 24 per cent of alcohol:				
335	Champagne, and all other sparkling, in bottles—				
	Containing ½ pint each or less..doz..	11, 205.07	41, 805.00	22, 591.34	3.72
	Containing more than ½ pint each and not more than 1 pint.....doz..	292, 552.16	2, 293, 712.35	1, 170, 268.64	7.60
	Containing more than 1 pint each and not more than 1 quart....doz..	193, 187.51	2, 871, 221.48	1, 585, 500.08	14.49
	Quantity in excess of 1 quart per bottle..............................galls..	852		2, 130.00	
336	Still wines:				
	In casks.........................galls..	3, 454, 078.22	2, 489, 203.39	1, 727, 030.14	.72
	In bottles or jugs—				
	Containing each not more than 1 pint..............................doz..	2, 810.28	8, 592.27	2, 255.49	3.05
	Containing each more than 1 pint and not more than 1 quart......doz..	339, 571.30	1, 875, 945.57	543, 314.11	5.52
	Quantity in excess of 1 quart or 1 pint per bottle..............pts..	7, 435		371.78	

DUTIES COLLECTED UNDER EXISTING LAW, ETC.—Continued.

Duties estimated under—		Rates of duty under—			Average ad valorem under—			Paragraph.
House bill.	Senate bill.	Present law.	House bill.	Senate bill.	Present.	House bill.	Senate bill.	
					Per ct.	*Per ct.*	*Per ct.*	
....	$3,123.09	2 cents per lb.	Free..........	25 per cent...	28.05	Free.	25	
....	2,334.63	....do	....do	....do	17.13	Free.	25	311
....	263.41	....do	....do	....do	24.33	Free.	25	
$6,186.44	6,186.44	15 cts. per lb..	} 20 per cent..	20 per cent...	{ 18.01	} 20	20	313
58,825.58	58,825.58	35 cts. per lb..			17.95			
6,350.00	5,859.37	3 cents per lb.	2 cts. per lb ..	....do	32.51	21.67	20	315
5,401.86	3,338.60	5 cents per lb.	3 cts. per lb ..	....do	53.93	32.34	20	
38,008.16	20,950.20	2 cents per lb.	2 cts. per lb..	30 per cent...	54.40	54.40	30	317
10,844.29	11,771.63	....do	....do	10 per cent...	9.21	9.21	10	318
28,542.91	24,609.62	....do	....do	5 per cent....	5.80	5.80	5	319
53,914.52	58,821.45	3½ cts. per lb..	3½ cts. per lb .	15 per cent...	13.75	13.75	15	320
22,233.94	16,911.90	1¼ cts. per lb.	1¼ cts. per lb.	30 per cent...	40.15	40.15	30	321
37,653.96	26,774.88	2 cts. per lb..	1 cent per lb.	....do	84.38	42.19	30	323
46,502.17	48,427.00	1½ cts. per lb.	....do	....do	43.51	20.60	30	324
70,012.96	51,853.11	10 cts. per lb.	10 cts. per lb.	25 per cent...	38.09	38.00	25	325
22,589.57	19,306.61	3½ cts. per lb.	3½ cts. per lb.	30 per cent...	35.10	35.10	30	326
3,623.24	1,905.96	3 cts. per lb..	1 cent per lb.	....do	171.10	57.03	30	
3,570.94	2,465.11	4 cts. per lb..	3 cts. per lb..	....do	57.94	43.46	30	
4,761.26	3,088.28	7½ cts. per gall	7½ cts. per gall	20 per cent...	27.40	27.40	20	327
7,960,748.17	8,808,097.30	....	....	....	33.32	21.58	22.38	
552,048.06	552,048.08	$2.50 per prf. gallon.	$1.80 per prf. gallon.	$1.80 per prf. gallon.	91.67	65.98	65.98	329
1,180,241.24	1,180,241.24	....do	....do	....do	293.26	211.14	211.14	
196,014.74	196,014.74	....do	....do	....do	366.91	264.06	264.06	
2,645.10	2,645.10	....do	....do	....do	97.63	70.27	70.27	331
353,049.39	353,049.39	....do	....do	....do	115.05	82.83	82.83	332
29,622.75	29,022.75	$1.50 per prf. gallon.	$1 per proof gallon.	$1 per proof gallon.	227.13	151.42	151.42	334
22,531.34	22,531.34	$2 per dozen..	$2 per dozen..	$2 per dozen..	53.82	53.82	53.82	335
1,170,208.64	1,170,208.64	$4 per dozen..	$4 per dozen..	$4 per dozen..	52.62	52.62	52.62	
1,585,500.08	1,585,500.08	$8 per dozen..	$8 per dozen..	$8 per dozen..	55.22	55.22	55.22	
2,130.00	2,130.00	$2.50 per gall.	$2.50 per gall.	$2.50 per gall.	....	....	....	
1,727,039.14	1,727,039.14	50 c. per gall..	50 c. per gall..	50 c. per gall..	69.39	69.39	69.39	336
2,255.42	2,255.42	80 cts. per doz.	80 c. per doz..	80 cts. per doz.	26.25	26.25	26.25	
543,314.11	543,314.11	$1.60 per doz.	$1.60 per doz.	$1.60 per doz .	28.96	28.96	28.96	
371.78	371.78	5 cts. per pint.	5 cts per pint.	5 cts. per pint.	....	....	....	

IMPORTED MERCHANDISE, 1893, WITH THE RATES AND

Paragraph.		Importations of fiscal year, June 30, 1893.			
		Quantities.	Values.	Duties.	Unit of value.
	SCHEDULE H.—SPIRITS, WINES, ETC.—Cont'd.				
	Vermuth, including ginger wine and ginger cordial:				
	In casks..........................galls..	773.50	$760.00	$386.75	$0.99
	In bottles or jugs—				
	Containing each not more than 1 pint..........................doz..	12	32.00	9.60	2.67
	Containing each more than 1 pint and not more than 1 quart.........doz..	56,432.58	169,155.17	90,292.14	3.00
	Bottles or jugs containing wines, cordials, brandy, or other spirituous liquors...No..	8,976,538	....	269,296.14	......
337	Malt liquors, viz, ale, beer, and porter:				
	In bottles or jugs..................galls..	1,230,327.50	1,193,215.08	495,731.00	.96
	Not in bottles or jugs............galls..	2,061,387	681,291.00	412,377.40	.33
338	Malt extract:				
	Fluid—				
	In bottles or jugs..............galls..	36,269	33,465.00	14,507.00	.92
	In casks.......................galls..	25,006	12,865.00	5,001.20	.51
	Solid or condensed....................	....	3,317.80	1,327.12	......
339	Beverages not elsewhere specified:				
	Cherry juice, and other fruit juice, not specially provided for—				
	Containing not more than 18 per cent of alcohol.................galls..	121,585.50	46,639.63	72,951.31	.38
	Containing more than 18 per cent of alcohol..........................galls..	35	58.00	87.50	1.66
	Prune juice or prune wine—				
	Containing not more than 18 per cent of alcohol...............galls..	27,741	24,065.12	16,644.60	.87
	Containing more than 18 per cent of alcohol..........................galls..	....	....	....	......
340	Ginger ale and ginger beer—				
	In plain, green, or colored, molded, or pressed glass bottles—				
	Containing each not more than ¾ of a pint..........................doz..	359,292	270,772.41	46,707.96	.75
	Containing more than ¾ of a pint each and not more than 1½ pints..........................doz..	121	86.90	31.46	.72
	Otherwise than in such bottles, or in such bottles containing more than 1½ pints each..................galls..	....	....	....	......
341	Mineral waters, and all imitations of natural mineral waters, and all artificial mineral waters not specially provided for—				
	In plain, green, or colored glass bottles—				
	Containing not more than 1 pint......................doz..	3,693.75	2,616.25	591.00	.71
	Containing more than 1 pint and not more than 1 quart....doz..	4,524	5,793.50	1,131.01	1.28
	Otherwise than in such bottles, or in bottles containing more than 1 quart......................galls..	39.60	33.00	7.92	.83
	Total Schedule H, spirits, wines, etc....	....	13,874,021.06	9,608,336.91	......
	SCHEDULE I.—COTTON MANUFACTURES.				
342	Cotton, manufactures of:				
	Thread, yarn, warp, or warp yarn, whether single or advanced beyond the condition of single by grouping or twisting two or more single yarns together, whether on beams or in bundles, skeins, or cops, or in any other form—				
	Valued at not exceeding 25 cents per pound..........................lbs..	392,458.30	87,143.60	39,243.83	.22
	Valued at over 25 and not exceeding 40 cents per pound............lbs..	689,318.12	242,718.00	124,077.26	.35
	Valued at over 40 and not exceeding 50 cents per pound............lbs..	184,315.43	84,498.00	42,392.56	.46

DUTIES COLLECTED UNDER EXISTING LAW, ETC.—Continued.

Duties estimated under—		Rates of duty under—			Average ad valorem under—			Paragraph.
House bill.	Senate bill.	Present law.	House bill.	Senate bill.	Present.	House bill.	Senate bill.	
					Per ct.	*Per ct.*	*Per ct.*	
$386.75	$386.75	50c. per gall..	50 c. per gall..	50 c. per gall.	50.49	50.49	50.49	
9.60	9.60	80 c. per doz..	83 c. per doz..	80 c. per doz..	30	30	30	
90,292.14	90,292.14	$1.60 per doz .	$1.60 per doz.	$1.60 per doz.	53.38	53.38	53.38	
134,648.07	....	3 cents each..	30 per cent...	Free........	*60	30	Free.	337
371,708.25	371,708.25	40c. per gall..	30 c. per gall.	30c. per gall..	41.56	31.17	31.17	
300,283.05	200,188.70	20c. per gall..	15c. per gall..	10c. per gall..	60.53	45.40	30.27	338
10,880.70	10,880.70	40c. per gall..	30 c. per gall.	30c. per gall..	43.35	32.51	32.51	
3,750.90	3,750.90	20c. per gall..	15 c. per gall	15c. per gall..	38.87	29.15	29.15	
905.34	905.84	40 per cent...	30 per cent...	30 per cent...	40	30	30	339
60,792.75	60,792.75	60c. per gall..	50c. per gall..	50c. per gall..	156.41	130.34	130.34	
63.00	63.00	$2.50 per pf. gallon.	$1.80 per pf. gallon.	$1.80 per pf. gallon.	150.86	108.54	108.54	
13,870.50	13,870.50	60c. per gall..	50 c. per gall .	50c. per gall..	69.16	57.97	57.9	
....	....	$2.50 per gall.	$1.80 per gall.	$1.80 per proof gallon.	......	......	......	340
54,154.48	54,154.48	13 cts. per doz	20 per cent...	20 per cent...	17.25	20	20	
17.38	17.38	26 cts. per doz	....do	....do	36.20	20	20	
....	....	50 cts. per gall	....do	....do	....	20	20	341
784.87	784.87	16 cts. per doz	30 per cent...	30 per cent...	22.50	30	30	
1,738.05	1,738.05	25 cts. per doz	....do	....do	19.52	30	30	
9.90	9.90	20 cts. per gall	....do	....do	24	30	30	
8,421,347.54	8,183,605.12	....	....	....	60.90	60.60	58.98	
								342
26,143.08	26,143.08	10 cts. per lb..	30 per cent...	30 per cent...	45.03	30	30	
84,951.30	84,951.30	18 cts. per lb..	35 per cent...	35 per cent...	51.12	35	35	
33,799.20	33,799.20	23 cts. per lb..	40 per cent...	40 per cent...	50.17	40	40	

* Bottles containing wines, cordials, etc., present duty estimated 60 per cent ad valorem.

IMPORTED MERCHANDISE, 1893, WITH THE RATES AND

Paragraph.		Importations of fiscal year, June 30, 1893.			
		Quantities.	Values.	Duties.	Unit of value.
	SCHEDULE I.—COTTON MANUFACTURES—Con'd. Cotton, manufactures of—Continued. Thread, yarn, warp, etc.—Continued. Valued at over 50 and not exceeding 60 cents per pound............lbs..	99,715.38	$57,024.00	$27,920.32	$0.57
	Valued at over 60 and not exceeding 70 cents per pound............lbs..	93,419.38	61,413.00	30,828.39	.66
	Valued at over 70 and not exceeding 80 cents per pound............lbs..	74,935.90	57,004.00	28,475.61	.76
	Valued at over 80 cents and not exceeding $1 per pound............lbs..	116,166.12	104,129.00	55,750.74	.90
343	Valued at over $1 per pound.....lbs.,	47,207.61	57,621.00	28,810.50	1.22
344	Thread on spools, 100 yards on each spool................................doz..	809,852	107,082.00	60,880.64	.12
	Cloth— Not exceeding 50 threads to the square inch, counting the warp and filling— Not bleached, dyed, colored, stained, painted, or printed, valued at 6½ cents or less per square yard............sq. yds..	354	17.00	7.08	.048
	Bleached, valued at 9 cents or less per square yard......sq. yds..	92,939	7,848.00	2,323.48	.084
	Dyed, colored, stained, painted, or printed, valued at 12 cents or less per square yard.sq. yds..	221,166	18,052.47	8,846.64	.086
345	Exceeding 50 and not exceeding 100 threads to the square inch, counting the warp and filling— Not bleached, dyed, colored, stained, painted, or printed, valued at 6½ cents or less per square yard............sq. yds..	10,199	562.00	229.49	.055
	Bleached, valued at 9 cents or less per square yard........sq. yds..	1,096,933.00	125,350.10	50,908.02	.062
	Dyed, colored, stained, painted, or printed, valued at 12 cents or less per square yard.sq. yds..	850,745.81	78,080.32	34,029.83	.092
	Not exceeding 100 threads to the square inch, counting the warp and filling— Not bleached, dyed, colored, stained, painted, or printed, valued at over 6½ cents per square yard............sq. yds..	210,366	19,355.70	6,774.50	.092
	Bleached, valued at over 9 cents per square yard........sq. yds..	372,226	50,154.12	17,553.94	.13
346	Dyed, colored, stained, painted, or printed, valued at over 12 cents per square yard..sq. yds..	333,715	56,598.70	19,800.54	.17
	Exceeding 100 and not exceeding 150 threads to the square inch, counting the warp and filling— Not bleached, dyed, colored, stained, painted, or printed, valued at 7½ cents or less per square yard............sq. yds..	141,853.50	8,060.00	4,255.61	.057
	Not bleached, dyed, colored, stained, painted, or printed, valued at over 7½ cents per square yard............sq. yds..	141,156	13,290.00	5,316.60	.094
	Bleached, valued at 10 cents or less per square yard..sq. yds..	2,376,266	191,652.00	95,048.25	.081
	Bleached, valued at over 10 cents per square yard......sq. yds..	977,530	121,493.00	48,597.20	.12
	Dyed, colored, stained, painted, or printed, valued at 12½ cents or less per square yard..sq. yds..	2,232,448	228,020.00	111,622.40	.10
	Dyed, colored, stained, painted, or printed, valued at over 12½ cents per square yard..sq. yds..	2,340,750	394,282.37	157,712.95	.17

DUTIES COLLECTED UNDER EXISTING LAW, ETC.—Continued.

Duties estimated under—		Rates of duty under—			Average ad valorem under—			Paragraph.
House bill.	Senate bill.	Present law.	House bill.	Senate bill.	Present.	House bill.	Senate bill.	
					Per ct.	Per ct.	Per ct.	
$22,809.60	$22,809.60	28 cts. per lb..	40 per cent...	40 per cent...	48.96	40	40	
24,565.20	24,565.20	33 cts. per lb.	....do	....do	50.19	40	40	
22,801.60	22,801.60	38 cts. per lb.	....do	....do	49.95	40	40	
41,651.00	41,651.00	48 cts. per lb .	....do	....do	53.55	40	40	
28,048.40	28,048.40	50 per cent..	....do	....do	50	40	40	
89,143.34	89,143.34	7 cts. per doz.	4½ cts. per doz	4½ cts. per doz	56.33	36.25	36.25	43, 44
3.54	3.54	2 c. per sq. yd	1 c. per sq. yd	1 c. per sq. yd	41.65	20.83	20.83	
1,161.74	1,161.74	2½ c. per sq. yd	1¼ c. per sq. yd	1¼ c. per sq. yd	29.61	14.80	14.80	
4,423.32	4,423.32	4 c. per sq. yd	2 c. per sq. yd	2 c. per sq. yd	46.68	23.34	23.34	345
127.48	127.58	2¼ c. per sq. yd	1¼ c. per sq. yd	1¼ c. per sq. yd	40.83	22.70	22.70	
29,954.00	29,954.00	3 c. per sq. yd	1½ c. per sq. yd	1½ c. per sq. yd	47.79	23.89	23.89	
23,395.50	23,395.50	4 c. per sq. yd	2¼ c. per sq. yd	2¼ c. per sq. yd	43.57	28.08	28.08	
3,871.14	3,871.14	35 per cent...	20 per cent...	20 per cent...	35	20	20	
12,538.53	12,538.53	....do	25 per cent...	25 per cent...	35	25	25	
16,970.61	16,970.61	....do	30 per cent...	30 per cent...	35	30	30	346
2,127.80	2,127.80	3 c. per sq. yd.	1½ c. per sq. yd	1½ c. per sq. yd	52.74	26.37	26.37	
3,322.50	3,322.50	40 per cent...	25 per cent...	25 per cent...	40	25	25	
59,405.15	59,405.15	4 c. per sq. yd.	2½ c. per sq. yd	2½ c. per sq. yd	49.59	30.96	30.96	
36,447.90	36,447.90	40 per cent...	30 per cent...	30 per cent...	40	30	30	
78,135.68	78,135.68	5 c. per sq. yd.	3½ c. per sq. yd	3½ c. per sq. yd	48.76	30.03	30.03	
137,908.83	137,908.83	40 per cent...	35 per cent...	35 per cent...	40	35	35	

IMPORTED MERCHANDISE, 1893, WITH THE RATES AND

Paragraph.		Importations of fiscal year, June 30, 1893.			
		Quantities.	Values.	Duties.	Unit of value.
	SCHEDULE I.—COTTON MANUFACTURES—Con'd. Cotton, manufactures of—Continued. Cloth—Continued.				
347	Exceeding 150 and not exceeding 200 threads to the square inch, counting the warp and filling— Not bleached, dyed, colored, stained, painted, or printed, valued at 8 cents or less per square yard..........sq. yds..	561,321.67	$29,161.00	$19,646.27	$0.052
	Not bleached, dyed, colored, stained, painted, or printed, valued at over 8 cents per square yard..........sq. yds..	120,944	12,188.00	5,484.60	.10
	Bleached, valued at 10 cents per square yard..........sq. yds..	2,287,630.25	166,008.75	102,043.42	.073
	Bleached, valued at over 10 cents per square yard......sq. yds..	1,705,719	230,897.56	103,903.90	.14
	Dyed, colored, stained, painted, or printed, valued at 12 cents or less per square yard.sq. yds..	3,807,101	417,564.01	214,340.57	.11
	Dyed, colored, stained, painted, or printed, valued at over 12 cents per square yard.sq. yds..	8,034,860	1,301,990.65	585,895.80	.16
348	Exceeding 200 threads to the square inch, counting the warp and filling— Not bleached, dyed, colored, stained, painted, or printed, valued at 10 cents or less per square yard..........sq. yds..	2,334,849	196,894.00	105,068.28	.084
	Not bleached, dyed, colored, stained, painted, or printed, valued at over 10 cents per square yard..........sq. yds..	175,040	20,689.00	9,310.05	.12
	Bleached, valued at 12 cents or less per square yard ..sq. yds..	1,867,240	186,104.00	102,696.70	.10
	Bleached, valued at over 12 cents per square yard......sq. yds..	1,147,025	190,815.88	85,867.15	.17
	Dyed, colored, stained, painted, or printed, valued at 15 cents or less per square yard..sq. yds..	7,449,602	928,746.00	502,848.18	.12
	Dyed, colored, stained, painted, or printed, valued at over 15 cents per square yard.sq. yds..	3,729,304	708,466.63	318,809.98	.19
	Bleached, dyed, colored, stained, painted, or printed, containing an admixture of silk, and not otherwise provided for.sq.yds..	198,802.63	74,814.98	46,065.56	*.38
349	Corsets not elsewhere specified....doz..	32,773.41	366,754.04	183,377.03	11.19
	Other articles of wearing apparel and ready-made clothing— Of which India rubber is a component material..............lbs..	1,966.75	2,519.00	2,252.88	1.27
350	All other not specially provided for.		1,288,105.43	644,052.74	
	Plushes, velvets, velveteens, corduroys, and all other pile fabrics composed of cotton or other vegetable fiber— Plushes, velvets, and velveteens— Not bleached, dyed, colored, stained, painted, or printed ....sq. yds..	1,496,490.83	284,215.00	206,492.08	.19
	Bleached..............sq. yds..	26,192	9,256.00	4,904.24	.35
	Dyed, colored, stained, painted, or printed..........sq. yds..	4,637,916	1,613,311.12	971,970.48	.35
	All other..............sq. yds..	56,341	46,483.00	18,593.20	.83
	Corduroys and other pile fabrics— Not bleached, dyed, colored, stained, painted, or printed ....sq. yds..	240,147.50	50,496.00	34,713.95	.21

DUTIES COLLECTED UNDER EXISTING LAW, ETC.—Continued.

Duties estimated under—		Rates of duty under—			Average ad valorem under—			Paragraph.
House bill.	Senate bill.	Present law.	House bill.	Senate bill.	Present.	House bill.	Senate bill.	
					Per ct.	Per ct.	Per ct.	347
$11,220.43	$11,220.43	3½ c. per sq. yd	2 c. per sq. yd	2 c. per sq. yd.	07.35	38.48	38.48	
3,656.40	3,656.40	45 per cent ..	30 per cent...	30 per cent...	45	30	30	
62,909.82	62,909.82	4½ c. per sq. yd	2⅜ c. per sq. yd	2⅜ c. per sq. yd	61.67	36.49	36.49	
80,814.14	80,814.14	45 per cent...	35 per cent...	35 per cent...	45	35	35	
165,026.92	165,026.92	5½ c. per sq. yd	4¼ c. per sq. yd	4¼ c. per sq. yd	51.33	38.44	38.44	
520,796.26	520,796.26	45 per cent...	40 per cent...	40 per cent...	45	40	40	348
70,045.47	70,045.47	4½ cts. per sq. yd.	3 cts. per sq. yd.	3 cts. per sq. yd.	53.36	35.58	35.58	
6,200.70	6,200.70	45 per cent...	30 per cent...	30 per cent...	45	30	30	
74,689.96	74,689.96	5½ cts. per sq. yd.	4 cts. per sq. yd.	4 cts. per sq. yd.	55.18	40.08	40.08	
66,785.55	66,785.55	45 per cent...	35 per cent...	35 per cent...	45	35	35	
428,352.12	428,352.12	6¾ cts. per sq. yd.	5¾ cts. per sq. yd.	5¾ cts. per sq. yd.	54.14	46.12	46.12	
283,380.65	283,380.65	45 per cent...	40 per cent...	40 per cent...	45	40	40	
29,925.97	29,925.97	10 cts. per sq. yd. and 35 per cent.	....do	....do	61.57	40	40	
146,701.61	146,701.61	50 per cent...	....do	....do	50	40	40	349
1,007.60	1,007.60	50 cents per pound and 50 per cent.	....do	....do	89.44	40	40	
515,242.17	515,242.17	50 per cent...	....do	....do	50	40	40	350
99,475.25	99,475.25	10 cts. per sq. yd. and 20 per cent.	35 per cent...	35 per cent...	72.65	35	35	
3,702.40	3,702.40	12 c. p. sq. yd. and 20 p. ct.	40 per cent...	40 per cent...	53.95	40	40	
645,324.44	645,324.44	14 c. p. sq. yd. and 20 p. ct.	....do	....do	60.25	40	40	
16,209.05	16,269.05	40 per cent...	35 per cent...	35 per cent...	40	35	35	
17,673.60	17,673.60	10 c. p. sq. yd. and 20 p. ct.	....do	....do	68.75	35	35	

IMPORTED MERCHANDISE, 1893, WITH THE RATES AND

Paragraph.		Importations of fiscal year, June 30, 1893.			
		Quantities.	Values.	Duties.	Unit of value.
	SCHEDULE I.—COTTON MANUFACTURES—C'td.				
	Cotton, manufactures of—Continued. Plushes, velvets, velveteens, corduroys, and all other pile fabrics composed of cotton or other vegetable fiber—Con'd.				
	Bleached................sq. yds..	8,105.50	$2,293.40	$1,431.34	$0.28
	Dyed, colored, stained, painted, or printed...............sq. yds..	1,150,081.37	397,530.41	240,601.47	.35
351	All other...............sq. yds..	48,436	25,796.71	10,318.68	.53
	Chenille curtains, table covers, and all goods manufactured of cotton chenille, or of which cotton chenille forms the				
352	" component material of chief value.....		38,999.00	23,309.40	......
	Stockings, hose and half hose, other, valued at not more than $1.50 per				
	dozen....................doz..	104,692	58,067.73	20,323.71	.56
	Shirts and drawers valued at not more than $1.50 per dozen...............doz..	30,601	39,629.45	13,870.31	1.30
	Knit goods made on knitting machines or frames—				
353	Shirts and drawers—				
	Valued at more than $1.50 and not more than $3 per dozen ....doz..	80,730.41	230,072.80	170,255.90	2.56
	Valued at more than $3 and not more than $5 per dozen...doz..	48,029.86	182,695.23	133,115.49	3.80
	Valued at more than $5 and not more than $7 per dozen...doz..	19,176.90	112,401.50	73,726.03	5.86
	Valued at more than $7 per dozen....................doz..	6,544.62	67,093.10	39,926.48	10.25
	Stockings, hose and half hose— Selvedged, fashioned, narrowed, or shaped wholly or in part by knitting machines or frames, or knit by hand, including such as are commercially known as seamless stockings, hose, or half hose, finished or unfinished—				
	Valued at not more than 60 cents per dozen pairs..........doz..	1,343,998.08	786,152.33	426,030.11	.59
	Valued at more than 60 cents and not more than $2 per dozen pairs....................doz..	3,780,115.28	4,511,010.70	3,246,362.01	1.19
	Valued at more than $2 and not more than $4 per dozen pairs ....doz..	117,221.57	319,247.36	215,615.14	2.72
	Valued at more than $4 per dozen pairs....................doz..	13,091.85	78,225.63	44,382.13	6.01
354	Cords, braids, boot, shoe, and corset lacings—				
	On which duty computed at 35 cents per pound is less than 40 per cent ad valorem...............lbs..	84,531	97,945.75	39,178.30	1.16
	All other..................lbs..	484,093	298,032.00	109,432.48	.02
	Gimps, galloons, webbing, goring, suspenders and braces, elastic or nonelastic..........................		421,353.97	168,541.59	......
	Damask............................		371,890.97	148,756.39	......
355	All other manufactures of cotton not specially provided for.............		2,171,430.56	868,575.83	......
	Total Schedule I, cotton manufactures.		20,510,438.98	11,333,605.23	......
	SCHEDULE J.—FLAX, HEMP, AND JUTE, AND MANUFACTURES OF—				
	Flax and hemp, and manufactures of flax, hemp, jute, and other vegetable fiber: Unmanufactured—				
358	Flax, hackled, known as "dressed line"...................tons..	1,306.04	815,290.00	87,803.91	623.96
360	Hemp, hackled, known as line of hemp....................tons..	98.11	21,012.00	4,903.29	214.17

DUTIES COLLECTED UNDER EXISTING LAW, ETC.—Continued.

Duties estimated under—		Rates of duty under—			Average ad valorem under—			Paragraph
House bill.	Senate bill.	Present law.	House bill.	Senate bill.	Present.	House bill.	Senate bill.	
					Per ct.	*Per ct.*	*Per ct.*	
$917.36	$917.36	12 c. p. sq. yd. and 20 p. ct.	40 per cent..	40 per cent...	62.42	40	40	
159,012.16	159,012.16	14 c. p. sq. yd. and 20 p. ct.	....do........	....do	60.52	40	40	
9,028.84	9,028.84	40 per cent...	35 per cent...	35 per cent...	40	35	35	
15,599.60	15,599.60	60 per cent...	40 per cent...	40 per cent...	60	40	40	351
17,420.32	17,420.32	35 per cent...	30 per cent...	30 per cent...	35	30	30	352
11,888.83	11,888.83	....do........	....do........	....do........	35	30	30	
92,029.12	92,029.12	$1 per dozen and 35 p. ct.	40 per cent...	40 per cent ..	74	40	40	353
75,078.09	75,078.09	$1.25 per doz. and 40 p. ct.	....do........	....do........	72.86	40	40	
44,960.00	44,960.00	$1.50 per doz. and 40 p. ct.	....do........	....do........	65.59	40	40	
26,837.24	26,837.24	$2 per dozen and 40 p. ct.	....do........	....do........	59.51	40	40	
314,400.93	314,400.93	20 cts. per doz. and 20 p. ct.	....do........	....do........	54.19	40	40	
1,804,406.68	1,804,406.68	50 cts. per doz. and 30 p. ct.	....do........	....do........	71.97	40	40	
127,698.94	127,698.94	75 cts. per doz. and 40 p. ct.	....do........	....do........	67.54	40	40	
31,390.25	31,390.25	$1 per doz. and 40 p. ct.	....do........	....do........	56.74	40	40	
34,281.01 104,311.20	34,281.01 104,311.20	40 per cent ... 35 cents per lb.	35 per cent... ....do........	35 per cent... ....do........	40 56.85	35 35	35 35	354
147,473.88 130,161.84	147,473.88 130,161.84	40 per cent ... .do........	....do........ ....do........	....do........ ....do........	40 40	35 35	35 35	
760,003.84	760,003.84	....do........	....do........	....do........	40	35	35	355
7,885,585.28	7,885,585.28				55.25	38.45	38.45	
43,902.95	43,902.95	3 cts. per lb ..	1½ cts. per lb..	1½ cts. per lb..	10.77	5.39	5.39	358
2,197.66	2,197.66	$50 per ton...	1 ct. per lb ...	1 ct. per lb ...	23.35	10.46	10.46	360

IMPORTED MERCHANDISE, 1893, WITH THE RATES AND

Paragraph.		Importations of fiscal year, June 30, 1893.			
		Quantities.	Values.	Duties.	Unit of value.
	SCHEDULE J.—FLAX, HEMP, AND JUTE, AND MANUFACTURES OF—Continued. Flax and hemp, and manufactures of flax, hemp, jute, and other vegetable fiber— Continued.				
361	Yarn, jute...................................lbs..	3,725,580	$717,984.00	$62,294.40	0.048
362	Cables, cordage and twine— Cables and cordage— Of hemp, untarred...........lbs..	31,290	3,521.00	782.24	.11
	Other, untarred, composed in whole or in part of istle or Tampico fiber, manila, sisal grass, or sunn..............lbs..	145,162	12,914.00	2,177.43	.080
	Tarred.........................lbs..	404,408	38,856.00	12,132.24	.000
	All other......................lbs..	3,611	288.39	54.17	.08
363	Hemp and jute carpets.............sq. yds..	391,266	148,268.00	23,475.00	.38
	Burlaps, of flax, jute, or hemp, or of which flax, jute, or hemp, or either of them, shall be the component material of chief value (except such as may be suitable for bagging for cotton)—				
364	Not exceeding 60 inches in width..lbs..	111,416,904	6,193,572.73	1,810,524.75	.056
365	Bags for grain made of burlaps......lbs..	26,832,234	1,199,804.25	530,644.68	.045
366	Bagging for cotton, gunny cloth, and all similar material for covering cotton, composed in whole or in part of hemp, flax, jute, or jute butts— Valued at 6 cents or less per square yard............................sq. yds..	730,224	35,932.00	11,683.00	.049
	Valued at more than 6 cents per square yard............................sq. yds..	71,517	4,881.00	1,287.30	.068
367	Gill netting, nets, webs, and seines of flax— Made of thread or twine from yarn of a number not higher than 20..lbs..	24,338	3,330.11	4,816.28	.137
	Made of thread or twine from yarn finer than No. 20.................lbs..	985.50	1,497.25	870.86	1.52
368	Hose, linen hydraulic, made in whole or in part of flax, hemp, or jute.......lbs..	19,132	11,153.35	3,820.40	.58
369	Oilcloths for floors, stamped, painted, or printed, including linoleum, corticene, cork carpets, figured or plain, and all other oilcloth (except silk oilcloth), and waterproof cloth, not specially provided for— Valued at 25 cents or less per square yard............................sq. yds..	870,838	100,321.00	64,128.40	.18
	Valued above 25 cents per square yard............................sq. yds..	462,609.75	255,389.00	146,008.17	.55
370	Manufactures—Yarns or threads— Flax or hemp— Valued at 13 cents or less per pound.........................lbs..	771,052	72,009.00	46,203.12	.004
	Valued at more than 13 cents per pound.........................lbs..	1,235,039	524,973.60	230,240.37	.43
	Manufactures of flax or hemp, or of which these substances, or either of them, is the component material of chief value..................		3,557,503.45	1,778,781.19	....
371	Manufactures of flax containing more than 100 threads to the square inch, counting both warp and filing (until January 1, 1895)........		11,491,780.77	4,022,123.27	....
372	Wearing apparel—. Collars and cuffs entirely of cotton.........................doz pcs..	929	419.00	280.00	.45
	Collars and cuffs, composed in whole or in part of linen............doz..	89,137.90	93,705.00	64,223.43	1.051
	Shirts and all articles of wearing apparel of every description, not specially provided for, composed wholly or in part of linen........	....	38,738.92	21,300.40	....

DUTIES COLLECTED UNDER EXISTING LAW, ETC.—Continued.

Duties estimated under—		Rates of duty under—			Average ad valorem under—			Paragraph.
House bill.	Senate bill.	Present law.	House bill.	Senate bill.	Present.	House bill.	Senate bill.	
					Per ct.	*Per ct.*	*Per ct.*	
$35,596.80	$35,596.80	35 per cent...	20 per cent...	20 per cent...	35	20	20	361 362
350.10	350.10	2¼ cts. per lb..	10 per cent...	10 per cent ..	22.34	10	10	
1,291.40	1,291.40	1¼ cts. per lb..	....do	....do	16.86	10	10	
3,885.60	3,885.60	3 cts. per lb...	....do	....do	31.23	10	10	
28.84	28.84	1¼ cts. per lb..	....do	....do	18.78	10	10	
29,653.60	29,653.60	6c. per sq. yd.	20 per cent...	20 per cent...	15.83	20	20	363
905,262.38	905,262.38	1⅛ cts. per lb..	15 per cent...	15 per cent...	29.23	15	15	364
239,960.85	269,955.95	2 cts. per lb..	20 per cent...	22½ per cent..	44.73	20	22.50	365 366
5,389.80	5,389.80	1₇⁄₁₀c. p. sq.yd.	15 per cent...	15 per cent...	32.52	15	15	
732.15	732.15	1₇⁄₁₀c. p. sq.yd.	....do	....do	26.37	15	15	367
999.03	1,165.54	15 cts. lb. and 35 per cent.	30 per cent...	35 per cent...	144.63	30	35	
449.18	524.03	20 cts. lb. and 40 per cent.	....do	....do	58.17	30	35	
3,903.67	3,346.00	20 cts. per lb.	35 per cent...	30 per cent...	34.31	35	30	368 369
48,096.30	32,064.20	40 per cent...	20 per cent...	20 per cent...	40	30	20	
76,616.70	89,386.10	15 cts. per sq. yard and 30 per cent.	....do	35 per cent...	57	30	35	370
18,152.25	18,152.25	6 cts. per lb..	25 per cent...	22 per cent...	63.92	25	25	
157,493.58	157,493.58	45 per cent...	30 per cent...	30 per cent...	45	30	30	
1,067,268.74	1,067,268.74	50 per cent...	....do	....do	50	30	30	
3,447,534.23	3,447,534.23	35 per cent...	....do	....do	35	30	30	371
146.65	146.65	15 cts. per doz. and 35 p. ct.	35 per cent...	35 per cent...	68.26	35	35	372
32,796.78	51,537.79	30 cts. per doz. and 40 p. ct.	....do	55 per cent...	68.54	35	55	
11,808.62	19,369.46	55 per cent...	....do	50 per cent...	55	35	55	

TA——13

IMPORTED MERCHANDISE, 1893, WITH THE RATES AND

Paragraph.		Importations of fiscal year, June 30, 1893.			
		Quantities.	Values.	Duties.	Unit of value.
	SCHEDULE J.—FLAX, HEMP, AND JUTE, AND MANUFACTURES OF—Continued. Flax and hemp, and manufactures of flax, hemp, jute, and other vegetable fiber—Continued.				
373	Laces, edgings, embroideries, insertings, neck ruflings, ruchings, trimmings, tuckings, lace window curtains, and other similar tamboured articles, and articles embroidered by hand or machinery, embroidered and hem stitched handkerchiefs, and articles made wholly or in part of lace, rufflings, tuckings, or ruchings, composed of flax, jute, or other vegetable fiber, except cotton, or of which either of these substances, except cotton, is the component material of chief value, not specially provided for..............	....	$2,564,900.99	1,538,940.59	....
	Laces, edgings, embroideries, insertings, neck ruflings, ruchings, trimmings, tuckings, lace window curtains, and other similar tamboured articles, and articles embroidered by hand or machinery, embroidered and hemstitched handkerchiefs, and articles made wholly or in part of lace, rufflings, tuckings, or ruchings, composed of cotton, or of which cotton is the component material of chief value, not specially provided for.............	....	12,813,997.65	7,688,398.62	....
	All other manufactures not specially provided for—				
374	Manufactures of jute, or of which jute is the component material of chief value, not specially provided for— Valued at 5 cents per pound or less...............................lbs..	2,099,318	75,828.00	41,966.36	$0.036
	Valued above 5 cents per pound ....lbs..	9,318,621	690,383.89	276,153.56	.074
	Manufactures of other vegetable fiber, except flax, hemp, or cotton, or of which other vegetable fiber, except flax, hemp, or cotton, is the component material of chief value, not specially provided for—				
	Valued at 5 cents per pound or less ....lbs..	15,679	597.00	313.58	.038
	Valued above 5 cents per pound..lbs..	....	160,281.00	64,112.40	....
	Burlaps, exceeding 60 inches in width ....lbs..	8,239,159	537,016.00	214,806.40	.065
	Total Schedule J, flax, hemp, etc	....	41,706,792.44	18,767,353.37	....
	SCHEDULE K.—WOOLEN GOODS.* Manufactures composed wholly or in part of wool, worsted, the hair of the camel, goat, alpaca, or other animals: Rags, mungo, flocks, noils, shoddy, and waste—				
†388	Shoddy ....lbs..	35	20.00	10.50	.57
	Top, slubbing, roving, ring, yarn, garnetted, and other wastes ..lbs..	93,477	33,564.00	28,043.10	.36
†389	Rags, mungo, and flocks..........lbs..	158,265.50	46,108.00	15,826.55	.29
390	Wools, etc., viz, roping, roving or tops, and all wool advanced by manufacture beyond washed or scoured condition:				
391	Yarns, woolen and worsted— Valued at not more than 30 cents per pound ....lbs..	871	98.30	273.93	.11
	Valued at more than 30 and not more than 40 cents per pound ......lbs..	22,404.50	8,822.63	10,481.41	.39
	Valued at more than 40 cents per pound ....lbs..	1,179,174.04	693,999.40	731,581.87	.59

* HOUSE OF REPRESENTATIVES.—The reduction of the rates of duty herein provided for manufactures of wool shall take effect July 1, 1894, and on all rates of duty in the woolen schedule, except on carpets, there shall be a reduction of 1 per cent ad valorem to take effect on the 1st day of July, 1896, and thereafter of a like amount on the 1st day of July, 1897, 1898, 1899, and 1900, respectively.

DUTIES COLLECTED UNDER EXISTING LAW, ETC.—Continued.

Duties estimated under—		Rates of duty under—			Average ad valorem under—			Paragraph.
House bill.	Senate bill.	Present law.	House bill.	Senate bill.	Present.	House bill.	Senate bill.	
					Per ct.	Per ct.	Per ct.	
$1,025,960.40	$1,025,960.40	60 per cent...	40 per cent...	40 per cent...	60	40	40	373
5,125,599.06	5,125,599.06	60 per cent...	40 per cent...	40 per cent...	60	40	40	
22,748.40	22,748.40	2 cts. per lb..	30 per cent...	30 per cent...	55.37	30	30	374
207,115.17	207,115.17	40 per cent...	....do	....do	40	30	30	
179.10	179.10	2 cts. per lb..	....do	....do	52.53	30	30	
48,084.30	48,084.30	40 per cent...	....do	....do	40	30	30	
161,104.80	161,104.80	....do	....do	....do	40	30	30	
12,724,279.49	12,779,029.03				45	30.51	30.35	
3.00	3.00	30 cents p. lb.	15 per cent...	15 per cent...	52.50	15	15	†388
5,034.60	5,034.60	....do	....do	....do	89.55	15	15	
6,916.20	6,916.20	10 cents p. lb.	....do	....do	34.32	15	15	†389 390
29.39	29.39	27½ c. p. & lb. 35 p. c.	30 per cent...	30 per cent...	278.66	30	30	391
2,646.79	2,646.79	33 c. p. lb. & 35 p. c.	....do	....do	118.79	30	30	
242,899.79	242,899.79	38½ c. p. lb. & 40 p. c.	....do	35 per cent...	105.42	35	30	

* SENATE.—The reduction of the rates of duty herein provided for manufactures of wool shall take effect December 2, 1894.
† Yarn and other wastes, rags and flocks are made free of duty by the proposed bill.

IMPORTED MERCHANDISE, 1893, WITH THE RATES AND

Paragraph		Importations of fiscal year, June 30, 1893.			
		Quantities.	Values.	Duties.	Unit of value.
	SCHEDULE K.—WOOLEN GOODS—Continued.				
392	Cloths, woolen or worsted:				
	Valued at not more than 30 cents per pound..........................lbs..	48,852.25	$13,097.00	$21,360.04	$0.27
	Valued at more than 30 and not more than 40 cents per pound.............lbs..	347,450.50	127,569.00	184,796.00	.37
	Valued above 40 cents per pound....lbs..	14,250,621.63	12,666,256.30	12,608,401.74	.89
	Shawls, woolen or worsted:				
	Valued at not more than 30 cents per pound............................lbs..				
	Valued at more than 30 and not more than 40 cents per pound...........lbs..	997	348.00	523.06	.35
	Valued at above 40 cents per pound..lbs..	266,912.52	304,222.98	269,552.98	1.14
	Knit fabrics, and all fabrics made on knitting machines or frames:				
	Valued at not more than 30 cents per pound............................lbs..				
	Valued at more than 30 and not more than 40 cents per pound...........lbs..	2.50	1.00	1.36	.40
	Valued at above 40 cents per pound..lbs..	11,531.09	15,732.50	12,940.27	1.36
	All knit wearing apparel............lbs..	992,221.15	1,440,688.25	1,355,502.52	1.45
	All other manufactures, not specially provided for:				
	Valued at not more than 30 cents per pound............................lbs..	10,601.41	2,925.00	4,668.47	.28
	Valued at more than 30 and not more than 40 cents per pound...........lbs..	57,878.10	21,720.00	30,971.11	.38
	Valued at above 40 cents per pound..lbs..	399,613.60	474,844.83	413,252.47	1.19
393	Blankets:				
	Valued at not more than 30 cents per pound............................lbs..	5,095	1,444.00	1,273.88	.28
	Valued at more than 30 and not more than 40 cents per pound..........lbs..	672.85	227.00	227.48	.34
	Valued at more than 40 and not more than 50 cents per pound..........lbs..	696.75	333.75	346.78	.48
	Valued at more than 50 cents per pound............................lbs..	3,940.75	3,762.25	3,022.17	.95
	Hats of wool:				
	Valued at not more than 30 cents per pound............................lbs..	18	5.35	4.58	.30
	Valued at more than 30 and not more than 40 cents per pound..........lbs..	23.75	7.32	7.78	.31
	Valued at more than 40 and not more than 50 cents per pound..........lbs..	3,954	1,885.00	1,964.57	.48
	Valued at more than 50 cents per pound............................lbs..	24,575.95	20,021.34	17,470.28	.81
	Flannels for underwear:				
	Valued at not more than 30 cents per pound............................lbs..	173	52.00	44.15	.30
	Valued at more than 30 and not more than 40 cents per pound..........lbs..	1,747	561.00	580.69	.32
	Valued at more than 40 and not more than 50 cents per pound..........lbs..	1,509.33	729.67	753.47	.48
	Weighing over 4 ounces per square yard..............................lbs..	79,722.43	75,372.83	72,764.29	.95
394	Dress goods, women's and children's, coat linings, Italian cloths, and goods of similar description:				
	Of which the warp consists wholly of cotton or other vegetable materials, with the remainder of the fabric composed wholly or in part of wool, worsted, the hair of the camel, goat, alpaca, or other animals—				
	Valued at not exceeding 15 cents per square yard.................sq. yds..	14,640,855.85	1,900,189.73	1,784,935.85	.13
	Valued at above 15 cents per square yard.......................sq. yds..	5,794,945.54	1,170,733.78	1,048,962.53	.20
	Weighing over 4 ounces per square yard..............................lbs..	6,253,665.74	5,109,203.70	5,396,214.82	.82

195

DUTIES COLLECTED UNDER EXISTING LAW, ETC.—Continued.

Duties estimated under—		Rates of duty under—			Average ad valorem under—			Paragraph.
House bill.	Senate bill.	Present law.	House bill.	Senate bill.	Present.	House bill.	Senate bill.	
					Per ct.	*Per ct.*	*Per ct.*	392
$5,238.80	$4,583.95	33 c. p. lb. & 40 p. c.	40 per cent...	35 per cent...	163.09	40	35	
51,027.60	44,640.15	38½ c. p. lb. & 40 p. c.	....do........	....do........	114.86	40	35	
5,066,602.52	4,433,180.70	44 c. p. lb. & 50 p. c.	....do........	....do........	99.50	40	35	
		33 c. p. lb. & 40 p. o.	....do........	....do........		40	35	
139.20	121.80	38½ c. p. lb. & 40 p. o.	....do........	....do........	150.30	40	35	
							35	
121,689.19	106,478.04	44 c. p. lb. & 50 p. c.	....do........	....do........	88.60	40		
							35	
....	....	33 c. p. lb. & 40 p. c.	....do........	....do........	....	40		
.40	.35	38½ c. p. lb. & 40 p.o.	....do........	....do........	136	40	35	
6,298.00	5,506.37	44 c. p. lb. & 50 p. c.	....do........	....do........	82.25	40	35	
576,275.30	504,240.88	49½ c. p. lb. & 60 p. c.	....do........	....do........	94.09	40	35	
1,170.00	1,023.75	33 c. per lb. and 40 p. c.	....do........	....do........	150.00	40	35	
8,683.00	7,602.00	38½ c. per lb. and 40 p. c.	....do........	....do........	142.50	40	35	
189,937.93	166,195.69	44 c. per lb. and 50 p. c.	....do........	....do........	87.03	40	35	393
361.00	361.00	16½ c. per lb. and 35 p. c.	25 per cent...	25 per cent...	88.22	25	25	
68.10	68.10	22 c. per lb. and 35 p. c.	30 per cent...	30 per cent...	100	30	30	
116.81	100.13	33 c. per lb. and 35 p. c.	35 per cent...	....do........	103.90	35	30	
1,316.78	1,128.67	38½ c. per lb. and 40 p. c.	....do........	....do........	80.33	35	30	
1.33	1.33	16½ c. per lb. and 35 p. c.	25 per cent...	25 per cent...	86	25	25	
2.20	2.20	22 c. per lb. and 35 p. c.	30 per cent...	30 per cent...	106.38	30	30	
650.75	565.50	33 c. per lb. and 35 p. c.	35 per cent...	....do........	104.22	35	30	
7,007.46	6,006.40	38½ c. per lb. and 40 p. c.	....do........	....do........	87.26	35	30	
13.00	13.00	16½ c. per lb. and 35 p. c.	25 per cent...	25 per cent...	84.00	25	25	
168.30	168.30	22 c. per lb. and 35 p. c.	30 per cent...	30 per cent...	103.51	30	30	
255.38	218.90	33 c. per lb. and 35 p. o.	35 per cent...	....do........	103.22	35	30	
30,149.13	22,611.85	38½ c. per lb. and 40 p. o.	40 per cent...	....do........	96.54	40	30	394
760,075.89	665,066.40	7 c. p. sq. yd. and 40 p.o.	....do........	35 per cent...	93.93	40	35	
468,293.51	409,751.82	8 c. per sq. yd. and 50 p. c.	....do........	....do........	89.60	40	35	
2,043,681.48	1,788,221.29	44 cts. per lb. and 50 p. c.	....do........	....do........	103.86	40	35	

IMPORTED MERCHANDISE, 1893, WITH THE RATES AND

Paragraph.		Importations of fiscal year, June 30, 1893.			
		Quantities.	Values.	Duties.	Unit of Value.
	SCHEDULE K.—WOOLEN GOODS—Continued.				
	Dress goods, womens' and childrens', coat linings, Italian cloths, and goods of similar description—Continued.				
395	Composed wholly or in part of wool, worsted, the hair of the camel, goat, alpaca, or other animals—				
	Weighing over 4 ounces per square yard......lbs..	1,488,242.45	$1,763,256.99	$1,536,455.17	$1.18
	All other......sq. yds..	38,794,768.68	7,878,190.11	8,594,460.64	.20
396	Other clothing, ready-made, and articles of wearing apparel (except knit goods), made up or manufactured wholly or in part......lbs..	304,772.13	742,354.87	596,275.12	2.44
	Felts, not woven......lbs..	43,657.81	65,305.65	60,784.07	1.50
	Plushes and other pile fabrics......lbs..	139,963.25	153,655.50	161,475.15	1.10
397	Cloaks, dolmans, jackets, talmas, ulsters, or other outside garments for ladies' and children's apparel, and goods of similar description, or used for like purposes.lbs..	160,111.42	373,255.35	303,208.41	2.33
398	Webbing, gorings, suspenders, braces, beltings, bindings, braids, galloons, fringes, gimps, cords, cords and tassels, dress trimmings, laces and embroideries, head nets, buttons, or barrel buttons, or buttons of other forms for tassels or ornaments, wrought by hand, or braided by machinery, which are elastic or nonelastic..lbs..	173,357.27	307,531.66	288,533.38	1.77
399	Carpets and carpeting—				
	Aubusson, Axminster, moquette, and chenille carpets, and carpets woven whole for rooms, and Oriental, Berlin, and other similar rugs......sq. yds..	441,750.32	1,271,036.87	773,464.93	2.88
400	Saxony, Wilton, and Tournay velvet carpets......sq. yds..	47,140.46	95,716.62	66,570.92	2.03
401	Brussels carpets......sq. yds..	67,744	71,821.00	56,532.77	1.06
402	Velvet and tapestry velvet carpets, printed on the warp or otherwise ......sq. yds..	36,992.25	46,447.60	33,375.70	1.26
403	Tapestry Brussels, printed on the warp or otherwise......sq. yds..	4,651.10	3,430.60	2,674.31	.74
404	Treble ingrain, three-ply, and all chain Venetian carpets......sq. yds..	33,484	27,603.63	17,403.41	.82
405	Wool, Dutch, and two-ply ingrain carpets......sq. yds..	33,721.50	19,079.00	12,352.61	.57
406	Druggets and bockings, printed, colored, or otherwise......sq. yds..	4,471.93	2,311.00	1,908.22	.52
	Felt carpeting......sq. yds..	6,836	3,331.00	2,084.36	.49
407	Carpets of wool, or in part of, not especially provided for......sq. yds..	10,691.83	15,839.00	7,919.50	1.48
408	Carpets and carpetings of cotton..........	....	18,698.00	9,349.00	......
	Total schedule K, wool, manufactures of..........	....	36,999,469.16	36,448,667.46	......
	SCHEDULE L.—SILK AND SILK GOODS.				
409	Silk, manufactures of:				
	Silk, not raw—				
	Partially manufactured from cocoons, or from waste silk, and not further advanced or manufactured than carded or combed silk......lbs..	476	387.00	238.00	.81
410	Sewing silk, and silk thread or yarns of every description......lbs..	16,740.13	37,327.33	11,196.20	2.23
	Spun silk, in skeins or cops or on beams......lbs..	758,502.56	1,338,851.88	468,598.16	1.77
	Thrown silk, not more advanced than singles, tram, or organzine, twist and floss......lbs..	15,482.87	25,297.00	7,589.10	1.63
411	Velvets, plushes, or other pile fabrics— Containing, exclusive of selvedges, less 75 per cent in weight of silk......lbs..	1,153,177.87	3,001,293.38	2,179,960.86	2.60

DUTIES COLLECTED UNDER EXISTING LAW, ETC.—Continued.

Duties estimated under—		Rates of duty under—			Average ad valorem under—			Paragraph.
House bill.	Senate bill.	Present law.	House bill.	Senate bill.	Present.	House bill.	Senate bill.	
								395
					Per ct.	*Per ct.*	*Per ct.*	
$705,302.80	$617,139.94	44 cts. per lb. and 50 p. c.	40 per cent	35 per cent	87.14	40	35	
3,151,276.04	2,757,366.54	12 c. p. sq. yd. and 50 p. c.	....do	....do	109.09	40	35	
334,059.69	296,941.94	49½ c. per lb. and 60 p. c.	45 per cent	40 per cent	80.32	45	40	396
29,387.54	26,122.26	....do	....do	....do	93.09	45	40	
69,144.97	61,462.20	....do	....do	....do	105.09	45	40	
167,964.90	149,302.14	....do	....do	....do	81.23	45	40	397
123,012.66	107,636.08	60 cts. per lb. and 60 p. c.	40 per cent	35 per cent	83.82	40	35	398
444,862.90	444,862.90	60 c. p. sq. yd. and 40 p. c.	35 per cent	....do	60.85	35	35	399
33,500.81	83,500.81	....do	....do	....do	60.55	35	35	400
21,546.30	21,546.30	44 cts. per sq. yd. and 40 per cent.	30 per cent	30 per cent	81.50	30	30	401
13,934.10	13,984.10	40 c. per sq. yd. and 40 p. c.	....do	....do	71.86	30	30	402
1,029.00	1,029.09	28 c. per sq. yd. and 40 p. c.	....do	....do	77.97	30	30	403
8,281.09	8,281.09	19 c. per sq. yd. and 40 p. c.	....do	....do	63.05	30	30	404
4,769.75	4,769.75	14 c. per sq. yd. and 40 p. c.	25 per cent	25 per cent	64.74	25	25	405
577.75	577.75	22 c. per sq. yd. and 40 p. c.	....do	....do	82.57	25	25	406
832.75	832.75	11 c. per sq. yd. and 40 p. c.	....do	....do	62.57	25	25	407
3,959.75	3,959.75	50 per cent	....do	....do	50	25	25	408
4,674.50	4,674.50	....do	....do	....do	50	25	25	
14,714,879.23	12,979,346.23				98.53	39.78	35.09	
								409
110.00	77.40	50 cts. per lb.	25 cents per pound.	20 per cent	60.50	30.25	20	
7,465.46	9,331.83	30 per cent	20 per cent.	25 per cent	30	20	25	410
267,770.37	334,712.97	35 per cent	....do	....do	35	20	25	
5,059.40	16,324.25	30 per cent	....do	....do	30	20	25	411
1,350,582.02	1,350,582.02	$1.50 per lb. and 15 p. c.	45 per cent	45 per cent	72.63	45	45	

IMPORTED MERCHANDISE, 1893, WITH THE RATES AND

Paragraph.		Importations of fiscal year, June 30, 1893.			
		Quantities.	Values.	Duties.	Unit of value.
	SCHEDULE L.—SILK AND SILK GOODS—Cont'd. Silk, manufactures of—Continued. Silk, not raw—Continued. Velvets, plushes, or other pile fabrics—Continued. Containing, exclusive of selvedges, 75 per cent or more in weight of silk..............lbs..	21,327.33	$181,116.00	$101,813.07	$8.49
412	Other...................................... Webbings, gorings, suspenders, braces, beltings, braids, bindings, galloons, fringes, cords and tassels, elastic or nonelastic............... Buttons..................................... Handkerchiefs............................		552,923.96 723,022.71 1,762.00 1,384,513.72	276,462.00 361,511.35 881.00 830,708.24	
413	Laces and embroideries, neck ruflings, and ruchings................................ Wearing apparel— Knit goods— Composed in part of Indian rubber.........................ozs..	1,470	4,931,757.39 549.00	2,059,054.38 447.00	.37
	Other...................................... Ready-made clothing and other— Composed in part of Indian rubber.........................ozs..	2,968	923,499.50 1,334.82	554,099.70 1,038.33	.45
414	Other...................................... Dress and piece goods................. Ribbons.................................... All other, not specially provided for........		1,485,027.21 9,192,902.27 2,203,695.83 11,934,627.92	891,016.32 4,506,481.14 1,101,847.92 5,967,313.97	
	Total Schedule L, silk and silk goods..		37,019,948.92	20,310,258.74	
	SCHEDULE M.				
415	Pulp of wood— Mechanically ground..............tons.. Chemical, unbleached............tons.. Chemical, bleached................tons..	10,980.80 42,617.43 10,034.29	190,137.12 2,066,257.67 652,712.00	27,452.00 255,704.97 70,240.01	17.32 48.48 65.05
416	Sheathing.................................. Sheathing, patent....................... Printing paper, suitable only for books and newspapers—		1,621.00 529.00	162.10 105.80	
417	Unsized........................lbs..	370,596	18,047.00	2,707.05	.049
418	Sized or glued................lbs..	936,125	66,362.00	13,272.40	.071
419	Paper, albumenized or sensitized............ Papers known commercially as copying paper, filtering paper, silver paper, and all tissue paper, white or colored, made up in copying books, reams, or in any other form.	1,091,981.87	233,025.16 185,313.46	81,558.80 115,155.59	.17
420	Papers known commercially as surface-coated papers, and manufactures thereof, cardboards, lithographic prints from either stone or zinc, bound or unbound (except illustrations when forming a part of a periodical, newspaper, or in printed books accompanying the same), and all articles produced either in whole or in part by lithographic process, and photograph, autograph, and scrap albums, wholly or partially manufactured.....................		1,855,980.58	649,593.18	
421	Envelopes..................................M..	3,041.92	3,625.00	760.51	1.10
422	Hangings, and paper for screens or fireboards..		123,196.25	30,798.82	
423	Books, pamphlets, bound or unbound, maps, charts, and all printed matter not specially provided for.................................. Engravings, bound or unbound, etchings, and photographs........................... Blank books, bound or unbound............		1,798,330.57 280,225.51 9,403.10	449,582.65 70,056.39 2,350.78	
424	Cards, playing.....................packs..	3,800	602.89	1,900.00	.17
425	Writing, drawing, and all other paper, not specially provided for........................ Other manufactures of paper, or of which paper is the component of chief value......		206,924.34 987,967.77	51,731.09 246,991.96	
	Total Schedule M, pulp, paper, etc....		8,680,319.32	2,070,124.10	

DUTIES COLLECTED UNDER EXISTING LAW, ETC.—Continued.

Duties estimated under—		Rates of duty under—			Average ad valorem under—			Paragraph.
House bill.	Senate bill.	Present law.	House bill.	Senate bill.	Present.	House bill.	Senate bill.	
					Per ct.	Per ct.	Per ct.	
$81,502.20	$81,502.20	$3.50 per lb. and 15 p. ct.	45 per cent...	45 per cent...	56.21	45	45	
248,815.78	248,815.78	50 per cent ..	....do	....do	50	45	45	
289,209.08	289,209.08	....do	40 per cent...	40 per cent...	50	40	40	412
704.80	704.80	....do	....do	45 per cent...	50	40	45	
692,256.86	623,031.16	60 per cent...	50 per cent...	....do	60	50	45	
2,465,878.69	2,219,290.82	....do	....do	....do	60	50	45	}413
274.50	247.05	8 cts. per oz. and 60 p. ct.	....do	....do	81.42	50	45	
461,749.75	415,574.77	60 per cent...	....do	....do	60	50	45	
667.41	600.67	8 cts. per oz. and 60 p. ct.	....do	....do	77.79	50	45	
742,513.60	668,262.24	60 per cent...	....do	....do	60	50	45	
4,136,833.02	4,136,833.02	50 per cent...	45 per cent...	....do	50	45	45	414
991,663.12	991,663.12	....do	....do	....do	50	45	45	
5,370,582.56	5,370,582.56	....do	....do	....do	50	45	45	
17,113,647.62	16,747,345.74				53.56	45.13	44.16	
								415
19,013.71	19,013.71	$2.50 per ton.	10 per cent...	10 per cent...	14.44	10	10	
206,625.75	206,625.75	$6 per ton....	....do	....do	12.38	10	10	
65,271.20	65,271.20	$7 per ton....	....do	....do	10.76	10	10	
162.10	162.10	10 per cent...	....do	....do	10	10	10	416
52.90	52.90	20 per cent...	....do	....do	20	10	10	
2,165.64	2,165.64	15 per cent...	12 per cent...	....do	15	12	10	417
9,054.30	9,854.30	20 per cent...	15 per cent...	....do	20	15	10	418
58,256.29	58,256.29	35 per cent...	25 per cent...	25 per cent...	35	25	25	419
46,328.36	55,594.03	8 cts. per lb. and 15 p. ct.	....do	30 per cent....	62.14	25	30	
463,995.15	556,704.17	35 per cent...	....do	....do	35	25	30	420
725.00	725.00	25 cts. per M.	20 per cent...	20 per cent...	20.98	20	20	421
24,639.05	24,639.05	25 per cent...	....do	....do	25	20	20	422
449,582.65	449,582.65	....do	25 per cent...	25 per cent...	25	25	25	423
70,056.39	70,056.39	....do	....do	....do	25	25	25	
1,880.62	1,880.62	....do	20 per cent...	20 per cent...	25	20	20	
711.45	711.45	50 cts. per pk.	10 cts. per pk. and 50 p. ct.	10 cts. per pk. and 50 p. ct.	236.70	107.24	107.24	424
41,384.86	41,384.86	25 per cent...	20 per cent...	20 per cent...	25	20	20	425
197,593.55	197,593.55	....do	....do	....do	25	20	20	
1,858,398.97	1,760,463.66				23.85	19.10	20.28	

IMPORTED MERCHANDISE, 1893, WITH THE RATES AND

Paragraph.		Importations of fiscal year, June 30, 1893.			
		Quantities.	Values.	Duties.	Unit of value.
	SCHEDULE N.—SUNDRIES.				
427	Brooms of all kinds............................	....	$4,572.60	$1,829.04	......
	Brushes of all kinds, including feather dusters and hair pencils in quills...............	....	819,194.56	327,677.83	......
428	Buttons and button forms: Button forms: Lastings, mohair cloth, silk, or other manufactures of cloth, woven or made in patterns of such size, shape, or form, or cut in such manner as to be fit for buttons exclusively.....	....	199,074.00	19,903.40	—
429	Agate buttons..................................	....	194,538.11	47,884.53	......
	Pearl and shell buttons..............line..	13,057,641.80	275,216.00	395,245.08	$0.021
430	Ivory, vegetable ivory, bone or horn buttons..	....	471,075.00	235,537.50	......
431	Shoe buttons, made of paper board, papier maché, pulp, or similar material, not specially provided for, valued at not exceeding 3 cents per gross..gross..	500,956	7,703.00	5,009.56	.015
434	Corks...lbs..	703,038.63	345,189.40	105,455.79	.49
435	Dice, draughts, chessmen, chess balls, and billiard, pool, and bagatelle balls, of ivory, bone, or other material....................	....	21,582.00	10,791.00	......
436	Dolls, doll heads, toy marbles of whatever material composed, and all other toys not composed of rubber, china, porcelain, parian, bisque, earthen or stone ware, and not specially provided for....................	....	2,827,044.21	989,465.48	......
437	Emery: Grains, and ground, pulverized, or refined...lbs..	668,065	26,522.00	6,680.65	.040
	Gunpowder, and all explosive substances:				
438	Firecrackers of all kinds...............lbs..	6,177,850.87	335,478.60	494,228.07	.054
439	Fulminates, fulminating powders, and all like articles, not specially provided for...	....	48,509.29	14,552.79	......
440	Gunpowder, and all explosive substances, used for mining, blasting, artillery, or sporting purposes— Valued at 20 cents or less per pound..lbs..	4,768	924.00	238.40	.19
	Valued at above 20 cents per pound ....lbs..	73,512	68,035.00	5,904.96	.92
	Coal and coke: Bituminous coal and shale..........tons..	1,090,374.12	3,599,037.72	817,780.59	3.30
	Slack, or culm of coal, such as will pass through a half-inch screen......tons..	14,692.55	15,366.55	4,407.75	1.05
	Coke..tons..	26,599.80	87,238.00	17,447.62	3.28
441	Matches, friction or lucifer, of all descriptions: In boxes containing not more than 100 matches per box.....................gross..	295,367	87,047.00	29,536.70	.29
	Otherwise than in boxes containing not more than 100 matches each......M..	977,195	46,105.00	9,771.95	.047
442	Percussion caps................................	....	74,639.70	29,855.88	......
443	Dressed, colored, or manufactured, including dressed and finished birds suitable for millinery ornaments: Ostrich feathers..............................	....	10,000.11	5,045.05	......
	All other.....................................	....	96,981.42	48,490.74	......
	Feathers and flowers, artificial and ornamental, or parts thereof, of whatever material composed, not specially provided for..	....	1,637,366.98	818,083.50	......
444	Furs dressed on the skin, but not made up into articles.....................................	....	4,174,230.29	834,846.05	......
	Furs, not on the skin, prepared for hatters' use..	....	1,887,612.00	377,522.40	......
445	Beads of glass, loose, unthreaded or unstrung.	....	44,371.75	4,437.17	......
446	Gun wads of all descriptions..................	....	946.98	331.44	......
447	Human hair: Clean or drawn, but not manufactured..	....	37,842.00	7,568.40	......
448	Haircloth, known as crinoline cloth.sq.yds..	177,560.50	50,742.00	14,204.84	.28
449	Haircloth, known as hair seating...sq.yds..	29,178	37,694.00	8,753.40	1.29

DUTIES COLLECTED UNDER EXISTING LAW, ETC.—Continued.

Duties estimated under—		Rates of duty under—			Average ad valorem under—			Paragraph.
House bill.	Senate bill.	Present law.	House bill.	Senate bill.	Present.	House bill.	Senate bill.	
					Per ct.	Per ct.	Per ct.	
$914.52	$914.52	40 per cent...	20 per cent...	20 per cent...	40	20	20	427
245,758.36	245,758.36	....do	30 per cent...	30 per cent...	40	30	30	
19,903.40	19,903.40	10 per cent...	10 per cent...	10 per cent...	10	10	10	428
47,884.53	47,884.53	25 per cent...	25 per cent...	25 per cent...	25	25	25	429
171,858.81	171,858.81	2½ cts. per line and 25 p. c.	1 ct. per line and 15 p. c.	1 ct. per line and 15 p. c.	143.61	84.50	84.50	
117,768.75	117,768.75	50 per cent...	25 per cent...	25 per cent...	50	25	25	430
1,925.75	1,925.75	1 ct. per gross	....do	....do	65.06	25	25	431
69,037.88	70,303.86	15 cts. per lb..	20 per cent...	10 cts. per lb..	30.55	20	20.37	434
10,791.00	6,474.60	50 per cent...	50 per cent...	30 per cent...	50	50	30	435
706,761.05	706,761.05	35 per cent...	25 per cent...	25 per cent...	35	25	25	436
6,080.05	5,304.40	1 cent per lb..	1 cent per lb..	20 per cent...	25.19	25.19	20	437
494,228.07	167,739.30	8 cts. per lb..	8 cts. per lb..	50 per cent...	147.32	147.32	50	438
14,552.79	14,552.79	30 per cent...	30 per cent...	30 per cent...	30	30	30	439
238.40	92.40	5 cts. per lb..	5 cts. per lb..	10 per cent...	25.80	25.80	10	440
5,904.96	6,803.50	8 cts. per lb..	8 cts. per lb..	....do	8.68	8.68	10	
	436,149.64	75 cts. per ton.	Free	40 cts. per ton.	22.72	Free.	12.12	
	2,203.78	30 cts. per ton.	Free	15 cts. per ton.	28.68	Free.	14.34	
	13,085.71	20 per cent...	Free	15 per cent...	20	Free.	15	
17,529.40	8,764.70	10 cents per gross.	20 per cent...	10 per cent...	33.93	20	10	441
9,221.00	4,610.50	1 ct. per thousand.	....do	....do	21.19	20	10	
22,391.90	22,391.91	40 per cent...	{30 per cent... {35 p. c. (blasting).	30 per cent. {35 per cent. }	40	{30 {35	30 } 35 }	442
3,531.54	3,531.54	50 per cent...	35 per cent...	....do	50	35	35	443
33,943.49	33,943.49	....do	....do	....do	50	35	35	
573,078.44	573,078.44	....do	....do	....do	50	35	35	
417,423.03	834,846.05	20 per cent...	10 per cent...	20 per cent...	20	10	10	444
188,761.20	188,761.20	....do	....do	10 per cent...	20	10	10	
4,437.17	4,437.17	10 per cent...	10 per cent...	....do	10	10	10	445
236.75	94.69	35 per cent...	25 per cent...	....do	35	25	10	446
7,568.40	7,568.40	20 per cent...	20 per cent...	20 per cent...	20	20	20	447
15,222.60	12,685.50	8 cts. per sq. yd	30 per cent...	25 per cent...	27.09	30	25	448
9,423.50	9,423.50	30 cents per sq. yd.	25 per cent...	....do	23.22	25	25	449

IMPORTED MERCHANDISE, 1893, WITH THE RATES AND

Paragraph		Importations of fiscal year, June 30, 1893.			
		Quantities.	Values.	Duties.	Unit of value.
	SCHEDULE N.—SUNDRIES—Continued.				
451	Hats, for men's, women's, and children's wear, composed of the fur of the rabbit, beaver, or other animals, or of which such fur is the component material of chief value, wholly or partially manufactured, including fur hat bodies	....	$201,435.39	$110,789.48	....
	Jewelry and precious stones, not elsewhere specified:				
452	Jewelry: All articles not specially provided for, composed of precious metals or imitations thereof, whether set with coral, jet, or pearls, or with diamonds, rubies, cameos, or other precious stones or imitations thereof, or otherwise, and which shall be known commercially as "jewelry," and cameos in frames	....	318,649.81	159,324.92	....
453	Pearls	....	6,926.00	692.60	....
454	Precious stones, and imitations of—				
	Cut, but not set	....	14,740,929.60	1,474,092.96	....
	Set, and not specially provided for	....	7,482.00	1,870.50	....
	Imitations of, not set, composed of paste or glass, not exceeding 1 inch in dimensions	....	104,983.74	10,496.37	....
	Diamonds and other precious stones, rough or uncut	....	597,010.00	....	....
	Leather, and manufactures of:				
455	Bend or belting, and sole	....	35,824.87	3,582.49	....
456	Calf skins, japanned	....	797,936.00	239,380.80	....
	Calf skins, tanned, or tanned and dressed	....	590,246.50	118,049.30	....
	Piano-forte and piano-forte action leather	....	582.00	203.70	
	Skins for morocco—				
	Finished	....	85,818.70	17,163.74	....
	Tanned, but unfinished	....	3,822,591.00	382,259.10	....
	Skins, chamois or other, not specially provided for; bookbinders' calf skins, kangaroo, sheep, and goat skins, including lamb and kid skins, dressed and finished	....	1,930,562.00	386,112.40	....
	Upper leather, dressed, including patent, enameled, and japanned leather, dressed or undressed, and finished	....	398,601.78	79,720.35	....
	All leather not specially provided for	....	53,010.00	5,301.00	....
	Boots and shoes	....	95,622.42	23,905.02	....
458	Gloves, composed wholly or in part of kid or other leather, and whether wholly or partly manufactured—				
	Ladies' and children's—				
	Fourteen inches and under in extreme length—				
	Schmaschen—				
	Plain ....doz	254,477.02	$45,015.00	445,333.01	$3.32
	Pique or prick seam, and embroidered with more than 3 single strands or cords ....doz	11,172.67	42,925.00	25,138.51	3.84
	Lined ....doz	1,226	5,190.00	3,371.50	4.23
	Lamb—				
	Plain ....doz	72,723.50	294,470.00	163,627.90	4.05
	Pique or prick seam, and embroidered with more than 3 single strands or cords ....doz	20,229	95,012.00	55,629.75	4.70
	Lined ....doz	2,822.75	14,237.00	9,173.95	5.04
	Kid—				
	Plain ....doz	182,320.17	975,057.00	592,540.57	5.35
	Pique or prick seam, and embroidered with more than 3 single strands or cords ....doz	18,049.60	109,957.00	67,685.99	6.09
	Lined ....doz	149	1,050.00	633.25	7.72
	Suedes and other, whether more or less than 14 inches in extreme length—				
	Plain ....doz	532,283.90	2,777,532.20	1,388,766.10	5.22

203

DUTIES COLLECTED UNDER EXISTING LAW, ETC.—Continued.

Duties estimated under—		Rates of duty under—			Average ad valorem under—			Paragraph
House bill.	Senate bill.	Present law.	House bill.	Senate bill.	Present.	House bill.	Senate bill.	
					Per ct.	*Per ct.*	*Per ct.*	
$60,430.02	$70,502.38	55 per cent...	30 per cent...	35 per cent...	55	30	35	451
111,527.43	111,527.43	50 per cent...	35 per cent...	....do........	50	35	35	452
1,038.90	692.60	10 per cent...	15 per cent...	10 per cent...	10	15	10	453
								454
4,422,278.88	2,211,139.44	....do........	30 per cent...	15 per cent...	10	30	15	
2,618.70	2,244.60	25 per cent...	35 per cent...	30 per cent...	25	35	30	
26,245.94	26,245.04	10 per cent...	25 per cent...	25 per cent...	10	25	25	
89,550.00	....	Free........	15 per cent...	Free........	Free.	15	Free.	
								455
3,582.49	3,582.49	10 per cent...	(sole) 5'per ct. 10 per cent..	10 per cent...	10	{5 {10	}10	456
119,690.40	159,587.20	30 per cent...	15 per cent ..	20 per cent...	30	15	20	
78,536.97	118,049.30	20 per cent...	....do........	....do........	20	15	20	
145.50	116.40	35 per cent...	25 per cent...	....do........	35	25	20	
12,872.80	17,163.74	20 per cent...	15 per cent...	....do........	20	15	20	
382,259.10	382,259.10	10 per cent...	10 per cent...	10 per cent...	10	10	10	
289,584.30	386,112.40	20 per cent...	15 per cent...	20 per cent...	20	15	20	
59,790.26	79,720.35	....do........	....do........	....do........	20	15	20	
5,301.00	5,301.00	10 per cent...	10 per cent...	10 per cent...	10	10	10	458
19,124.48	19,124.48	25 per cent...	20 per cent...	20 per cent...	25	20	20	
			Ladies' or childrens' "glace" finish.—Schmaschen—					
338,006.00	338,006.00	$1.75 per doz.	Not over 14 in. $1 p. doz. prs.		52.70	40	40	
17,170.00	17,170.00	$2.25 per doz.	Over 14 in. and not over 17, $1.50 p. doz. prs.;		58.56	40	40	
2,076.00	2,076.00	$2.75 per doz.	Over 17 in., $2 p. doz. prs.		64.06	40	40	
117,788.00	117,788.00	$2.25 per doz.	Men's,$2 p.doz.prs."glace" finish, lamb or sheep;		55.57	40	40	
38,004.80	38,004.80	$2.75 per doz.	Not over 14 in. $1.75 p. doz. prs.;		58.55	40	40	
5,694.80	5,694.80	$3.25 per doz.	Over 14 and not over 17, $2.75 p. doz. prs.;		64.44	40	40	
390,022.80	390,022.80	....do........	Over 17 in., $3.75 p.doz.prs.		60.77	40	40	
43,982.80	43,982.80	$3.75 per doz.	Men's, $3 p. doz. "glace" finish, goat, kid, or other;		61.56	40	40	
460.00	460.00	$4.25 per doz.	Not over 14 in., $2.25 per doz. prs.;		57.07	40	40	
1,111,012.88	1,111,012.88	50 per cent...	Over 14 and not over 17, $3 per doz. prs.;		50	40	40	

IMPORTED MERCHANDISE, 1893, WITH THE RATES AND

Paragraph.		Importations of fiscal year, June 30, 1893.			
		Quantities.	Values.	Duties.	Unit of value.
	SCHEDULE N.—SUNDRIES—Continued.				
	Gloves composed wholly or in part of kid or other leather, and whether wholly or partly manufactured—Continued.				
	Ladies' and children's—Continued.				
	Fourteen inches and under in extreme length—Continued.				
	Suedes and other, whether more or less than 14 inches in extreme length—Continued.				
	Pique or prick seam, and embroidered with more than 3 single strands or cords ....doz..	24,945	$150,412.10	$92,178.55	$6.39
	Lined ....doz..	5,672.64	24,519.50	17,932.38	4.32
	Ladies' and children's, on which the above rates of duty do not equal a duty of 50 per cent ....doz..	183,455.31	876,315.71	438,157.85	4.78
	Men's gloves—				
	Fourteen inches and under in extreme length, plain ....doz..	5,911.16	46,062.50	23,031.25	7.79
	Over 14 inches in extreme length—				
	Plain.........................doz..	39,655.56	195,412.50	137,361.84	4.93
	Pique or prick seam, and embroidered with more than 3 single strands or cords..........................doz..	57,692.87	368,011.05	270,544.88	6.37
	Lined........................doz..	407.77	2,778.00	2,204.56	6.81
	Do......................doz..	2,141.17	20,895.00	15,800.42	9.76
	Do......................doz..	.06	1.00	.75	12.50
459	Miscellaneous manufactures:				
	Alabaster and spar, manufactures of.....		43,227.00	10,806.75	
	Amber, manufactures of.................		4,872.00	1,218.00	
	Asbestos, manufactured		7,971.00	1,902.75	
	Bladders, manufactures of		56.00	14.00	
	Coral, manufactures of		657.25	164.31	
	Catgut or whipgut or wormgut, manufactures of		1,497.00	374.25	
	Jet manufactures......................		8,812.60	2,203.15	
	Paste, manufactures of.................		3,710.00	920.75	
	Wax, manufactures of..................		16,694.25	4,173.56	
	Candles and tapers of wax..............		11,973.00	2,993.25	
	Osier or willow, prepared for basketmakers' use.		64,427.00	19,328.10	
	Osier or willow, manufactures of........		125,916.75	50,366.70	
460	Bone and horn, manufactures of		273,944.73	82,182.42	
	Chip, manufactures of (baskets)		703.00	237.00	
	Grass, manufactures of		31,768.07	9,530.43	
	India rubber..........................		265,155.10	79,546.53	
	Palm leaf, manufactures of.............		118,902.44	35,697.73	
	Straw, manufactures of		965,482.54	289,644.78	
	Do for julips...................		1,250.00	375.00	
	Whalebone, manufactures of............		4,756.00	1,476.80	
461	Leather, all manufactures of		636,495.61	223,473.48	
	Fur, manufactures of		136,183.27	47,046.06	
	India rubber, vulcanized, known as hard rubber		58,680.35	20,538.14	
	Gutta-percha..........................		81,288.10	28,450.84	
	Hair, manufactures of.................		24,509.49	8,578.32	
	Papier-maché, manufactures of...........		74,698.33	26,144.42	
462	Ivory and vegetable ivory, manufactures of..		66,804.66	26,721.86	
	Shell and mother-of-pearl, manufactures of ..		263,842.43	113,586.98	

DUTIES COLLECTED UNDER EXISTING LAW, ETC.—Continued.

Duties estimated under—		Rates of duty under—			Average ad valorem under—			Paragraph.
House bill.	Senate bill.	Present law.	House bill.	Senate bill.	Present.	House bill.	Senate bill.	
					Per ct.	*Per ct.*	*Per ct.*	
$63,764.84	$63,764.84	50c. per doz. and 50 p. ct.	Over 17 in., $4 p.doz. prs. oz. Men's, $3 per doz. prs. Ladies' or children's, of sheep origin—		57.82	40	40	
9,807.80	9,807.80	$1 per dozen 50 and p. ct.	Not over 14 in., $1.75 p. doz. prs.;		73.13	40	40	
			Over 14 and not over 17, per doz. prs. $2.75;		50	40	40	
350,526.28	350,526.28	50 per cent...	Over 17 in., $3.75 p. doz. prs.; Men's $3 per doz. prs. Ladies', etc., kid, goat, etc.—		50	40	40	
18,425.00	18,425.00	50 per cent...	Not over 14 in., $2.25 p. doz. prs.;		70.29	40	40	
78,165.00	78,165.00	$1 per dozen and 50 p. c.	Over 14 and not over 17, $3 per doz. prs.		73.52	40	40	
147,204.42	147,204.42	$1.50 per doz. and 50 p. c.	Over 17 in., $4 p. doz. prs.		79.36	40	40	
1,111.20	1,111.20	$2 per dozen and 50 p. c.	Men's $3 per doz. prs.		75.62	40	40	
8,358.00	8,358.00	$2.50 per doz. and 50 p. c.	All leather gloves, when lined, 50c. p. doz. additional. NOTE: Owing to change in classification of sizes, no comparison can be given. (Estimated rate by proposed bill=40 p. c. on all.)		75	40	40	
.40	.40	$3 per dozen and 50 p. c.						
12,968.10	12,968.10	25 per cent...	30 per cent...	30 per cent...	25	30	25	459
1,218.00	1,218.00	....do	25 per cent...	25 per cent...	25	25	25	
1,992.75	1,992.75	....do	....do	....do	25	25	25	
14.00	14.00	....do	....do	....do	25	25	25	
164.31	164.31	....do	....do	....do	25	25	25	
374.25	374.25	....do	....do	....do	25	25	25	
2,203.15	2,203.15	....do	....do	....do	25	25	25	
929.75	929.75	....do	....do	....do	25	25	25	
4,173.56	4,173.56	....do	....do	....do	25	25	25	
2,993.25	2,993.25	....do	....do	....do	25	25	25	
12,885.40	12,885.40	30 per cent...	20 per cent...	20 per cent...	30	20	20	
31,479.19	31,479.19	40 per cent...	25 per cent...	25 per cent...	40	25	25	
68,486.18	68,486.18	30 per cent...	....do	....do	30	25	25	460
198.25	198.25	....do	....do	....do	30	25	25	
7,942.02	7,942.02	....do	....do	....do	30	25	25	
66,538.77	66,538.77	....do	....do	....do	30	25	25	
20,998.11	20,998.11	....do	....do	....do	30	25	25	
241,370.63	241,370.63	....do	....do	....do	30	25	25	
312.50	312.50	....do	....do	....do	30	25	25	
1,189.00	1,189.00	....do	....do	....do	30	25	25	
119,548.68	119,548.68	35 per cent...	30 per cent...	30 per cent...	35	30	30	461
40,839.98	40,839.98	....do	....do	....do	35	30	30	
17,604.10	17,604.10	....do	....do	....do	35	30	30	
24,386.43	24,386.43	....do	....do	....do	35	30	30	
7,352.84	7,352.84	....do	....do	....do	35	30	30	
22,409.50	22,409.50	....do	....do	....do	35	30	30	
23,381.63	23,381.63	40 per cent...	35 per cent...	35 per cent...	40	35	35	462
99,344.85	99,344.85	....do	....do	....do	40	35	35	

IMPORTED MERCHANDISE, 1893, WITH THE RATES

Paragraph.		Importations of fiscal year, June 30, 1893.			
		Quantities.	Values.	Duties.	Unit of value.
	SCHEDULE N.—SUNDRIES—Continued.				
463	Masks, composed of paper or pulp		$9,840.86	$3,444.30	
464	Matting and mats made of cocoa fiber or rattan:				
	Matting ....sq. yds..	101,998	17,028.00	12,239.76	$0.16
	Mats ....sq. yds..	10,592.09	2,063.00	855.36	.18
	Floor matting manufactured from round or split straw, including what is commonly known as Chinese matting		1,666,384.69		
466	Pencils:				
	Wood filled with lead or other material, and pencils of lead..............gross..	28,594.40	81,509.00	43,749.90	2.11
	Slate pencils ....gross..	467,153	39,278.00	18,686.12	.084
467	Pencil leads, not in wood.		20,861.00	2,086.10	
468	Pipes and smokers' articles:				
	Common pipes of clay............gross..	185,327.78	55,476.90	27,709.17	.30
	Pipes, pipe bowls of all materials, and all smokers' articles whatsoever, not specially provided for, including cigarette books, cigarette book-covers, pouches for smoking or chewing tobacco, and cigarette paper in all forms		378,654.01	265,057.76	
470	Umbrellas, parasols, and sunshades, and sticks for:				
	Umbrellas, parasols, and sunshades—				
	Covered with silk or alpaca		26,423.26	14,532.79	
	Covered with other materials		2,372.90	1,067.81	
471	Sticks for umbrellas, parasols, and sunshades—				
	Carved		6,360.00	3,180.00	
	Plain		110,898.00	38,814.30	
472	Waste, all not specially provided for		152,974.54	15,297.46	
	Total Schedule N, sundries		54,057,663.86	13,981,275.89	
	Section 4. (Act of Oct. 1, 1890):				
	Unmanufactured		145,036.92	14,503.69	
	Manufactured		1,285,569.34	257,113.81	
	Repairs on vessels		2,054.26	1,027.12	
	Total		1,432,660.52	272,644.62	

AND DUTIES COLLECTED UNDER EXISTING LAWS, ETC.—Continued.

Duties estimated under—		Rates of duty under—			Average ad valorem under—			Paragraph.
House bill.	Senate bill.	Present law.	House bill.	Senate bill.	Present.	House bill.	Senate bill.	
					Per ct.	Per ct.	Per ct.	
$2,460.21	$2,460.21	35 per cent...	25 per cent ..	25 per cent...	35	25	25	463
3,405.60	3,405.60	12 c per sq. yd	20 per cent ..	20 per cent...	71.87	20	20	
412.60	412.60	8 c per sq. ft..	....do	....do	41.46	20	20	
....	333,276.93	Free....;......	Free..........	....do	Free.	Free.	20	464
28,528.15	32,603.60	50 c per gross and 30 per c.	35 per cent...	40 per cent ..	53.67	35	40	466
9,819.50	11,783.40	4 c per gross .	25 per cent ..	30 per cent ..	47.57	25	30	
2,086.10	2,086.10	10 per cent...	10 per cent ..	10 per cent ..	10	10	10	467
18,532.78	5,547.69	15 c per gross.	10 c per gross.	..... do	50.11	33.41	10	468
189,327.01	189,327.01	70 per cent..	50 per cent ..	50 per cent ..	70	50	50	
11,890.46	11,890.46	55 per cent ..	45 per cent...	45 per cent ..	55	45	45	470
830.20	830.20	45 per cent ..	35 per cent...	30 per cent ..	45	35	30	
1,908.00	1,908.00	50 per cent ..	30 per cent...	....do	50	30	30	471
33,260.40	33,269.40	35 per cent ..	....do	....do	35	30	30	
15,297.46	15,297.46	10 per cent...	10 per cent...	10 per cent...	10	10	10	472
12,794,208.78	11,551,909.95	....	....	....	27	26.28	21.37	
14,503.69	14,503.69	10 per cent...	10 per cent...	10 per cent...	10	10	10	
257,113.81	257,113.81	20 per cent...	20 per cent...	20 per cent...	20	20	20	
1,027.12	1,027.12	50 per cent...	50 per cent...	50 per cent...	50	50	50	
272,644.62	272,644.62	....	....	....	19.03	19.03	19.03	

TA——14

ARTICLES TRANSFERRED FROM

Paragraph		Importations of 1893.	
		Quantities.	Value.
	SCHEDULE A.—CHEMICALS, OILS, AND PAINTS.		
5	Acid, sulphuric or oil of vitriol, not otherwise specially provided for..lbs..	634	$43.00
	Ammonia:		
10	Carbonate of..lbs..	551,824	36,352.00
10	Muriate of, or sal ammoniac...........................lbs..	4,217,025	208,068.00
10	Sulphate of..lbs..	14,025,750	315,802.00
13	Copper, sulphate of or blue vitriol ....lbs..	8,941	363.00
14	Borax: Crude, or borate of soda, or borate of lime.........lbs..	543,067	13,659.00
15	Camphor, refined ....lbs..	156,291	51,229.33
19	Coal tar, all preparations of, not colors or dyes, not specially provided for..lbs..		158,713.04
	Oils, mineral—		
	Naphtha, benzine, benzole, dead oil, and similar products of coal tar..galls..	694,167	41,103.00
	All other..galls..	454,312	18,423.00
20	Cobalt, oxide of..lbs..	35,729.75	55,742.00
23	Iron, sulphate of, or copperas.............................lbs..	1,010,039	4,099.00
24	Barks, beans, berries, balsams, buds, bulbs, and bulbous roots, and excrescences, such as nutgalls, fruits, flowers, dried fibers, grains, gums, and gum resins, herbs, leaves, lichens, mosses, nuts, roots, and stems, spices, vegetables, seeds (aromatic, not garden seeds), and seeds of morbid growth, weeds, woods used expressly for dyeing, and dried insects, any of the foregoing which are not edible, but which have been advanced in value or condition by refining or grinding, or by other process of manufacture...		69,678.25
29	Indigo—		
	Carmined..lbs..	29,687	35,304.00
	Extracts or pastes of.....................................lbs..	1,317,835	101,347.00
31	Iodine, resublimed...lbs..	6	25.00
34	Magnesia, sulphate of, or epsom salts.................lbs..	61,337	480.00
	Oils—		
39	Cotton seed ....galls..	5,104	1,858.00
40	Croton ....lbs..		
54	Paints, colors, etc.—		
	Baryta, sulphate of, or barytes, including barytes earth, unmanufactured...tons..	2,709.25	6,995.00
	Ocher and ochery earths, dry..........................lbs..	7,167,847	71,230.00
	Sienna and sienna earths, dry........................lbs..	1,297,870	29,538.00
	Umber and umber earths, dry........................lbs..	1,399,075	15,494.00
70	Potash, caustic or hydrate of, refined in sticks or rolls...lbs..	9,513	1,781.00
85	Soda, sulphate of—		
	Glauber salts..tons..	218.66	4,012.53
	Salt cake, or niter cake................................tons..	19,723.37	221,846.00
88	Sulphur, refined...tons..	5.05	118.00
	Total Schedule A transferred to free list		1,463,309.15
	SCHEDULE B.—EARTH, EARTHENWARE, AND GLASSWARE.		
98	Clays or earths, unwrought or unmanufactured......tons..	20,650.25	157,084.00
	Stone:		
126	Burr stone, manufactured or bound up into millstones.....		630.00
127	Freestone, granite, sandstone, limestone, and other building or monumental stone, except marble unmanufactured or undressed...cu. ft..	147,416.11	47,131.00
	Total Schedule B transferred to free list		204,851.00
	SCHEDULE C.—METALS, AND MANUFACTURES OF.		
	Iron ores:		
132	Chromate of iron, or chromic ore.....................tons..	6,000.34	54,698.00
140	Cotton ties of iron or steel:		
	Not thinner than No. 10 wire gauge................lbs..	1,017,586	30,505.00
	Thinner than No. 10 and not thinner than No. 20......lbs..	999,225	25,803.00
187	Antimony, as regulus or metal ....lbs..	3,802,153	352,531.00
	COPPER, AND MANUFACTURES OF:		
	Ores (fine copper contained therein) ....lbs..	7,465,101	454,228.00
	Regulus of, and black or coarse copper, and copper cement, fine copper contained therein ....lbs..	2,109,847	139,080.00
191 to 195	Old, fit only for remanufacture, and clippings from new copper..lbs..	72,373	7,352.45
	Composition metal, of which copper is a component material of chief value, not specially provided for......lbs..	38,679	5,063.00
	Plates, not rolled, bars, ingots, Chile or other pigs, and in other forms, not manufactured, not specially provided for...lbs..	576,075	61,020.00

DUTIABLE TO FREE LIST.

Importations of 1893.		Rates.			Equivalent ad valorem.			Paragraph.
Duties.	Unit of value.	Present.	House.	Senate.	Present.	House.	Senate.	
					Per ct.			
$1.59	$0.068	¼ cent per pound	Free..	Free..	3.07	Free..	Free..	5
9,656.94	.066	1¾ cents per pound	..do ...	..do ...	20.56	..do ...	..do ...	10
31,627.72	.049	¾ cent per pound	..do ...	..do ...	15.20	..do ...	..do ...	10
70,128.78	.023	½ cent per pound	..do ...	..do ...	22.21	..do ...	..do ...	10
178.82	.041	2 cents per pound	..do ...	..do ...	49.26	..do ...	..do ...	13
16,319.01	.025	3 cents per pound	..do ...	..do ...	119.47	..do ...	..do ...	14
6,251.64	.33	4 cents per pound	..do ...	..do ...	12.20	..do ...	..do ...	15
31,742.61		20 per cent	..do ...	..do ...	20	..do ...	..do ...	19
10,275.75	.059	25 per cent	..do ...	..do ...	25	..do ...	..do ...	
3,684.60	.041	20 per cent	..de ...	..do ...	20	..do ...	..do ...	
10,718.93	1.56	30 cents per pound	..do ...	..do ...	19.23	..do ...	..do ...	20
3,030.12	.004	1/10 cent per pound	..do ...	..do ...	73.92	..do ...	..do ...	23
6,967.83		10 per cent	..do ...	..do ...	10	..do ...	..do ...	24
2,968.70	1.19	10 cents per pound	..do ...	..do ...	8.41	..do ...	..do ...	29
9,883.80	.077	¾ cent per pound	..do ...	..do ...	9.75	..do ...	..do ...	
1.80	4.17	30 cents per pound	..do ...	..do ...	7.20	..do ...	..do ...	31
184.03	.008	1/10 cent per pound	..do ...	..do ...	38.34	..do ...	..do ...	34
510.40	.36	10 cents per gal	..do ...	..do ...	27.47	..do ...	..do ...	39
		30 cents per pound	..do ...	..do ...		..do ...	..do ...	40
3,034.36	2.58	$1.12 per ton	..do ...	..do ...	43.38	..do ...	..do ...	54
17,919.64	.010	¼ cent per pound	..do ...	..do ...	25.16	..do ...	..do ...	
3,214.70	.023	...do	..do ...	..do ...	10.98	..do ...	..do ...	
3,497.69	.011	...do	..do ...	..do ...	22.57	..do ...	..do ...	
95.13	.19	1 cent per pound	..do ...	..do ...	5.34	..do ...	..do ...	70
273.34	18.35	$1.25 per ton	..do ...	..do ...	6.81	..do ...	..do ...	85
24,554.24	11.25	...do	..do ...	..do ...	11.11	..do ...	..do ...	
40.40	23.37	$8 per ton	..do ...	..do ...	34.23	..do ...	..do ...	88
271,892.57					18.58			
30,975.43	7.61	$1.50 per ton	Free..	Free..	19.72	Free..	Free..	98
95.40		15 per cent	..do ...	..do ...	15	..do ...	..do ...	126
16,215.77	.32	11 cts. per cub. ft	..do ...	..do ...	34.41	..do ...	..do ...	127
47,286.60					23.08			
8,204.70	9.12	15 per cent	Free..	Free..	15	Free..	Free..	132
12,211.02	.030	1/10 cents per pound	..do ...	..do ...	40.03	..do ...	..do ...	140
12,089.92	.026	1/10 cents per pound	..do ...	..do ...	50.23	..do ...	..do ...	
28,516.13	.093	¾ cent per pound	..do ...	..do ...	8.09	..do ...	..do ...	137
37,325.53	.061	½ cent per pound	..do ...	..do ...	8.22	..do ...	..do ...	
21,003.47	.06	1 cent per pound	..do ...	..do ...	15.17	..do ...	..do ...	
723.73	.10	...do	..do ...	..do ...	9.84	..do ...	..do ...	101 to 195
386.79	.15	...do	..do ...	..do ...	6.49	..do ...	..do ...	
7,200.94	.11	1¼ cents per pound	..do ...	..do ...	11.80	..do ...	..do ...	

Articles transferred from

Paragraph.		Importations of 1893.	
		Quantities.	Value.
	SCHEDULE C.—METAL, AND MANUFACTURES OF—Cont'd.		
202	Metals unwrought, and metallic mineral substances, in a crude state, not specially provided for		$29,529.00
	Mica..lbs..	930,707	214,679.99
203	Nickel, nickel oxide, alloy of any kind in which nickel is the material of chief value..lbs..	310,902	130,797.00
207	Quicksilver...lbs..	94,457	38,100.00
	Total Schedule C transferred to free list............		1,544,346.44
	SCHEDULE D.—WOOD, AND MANUFACTURES OF.		
	Timber:		
216	Used for spars and in building wharves..............cu. ft..	78,452	9,431.85
217	Hewn and sawed....................................cu. ft..	1,419,484	62,867.83
218	Squared or sided, not specially provided for........cu. ft..	65,139	b 491.64
	Lumber:		
	Boards, planks, deals, and other sawed lumber—		
	Of hemlock, white wood, sycamore, white pine, and basswood—		
	Not planed or finished......................M ft..	514,939.12	6,183,030.36
	All sawed lumber, not specially provided for—		
	Not planed or finished......................M. ft..	154,111.09	1,440,203.30
219	Paving posts, railroad ties, and telephone and telegraph poles of cedar...No..	1,815,949	271,235.91
220	Sawed boards, planks, deals, and all forms of sawed cedar, lignum vitæ, lancewood, ebony, box, granadilla, mahogany, rosewood, satinwood, and all other cabinet woods not further manufactured than sawed...M ft..	365.72	24,204.61
	Unmanufactured, not specially provided for...............		25,952.20
	Veneers of wood...		750.00
	Clapboards—		
221	Pine..M..	67.99	2,003.40
222	Spruce..M..	6,907.44	111,985.00
223	Hubs for wheels, posts, last, wagon, oar, gun, and heading blocks, and all like blocks or sticks, rough hewn or sawed only		28,227.30
224	Laths..M..	327,441.83	462,140.04
225	Pickets and palings.................................M..	5,483.09	36,099.93
226	Shingles—		
	White pine..M..	216,780.75	397,313.95
	All other..M..	253,220.70	519,445.00
227	Staves of all kinds...		646,613.40
	Total Schedule D transferred to free list............		10,222,505.72
	SCHEDULE G.—AGRICULTURAL PRODUCTS, ETC.		
268	Milk, fresh..galls..	6,265	1,429.75
272	Broom corn..tons..	12.25	524.00
273	Cabbages..No..	328,683	13,178.34
274	Cider..galls..	13,145.50	3,549.00
275	Eggs..doz..	3,295,842.13	302,610.90
276	Eggs, yolk of...		12.00
281	Pease, green, in bulk or packages.........................bush..	845.19	508.39
282	Plants, trees, shrubs, and vines.............................		139,004.15
286	Garden seeds, agricultural and other seeds, n. s. p......		338,013.25
289	Straw..tons..	8,890.33	30,681.33
290	Teazles...		6,508.00
	Fish, fresh:		
294	Herring..lbs..	383,610	4,937.00
293	Salmon..lbs..	1,238,605	110,124.00
293	All other..lbs..	9,909,522	408,717.81
310	Bacon and hams...lbs..	247,783.75	47,530.90
312	Meats, dressed or undressed, but not otherwise prepared..lbs..		28,301.30
	Meats of all kinds, prepared or preserved..................lbs..		104,433.34
314	Lard..lbs..	6,051	510.10
316	Tallow..lbs..	48,300	5,087.00
	Grease of wool, known as degras..........................lbs..	11,693,850	196,848.00
322	Salt:		
	In bags, sacks, barrels, or other packages...............lbs..	130,678,356	446,273.03
	In bulk..lbs..	181,443,328	176,320.94
	Total Schedule G transferred to free list............		2,461,238.49

dutiable to free list—Continued.

Importations of 1893.		Rates.			Equivalent ad valorem.			Paragraph.
Duties.	Unit of value.	Present.	House.	Senate.	Present.	House.	Senate.	
					Per ct.			
$5,905.80		20 per cent	Free	Free	20	Free	Free	202
75,137.98	$0.23	35 per cent	..do	...do	35	..do	...do	
31,090.20	.42	10 cents per pound	..do	...do	23.77	..do	...do	203
9,445.70	.40	......do	..do	...do	24.79	..do	...do	207
250,230.91					16.20			
943.13	.12	10 per cent	Free	Free	10	Free	...do	216
6,286.79	.044	......do	..do	...do	10	..do	...do	217
b 325.63	.008	¼ cent per cubic foot	..do	...do	66.25	..do	...do	218
514,039.12	12.01	$1 per M feet	..do	...do	8.33	..do	...do	
308,222.19	9.35	$2 per M feet	..do	...do	21.40	..do	..do	
54,247.19	.15	20 per cent	..do	...do	20	..do	...do	219
3,630.60	06.18	15 per cent	..do	...do	15	..do	...do	220
5,190.44		20 per cent	..do	...do	20	..do	..do	
150.00		......do	..do	...do	20	..do	...do	
67.90	29.47	$1 per M	..do	...do	3.39	..do	...do	221
10,406.19	16	$1.50 per M	..do	...do	9.37	..do	...do	222
5,645.46		20 per cent	..do	...do	20	..do	...do	223
49,110.34	1.41	15 cents per M	..do	...do	10.63	..do	..do	224
3,670.00	6.69	10 per cent	..do	...do	10	..do	...do	225
43,356.15	1.83	20 cents per M	..do	...do	10.91	..do	...do	226
75,966.20	2.05	30 cents per M	..do	...do	14.62	..do	..do	
64,661.34		10 per cent	..do	...do	10	..do	...do	227
1,146,915.03					11.22			
313.25	.23	5 cents per gallon	Free	Free	21.91	Free	Free	268
98.02	42.77	$8 per ton	..do	...do	18.71	..do	...do	272
9,800.49	.040	3 cents each	..do	...do	74.82	..do	...do	273
657.28	.27	5 cents per gallon	..do	...do	18.52	..do	...do	274
164,792.12	.12	5 cents per dozen	..do	...do	41.20	..do	...do	275
3.00		25 per cent	..do	...do	25	..do	...do	276
138.07	1.65	40 cents per bushel	..do	...do	24.29	..do	...do	281
27,800.73		20 per cent	..do	...do	20	..do	...do	282
67,602.65		...do	..do	...do	20	..do	...do	286
9,204.40	3.45	30 per cent	..do	...do	30	..do	...do	289
1,970.40		...do	..do	...do	30	..do	...do	290
959.05	.013	¼ cent per pound	..do	...do	19.43	..do	...do	294
9,289.55	.094	¾ cent per pound	..do	...do	8	..do	...do	293
74,321.52	.041	...do	..do	...do	18.18	..do	...do	293
12,380.19	.19	5 cents per pound	..do	...do	26.06	..do	...do	310
2,830.14		10 per cent	..do	...do	10	..do	...do	}312
26,108.35		25 per cent	..do	...do	25	..do	...do	
121.02	.084	2 cents per pound	..do	...do	23.72	..do	...do	314
483.00	.11	1 cent per pound	..do	...do	9.49	..do	...do	316
58,460.28	.017	½ cent per pound	..do	...do	29.70	..do	...do	322
156,813.97	.003	12 cents per 100 pounds	..do	...do	35.14	..do	...do	
145,158.63	.001	8 cents per 100 pounds	..do	...do	82.33	..do	...do	
769,364.01					31.26			

Articles transferred from

Paragraph		Importations of 1893.	
		Quantities.	Value.
	SCHEDULE H.—SPIRITS, WINES, ETC.		
340	Lemonade, soda water, and other similar waters: In plain, green, or colored, molded, or pressed glass bottles—		
	Containing each not more than three-fourths of a pint ....doz..	44,794.50	$31,240.00
	Containing more than three-fourths of a pint each and not more than one and one-half pints............doz..	224	240.00
	Otherwise than in such bottles, or in such bottles containing more than one and one-half pints each............galls..	30	10.00
	Total Schedule H transferred to free list.................		31,490.00
	SCHEDULE J.—FLAX, HEMP, JUTE, ETC.		
	Flax:		
356	Straw...tons..	153.10	4,099.00
357	Not hackled or dressed..............................tons..	3,260.70	759,421.00
358	Tow of...tons..	1,924.81	291,337.60
359	Hemp, tow of...tons..	524.84	64,139.00
360	Hemp...tons..	4,239.79	607,372.00
362	Twine, manufactured in whole or in part of istle or Tampico fiber, manila, sisal grass, or sunn:		
	Binding...lbs..	35,684	3,863.00
	Total Schedule J transferred to free list............		1,730,231.60
	SCHEDULE K.—WOOL.		
	Wools, hair of the camel, goat, alpaca, and other like animals, and manufactures of:		
	Unmanufactured—		
384	Class 1: Merino, mestiza, metz, or metis wools, or other wools of merino blood, immediate or remote, Down clothing wools, and wools of like character with any of the preceding, including such as have been heretofore usually imported into the United States from Buenos Ayres, New Zealand, Australia, Cape of Good Hope, Russia, Great Britain, Canada, and elsewhere, and also including all wools not hereinafter described or designated in classes 2 and 3—		
	Unwashed wool................................lbs..	35,322,611.50	6,516,121.92
	Washed wool..................................lbs..	6,123	2,757.00
	Scoured wool.................................lbs..	74,287	36,761.00
384	Class 2: Leicester, Cotswold, Lincolnshire, Down combing wools, Canada long wools, or other like combing wools of English blood, and usually known by the terms herein used, and also all hair of the camel, goat, alpaca, and other like animals—		
	Wool, unscoured ....lbs..	5,740,629.37	1,225,165.00
	Wool, scoured ....lbs..	304	251.00
	Wool, sorted ....lbs..	15,322	4,011.00
	Camel's hair, unscoured ....lbs..		
	Hair of the goat, alpaca, and other like animals, unscoured..lbs..	1,278,932	306,164.00
	Hair of the goat, alpaca, and other like animals, scoured...lbs..	852	221.00
	Class 3: Donskoi, native South American, Cordova, Valparaiso, native Smyrna, Russian camel's hair, and including all such wools of like character as have been heretofore usually imported into the United States from Turkey, Greece, Egypt, Syria, and elsewhere—		
385	Value 13 cents or less per pound—		
	Wool ....lbs..	125,611,283	9,504,403.00
	Wool, sorted ....lbs..	153,467	14,365.00
	Camel's hair, Russian ....lbs..	4,380,714	325,550.00
386	Value over 13 cents per pound—		
	Wool ....lbs..	3,041,337	466,102.00
	Wool, sorted ....lbs..	10,760	1,817.00
	Camel's hair, Russian ....lbs..		
	Manufactures composed wholly or in part of wool, worsted, the hair of the camel, goat, alpaca, or other animals—		
	Rags, flocks, noils, and waste—		
388	Noils...lbs..	40,777	13,193.00
388*	Yarn and other wastes........................lbs..		
389*	Rags and flocks ....lbs..		
	Total Schedule K transferred to free list		18,416,881.92

* No data—included in dutiable estimate of reduction, page 159.

dutiable to free list—Continued.

Importations of 1893.		Rates.			Equivalent ad valorem.			Paragraph.
Duties.	Unit of value.	Present.	House.	Senate.	Present.	House.	Senate.	
					Per ct.			
$5,823.29	$0.70	13 cents per dozen	Free..	Free..	18.64	Free..	Free..:	340
58.24	1.07	26 cents per dozen	..do...	..do...	24.27	..do....	..do...	
15.00	.33	50 cents per gall	..do...	..do...	15.00	..do....	..do...	
5,896.53					18.72			
765.52	26.77	$5 per ton	Free..	Free..	18.68	Free..	Free..	356
73,039.79	232.90	$22.40 per ton	..do...	..do...	10.77	..do....	..do...	357
21,567.81	151.36	$11.20 per ton	..do...	..do...	7.40	..do....	..do...	{358
5,878.26	122.21	......do......	..do...	..do...	9.16	..do....	..do...	{359
105,994.82	143.25	$25 per ton	..do...	..do...	17.45	..do....	..do...	360
249.79	.11	$\frac{7}{10}$ cent per pound.'	..do...	..do...	6.47	..do....	..do...	362
207,485.99					11.99			
3,885,487.27	.18	11 cents per pound	Free..	Free..	59.63	Free..	Free..	384
1,347.06	.45	22 cents per pound	..do...	..do...	48.86	..do....	..do...	
24,514.71	.49	33 cents per pound	..do...	..do...	66.69	..do....	..do...	
688,875.53	.21	12 cents per pound	..do...	..do...	56.23	..do....	..do...	384
109.44	.83	30 cents per pound	..do...	..do...	43.60	..do....	..do...	
3,677.28	.26	24 cents per pound	..do...	..do...	91.68	..do....	..do...	
		12 cents per pound	..do...	..do...		..do....	..do...	
153,471.84	.24	......do......	..do...	..do...	50.13	..do....	..do...	
90.72	.88	36 cents per pound	..do...	..do...	41.05	..do....	..do...	
3,041,408.94	.076	32 per cent	..do...	Free..	32	..do....	..do +..	385
9,193.60	.094	64 per cent	..do...	..do...	64	..do....	..do...	
104,176.00	.074	32 per cent	..do...	..do...	35	..do....	..do...	
233,051.00	.15	50 per cent	..do...	..do...	50	..do....	..do...	386
1,817.00	.17	100 per cent	..do...	..do...	100	..do....	..do...	
		50 per cent	..do...	..do...		..do....	..do...	
12,233.10	.32	30 cents per pound	Free..	Free..	92.72	Free..	Free..	388
		......do......	..do...	..do...		..do....	..do...	*388
		10 cents per pound	..do...	..do...		..do....	..do...	*389
8,159,453.49					44.30			

Articles transferred from

Paragraph.		Importations of 1893.	
		Quantities.	Value.
	SCHEDULE N.—SUNDRIES.		
426	Bristles ....lbs..	1,608,688.01	$1,508,115.00
434	Cork bark, cut into squares or cubes.......................lbs..	24.00	25.00
443	Feathers and downs, crude, not dressed:		
	Ostrich feathers..	....	545,437.00
	All other	....	268,064.00
450	Curled hair, suitable for beds or mattresses	....	3,843.00
465	Paintings, in oil or water colors	....	2,086,764.60
	Statuary..	....	175,002.16
469	Hatters' plush, black, composed of silk, or of silk and cotton...	....	120,428.00
	Total Schedule N transferred to free list..............	....	4,707,678.76
	Articles under section 3, act of Oct. 1, 1890:		
	Coffee..lbs..	19,757,574	3,305,105.00
	Goatskins, raw ....lbs..	1,825,624	398,614.00
	Hides, raw or uncured, whether dry, salted, or pickled, and other skins, except sheepskins with the wool on .....lbs..	6,494,611	685,288.00
	Total	....	4,389,007.00
	Total transfers from dutiable to free list............	....	45,171,630.08

dutiable to free list—Continued.

Importations of 1893.		Rates.			Equivalent ad valorem.			Paragraph.
Duties.	Unit of value.	Present.	House.	Senate.	Present.	House.	Senate.	
				Per ct.				
$160,868.83	$0.04	10 cents per pound	Free..	Free..	10.67	Free..	Free..	426
2.40	1.04	....do....................	..do ...	..do ...	9.60	..do ...	..do ...	434
								443
54,543.70		10 per cent..............	. do ...	.do ...	10	..do ...	..do ...	
26,806.40		....do....................	..do ...	..do ...	10	..do ...	..do ...	
576.45		15 per cent..............	..do ...	..do ...	15	..do ...	..do ...	450
313,014.71		....do....................	..do ...	..do ...	15	..do ...	..do ...	465
26,250.32		....do....................	..do ...	..do ...	15	..do ...	..do ...	
12,042.80		10 per cent..............	..do ...	..do ...	10	..do ...	..do ...	469
504,105.61					12.02			
592,727.22	.17	3 cents per pound	Free..	Free..	17.93	Free..	Free..	
27,354.38	.22	1½ cents per pound........	..do ...	..do ...	6.87	..do ...	..do ...	
97,419.19	.11	....do....................	..do ...	..do ...	14.22	..do ...	..do ...	
717,530.79					16.35			
12,170,167.53					26.94			

RECAPITULATION.

Schedules.		Importations of the fiscal year, June 30, 1893.		Duties estimated under bill H. R. 4864.			Average ad valorem under—		
		Value.	Duty received.	House.	Senate.		Present law.	House.	Senate.
							Per cent.	Per cent.	Per cent.
A	Chemicals, oils, and paints	$29,315,095.67	$6,122,059.85	$5,090,316.00	$5,103,006.20		32.04	25.09	25.12
B	Earths, earthenware, and glassware	23,513,506.16	12,101,651.60	8,076,228.11	8,731,495.00		51.46	34.57	37.13
C	Metals, and manufactures of	46,173,495.23	27,003,537.41	15,769,653.89	14,555,313.28		58.48	33.06	34.52
D	Wood, and manufactures of	2,864,432.36	935,381.08	648,451.22	653,710.13		32.66	22.64	22.82
E	Sugar	118,981,131.14	193,294.48	10,832.14	11,822,623.01		14.55	22.43	35.36
F	Tobacco, and manufactures of	12,568,407.12	14,831,089.09	11,528,783.11	11,528,783.11		117.83	91.68	91.68
G	Agricultural products and provisions	39,337,409.55	12,122,403.81	7,060,748.17	8,868,607.30		63.32	21.68	22.38
H	Spirits, wines, and other beverages	13,574,931.06	9,088,330.91	8,431,317.64	8,182,005.12		69.90	60.69	68.98
I	Cotton manufactures	20,510,438.98	11,332,605.23	7,885,585.28	7,885,585.28		65.25	38.45	38.45
J	Flax, hemp, and jute, and manufactures of	41,706,792.44	18,767,353.37	12,734,279.49	12,777,037.08		45.00	30.51	30.35
K	Wool, and manufactures of	36,993,460.16	36,448,677.46	14,714,879.23	12,973,340.23		98.50	39.78	35.00
L	Silk, and silk goods	37,019,948.02	20,310,258.74	17,113,647.62	16,747,145.74		53.50	45.13	44.16
M	Pulp, papers, and books	8,640,310.32	2,070,124.10	1,658,208.97	1,760,463.66		23.85	10.10	20.28
N	Sundries	54,657,663.86	13,081,275.89	12,784,208.78	11,651,960.95		27.	26.28	21.37
Sec. 4.	Unenumerated	1,432,660.52	272,644.62				10.03	10.03	10.03
	Articles transferred to the free list	45,171,630.08	12,170,167.53	272,644.62	272,644.62		20.94		
		523,441,241.57	198,373,452.97	124,093,004.17	163,361,018.35		49.58	35.52	34.15

NOTE.—The computations of the average ad valorem rates of duty are calculated upon the dutiable value only. The value of the articles that are free of duty by either the present law, House, or Senate bills are omitted.

	Value.	Duty.	Ad valorem rate.	Amount of decrease.
			Per cent.	
Dutiable—Under present law	$400,069,658.48	$198,373,452.97	40.58	
Dutiable—Under House bill	351,041,963.12	124,093,004.17	35.52	$73,680,418.80
Dutiable—Under Senate bill	478,209,611.49	163,361,018.35	34.15	35,012,434.62

The estimated revenue by this bill:
From customs $163,361,018.35
Internal revenue, additional from—
  Income $30,000,000
  Spirits 20,000,000
  Playing cards 3,000,000
                                                        53,000,000.00
                                                        216,361,018.35

ARTICLES TRANSFERRED FROM THE FREE LIST TO THE DUTIABLE LIST BY THE SENATE BILL.

	Rate of duty under—		
	Present law.	House.	Senate.
Floor matting, commonly known as Chinese matting	Free	Free	20 per cent.
Fruits and nuts:			
Dates	do	do	Do.
Olives, green or prepared	do	do	Do.
Cream or Brazil nuts	do	do	Do.
Orchids or lily of the valley, azaleas, etc	do	do	10 per cent.
Sugar	do	do	1 cent per lb. not over 80°, etc.
Molasses	do	do	2 and 4 cents per gallon.

ARTICLES TRANSFERRED FROM THE FREE LIST OF THE HOUSE BILL TO THE DUTIABLE LIST OF THE SENATE BILL.

Bone char, suitable for use, etc	25 per cent	Free	20 per cent.
Iron ore	75 cents per ton	do	40 cents per ton.
Apples, green or ripe	25 cents per bushel	do	20 per cent.
Apples, dried, evaporated, etc	2 cents per pound	do	Do.
Beef	do	do	25 per cent.
Mutton	do	do	Do.
Pork	do	do	Do.
Coal, bituminous	75 cents per ton	do	40 cents per ton.
Coal, slack or culm of	30 cents per ton	do	15 cents per ton.
Coke	20 per cent	do	15 per cent.
Sugar, raw, refined	Free: ½ cent per pound	do	1 c. per lb., not over 80°, etc.

ARTICLES TRANSFERRED FROM THE DUTIABLE LIST OF THE HOUSE BILL TO THE FREE LIST OF THE SENATE BILL.

Bottles containing wines, spirits, etc	3 cents each	30 pr. ct.	Free.
Diamonds and other precious stones, rough or uncut	Free	15 pr. ct.	Do.

ARTICLES TRANSFERRED FROM THE FREE LIST TO THE DUTIABLE BY BOTH HOUSE AND SENATE BILLS.

Currants, Zante	Free	10 pr. ct.	30 per cent.
Opium, crude, etc	do	$1 pr. lb.	$1 per pound.

INDEX.

	Paragraphs, present law.	Paragraphs, proposed law.
A.		
Abortion—articles, drugs, medicines to cause	Pages 93, 94	Secs. 10, 11, 12.
Absinthe	332	240
Abstract of decisions of appraisers to be made and published once each week	Page 116.	Sec. 39.
Academies, articles for	602	603
Acetate of lead:		
brown	62	49
white	62	49
Acid—		
acetic	1	1
boracic	2	2
chromic	3	3
citric	4	4
pyroligneous	1	1
sulphuric	5, 728	643
tannic	6	5
tartaric	7	6
Acids	473	363
Aconite	474	364
Acorus	321, 475	231, 365
Adhesive felt	569	479
Additional papers and declarations required with invoice of consigned goods at time of entry	Page 108.	Sec. 8:
Administrative customs provisions—		
Appeal to circuit court, regulations	Page 112.	Sec. 35.
Appeal must be taken within ten days	Page 112.	Sec. 35.
Appeal from decision of collector	Page 112.	Sec. 35.
Appeal on classification, mode of	Page 114.	Sec. 36.
Appraisers, nine to be appointed	Page 111.	Sec. 34.
Appraising officers and collectors duties in ascertaining actual market values imported merchandise	Page 109.	Sec. 31.
Appraisers to be employed at such ports as Secretary of Treasury may prescribe	Page 110.	Sec. 33.
Appraisers' decisions to be reported with samples, whom to	Page 116.	Sec. 39.
Appraisers' decisions final as to dutiable value	Page 111.	Sec. 34.
Appraisers' duties prescribed	Page 111.	Sec. 34.
Appraisers' decisions to be filed	Page 116.	Sec. 39.
Baggage, transit to foreign countries	Page 120.	Sec. 49.
Bonded warehouse, withdrawal warehouse	Page 117.	Sec. 41.
Bribes, penal offense	Page 119, 120	Secs. 47, 48.
Classifications and rates of duty, decisions rendered	Page 119.	Sec. 46.
Coverings, duty on	Page 116.	Sec. 40.
Damage allowance abolished	Page 118.	Sec. 44.
Declarations of consigned goods at time of entry	Page 108.	Sec. 8.
Declarations on invoices, how indorsed	Page 100.	Sec. 25.
Declarations, forms of, prescribed	Page 104.	Sec. 27.
Examination of parties by collector	Page 101.	Sec. 26.
Fees abolished in customs cases	Page 107.	Sec. 43.
Forfeiture, to what shall apply	Page 107.	Sec. 29.
Invoice, purchased goods, method	Page 107.	Sec. 29.
Invoice must accompany merchandise admitted to entry	Page 101.	Sec. 26.
Invoice value	Page 107.	Sec. 29.

	Paragraphs, present law.	Paragraphs, proposed law.
Administrative customs provisions—Continued.		
Invoices, how made out	Page 99.	Sec. 24.
Market value, definition of	Page 116.	Sec. 40.
Merchandise admitted to entry must be accompanied by invoice	Page 101.	Sec. 26.
Oaths administered by general appraisers	Page 115.	Sec. 37.
Oaths, declarations substituted for	Page 117.	Sec. 43.
Overpayment	Page 118.	Sec. 45.
Owner of imported goods, who	Page 99.	Sec. 23.
Owner may abandon goods to Government, if amounting to 10 per cent or over of invoice	Page 118.	Sec. 44.
Papers, production of	Page 115.	Sec. 37.
Papers compelled to be produced by collector	Page 101.	Sec. 26.
Penalty for fraudulent acts in connection with preceding sections	Page 108.	Sec. 30.
Penalty for undervaluation under 10 per cent	Page 107.	Sec. 29.
Penalties of section 6 applied to declarations substituted for oaths	Page 117.	Sec. 43.
Permanent board at port of New York	Page 110.	Sec. 33.
Penalty for violation of preceding section	Page 115.	Sec. 38.
Penalty for false declarations	Page 106.	Sec. 28.
Penalty for false swearing	Page 115.	Sec. 38.
Procedure, mode of, when market value can not be ascertained	Page 109.	Sec. 32.
Proofs in customs cases, where placed	Page 117.	Sec. 42.
Publications of appraisers	Page 116.	Sec. 39.
Purchased goods, invoice value	Page 107.	Sec. 29.
Rates and classifications of duty, decisions rendered	Page 119.	Sec. 46.
Reappraisement, mode of	Page 112.	Sec. 34.
Refunds, statement of	Page 118.	Sec. 45.
Repealing section	Page 121.	
Sample place at port of New York	Page 110.	Sec. 33.
Testimony in writing	Page 115.	Sec. 37.
Undervaluation of goods	Page 107.	Sec. 29.
Values, decisions rendered	Page 119.	Sec. 46.
Withdrawal from bonded warehouse	Page 117.	Sec. 41.
Advertisements, obscene	Page 93.	Secs. 11, 12, 13.
Agates, unmanufactured	476	366
Agate buttons	429	316
Agricultural seeds	286	611
Agricultural drills, duty on	215	591
Alabaster:		
manufactures of	459	351
casts	677	585
Albata	188	158
Albumen	477	367
Albumenized papers	419	307
Albums	420	308
Alcohol, amylic	42	30
Alcoholic—		
compounds	8	7
perfumery	8	7
preparations	74	58
Ale	337	245
ginger	340	248, 555
Alizarin, yellow, orange, green, blue, brown, black	478	368
assistant	36	26
colors or dyes	478	368
Alkalin silicate	84	68
Alkalies	76	60
Alkaloids	76	60
of chinchona bark	690	601
salts of chinchona bark	690	601
Alloy of any kind, composed of nickel	203	563
Alloys of aluminum	186	157
Almond oil	661	568

	Paragraphs, present law.	Paragraphs, proposed law.
Almonds	306	221
Alum, alum cake	9	8
in crystals or ground	9	8
patent	9	8
Alumina	9	8
sulphate of	9	8
Aluminium	186	157
in leaf	190	160
Aluminous cake	9	8
Amber, unmanufactured	479	369
manufactures	459	351
oil	661	568
Ambergris	480	370
oil	661	568
American—		
artists, productions of	757	686
fisheries, products of	571	481
vessels, repair of	Page 91.	Sec. 8.
Ammonia—		
carbonate	10	371
muriate of	10	371
sulphate of	10	371
Amylic alcohol	42	30
Anatomical preparations	707	619
Anchors	153	126
Anchovies	291	208
Angora goatskins, unmanufactured	605	505
Andirons	161	134
Aniline—		
arseniate of	490	383
oil	661	568
salts	481	372
Animal carbon	511	408
Animals	247–251	189
for breeding	482	373
for exhibition	483	374
for racing	483	374
zoological collections	483	374
integuments of	507	403
of immigrants	483	374
Anise oil	661	568
Anise-seed oil	661	568
Annatto	484	375
Anthoss oil	661	568
Anthracite coal	536	441
Antimony	187	376
ore	485	376
regulus of	187	376
sulphite of	485	376
Antiquities, collections of	524	426
Anvils	155	128
Apatite	486	377
Apparatus—		
life-saving	633	535
philosophical	677	585
Apparel—		
children's	397	285
theatrical	686	596
wearing	752	669
Appeal from Board of General Appraisers, how made	Page 114.	Sec. 36.
Appendix. Comparison of income tax law with proposed law		Page 279.
Apples	297, 298	213, 378, 379
dried, desiccated, evaporated, or prepared in any manner	298	213, 379

	Paragraphs, present law.	Paragraphs, proposed law.
Apples—Continued.		
green or ripe	297	213, 378
dried	298	213, 379
desiccated	298	213, 379
evaporated	298	213, 379
prepared in any manner	298	213, 379
Appraisement of value (similitude)	Page 89.	Sec. 4.
Appraisers—		
authorizes passage of baggage to transit to a foreign country without payment of duty	Page 120.	Sec. 49.
hearings before	Page 114.	Sec. 36.
nine general, authorized to be appointed by the President	Page 110.	Sec. 33.
penalty for undervaluation	Page 107.	Sec. 29.
regulations regarding	Page 110.	Sec. 33.
to be employed at such ports as Secretary of Treasury may prescribe	Page 110.	Sec. 33.
Argal	487	380
Argentine	188	158
Argol	487	380
Aromatic seeds	24	470
Arrack	332	240
Arrowroot	488	381
Arseniate of aniline	490	383
Arsenic	489	382
sulphide of	489	382
Art squares	408	296
educational stops	491	384
Art, works of	465, 757–759	575, 686–688
Articles—		
domestic growth	493	387
domestic manufacture	493	387
domestic production	493	387
domestic reimported	Page 96.	Sec. 19.
imported by the United States		385
manufactured, withdrawal from warehouse	Page 91.	Sec. 8.
manufactured of imported materials, regulations regarding	Page 91.	Sec. 8.
of foreign production, and machinery—when free	Page 90.	Sec. 7.
unenumerated	Page 89.	Sec. 3.
used in dyeing	24, 26, 492	470, 18, 386
tanning	26, 492	18, 386
Articles of glass—		
painted	111	90
colored	111	90
printed	111	90
stained	111	90
etched	111	90
otherwise ornamented or decorated	111	90
cut	111	90
engraved	111	90
Artificial mineral waters	341	249
Artificial and ornamental—		
feathers and flowers	443	328
parts of	443	328
Artistic copies of antiquities	759	688
Artists' colors	61	48
water-color paints	61	48
Asbestos	459, 494	351, 388
Ashes—		
beet root	495	389
lye of wood	495	389
wood	495	389
Asphaltum	496	390
Aspic oil	661	568
Assafœtida	497	391

	Paragraphs, present law.	Paragraphs, proposed law.
Asses' skins	605	505
Aubusson carpets	399	287
Autograph albums	420	308
Axles—		
bars	154	127
blanks	154	127
iron or steel	154	127
parts of	154	127
forgings	154	127
Axminster carpets	399	287
Azaleas	666	234½, 572

B.

	Paragraphs, present law.	Paragraphs, proposed law.
Bacon	310	392
Bagatelle balls	435	320
Bagging	366	271
Bags	365	270
domestic	493	387
Balls—		
bagatelle	435	320
billiard	435	320
chess	435	320
pool	435	320
Balm of Gilead	498	393
Balsams	24, 560	470
Bamboo reeds, sticks, etc	756	684
unmanufactured	756	684
Band iron	140	116
Bar iron	135	112
Bark, cinchona	499	394
Barks	24, 560	470
extracts of, used in tanning	26	18
used in manufacture of quinia	499	394
Barley	252	191
malt	253	190
pearled, patent, or hulled	254	191
Barrels	228	180
domestic	493	387
Bars of copper	194	454
lead	200	166
Bars or pigs of brass	189	159
Bars, iron and steel, for vessels	Page 90.	Sec. 7.
Baryta—		
carbonate of	500	395
sulphate of	49	37
Barytes	49	37
artificial, sulphate of	51	39
unmanufactured	500	395
Basswood lumber	218	168, 676
Bauxite	501	396
Bay rum	334	242
Bay water	334	242
Bead or beaded trimmings, manufactures	462	354
Beaded silk goods	413	301
Beads, glass	445	99
Beans	24, 270, 271, 560	197, 198, 470
prepared and preserved	271	198
tonka	739	656
tonqua	739	656
tonquin	739	656
Beauxite	500	395
Bed—		
down	567	477
feathers	567	477

T A——15

	Paragraphs, present law.	Paragraphs, proposed law.
Bedsides	408	296
Beef	311	224¼, 392
mutton and pork	310	224¼, 392
Beer	337	245
coloring	22	16
ginger	340	248
Beeswax	502	397
Beet root ashes	495	389
Beet juice	726	182½, 644
Bell metal	503	398
Bells, broken	503	398
Beltings	398, 412	286, 300
Belt pins	206	170
Bene oil	661	568
Bent glass	122	102
Bergamot oil	661	568
Berlin blue	50	38
Berries	24, 560	470
Bicarbonate of soda	80	64
Bichromate of potash	69	54
Bichromate of soda	82	66
Billets	136	111
Billiard balls	435	320
Binding twine	362	268, 399
Bindings	398, 412	286, 300
Birds	504, 505	400, 401
dressed and finished	443	328
stuffed and skins	504	400
Bismuth	506	402
Bisque ware	100, 101	84, 85, 86
Bitters	332	240
spirituous	332	240
Bitumen	496	390
Bituminous coal	432	318½, 441
Black—		
bone	52	40
copper	193	453
oxide of tin	209	653
salts	685	595
Blacking	11	9
Blacksmiths' hammers and sledges—		
iron	156	129
steel	156	129
Bladders	507	403
fish	507	403
manufactures of	459	351
salted for preservation	507	403
Blanc fixe	51	39
Blank books	423	311
Blankets	393	282
Bleaching powder	635	537
Blocks of lead	200	166
rough hewn or sawed only	223	679
Blood—		
dragon's	559	469
dried	508	404
Blooms	136	111
Blown glass	108, 109	102
Blue vitriol	12	405
wash	55	43
Blues	50	38
Blue clay	535	439
Blue wash	58	43
Blue, ultramarine	55	43
Boards, sawed	218, 220	676
Boats, life	633	535

	Paragraphs, present law.	Paragraphs, proposed law.
Bockings	406	294
Bodkins	178	150
Boiler—		
iron	138	114
tubes, flues, stays, pipes	157	130
Bologna sausages	509	406
Bolt blanks	158	131
Bolting cloths	510	407
Bolts—		
handle	755	673
heading	755	673
iron and steel, for vessels	Page 90.	Sec. 7.
shingle	755	673
stave	755	673
Bolts and bolt blanks—		
iron	158	131
steel	158	131
Bond, internal-revenue, manufacturer's	Page 92.	Sec. 9.
when canceled, invoices	Page 101.	Sec. 26.
Bonded warehouse, manufacture of goods in	Page 97.	Sec. 21.
withdrawals from	Page 97.	Sec. 20.
Bone—		
ash	511	408
black	52	40
buttons	430	317
char	13	11, 409
dust	511	408
manufactures of	435, 460	320, 352
Bones	511	408
not burned	511	408
calcined	511	408
ground	511	408
steamed	511	408
otherwise manufactured	511	408
Bonnet pins	206	170
Bonnets, materials for	518	417
Bookbinders' skins	456	341
Books	428, 512, 513, 515, 516	311, 410, 411, 413, 414
obscene	Pages 93, 94.	Secs. 11, 12, 13.
professional	686	596
Boots	456	341
Boracic acid	2	2
Borate of lime	14	10, 415
soda	14	415
Borax—		
crude	14	10, 415
refined	14	10, 415
Bort	557	467
Botanical and mineralogical specimens	712	625
Bottles, glass	103, 104, 336	88, 244
Bottles or jugs, no duty on	329	237
Bottles, vials, etc	103	88
Bounty, sugar, repeal of	232	182
Box—		
chronometers	210	172
lumber	220	684
wood	756	684
Braces	412	300
wool	398	286
Brads, cut	177	149
Braids	518	417
cotton	354	263
for hats, bonnets, and hoods	518	417
silk	412	300
wool	398	286

	Paragraphs, present law.	Paragraphs, proposed law.
Branding and labeling foreign manufactures	Page 90.	Sec. 5.
Brandy and other spirituous liquors	329	237
coloring for	22	16
Brass	189	159
Brazil—		
nuts	583	491
paste	517	416
pebbles	519	418
Bread knives	167	140
Breadstuffs, etc	252–265	190–193
Breadstuffs and farinaceous substances—		
buckwheat	255	190
corn or maize	256	190
corn meal	257	190
oats	259	190
oatmeal	260	190
rye	262	190
rye flour	263	190
wheat	264	190
wheat flour	265	190
Breccia	520	419
Brier-root	756	684
wood	756	684
Brick	93	76
fire	93	76
magnesic	93	77
Brimstone	727	642
Bristles	426	420
Britannia metal	676	584
British gum	324	233
Bromine	521	421
Bronze—		
casts	677	585
metal	190	160
powder	190	160
Broom corn	272	422
Brooms	427	314
Brown wool grease	316	645
Brushes	427	314
Brussels carpets	401, 403	289, 291
Buckwheat	255	190
Buds	24, 560	470
Building stone	127, 128	638, 106
Bulbous roots	24, 560, 699	470, 611
Bulbs	24, 560, 699	470, 611
Bullions	196	162
Bullion—		
gold	532	423
silver	522	423
Bunting	395	283
Burden of proof in customs cases to lie on the claimant of goods	Page 117.	Sec. 42.
Burgundy pitch	523	424
Burlaps	364	270
Burnt pyrites, dross from	133	109¼, 518
dross or residuum of	133	109¼, 518
Burnt starch	324	233
Burr—		
stone	126, 723	638
stones	126, 723	638
waste		685
Butchers' knives	167	140
Butter	266	194
knives	167	140
substitutes for	266	194
Button forms	428	315

	Paragraphs, present law.	Paragraphs, proposed law.
Buttons	398, 429	286, 316
agate	429	316
barrel	398	286
bone	430	317
cloth for	428	315
glass	430	317
horn	430	317
ivory	430	317
pearl	429	316
shell	429	316
shoe	431	318
vegetable ivory	430	317

C.

	Paragraphs, present law.	Paragraphs, proposed law.
Cabbages	273	425
Cabinet woods	220, 756	684
Cabinets—		
of coins	524	426
furniture	230	181
of medals	524	426
Cables, tarred	362	268, 399
Cacao—		
crude	542	447
fiber	542	447
leaves	542	447
shells	542	447
Cadmium	525	427
Cajeput oil	661	568
Cake—		
niter	85	622
oil	661	568
salt	85	622
Calamine	526	428
Calfskins	456	341
japanned	456	341
Calomel	75	59
Cameos in frames	452	336
Camel's hair, third class	385, 386	685
Camphor	15	429
crude	527	429
Candy, sugar	238	183
Cane juice	726, 64	182½
Canes, walking-sticks	756	684
Cans, tin	296	212
Capsicum	326	235
Caps, percussion	442	327
Carbon, animal	511	408
Carbonate—		
of ammonia	10	371
of baryta	500	395
of magnesia	34	24
of potash, crude or fused	685	595
of strontia	725	640
Carbonized—		
wool	388	278
noils	388	278
Carboys—		
domestic	493	387
glass	103	88
Card—		
boards	420	308
clothing	159	132
waste	388	685
Cards, playing	424	312
Carpets	399–408	287–296

	Paragraphs, present law.	Paragraphs, proposed law.
Caraway oil	661	568
Casks	228	180
domestic	493	387
Cast-iron articles	160–163	133–136
Castile soap	79	63
Castor or castoreum	528	430
beans	284	205
oil	37	27
seed	284	205
Casts—		
alabaster	677	585
bronze	677	585
immoral	Pages 93, 94.	Secs. 11, 12, 13.
marble	677	585
obscene	Pages 93, 94.	Secs. 11, 12, 13.
plaster of Paris	677	585
Cassada	730	646
Cassava	730	646
Cassia	713	626
buds	713	626
oil	661	568
vera	713	626
Cassiterite	209	653
Catgut	529	431
manufactures of	459	351
Cattle, neat	Page 96.	Secs. 17, 18.
hides of	Page 96.	Secs. 17, 18.
regulations	482	373
more than one year old	248	189
Caustic—		
potash	70, 685	595
soda	81	65
Cayenne pepper	326	235
Cedar	219	684
paving posts	219	684
railroad ties	219	684
telephone poles	219	684
telegraph poles	219	684
plank	220	684
deals	220	684
sawed	220	684
wood	756	684
Cedrat oil	661	568
Cement	95	79
copper	193	453
Cerium	530	432
Certified invoice or affidavit must accompany merchandise admitted to entry	Page 101.	Sec. 26.
Chain or chains, iron or steel	164	137
Chair cane	229	170, 684
Chalk	16, 531	11, 433
preparations of, all	16	11
prepared	16	11
precipitated	16	11
French	16	11
red	16	11
Chamois skin	456	341
Chamomile oil	661	568
Champagne	335	243
Charcoal	532	434
Charms	100	84
Charts	423, 512	311, 410
Cheese	267	195

	Paragraphs, present law.	Paragraphs, proposed law.
Chemical—		
apparatus	682	590
compounds	76	60
glassware	107	102
salts	76	60
vessels and parts of	682	590
wood pulp	415	303
Chenille carpets	309	487
cotton	351	260
goods	351	260
Chenilles	411	299
curtains	351	269
table covers	351	260
Cheroots	246	188
Cherry juice	339	247
Chess—		
balls	435	320
men	435	320
Chicory root	317, 533	227, 435
burnt or roasted	317	227
ground or granulated	317	227
in rolls	317	227
Children's hats	451	335
Chimney pieces, slate	130	108
Chimneys, glass	108	102
China—		
clay	98	82
ware	99–101	83, 84, 85, 86
Chili or other pigs	194	454
Chinese blue	50	38
matting	464	356
matting	575	485, 464
Chip braids, plaits, and laces	518	417
Chip, manufactures of	460	352
Chloral hydrate		12
Chlorate—		
of potash	685	595
of soda	709	621
Chloride of lime	635	537
Chloroform	17	13
Chocolate	318	228
confectionery	239, 318	183, 228
Chromate—		
of iron	132	438
of potash	69	54
of soda	82	66
Chrome colors	53	41
Chromic—		
acid	3	3
ore	132	438
Chronometers, box or ship's	210	172
parts of	210	172
Cider	274	436
Cigarette-books	468	350
covers	468	359
Cigarette paper	468	359
Cigarettes, internal revenue tax on	Page 122.	Sec. 53.
Cigarettes	246	188
Cigars	246	188
Cinchona bark	499	394
Cinchona bark—		
alkaloids of	690	601
salts of	690	601
Cinnamon	714	627
chips	714	627
oil	661	568

	Paragraphs, present law.	Paragraphs, [proposed law.
Circulars, obscene	Pages 93, 94.	Secs. 11, 12, 13.
Citrate of lime	634	536
Citric acid	6	4
Citronella oil	661	568
Civet, crude	534	437
oil	661	568
Clapboards	221, 222	677, 678
pine	221	677
spruce	222	678
Clay, china or earth	98	82
Clay pipes and pipe bowls	468	359
common blue	535	439
Clays	98, 535	82, 439, 440
Cliff-stone	723	638
Clippings, brass and copper	189, 192	159, 452
Dutch-metal	189	159
clippings	670	577
Cloaks of wool	397	285
Clocks or parts thereof	211	173
Cloth—		
bolting	510	407
cotton	345–349	253–258
crinoline	448	333
hair	448, 449	333, 334
mohair	428	315
oil	661	568
woolen	392	281
Clothing—		
card	159	132
ready-made	349, 396, 413	258, 284, 301
rubber	349, 413	258, 301
Clove stems	715	628
Cloves	715	628
Coal—		
anthracite	536	441
bituminous	432	318¼, 441
culm or slack	432	318¼, 441
stores	537	
Coal-tar—		
colors	18	14
crude	538	443
dyes	18	14
pitch	731	647
preparations of	18, 19	14, 443
Coat linings of wool	394, 395	283
Coarse copper	193	453
Cobalt	539	444
ore of	539	444
oxide of	20	444
Cocculus indicus	540	445
Cochineal	541	446
Cocoa, prepared or manufactured	319	229
butter or butterine	320	230
crude	542	447
fiber	542	447
leaves	542	447
cables and cordage of hemp	362	268, 399
shells	542	447
Cocoa fiber matting	464	356
mats	464	356
Cocoanut oil	661	568
Cocoanuts	582	491
Cocoons, silk	705	617
Cod-liver oil	38	28
Coffee	543	448
substitutes for	321	231

	Paragraphs, present law.	Paragraphs, proposed law.
Cogged ingots	146, 185	122, 156
Coins	544	449
cabinets of	524	426
gold	544	449
silver	544	449
copper	544	449
Coir	545	450
yarn	545	450
Coke	433	318¼, 442
Collars and cuffs	372	275
Collections of antiquities	524	426
Collector's account of bonded merchandise	Page 92.	Sec. 9.
Collector authorized to examine parties under oath	Page 101.	Sec. 26.
Collector authorized to compel production of papers	Page 101.	Sec. 26.
Collodion	21	15
Cologne water	8	7
Coloring for brandy	22	16
Colors	49, 61, 478	37, 48, 368
chromium	53	41
coal-tar	18	14
containing quicksilver	57	45
Comfits	303	218
Composition—		
metal composed of copper	192	452
metal for vessels	546	451
sheathing or yellow metal	195	161
Compounds alcoholic	8, 74	7, 58
chemical	76	
Common window-glass	112	91
Concentrated melada	726	641, 182½
Concrete and concentrated molasses	726	641, 182½
Confectionery	238, 239	183
chocolate	318	228
Congressional Library, books for	514	412
Copper—		
articles of	191–195	161, 451–454
bars	191–195	161, 451–454
black or coarse	191–195	161, 451–454
bottoms	191–195	161, 451–454
braziers'	191–195	161, 451–454
cement	191–195	161, 451–454
clippings	191–195	161, 451–454
coins	544	449
composition metal	192	452
for vessels	Page 90.	Secs. 6, 7.
ingots	191–195	161, 451–454
manufactures of	191–195	161, 451–454
medals	648	551
old	546	451
ore	191–195	161, 451–454
pigs	191–195	161, 451–454
pipes	191–195	161, 451–454
plates	191–195	161, 451–454
regulus, of	191–195	161, 451–454
rods	191–195	161, 451–454
sheets	191–195	161, 451–454
subacetate of	749	666
sulphate of	12	405
Copperas	23	455
Copying paper	419	307
Coral, manufactures of	459	351
marine	547	456
uncut	547	456
unmanufactured	547	456
Cordage	362	268, 399
Cordials	332	240

	Paragraphs, present law.	Paragraphs, proposed law.
Cords and tassels of wool	398	286
cotton	354	263
and tassels of silk	412	300
Corduroys, cotton	350	259
Cork—		
bark manufactures	434	319, 457
unmanufactured	548	457
carpets	369	273
wood	548	457
unmanufactured, cut into squares or cubes	548	457
manufactures of	434	319, 457
Corn	256	190
meal	257	190
Corticene	369	273
Cosmetics	77	61
Cotton	549	458
and silk hatters' plush	469	593
bagging	366	271
boot lacings	354	263
braces	354	263
braids	354	263
carpeting	407	295
chenille and chenille goods	349, 351	258, 260
cloth	344–348	252–256
clothing, ready made	349	258
collars and cuffs	372	275
cords	354	263
corduroy	350	259
corset lacings	354	263
damask	355	264
drawers	352, 353	261, 262
duck	346	254
embroideries	373	276
flocks	549	458
galloons	354	263
gimps	354	263
gins, duty on	215	591
goods, knit	351, 352	260, 261
goring	354	263
hemmed handkerchiefs	349	258
hemstitched handkerchiefs	373	276
hose and half hose	352, 353	261, 262
insertings	373	276
knit goods	352, 353	261, 262
lace window curtains	373	276
laces	373	276
manufactures of	342–355	250–264
neckties	349	258
pile fabrics	350	259
plushes	350	259
seed oil	39	568
shoe lacings	354	263
shirts	352, 353	261, 262
stockings	352, 353	261, 262
suspenders	354	263
table covers of chenille	351	260
thread	342, 343	250, 251
ties, iron or steel	140	459
trimmings	373	276
velvet	350	259
velveteens	350	259
warps	342	250
warp yarn	342	250
waste	549	458
wearing apparel	349, 372	258, 275
webbing	354	263

	Paragraphs, present law.	Paragraphs, proposed law.
Cotton—Continued.		
wire	148	124
woven fabrics		257
yarn	342	250
Covers	408	296
Coverings not dutiable	Page 116.	Sec. 40.
Corrugated iron	142	118
Cream nuts	584	491
Cream of tartar	90	73
Crinoline cloth	448	333
wire	148	124
Crockery ware	100, 101	84, 85, 86
Croton oil	40	568
seed	699	611
Crowbars—		
iron	156	129
steel	156	129
Crown glass	112	91
Crucibles	90	83
Crucible clay	535	439
Crude mineral substances	202	552
borax	14	415
civet	534	437
coal tar	538	443
gum	479	369
tartar	487	380
oil, petroleum		568
Cryolite	550	460
Cubic nitrate	709	621
Cudbear	551	461
Culm, coal	432	318½, 441
Cultivators, duty on	215	591
Curling stones	552	462
Curling-stone handles	552	462
Curled hair suitable for beds or mattresses	604	504
Currants, Zante	302	217
Zante or other	578	213, 217
Currency valuations of merchandise	Page 121.	Sec. 52.
Curry	553	463
powder	553	463
Curtains, cotton lace window	373	276
chenille	351	260
Cutch	554	464
Cut glass	111	90
Cutlery	165	138
Cuttle-fish bone	555	465
Cyanite	625	526
Cylinder glass	112, 113	91, 92

D.

Dairy products	266, 269	194, 196
Damage on iron and steel, none allowed	149	125
allowance abolished	Page 118.	Sec. 44.
Damask cotton	355	263
Dandelion root	556, 321	466, 231
Dates	579	213, 488
Decisions of general appraisers to be reported to the Secretary of the Treasury and board of general appraisers with samples	Page 116.	Sec. 39.
Decisions of general appraisers to be filed, and to be opened to public inspection	Page 116.	Sec. 39.
Decision of board of appraisers final as to dutiable value	Page 111.	Sec. 34.
Decision of collector conclusive unless appeal is taken within ten days	Page 112.	Sec. 35.

	Paragraphs, present law.	Paragraphs, proposed law.
Decision of board conclusive unless appeal to circuit court is taken as prescribed in section 15	Page 112.	Sec. 35.
Declarations substituted for oaths	Page 117.	Sec. 43.
forms of, prescribed	Page 104.	Sec. 27.
Decorated glassware	105, 106	89
Definition of "value" or "actual market value" as used in this act	Page 116.	Sec. 40.
Degras	316	645
Demijohns, glass	103	88
Dentifrices	77	61
Dextrine	324	233
Diamond dust	557	467
Diamonds	557	467
miners	557	467
Dice	435	320
Discriminating duty	Page 112.	Sec. 35.
Distilled spirits	331	239
Distilled oils	76	60
Divi-divi	558	468
Dollheads	436	321
Dolls	436	321
Dolmans, of wool	397	285
Domestic—		
animals, regulations	482	373
articles returned	493	387
bags	493	387
barrels	493	387
carboys	493	387
casks	493	387
manufactures	493	387
products	493	387
vessels	493	387
Downs, bed	567	477
crude, not dressed, colored or manufactured	567	477
of all kinds	443	328
Dragon's blood	559	469
Drawback	Page 117.	Sec. 43.
Drainings of sugar	726	641, 182½
Drawing paper	422	310
Drawings	677, 758	585, 687
Draughts	435	320
Dress goods—		
trimmings	398	286
worsted	394, 395	283
wool	394, 395	283
Dressed upper leather	456	341
Dross from burnt pyrites	133	518
Druggets	406	294
Drawback, provision for	493	387
on tin plate	328	
on imported materials	Page 117.	Sec. 43.
Drugs such as barks, beans, berries, etc	24, 560	470
to prevent conception	Pages 93, 94.	Secs. 11,12, 13.
Dutch metal	190	160
Dutch wool carpets	405	293
clippings	189	159
Duty, discriminating	Page. 95.	Sec. 14.
not to be assessed on less than invoice value	Page. 107.	Sec. 29.
on unusual coverings	Page. 116.	Sec. 40.
Dyeing, articles used in	492	386
Dyeing, articles in a crude state	492	386
Dyes, coal-tar	18	14
Dyewoods, extracts and decoctions	26	18

	Paragraphs, present law.	Paragraphs, proposed law.
E.		
Earthenware	99–101	83, 84, 85, 86
yellow	83	83
Earths or clays	98	82
unwrought or unmanufactured	98	440
Earths—		
ochery	54	42, 566
sienna	54	42, 566
umber	54	42, 566
Ebony wood	220, 756	684
Edgings	373	276
Effects, personal	752	669
Eggs	275	471
birds', fishes', and insects'	561	471
silkworms'	706	618
and yolks of	561	471
Egg yolks	276	471
Embroideries	373	276
cotton	373	276
flax	373	276
linen	373	276
silk	413	301
wool	398	286
Embroidered articles or fabrics	413	301
Emery—		
grains	437	322
ground	437	322
manufactured	437	322
ore	562	472
pulverized	437	322
refined	437	322
Enamel, fusible	122	101
Enameled ironware	171, 172	144
Engravers' diamonds	557	467
Engravings	758, 423, 511	687, 311, 408
Envelopes, paper	421	309
Epaulets	196	162
Epsom salts	34	24
Erasers	165	138
Ergot	563	473
Essences	25	17
fruit	25	17
Essential oils	76	60
Etchings	512, 677, 423, 465	410, 585, 311, 575
proofs of	465	575
Ether	25	17
fruit	25	17
nitrous, spirits of	25	17
sulphuric	25	17
Excrescences	24, 560	470
Exhibition—		
articles for		
paintings for	758, 759	687, 688
photographic pictures for		
statuary for		
Explosive substances	438–442	323–327
Expressed oils	76	60
Extract—		
of annato	484	375
of hemlock and other barks used in tanning	26	18
of indigo	29	514
of licorice	33	23
of madder	639	541
of meat	313	225

	Paragraphs, present law.	Paragraphs, proposed law.
Extract—Continued.		
and decoctions	26	18
of opium	47	35
of orleans	484	375
of rocou	484	375
of roncou	484	375
of safflower	694	605
saffron	694	605
sumac	26	18
Extracts, other	26	18
and pastes of indigo	614	514
Eyeglasses	119	98

F.

	Paragraphs, present law.	Paragraphs, proposed law.
Fans, palm-leaf	564	474
of all kinds		330
Farina	565	475
Farm and field products	270–283	197–204, 422, 425, 436, 471, 587, 581
Fashion-plates	566	476
Feather dusters	427	314
Feathers	443	328
crude, not dressed, colored, or manufactured	477	367
bed	567	477
dusters	427	314
Fees abolished in customs cases	Page 117.	Sec. 43.
Feldspar	568	478
Felt, adhesive	569	479
carpeting	406	294
Felt and felt fabrics	396	284
for papermakers' use	398	282
Fence wire rods	147	123
Fence posts	755	673
Fennel oil	661	568
Fibers	592–597, 670	487, 577
dried	24	470
Fibrin	570	480
Fibrous vegetable substances	597	487
Figs	300	215
Filberts	307	222
Files and file blanks	168	141
Filtering paper	419	307
Fine-art societies or institutions	677, 692, 758, 759	585, 603, 687, 688
Fire—		
arms	169, 170, 702	142, 143, 614
boards, paper for	422	310
brick	93	76
crackers	438	323
wood	755	673
Fish	291, 296, 571	208, 212, 481
bait	572	482
bladders	507	403
cans	296	212
fresh	293, 571	209, 481
frozen	571, 293	209, 481
glue	27	19
herrings	294	210
in cans or packages	295	211
packed in any other manner	295	211
mackerel	292	209, 210
oil	46, 661	34, 568
pickled	292	209, 210
salmon	292	209, 210

	Paragraphs, present law.	Paragraphs, proposed law.
Fish—Continued.		
salt-water, frozen	294	210
shell and shrimps	703	615
skins	573	483
smoked, dried, salted, or pickled	293	209, 481
sounds	507	403
prepared	27	19
Fisheries, products of American	571	481
Flatirons	135	112
Flannels	393	282
Flax—		
carpeting	407	295
embroideries	373	276
gill netting	367	272
hackled	358	265
hemp and jute	356–374	265–277, 497, 399
insertings	373	276
laces	373	276
linen hydraulic hose	368	275
manufactures of	371	277
nets	367	272
not hackled	357	497
oilcloths, etc	369	273
or hemp tow	359	497
seed	285	206
oil	41	29
seines	367	272
straw	356	497
tow of	359	497
wearing apparel	372	275
webs	367	272
Flints, flint, and flint stones	574	484
Flint glassware	103–105	88
Flitters or metallics	190	160
Floats	168	141
Flocks	389	685
Flocks, cotton	549	458
woolen	389	278
Floor matting	464	356
of straw	575	464, 485
Floor rugs	408	296
Floss, silk	410	298
Flour—		
rye	263	190
sago	695	606
wheat	265	190
Flowers	24, 560	470
Flowers of sulphur	88	71, 642
Flues, boiler	157	130
Fluted glass	114	93
Foreign manufactures, branding and labeling same	Page 90.	Sec. 5.
Foreign vessels	Page 95.	Sec. 16.
Foreign coin to be estimated quarterly	Page 121.	Sec. 52.
Forfeiture to attach to goods *undervalued* more than 40 per cent	Page 107.	Sec. 29.
when shall apply	Page 107.	Sec. 29.
Forged iron	130	115
Forgings of iron or steel	139, 158	115, 126
Forks	167	140
Forms for buttons	428	315
Fossils	576	486
Fowls, land and water	505	401
Frames, spectacle and eyeglass	119	98
Free list	Page 65.	Sec. 2.
Freestone	127, 128	638, 106

	Paragraphs, present law.	Paragraphs, proposed law.
French chalk	16	11
Fresh milk	268	554
Fringes	398, 412	286, 300
Fruit and nuts	297–309, 578–586	213–224, 378, 379, 213, 217, 483–491
essences	25	17
ethers	25	17
green, ripe, or dried	580	489
juice	339	247
excrescences	24	470
oils	25	17
plants	577	487
preserved	304	219
Fruits, preserved in sugar	303	218
sirup	303	218
molasses	303	218
spirits	303	218
Fruits	443	328
Fulminates	439	324
Fulminating powders	439	324
Fur—		
articles of	461	353
hats	451	335
hatters'	451	335
skins of all kinds, not dressed	588	493
undressed	587	492
Furs	444	329
not on the skin, for hatters' use	444	329
Furniture, cabinet	230	181
and similar household effects	516	414
Fusel oil	42	30

G.

Galloons—		
cotton	354	263
silk	412	300
wool	398	286
Galvanized iron	143	119
Gambier	589	494
Garden seeds	286	611
Garments, outside	397	285
Gas-retorts	102	87
Gelatine	27	19
manufactures of	462	354
General appraisers, regulations regarding	Page 110.	Sec. 33
authorized to administer oaths, and cite parties before them; and with power to compel production of papers, and to take testimony in writing	Page 115.	Sec. 37
German silver	188	158
Gilead, balm of	498	393
Gill netting	367	272
Gimps of wool	398	286
cotton	354	263
Ginger—		
ale	340	248, 555
beer	340	248, 555
cordial	336	244
root	716	620
wine	336	244
Giving or soliciting of bribes or presents to or by officers of United States a penal offense	Pages 119, 120	Secs. 26, 27
Glass and glassware—		
beads	445	99
bent	122	102
beveled, enameled, etc.	118	97

	Paragraphs, present law.	Paragraphs, proposed law.
Glass and glassware—Continued.		
blown	108, 109	102
bottles	103, 104	88
bottles, etc., filled	104	88
broken	590	495
carboys	103	88
chemical	107	102
chimneys	108	102
colored	103	88
common window	112	91
crown	112, 113	91, 92
cut, engraved, etc	111, 118	90, 97
cylinder	112, 113	91, 92
decanters	111	90
demijohns	103	88
disks	591	496
flint	103, 104, 105	88
green	103	88
headed pins	206	170
lime	103, 104, 105	88
lenses	120, 121	100, 101
looking-glass plates	116, 117	95, 96
manufactures of	108, 122	102
mirrors	116, 119, 122	95, 98, 102
not cut, engraved, etc	105	88
old	590	495
obscured, or ground	114, 118	90, 97
opal	110	90
plate	114, 115, 116	93–95
plates or disks	591	496
porcelain	110	90
silvered	116, 117, 118	95, 96, 97
spectacles and eyeglasses	119, 121, 591	98, 101, 496
stained	106, 118	89, 97
stained and painted	677	585
stained or painted	122	102
vials	103	88
window	113, 118, 122	92, 97, 102
Glassware	103–122	88–102
chemical	107	102
chimneys	108	102
decorated	105, 106	88, 89
flint and lime	103, 104, 105	88
painted	111	90
pressed	105	88
Glaziers' diamonds	557	467
lead	201	167
Gloves—		
kid	458	343–350
leather	458	343–350
Glucose or grape sugar	240	183
Glue	27	19
fish or isinglass	27	19
stock	606	506
Glycerine—		
crude	28	20
refined	28	20
Goatskins	456	341
Angora	605	505
Gold—		
articles of	215	177
beaters' molds	598	498
skins	598	498
bullion	522	423
coins	544	449
leaf	197	163

T A——16

	Paragraphs, present law.	Paragraphs, proposed law.
Gold—Continued.		
medals	648	553
ore	667	571
pens	205	146
size	56	496
sweepings	729	44
Goods in bonded warehouse may be withdrawn within three years from entry on payment of duty in force at time of withdrawal	Page 117.	Sec. 41.
Goods in bond	Page 117.	Sec. 41.
manufactured in bonded warehouse, provisions for	Page 92.	Sec. 9.
to be manufactured in warehouse, regulations for	Page 92.	Sec. 9.
Goods, product of convict labor, importation prohibited	Page 121.	Sec. 51.
Goring, silk	412	300
Gorings, wool	398	286
Grain bags	365	270
Grains	443	328
Grains—excrescences	24	470
Granadilla wood	220, 756	684
Granite	127, 128, 728	106, 638
Grape sugar or glucose	240	183
Grapes	299	214
Grass—		
braids, etc., suitable for ornamenting hats	518	417
and straw, definition of	460	352
grasses and fibers	592, 597, 670	497, 577
manufactures	460	352
Grasses	597	497
Grease	599	499
grease from wool	316	645
Green pease	203	581
Grindstones	129	107
Guano	600	500
Gum	24, 560	470
British	324	233
resin	24, 560	470
substitute	324	233
Gun—		
blocks	223	679
powder	440	325
wads	446	331
Gunny—		
bags	601, 670	501, 577
cloth	366, 601, 670	271, 501, 577
Gut, cat, unmanufactured	529	431
whip	529	431
worm	529	431
Gutta-percha, crude	603	503
manufactures	461	353
Guts, salted	602	502
Gypsum	97	81

H.

Hair	604	504
alpaca	375	278, 685
animals, unmanufactured	391, 604	280, 504
of the camel	685	375–387
of the camel	389	278
of the camel	375, 377	685, 278
cattle	604	504
cloth	448, 449	333, 334
curled, for beds and mattresses	450	504
goat	375, 377	278, 685
horse	604	504
human	447, 604	332, 504

	Paragraphs, present law.	Paragraphs, proposed law.
Hair—Continued.		
on the skin	387	685
of the first class	384	685
of the second class	384	685
pencils	427	314
pins	206	170
seating	449	334
wood sticks	756	684
Hams	310	392
Hammers and sledges	156	129
Handkerchiefs—		
hemmed	349	268
hemstitched	373	276
flax, jute, or hemp	373	276
silk	413	301
Handle bolts	755	673
Hangings, paper	422	310
Hard rubber manufactures	461	353
Hard woods of various kinds, unmanufactured	756	684
Harness:		
of immigrants	463	374
Harvesters, duty on	215	591
Hassocks	408	296
Hat bodies of fur	451	335
bands, bindings, linings, etc., of silk, satin, or cotton	518	417
Hats	451	335
pins	206	170
materials for	518	417
wool	303	282
Hatters'—		
furs	444	329
irons	161	134
plush	469	593
plush of silk	469	593
Hay	277	199
Head-nets	398	286
Heading—		
blocks	223	679
bolts	755	673
Hemlock bark, extract of	26	18
Hemlock lumber	218	178, 676
Hemp (see Flax)	360	266, 497
cables and cordage of	362	268, 399
carpeting	363	269
hackled	360	266, 497
line of	360	266, 497
manufactures of	371	277
New Zealand	362	268, 399
not hackled	357	497
seed	699	611
oil	43	31
tow of	359	497
Herbs	24, 560	470
Herrings	294	216
pickled or salted	294	210
fresh	294	210
frozen	294	210
Herring oil	46	34
Hide—		
cuttings	606	506
rope	607	507
Hides	605	505
Hinges and hinge-blanks	158	131
Hob-nails	174	146
Hogs	249	189

	Paragraphs, present law.	Paragraphs, proposed law.
Hollow-ware	163	136
Hones	608	508
Honey	278	200
Hoods, materials for	518	417
Hoofs, unmanufactured	609	509
Hoop iron	140	116
Hoops, iron	140	116
Hop—		
poles	755	673
roots	610	510
Hops	279	201
Horse—		
shoe nails	174	146
shoes, wrought	176	148
Horses	247	189
Horn—		
buttons	430	317
manufactures of	460	352
strips	611	511
tips	611	511
Horns, and parts of, unmanufactured	611	511
Horse-rakes, duty on	215	591
Horses, regulations	482	373
Hose—		
linen hydraulic	368	275
cotton	352, 353	261, 262
Hosiery	352, 353	261, 262
House furniture	230	181
Household effects	516, 675	414, 583
Hubs for wheels	223	679
Human hair	447, 604	332, 504
Hunting knives	167	140
Hydrate, chloral		12
of potash	70	595
of soda	81	65
Hydraulic cement	95	79
Hydriodate of potash	71	55
Hydrographic charts	512	410
I.		
Ice	612	512
Images, obscene	Pages 93, 94	Secs. 11, 12, 13.
Immoral articles, casts, instruments	Pages 93, 94	Secs. 11, 12, 13.
Implements, professional	686	596
Importation of articles by the United States		385
Income tax	Pages 122-129	Secs. 54 to 68
India rubber	613	513
malacca joints	756	684
manufactures	460, 461	352, 353
milk of	613	513
old scrap	613	513
refuse	613	513
Indian peltries	674	582
Indians, goods and effects of	674	582
Indigo	29, 614	514
carmined	29	514
extracts of	29	514
Indurated fiber ware	461	353
Ingots, steel and cogged	146, 185	122, 156
of copper	194	454
Ingrain carpets, treble	404	292
Ingrain two-ply carpets	405	293
Ink powders	30	21

	Paragraphs, present law.	Paragraphs, proposed law.
Inks	30	21
Insects, dried	24, 560	470
Insertings—		
cotton	373	276
flax	373	276
Instruments—		
philosophical	677	585
professional	686	596
Integuments of animals	507	403
Internal-revenue manufactures in bond	Page 91.	Sec. 8.
Internal revenue—		
tax on cigarettes	Page 122.	Sec. 53.
income tax	Pages 122-129	Secs. 54–68.
and income tax, upon what levied	Page 122.	Sec. 54.
amount of tax	Page 122.	Sec. 54.
limitation of amount	Page 122.	Sec. 54.
when levied, collected, and paid	Page 122.	Sec. 54.
gains, profits, and income, how estimated	Page 122.	Sec. 55.
what deductions shall be allowed	Page 122.	Sec. 55.
when salaries shall be included in tax	Page 122.	Sec. 55.
who must render returns	Page 123.	Sec. 56.
penalty for refusing to make returns	Page 123.	Sec. 56.
how appeals may be taken from decisions of officers	Page 123.	Sec. 56.
how notice shall be served	Page 123.	Sec. 56.
relative to affidavits or depositions	Page 123.	Sec. 56.
when penalty shall be assessed	Page 123.	Sec. 56.
when income is due and payable	Page 124.	Sec. 57.
exemption to nonresident	Page 124.	Sec. 58.
what part of income nonresidents must pay tax on	Page 124.	Sec. 58.
income tax on corporations	Page 125.	Sec. 59.
what shall be liable	Page 125.	Sec. 59.
how returns shall be made	Page 125.	Sec. 59.
relative to building associations	Page 125.	Sec. 59.
what deductions may be made by corporations	Page 125.	Sec. 59.
returns of dividends, when to be made	Page 125.	Sec. 59.
returns of tax, when to be made by corporations	Page 125.	Sec. 59.
building associations exemptions	Page 125.	Sec. 59.
further returns from corporations as to surplus of dividends, how made	Page 126.	Sec. 60.
what deductions shall not be permitted by corporations	Page 126.	Sec. 61.
methods for preventing payment of dutiable tax by corporations	Page 126.	Sec. 61.
failure for making returns, penalty	Page 126.	Sec. 61.
exemption of charitable and other corporations from tax	Page 126.	Sec. 61.
tax upon national officials, how deducted and paid	Page 127.	Sec. 62.
penalty for divulging secrets of business by Government officials	Page 127.	Sec. 63.
inquiries to be made by collector and his deputies, when and how	Page 127.	Sec. 63.
when returns shall be made for income and special tax	Page 127.	Sec. 63.
penalty for making returns by partnerships and corporations	Page 127.	Sec. 63.
power of collector to cease from examining books	Page 127.	Sec. 63.
power of collector or deputy collector to enter premises	Page 127.	Sec. 63.
penalty for fraudulent valuation	Page 127.	Sec. 63.
penalty for fraudulent valuation, how collected	Page 127.	Sec. 63.
returns to be made by corporations doing business for profit	Page 129.	Sec. 64.
returns by corporations doing business for profit, how made and when	Page 129.	Sec. 64.
books of account to be kept by corporations doing business for profit	Page 129.	Sec. 65.
books open to inspection to internal revenue officers	Page 129.	Sec. 66.

	Paragraphs, present law.	Paragraphs, proposed law.
Internal revenue—Continued..		
further requirements in regard to income tax upon aliens and corporations	Page 129.	Sec. 67.
receipt to be made by collector	Page 129.	Sec. 68.
application of tax as between debtor and creditor	Page 129.	Sec. 68.
regulations of commissioner of internal revenue, invalid unless approved by Secretary	Page 130.	Sec. 69.
penalty for false swearing	Page 130.	Sec. 70.
release from forfeitures and penalties	Page 130.	Sec. 71.
Internal revenue tax—		
on playing cards	Page 130.	Sec. 72.
stamp tax on playing cards	Page 130.	Sec. 72.
how stamps shall be cancelled	Page 130.	Sec. 73.
registrative record by manufacturer of playing cards	Page 130.	Sec. 74.
penalty for failure to register	Page 130.	Sec. 74.
commissioner authorized to prepare stamps, where stamps shall be for sale	Page 130.	Sec. 75.
account of sales to be kept by collector	Page 130.	Sec. 75.
penalty for forging and counterfeiting stamps	Page 130.	Sec. 76.
penalty for removing or altering marks on stamps	Page 130.	Sec. 76.
possession of altered stamps, prima facie evidence of guilt	Page 130.	Sec. 76.
penalty for removal or sale of playing cards without paying tax	Page 131.	Sec. 77.
how playing cards can be removed from manufactory	Page 131.	Sec. 77.
penalty for removing stamps of manufacturer from cards	Page 131.	Sec. 78.
penalty for hiding or concealing untaxed cards	Page 132.	Sec. 79.
who shall pay the tax	Page 132.	Sec. 80.
penalty for selling cards without stamps	Page 132.	Sec. 80.
assessment for failure to stamp cards, how made	Page 132.	Sec. 81.
on distilled spirits	Page 132.	Sec. 82.
tax on	Page 132.	Sec. 82.
how computed	Page 132.	Sec. 82.
stamps for payment of same	Page 132.	Sec. 82.
mode of gauging	Page 132.	Sec. 82.
who shall pay the tax	Page 132.	Sec. 82.
when tax shall be paid	Page 132.	Sec. 82.
length of bonded period under distilled spirits	Page 132.	Sec. 82.
warehousing transportation bonds, conditions	Page 133.	Sec. 83.
when given and how	Page 133.	Sec. 83.
on what gauge tax shall be estimated	Page 133.	Sec. 83.
bonds for additional tax, forms and methods of giving	Page 133.	Sec. 83.
penalty for refusing to give additional tax bonds	Page 133.	Sec. 83.
provisions for execution of annual bond	Page 133.	Sec. 83.
notice by owner for regauging of spirits within four years	Page 134.	Sec. 84.
what tax shall be collected upon such regauging	Page 134.	Sec. 84.
allowance for loss of spirits	Page 134.	Sec. 84.
when tax shall be collected on original gauge	Page 134.	Sec. 84.
difference in allowance between different size of package	Page 134.	Sec. 84.
establishment of general bonded warehouses for fruit	Page 135.	Sec. 85.
officers in charge general bonded warehouses for fruit	Page 135.	Sec. 85.
shall be kept securely locked	Page 135.	Sec. 85.
under regulations by the commissioner	Page 135.	Sec. 85.
method of removal of distilled spirits from distillery warehouses	Page 135.	Sec. 86.
stamps to be affixed before removal from distillery warehouse	Page 135.	Sec. 87.
method of removal in bond to general warehouse	Page 135.	Sec. 88.
period of limitation as to payment of tax by bondsmen	Page 135.	Sec. 88.
spirits can be withdrawn but once from general bonded warehouse	Page 135.	Sec. 89.
bonds for spirits in general warehouse to be renewed whenever required by the commissioner	Page 135.	Sec. 89.

	Paragraphs, present law.	Paragraphs, proposed law.
Internal revenue tax—Continued.		
existing provisions of law in regard to withdrawals extended in this act	Page 135.	Sec. 90.
when warehouses may be discontinued, and transfer made by commissioner	Page 136.	Sec. 91.
how collector may distrain for failure to pay tax	Page 136.	Sec. 92.
provisions in regard to excessive wastage	Page 136.	Sec. 93.
penalty for failure to deposit bonded spirits after withdrawal from distillery warehouse	Page 136.	Sec. 93.
increased tax shall apply to all spirits	Page 136.	Sec. 94.
when distillers may not pay special tax	Page 136.	Sec. 95.
compensation of storekeepers and gaugers	Page 136.	Sec. 96.
assignment of storekeeper and gauger	Page 136.	Sec. 97.
bond to be given by storekeeper	Page 136.	Sec. 97.
assignment of gaugers by Commissioner	Page 137.	Sec. 98.
method of gauging on premises of rectifier	Page 137.	Sec. 99.
conviction of illicit distilling and power to license, of distiller	Page 137.	Sec. 100.
wines of domestic production, fortification of sweet wines	Page 137.	Sec. 101.
Tobacco:		
who shall be regarded as manufacturer of	Page 137.	Sec. 102.
what shall be construed as manufactured tobacco.	Page 137.	Sec. 102.
farmers and growers shall be regarded as manufacturers	Page 137.	Sec. 102.
reciprocity repeal of all agreements made with other countries under section 3, act of 1890	Page 138.	Sec. 104.
repealing clauses	Page 138.	Sec. 105.
Inventions, models of	652	557
Invoices—		
declarations on, how indorsed, and what it shall embody	Page 100.	Sec. 25.
how made out	Page 99.	Sec. 24.
when bond may be canceled	Page 101.	Sec. 26.
when consuls shall refuse certification	Page 100.	Sec. 25.
Iodate of potash	71	55
Iodide of potash	71	55
Iodine—		
crude	615	515
resublimed	31	515
Iodoform	32	22
Ipecac	616	516
Iridium	617	517
Iron—		
angles	137	113
articles, cast	160–163	133–136
articles of	215	177, 591
axles	154	127
parts of	154	127
forgings	154	127
band	140, 143	116, 119
bar	135, 136	111
bars	136	111
beams	137	113
billets	136, 146	111, 122
blacksmiths' hammers and sledges	156	129
blooms	136	111, 112
boiler	138	114
boiler tubes, flues, or stays	157	130
bolt and bolt blanks	158	131
bolts and other metal manufactures for vessels	Page 90.	Sec. 7.
brads, cut	177	149
building forms	137	113
car-truck channels	137	113
castings of	160, 161, 162	133–135
chain or chains	164	137

	Paragraphs, present law.	Paragraphs, proposed law.
Iron—Continued.		
channels	137	113
chromate of	132	438
columns and posts	137	113
cotton-ties (hoop iron)	140	459
crowbars	156	129
cut nails and spikes	173	145
damage allowance prohibited	177	149
deck and bulb beams	137	113
duty to take effect, when	142	118
ferromanganese	134	110
ferrosilicon	134	110
flat rails	141	117
flats	135	112
forged	139	115
forgings	139, 153	115, 126
girders	137	113
hatters' irons	161	134
hoop	140, 143	116, 119
hoops	140	119
joists	137	113
kentledge	134	110
loops	136	111, 112
limitation of duty	151	....
malleable, castings	162	135
nuts	176	148
ore	133	109½, 518
manganiferous	133	109½, 518
pigs	134	110
pipe, cast	160	133
plate	138, 143, 144, 145, 171	114, 119 119–121, 144
railway bars	141	117
railway fish plates	181	152
rivets	182	153
rods	136, 147	111, 112
rods for rivets, screws, nails, and fence wires	147	123
rolled	135, 136, 144	111, 112, 120
round, in coils or rods	135, 136	111, 112
scrap	134	110
scroll	140	116
sheet	142, 143, 144, 171, 172.	118–120, 144
sheets	143, 171, 172	118, 119, 144
and steel shotguns, muzzle-loading	169	142
skelp	138, 142	114, 118
slabs	136	111, 112
spiegeleisen	134	110
spikes	170, 173	145, 143
sprigs, cut	177	149
square	135	112
structural shapes	137	113
sulphate of	23	455
sulphuret of	133	109½, 518
TT, columns and posts	137	113
tacks, cut	177	149
taggers	142–145	118–121
tee rails	141	117
track tools	156	129
washers	176	148
wedges	156	129
wrought, for ships	153	126
wrought, horse-shoe nails	174	146
wrought, nails	174	146
wrought, pipes	157	130
wrought, tubes	157	130
Isinglass, or fish glue	27	19

	Paragraphs, present law.	Paragraphs, proposed law.
Istle	399, 592	287, 497
Italian cloths	394, 395	283
Ivory	618	519
buttons	430	317
cut into logs	618	519
drop black	52	40
vegetable	618	519
manufactures	435, 462	320, 354

J.

Jackets, woolen	397	285
Jalap	619	520
Japans	56	44
Japanned calfskins	456	341
Jasmine oil	661	568
Jellies	303	218
Jet	620	521
manufactures of	459	351
Jewelry	452, 453, 454	336–338
Jewels, used in manufacture of watches	557	467
Joss, light or stick	621	522
Juglandium oil	661	568
Jugs or bottles, no duty on	329	237
Juice—		
fruit	339	247
lemon, or sour orange	631	533
lime	631	533
Juniper oil	661	568
Junk, old	622	523
Jute	593	497
bags, for grain	365	270
bagging	366	271
burlaps	364	270
butts	594	497
carpeting	363	269
manufactures of	374	277
yarn	361	267

K.

Kainite	625	526
Kangaroo skins	456	341
Kaolin	98	82
Kelp	623	524
Kentledge, iron	134	110
Kernels, palm-nut	586	491
Kid gloves	458	343–350
skins	456	341
Kieserite	624	525
Kirschwasser	332	240
Kitchen knives	167	140
Knit goods—		
cotton or linen	352, 353	261, 262
silk	413	301
worsted or woolen	392	281
Knitting machines, cotton goods made on	352, 353	261, 262
needles	178, 179	150
Knives—		
butcher's	167	140
hunting	167	140
kitchen	167	140
pen	165	138
pocket	165	138
table	167	140
Kryolith	550	460
Kyanite	625	526

	Paragraphs, present law.	Paragraphs, proposed law.
L.		
Lac—		
spirits	627	528
sulphur	727	642
Lac dye—		
button, crude, seed, shell, stick	626	527
Lace window curtains, cotton	373	276
Lace articles	413	301
Laces—		
cotton	373	276
flax	373	276
for hats, bonnets, and hoods	518	417
linen	373	276
silk	413	301
wool	398	286
Lactarine	628	529
Lahn	737	654
Lambskins	456	341
Lambskin gloves	458	343–350
Lame	737	654
Lampblack	52	40
Lancewood	220, 756	684
Lard	314	530
Last blocks	223	679
Lastings	428	315
Laths	224	680
Laudanum	47	35
Lava, unmanufactured	629	531
tips	101	86
Lavender oil	661	568
Lead	199, 200, 201	165–167
acetate of	62	49
articles of	215	177
in bars	200	166
blocks	200	166
dross	199	165
molten	200	166
nitrate of	64	50
ore	199	165
in pigs	200	166
pipes	201	167
products	62, 67	49, 52
red	66	51
refuse	200	166
scrap	200	166
sheets	201	167
shot	201	167
type metal	208	171
white	67	52
wire	201	167
for pencils	467	358
Leaf—		
bronze or Dutch metal	190	160
gold	197	163
silver	198	164
tobacco	242	184
Leather	455–461	339–353, 458
bend or belting	455	339
manufactures of	461, 455–458	339–350, 353
bookbinders' calfskin	456	341
boots and shoes	456	341
calfskins	456	341
chamois skins	456	341
dressed upper	456	341
enameled	456	341
for uppers or vamps	457	342

	Paragraphs, present law.	Paragraphs, proposed law.
Leather—Continued.		
gloves	458	343–350
japanned calfskin	456	341
kangaroo skins	456	341
manufactures	455–457, 461	339–342, 353
morocco	456	341
not specially provided for	455	339, 340
patent	456	341
pianoforte	456	341
pianoforte action	456	341
sheep and goat skins	456	341
sole	455	339
upper	456	341
Leaves	24, 560	328, 470
Leeches	630	532
Lees crystals	91	74
Lemon—		
grass oil	661	568
juice	631	533
oil	661	568
peel	305, 570	220, 664
Lemons	301	216
Lemonade	340	248, 555
Lenses	120, 121	100, 101
Letter-press copying paper	422	310
Liability of collector prohibited for acts performed or decisions rendered in connection with values and classifications and rates of duty	Page 119.	Sec. 46.
Libraries or parts of	516	414
Library, Congressional	514	412
License regulation	Page 121.	Sec. 50.
Lichens	24, 560	470
Licorice—		
extracts of	33	23
juice	33	23
paste or roll	33	23
root, unground	632	534
Life—		
boats	633	535
saving apparatus	633	535
Lignum vitæ	756	684
Lily of the valley	666	234½, 572
Lime	96	80
borate of	14	10, 415
chloride of	635	537
citrate of	634	536
glassware	103–105	88
juice	631	533
sulphate	680	588
Limes	301	216
oil of	661	568
Limestone	127, 128	106, 638
Linen—		
brown and bleached	350	259
cloth	371	277
collars and cuffs	372	275
embroideries	373	276
hemstitched handkerchiefs	373	276
hydraulic hose	368	275
insertings	373	276
laces	373	276
manufactures of, embroidered	373	276
neck ruflings	373	276
ruchings	373	276
shirts	372	275
wearing apparel	372	275

	Paragraphs, present law.	Paragraphs, proposed law.
Lined gloves	458	343–350
Linoleum	369	273
Linseed	285	206
oil	41	29
Liquors	330, 332, 336	238, 240, 244
Literary societies and institutions	515, 692	413, 603
educational	515	413
philosophical	515	413
literary	515	413
religious	515	413
Litharge	62, 63	49
Lithographic stones	636	538
prints	420, 515	308, 413
Lithographs	420	308
Litmus	637	539
Lignum-vitæ	220	684
Loadstones	638	540
Logs	754	672
Logwood extracts	26	18
Longitudinal ribs for fence wire	147	123
Looking-glass plates	117	96
Loops, iron and steel	136	111
Lumber	218, 220	178, 676, 684
sawed	218	676
planed	218	178, 676
finished	218	178, 676
planed and tongued and groved	218	178, 676
for vessels	Page 90.	Sec. 7.

M.

Macaroni	258	192
Mace	717	630
oil	661	568
Machinery for repair	Page 94.	Sec. 13.
and articles of foreign production, when free	Page 90.	Sec. 7.
patterns	652	557
unfinished parts of	161	134
Mackerel	292	209, 210
Madder	639	541
Indian	639	541
Magic-lantern slides	121	101
Magnesia—		
calcined	34	24
carbonate of	34	24
medicinal	34	24
sulphate of	34	24
Magnesic fire-brick		77
Magnesite	640	543
Magnesium	641	544
Magnets	642	545
Mahogany wood	220, 756	684
Maize	256	190
Malacca joints, India	756	684
Melada	726, 237	182½, 641
Malleable iron castings	162	135
Malt extract	338	246
Manganese, ore, oxide	643	546
Manganiferous iron ore	133	518, 109½
Manila	595	497
binding twine	362	268, 399
cable and cordage	362	268, 399
for vessels	Page 90.	Sec. 7.
manufactures of	362	268, 399
Manna	644	547
Mantels	130	108

	Paragraphs, present law.	Paragraphs, proposed law.
Manufactures of—		
aluminum	215	177
alabaster	459	351
amber	459	351
asbestos	459	351
bladders	459	351
bone	460	352
catgut	459	351
china and earthenware	99–110	83–102
chip	460	352
copper	215	177
coral	459	351
corks	434	3, 9, 457
cotton	342–355	250–263
flax, jute, or hemp	358–374	265–277, 399, 497
fur	461	353
gelatine	462	354
glass	103–122	88–102
gold	215	177
grass	460	352
gutta-percha	461	353
hard rubber	461	353
horn	460	352
human hair	461	353
India rubber	460	352
indurated fiber ware	461	353
iron and steel and other metals	132–215	110–177, 376, 591
ivory	430, 462	354, 317, 552, 519
jet	459	351
jewelry	452–454	336–338
lead	62–67, 200, 201, 208, 215	49–52, 166, 167, 171, 177
leather	455–458, 461	339–350, 353
marble	124, 125	104, 105
metals	215	177
metallic articles	648	551
mother-of-pearl	462	354
miscellaneous manufactures of metal	186–215	157–177, 376, 451–454, 552, 563, 599, 653
nickel	203, 215	177, 563
osier	459	179
palm-leaf	460	352
paper	416–425	304–313
papier-maché	461	353
paste	459	351
pewter	215	177
platinum	215	177
shell	462	354
silk	409–414	298–302
silver	215	177
slate	130, 131	108, 109
spar	450	351
straw	460	352
stone	128	106
tin	143	119
tobacco	242–246	184–188
unenumerated	Page 89.	Sec. 3.
vegetable ivory	462	354
vulcanized India rubber	461	353
wax	459	351
weeds	460	352
whalebone	460	352

	Paragraphs, present law.	Paragraphs, proposed law.
Manufactures of—Continued.		
whip-gut	459	351
willow	459	351
wood	216–230	178–181, 674–684
other pulp	461	353
wool	391–408	280–296
felt for paper-makers' use	393	282
reduction of duty on, when to take effect		297
worm-gut	459	351
zinc	212, 213, 214, 215	174–177–591
Manufacturing purposes, acids	473	363
Manure, substances used for, and manures	511, 600	408, 500
Manuscripts	645	548
Maple-sugar bounty	231–237	182
Maps	423, 512	311, 410
Marble	123–125	103–105
casts	677	585
manufactures of	124	104
mosaic cubes	124	104
paving-tiles	124	104
slabs	124	104
Marbles	436	321
Market value, definition of	Page 116.	Sec. 40.
Marking or branding, etc	Page 90.	Sec. 5.
Marrow, crude	646	549
Marsh-mallows	647	550
Masks	463	355
Matches	441	326
Materials used in the manufacture of imported goods	Page 92.	Sec. 9.
Mats	408, 464	296, 356
Matting, floor	464	356
Chinese	575	485, 464
Meat, extract of	313	225
products	310–316	224½, 225, 226, 392, 530, 645
Meats, prepared or preserved	312	392
Medals	648	551
cabinets of	524	426
Medicinal acids	473	363
preparations	74–77	58–61
Meerschaum	649	553
Melada	726	641, 182½
concentrated	726	641, 182½
Men's hats	451	335
Merchandise, foreign, estimation of value	Page 121.	Sec. 52.
Merchandise taken from wrecks	Page 97.	Sec. 20.
Merchandise on board	Page 121.	Sec. 50.
Merchandise on board, duty to be paid on weight at withdrawal	Page 117.	Sec. 41.
Merchandise in sunken vessels	Page 97.	Sec. 20.
Mercurial preparations	75	59
Metal—		
bronze or Dutch	190	160
manufactures	215	177
threads	196	162
type	208	171
yellow or sheathing	189	159
unwrought	202	552
bells, broken	503	398
Metallic articles manufactured as trophies	648	551
mineral substances	202	552
crude	202	552
pins	206	170

	Paragraphs, present law.	Paragraphs, proposed law.
Metallics or flitters	190	160
Methods of making additions to invoice value of purchased goods	Page 107.	Sec. 29.
Mica	202	552
Milk	268, 269	196, 554
fresh	268	554
preserved	269	196
condensed	269	196
of Indian rubber	613	513
sugar of	269	196
Mill—		
cranks	153	126
irons	153	126
stones	723	638
Mineral—		
carbonate of magnesia	640	543
orange	65	51
salts, product of mineral spring	650	555
substances, crude	202, 651	552, 556
waters	341, 650	240, 555
wax	751	668
Mineralogical specimens	712	625
Minerals, crude	651	556
Mirrors, pocket and other	122	101, 102
Mode of appeal and time within which it must be taken from decision of collector	Page 112.	Sec. 35
on question of classification to the circuit court, and thence to the Supreme Court, and how final judgment shall be satisfied	Page 114.	Sec. 36
Mode of procedure when such actual market value can not be ascertained satisfactorily under provisions of section 10	Page 109.	Sec. 32
Mode of reappraisement	Page 111.	Sec. 34
Models	652	557
Mohair cloth	428	315
Molasses	726	641, 1823
concentrated	726	641, 1824
concrete	726	641, 1824
Molds, gold-beaters'	598	498
Molten lead	200	166
Monumental stone	128	106, 638
Morphia, and salts of	35	25
opium, containing 9 per cent and over	48	36
Morphine, and salts of	35	25
Moquette carpets	390	287
Morocco, skins for	456	341
Mosaic cubes	124	104
Mosses	653	558
Mother-of-pearl	462, 673	354, 580
Mowers, duty on	215	591
Mule-shoes, wrought	176	148
Mules	247	189
Mungo, woolen	389	278
Municipal corporations	757	686
Munjeet	639	541
Mushrooms	271	198
Music, raised print	513	411
Musk, crude	654	559
Muriate of potash	685	535
Muskets	169	142
Mustard	325	234
Mutton	311	224½, 392
Myrobolan	655	560
Myrtle sticks	756	684

	Paragraphs, present law.	Paragraphs, proposed law.
N.		
Nails	173, 174	145, 146
hob	174	146
horseshoe	174	146
wire	175	147
wrought-iron or steel	174, 175	146, 147
Natural history specimens	712	625
Neat cattle	Page 96.	Secs. 17, 18
hides of	Page 96.	Secs. 17, 18
Neckties	349	258
Neckwear, composed of cotton or other vegetable fiber	349	258
Needles	178, 179	150
hand-sewing and darning	656	561
Neroli oil	661	568
Nets, flax	367	272
Newspapers	657	562
New Zealand cordage, hemp	362	268, 399
Nickel	203, 667	563, 573
articles of	215	177
matte	667	573
ores	667	573
oxide	203	563
alloy of	203	563
manufactures of	215	177, 591
Niter cake	85	622
Nitrate:		
cubic	709	621
of soda	709	621
of lead	64	50
of potash, crude	685	595
refined	72	56
Nitrous ether, spirits of	25	17
Noils	388	685
Nonenumerated articles	Page 89.	Sec. 3.
Nursery stock	282	587
Nutgalls	24, 560	470
Nutmegs	718	631
Nuts	158, 306–309	131, 221–224
and washers	176	148
kernels, palm	582	491
Brazil	583	491
cocoa	582	491
cream	584	491
oil	661	568
excrescences	24	470
palm	582	491
of all other kinds	309	224
palm	585	491
Nux vomica	658	564
O.		
Oakum	659	565
Oar blocks	223	679
Oatmeal	260	190
Oats	259	190
Obscene advertisements, etc	Page 93, 94.	Secs. 11, 12, 13
Ocher and ochery earths	54	42, 566
Oil	36–46, 661	26–34, 568
almond	661	568
amber	661	568
ambergris	661	568
aniline	661	568
anise	661	568
anise seed	661	568
anthoss	661	568

	Paragraphs, present law.	Paragraphs, proposed law.
Oil—Continued.		
aspic	661	568
bene	661	568
bergamot	661	568
cajeput	661	568
cake	661	568
caraway	661	568
cassia	661	568
castor	37	27
cedrat	661	568
chamomile	661	568
cinnamon	661	568
citronella	661	568
civet	661	568
cloth, etc	369	273
cocoanut	661	568
cod-liver	38	28
cotton-seed	39	568
croton	40	568
crude petroleum		568
fennel	661	568
fish	46, 661	34, 568
flaxseed	41	29
fruit	25	17
fusel	42	30
hempseed	43	31
herring	46	34
jasmine	661	568
juglandium	661	568
juniper	661	568
lavender	661	568
lemon	661	568
grass	661	568
limes	661	568
linseed	41	29
mace	661	568
neroli	661	568
nut-oil	661	568
olive	44, 661	32, 568
orange	661	568
orange flower	661	568
origanum	661	568
palm	661	568
peppermint	45	33
petroleum		568
poppy-seed	41	29
rape-seed	43	31
roses	661	568
rosemary	661	568
seal	46	34
seeds	285	206
sesame	661	568
sesamum-seed	661	568
soluble	36	26
spermaceti	661	568
spike lavender	661	568
thyme	661	568
turkey-red	36	26
valerian	661	568
whale	46, 661	34, 568
Oils	25, 36–46, 76, 661	60, 568, 17, 29, 30, 31, 32, 33, 34
distilled	76	60
essential	76	60
expressed	76	60

	Paragraphs, present law.	Paragraphs, proposed law.
Oils—Continued.		
for dressing leather or wire drawing	599	409
fruit	25	17
of vitriol	5	613
rendered	76	60
soluble	36	26
Old copper	452	546
Old sheathing	189	159
Olives, green or prepared	662	215¼, 569
Olive oil	44	32
Onions	280	202
Opal glassware	110	90
Opium:		
aqueous extract of	47	35
crude	48, 663	36
for smoking	48	36
liquid preparations of	47	35
not adulterated, unmanufactured	47	35
other preparations of	47, 48	35, 36
tincture of	47	35
Optical instruments, disks for	591	496
lenses for	120, 121, 591	100, 100, 496
Orange—		
flower oil	661	568
mineral	65	51
oil	661	568
peel, preserved, etc	305	220
not preserved	664	570
sticks	756	684
Oranges	301	216
Oranges, lemons, and limes, duty on boxes	301	216
Orchids	666	234¼, 572
Orchil	665	571
liquid	665	571
Ore—		
antimony	485	376
chromic	132	438
cobalt	539	444
copper	191	451
imported in form of	546	451
emery	562	472
gold	667	573
iron	133	518, 109¼
lead	199	165
manganese	643	546
manganiferous	133	518, 109¼
nickel	667	573
silver	667	573
sulphur	727	642
as pyrites	133	518
tin	209, 736	653
Organzine, silk	410	298
Origanum oil	661	568
Orleans or rocou	484	375
extracts	484	375
Ornaments	100	84
wool	398	286
Orpiment	489	382
Osier—		
articles of	459, 518	351, 179, 417
manufactures	459	351, 179
prepared	459	351, 179
Osier or willow—		
for basketmakers' use	459	179
manufactures of	459	179

	Paragraphs, present law.	Paragraphs, proposed law.
Osmium	668	574
Other live animals	251	189
Other vessels, American manufacture	493	387
Ottar of roses	661	568
Outside covers not dutiable	Page 116.	Sec. 40.
Owner of imported goods, who	Page 99.	Sec. 23.
Owner may abandon goods to Government if amounting to 10 per cent or over of invoice	Page 118.	Sec. 44.
Ox shoes, wrought	176	148
Oxide—		
of cobalt	20	444
of manganese	643	546
of nickel	203	563
of strontia	725	610
of uranium	746	663
of zinc	60	47

P.

Paddy	261	193
Packing boxes of wood	228	180
Packing box shooks	228	180
Paint, white, containing zinc	60	47
Paintings	465, 677, 757, 758, 759	575, 585, 686, 687, 688
Paintings, definition of	465	575
on glass	757	686
Paints	49–61	37–48, 566
Palings	225	681
Palladium	669	576
Palms	666	572, 231½
Palm-leaf—		
braids, etc., suitable for ornamenting hats	518	417
manufactures of	460, 518	352, 417
fans	564	474
unmanufactured	564	474
Palm-nuts	585	491
kernels	586	491
oil	661	568
Pamphlets	513, 423	411, 311
Paper	416–425	304–313
drawing	422	310
envelopes	421	309
for fire-boards	422	310
for screens	422	310
hangings	422	310
manufactures of	421, 425	309, 313
old	670	577
sheathing	416	304
stock	670	577
Paper—		
albumenized and sensitized	419	307
albums	420	308
books	423	311
card-boards	420	308
cigars and cigarettes	246	188
copying	419	307
etchings, map charts, etc	423	311
filtering	419	307
letter-press copying	419	307
lithographic prints	420, 515	308, 413
pamphlet and engraving	423	311
photographs	423	311
playing-cards	424	312
printing-paper	417, 418	305, 306
silver	419	307

	Paragraphs, present law.	Paragraphs proposed law.
Paper—Continued.		
surface-coated paper	420	308
tissue	419	307
writing and drawing	422	310
Papers, obscene	Pages 93, 94.	Secs. 11, 12, 13
Papier-maché	461	353
Paraffine	671	578
Parasol sticks	471, 756	361, 684
Parasols and parts	470	360
Parchment	672	579
Parian ware	100–101, 759	84, 86, 688, 85
Paris, plaster of	461	353
Paris, white	59	46
Partridge sticks	756	684
Paste, Brazil	517	416
Pastes	77	61
Paste, manufactures of	459	351
Pastes of indigo	614	514
Patterns for machinery	652	557
Paving posts of cedar	219	684
Paving tiles, marble	124	104
Peanuts, or ground beans	308	223
Pearl, mother-of	673	580
Pearl buttons	429	316
Pearls	453	337
Pease, prepared or preserved	271	198
dried	281	203, 581
green	281	203, 581
Pease in cartons, papers, or other small packages	281	203, 581
split	281	203, 581
Pebbles, Brazilian	519	418
Peel—		
lemon	664	570
orange	664	570
Peltries, Indian	674	582
Penalty for violation of preceding section	Page 115.	Sec. 38.
for false swearing	Page 115.	Sec. 38.
for fraudulent acts in connection with preceding sections	Page 108.	Sec. 30.
to attach for undervaluation under 10 per cent	Page 107.	Sec. 29.
for making false declarations	Page 106.	Sec. 28.
Penalties of section 6 applied to declarations substituted for oaths	Page 117.	Sec. 43.
Penholders and parts thereof	205	169
Penknives	165	138
Pencils of wood	466	357
Pencil leads not in wood	467	358
Pencils of lead	466	357
slate	466	357
hair	427	314
Penholder tips	205	169
Pens, metallic	204	168
Pepper	719	632
Pepper, Cayenne	326	235
Pepper, red	236	235
Peppermint oil	45	33
Percussion caps	442	327
Periodicals	657	562
Perfumery	8	7
Perfumery, articles of	77	61
Permanent board to be established at the port of New York	Page 110.	Sec. 33.
Personal effects	675, 752	583, 669
Personal effects, limit of value	752	670
Petroleum oil		568

	Paragraphs, present law.	Paragraphs, proposed law.
Pewter—		
manufactures of	215	177
old	676	584
Philosophical—		
apparatus	758, 677	687, 585
instruments	677	585
preparations	677	585
societies and institutions	677	585
Phosphates, crude or native	678	586
Phosphorus	68	53
Photograph albums	420	308
Photographs	423, 512, 758	311, 410, 687
	759	688
Photographic pictures for exhibition	758, 759	687, 688
Pianoforte action leather	456	341
Pickets	225	681
Pickles	287	198
Pigments	61	48
Pigs of copper	194	454
Pig iron	134	110
Pipe—		
bowls	468	359
bowls of clay	468	359
cast-iron	160	133
Pipes	468	359
clay	468	359
iron or steel	157, 160	130, 133
lead	201	167
Piments	720	633
sticks	756	684
Pine clapboards	221	677
Pins	206	170
metallic	206	170
solid head	206	170
other	206	170
hair	206	170
safety	206	170
hat	206	170
bonnet	206	170
shawl	206	170
belt	206	170
Pique or prick seam gloves	458	343–350
Pistols	170	143
Pitch	731	647
Burgundy	523	424
Place of sample to be be established at the port of New York	Page 110.	Sec. 33.
Placques	100	84
Plaits for hats, bonnets, and hoods	518	417
Planking, ship	755	673
Planks, deals, etc	218	676, 178
Planters	215	591
Plants	282, 679	587
Plants:		
fruit	577	487
Plants used for forcing under glass	572	234½
Plaster of Paris	461, 680	353, 588
Plaster of Paris casts	677	585
Plate—		
glass	114–118	93–97
polished	115, 118	94–97
Plates—		
cast iron	161	134
of copper	194	454
electrotype	180	151
fashion	566	476

	Paragraphs, present law.	Paragraphs, proposed law.
Plates—Continued.		
lithograph	180	451
saw	146	122
steel, engraved	180	151
stereotype	180	151
stove	161	134
Platina	681	589
Platinum, unmanufactured	682	590
articles of	215	177
Playing cards	424	312
Plows	215	591
Plumbago	683	592
Plums	299	214
Plums, prunes, figs, raisins	302	217
Plush, black, known as hatters' plush, silk	469	593
Plush (hatters'), silk	350, 469	259, 593
Plushes, wool	396	284
silk	411	299
Pocketknives	165	138
Poles, hop	755	673
Polishing stones	684	594
Pomades	77	61
Pool balls	435	320
Poplar wood	670	577
Poppy oil	41	29
seed	285	206
Porcelain ware	100, 101, 110, 759	84, 85, 86, 90, 688
Pork	311	224½
Porter	337	245
Portland cement	95	79
Posts	223	679
Potash—		
bichromate of	69	54
carbonate of, crude or fused	685	595
caustic	70	595
chlorate of	685	595
chromate of	69	54
hydrate of	70	595
hydriodate of	71	55
iodate and iodide of	71	55
muriate of	685	595
nitrate of, crude	685	595
refined	72	56
prussiate of, red	73	57
yellow	73	57
sulphate of	635	595
Potassa, tartrate of	92	75
Potatoes	283	204
Pottery works	759	688
Pouches for tobacco	468	359
Poultry	315	226
Powder—		
bleaching	635	537
bronze	190	160
gun	440	325
Powders—		
fulminating	430	324
Precious stones	454, 557	338, 467
imitations	454	338
Preparations, medicinal	74–77	58–61
alcoholic	74	58
of anatomy	707	619
of coal tar	19	443
toilet	77	61
Printed matter	423	311

	Paragraphs, present law.	Paragraphs, proposed law.
Printer's ink	30	21
Printing paper, sized	418	306
unsized	418	306
Products of coal tar, not colors or dyes	538	443
Professional implements	686	596
instruments	686	596
books	686	596
tools of trade	686	596
Proprietary preparations	74, 75	58, 59
Proto oxide of strontian	725	640
Prunes	299	214
Prune juice	339	247
wine	339	247
Prussian blue	50	38
Prussiate of potash—		
red	73	57
yellow	73	57
Publications	512	410
Pulp, paper, and books	415-425	303-313
Pulp, wood	415	303
Putty	59	46
Pulu	687	597
Pumice	688	598
stone	723	638
Pyrites	133, 727	518, 642
Pyrites, residuum	133	518, 109¼
Pyroligneous acid	1	1
Pyroxyline, compounds	21	15
Q.		
Quicksilver	207	599
colors	57	45
Quills	689	600
Quilts of down	443	328
Quinia, sulphate of	690	601
Quoits	552	462
R.		
Rags	670, 691	577, 602, 685
woolen	389	278
Railroad-ties	755	673
of cedar	219	684
Railway:		
bars, iron or steel	141	117
fish plates	181	152
Raisins	302	217
Rape-seed	699	611
oil	43	31
Rasps	168	141
Ratafia	332	240
Rattan braids, plaits, laces, etc	518	417
mattings and mats	464	356
Rattans	229, 756	179, 684
Razors	165	138
Razor blades	165	138
Ready-made clothing, wholly or in part of wool	396	284
composed of cotton or other vegetable fiber, etc	349	258
Reapers	215	591
Red chalk	16	11
Red lead	66	51
Red pepper	326	235
Reeds and bamboo	756	684
Reeds, wrought or manufactured	229	179, 684
Refined sulphur	727	642
Refund in excess of overpayment in customs duties, permanent appropriation	Page 118	Sec. 45.

	Paragraphs, present law.	Paragraphs, proposed law.
Refunds. Secretary of Treasury to give a yearly detailed statement of such	Page 118.	Sec. 45.
Refuse lead	200	166
Regalia, gems, etc	692	603
Regulations concerning licenses	Page 121.	Sec. 50.
Regulus of antimony	187	376
Regulus of copper	193	453
Reimportation of articles	Page 96.	Sec. 19.
Religious societies and institutions	677, 692	585, 603
Rendered oils	76	60
Rennets	693	604
Repair, machinery for	Page 94.	Sec. 13.
Repealing section	Page 138.	Sec. 105.
Residuum from burnt pyrites	133	518
Rosin, gum	24, 560	470
Resublimed iodine	515, 615	515
Retorts	682	590
gas	102	87
Revolvers	170	143
Rice	261	193
cleaned	261	193
uncleaned	261	193
broken	261	193
flour and meal	261	193
Rifles, sporting	169	142
Rochelle salts	92	75
Rivets, iron or steel	182	153
Rocoa, or Orleans	484	375
Rolled plates	195	161
Roman cement	95	79
Rope—		
ends	670	577
hide	607	507
waste	670	507
Roofing slate	131	109
Root—		
arrow	488	381
dandelion	321, 556	231, 466
ginger	716	629
licorice	632	534
Roots	24, 560, 679	470, 587
bulbous	699	611
hop	610	510
Rosemary oil	661	568
Roses, ottar of	661	568
Rosewood	220, 733	684, 650
Rotten-stone	723	638
Roucou, extracts of	484	375
Round iron in coils	136	112
Round iron	135	112
Rubber	460, 461, 613	352–353, 513
clothing	349, 413	258, 301
Ruchings	373	276
silk	413	301
Rufflings	373	276
silk	413	301
Rugs	399, 408	287, 296
Rum, bay	334	242
Rye	262	190
flour	263	190
S.		
Sadirons	161	134
Safety pins	206	170
Safflower, extract of	694	605
Saffron	694	605

	Paragraphs, present law.	Paragraphs, proposed law.
Saffron cake	694	605
Sago	326	235
Sago, crude	695	606
flour	695	606
Salacine	696	607
Salammoniac	10	371
Saleratus	80	61
Salmon	292	209, 210
Saloup	700	612
Sal-soda	83	67
Salts in bulk, bags, etc.	322	608
cake	85	622
Saltpeter—		
crude	685	595
refined	72	56
Salts	76	60
black	685	595
Epsom	34	24
morphia	35	25
of quinia	690	601
of santonin	78	62
Rochelle	92	75
strychnia	87	70
Sand	723	638
Sandstone	723, 128	638, 106
Santonin	78	62
Sardines	291	208
Satin, white	51	39
Satinwood	220, 756	684
Sances	271, 287	198
Sauerkraut	697	609
Sausage—		
Bologna	509	406
skins	698	610
Sawed boards, planks, deals, or other lumber	218	676, 178
Saws	183	154
back	183	154
circular	183	154
crosscut	183	154
drag	183	154
hand	183	154
mill	183	154
pit	183	154
Saw plates, steel	146–152	122
Saxony carpets	400	288
Scenery, theatrical	686	596
Schmaschen gloves	458	343–350
Scientific apparatus, instruments, preparations for societies and institutions	677	585
Scissors and shears	165	138
Scrap iron and steel	134	110
Scrap albums	420	308
Scrap lead	200	166
Screens	408	296
paper for	422	310
Screws	184	155
wire rods	147	123
Scroll iron	140	116
Sculpture, specimens of	692	603
Sea-weeds	653	558
Seal oil	46	34
Seed—		
agricultural	286	611
all other	286	611
anise	699	611
canary	699	611

	Paragraphs, present law.	Paragraphs, proposed law.
Seed—Continued.		
cane	679	587
caraway	699	611
cardamon	699	611
castor	284	205
coriander	699	611
cotton	699	611
cummin	699	611
fennel	699	611
fenugreek	699	611
flax	285	206
flower	699	611
garden	286	611
grass	699	611
hemp	699	611
hoarhound	699	611
lin	285	206
mustard	699	611
poppy	285	206
rape	699	611
Saint John's bread or bean	699	611
sugar-beet	699	611
Seeds	679, 271, 284–286, 699	205, 206, 611, 587
aromatic	24, 560	470
croton	699	611
garden	286	611
mangel-wurzel	— 699	611
of all kinds not specially provided for	699	611, 634
of morbid growth	24, 560	470
oil	285	206
Seines	367	272
Selep	700	612
Sensitized paper	419	307
Sesame oil	661	568
Sesamum seed oil	661	568
Sewing silk	410	298
Shawl pins	206	170
Shears and scissors	165	138
Sheathing	195	161
Shell, manufactures of	462	354
Sheep	250	189
regulations	482	373
skins	456	341
Shale, coal	432	318½, 441
Shavings	670	577
Shawls of wool, etc	392	281
Sheathing, metal	195	161
paper	416	304
felt	569	479
Sheet iron	142, 143, 144	118, 119, 120
polished, planished, or glanced	144, 152	120
Sheet and plate iron and steel	142	118
standard gauge	142	118
Sheets of lead	201	167
Shell—		
buttons	429	316
fish	703	615
fish, in cans or packages of tin or other metal	296	212
Shells	701	613
Shingle bolts	755	673
Shingles	226	682
Ship—		
irons	153	126
planking	755	673
timber	755	673
Ship's chronometers	210	172

	Paragraphs, present law.	Paragraphs, proposed law.
Shirts and wearing apparel	372	275
Shoddy, woolen	388	278
Shoe buttons	431	318
of paper	431	318
of board	431	318
of papier-maché	431	318
of pulp	431	318
Shoe uppers or vamps of leather	457	342
Shoes	456	341
Shooks	228	180
Shot	201	167
guns	170	143
guns, muzzle-loading	169	142
gun barrels	702	614
Shrimps	703	615
Shrubs	282, 679	587
Side arms	166	139
Sienna and sienna earths	54	42, 566
Silicate—		
alkaline	84	68
of soda	84	68
Silk—		
and silk goods	414	302
as reeled from cocoon	704	616
braces, beltings, etc	412	300
button forms	428	315
carded	409	298
chenilles	411	299
clothing, ready-made, and wearing apparel	413	301
cocoons	705	617
combed	409	298
floss	410	298
goods, beaded	413	301
gorings	412	300
hatter's plush	469	593
knit goods	413	301
laces, embroideries, etc	413	301
manufactures of	414	302
organzine	410	298
partly manufactured	409	298
pile fabrics	411	299
plushes	411	299
raw	704	616
rubber clothing	413	301
sewing	410	298
singles	410	298
spun	410	298
suspenders	412	300
threads	410	298
thrown	410	298
tram	410	298
twist	410	298
velvets	411	299
waste	705	617
webbing	412	300
worms' eggs	706	618
yarns	410	298
Silver—		
articles of	215	177
bullion	522	423
coin	544	449
German	188	158
leaf	198	164
medals	648	551
ore	667	573
paper	419	307
sweepings	729	644

	Paragraphs, present law.	Paragraphs, proposed law.
Similitude clause	Page 89.	Sec. 4.
Sirups of sugar-cane juice or beet juice	726	641, 182½
Sisal grass	397, 596	285, 497
cable, cordage, and twine	362	268, 399
Size, gold	56	44
Skeletons	707	619
Skelp iron	142, 138	118, 114
Skins	456, 573, 605	341, 483, 505
Angora goat	605	505
asses	605	505
fish	573	483
fur	588	493
goat	605	505
gold-beaters'	598	498
sausage	698	610
Slack, coal	432	318½, 441
Slate—		
chimney pieces	130	108
mantels	130	108
pencils	466	357
slabs for table	130	108
other manufactures	130	108
Slates	130	108
roofing	131	109
Sledges	156	129
Slides for magic lanterns	121	101
Smelting in bonded warehouses	Page 97.	Sec. 21.
Smokers' articles	468	359
Smoking opium	48	36
Snails	708	620
Snuff and snuff flour—		
manufactured of tobacco	245	187
ground dry	245	187
ground damp	245	187
pickled	245	187
scented	245	187
of all descriptions	245	187
Soap—		
castile	79	63
fancy	79	63
other	79	63
Soda	80–85	64–68, 622
and potassa tartrate	92	75
ash	83	67
bicarbonate of	80	64
bichromate and chromate of	82	66
borate of	14	10, 415
caustic	81	65
chlorate of	709	621
crystals	83	67
hydrate	81	65
nitrate of	709	621
oleates of	36	26
sal	83	67
silicate of	84	68
sulphate of	85	622
supercarbonate of	80	64
water	340	248, 555
Sodium	710	623
Solid head pins	206	170
Sorghum for seed	699	611
Sour orange juice	631	533
Spar manufacture	459	351
Sparkling wines, in bottles	335	243
Sparterre	711	624

	Paragraphs, present law.	Paragraphs, proposed law.
Spectacles and frames	119	98
and eyeglass lenses	121	101
Specimens of natural history, botany, or mineralogy, etc..	712	625
Specimens of sculpture	692	603
Spermaceti oil	661	568
Spices	24, 326, 713-720	470, 235 626-633
Spiegeleisen	134	110
Spike lavender oil	661	568
Spikes, iron and steel, for vessels	Page 90.	Sec. 7.
Spirit varnishes	56	44
Spirits	329-334	237-242
from grain	329	237
rule for assessing duties	330	238
Spirituous beverages	332	240
Splice bars, railway	181	152
Sponges	86	69
Spool thread, cotton	343	251
Spruce clapboards	222	678
Spun silk	410	298
Spunk	721	635
Spurs for crockery	722	636
Square iron	135	112
Stained and painted glass	677	585
Stamping, branding, etc	Page 90.	Sec. 5.
Starch	323	232
burnt	324	233
Statuary	465, 677, 692, 758	575, 585, 603, 687
for exhibition	692, 758, 759	603, 687, 688
Statues	692	603
Statuettes	100	84
Stave bolts	755	673
Staves of wood	227	683
Stays, boiler	157	130
Steel (*see* Iron)—		
alloys	146	122
angles	137	113
articles of	215	177
axles	154	127
parts of	154	127
forgings	154	127
bands	140, 143	116, 119
bars	146, 152	122
splice	181	152
beams	137	113
billets	146	122
blacksmiths' hammers and sledges	156	129
blooms	146	122
boiler tubes, flues, or stays	157	130
bolts and bolt blanks	158	131
bolts for vessels	Page 90.	Sec. 7.
building forms	137	113
car-truck channels	137	113
castings	146	122
chain or chains	164	137
channels	137	113
circular-saw plates	152	129
connecting rods	146	122
cotton ties	140	459
crank and other shafts	146	122
crank pins	146	122
crowbars	156	129
cut nails and spikes	173	145
deck and bulb beams	137	113

	Paragraphs, present law.	Paragraphs, proposed law.
Steel (*see* Iron)—Continued.		
definition of	150	....
die blocks or blanks	146	122
forging	153, 139	126, 115
girders	137	113
gun molds	146	122
hammer molds	146	122
hoops	140, 143	119, 459
in all forms	146	122, 156
ingots	146, 185	122, 156
cogged	146	122
joists	137	113
nails	173, 174, 175	145–147
nails for vessels	Page 90.	Sec. 7.
nuts, wrought	176	148
piston rods	146	122
plates	138, 143, 146, 171, 172	114, 119, 122, 144
plates, engraved	180	151
rails, flat	141	117
rails, tee	141	117
railway bars	141	117
railway fish plates	181	152
rivets	182	153
rods	147	123
rods for rivets, screws, nails, and fence wire	147	123
rods for vessels	Page 90.	Sec. 7.
scrap	134	110
shafts and shafting	146	122
shapes or blanks	146	122
sheets	142, 145, 171, 172	118, 121, 144
slabs	146	122
spikes for vessels	Page 90.	Sec. 7.
spikes, wrought	176	148
strips	....	152
structural shapes	137	113
swaged	146	122
TT, columns and posts	137	113
track tools	156	129
washers, wrought	176	148
wedges	156	129
wheels	185	156
wire card clothing	159	132
wristpins	146	122
Steels	167	140
Stems	24, 560	470
suitable for millinery use	443	328
tobacco	738	655
Stereotype plates	180	151
Sticks, walking	756	684
Sticks	756	684
of partridge	756	684
of hairwood	756	684
of pimento	756	684
of orange	756	684
of myrtle	756	684
of other woods not specially provided for	756	684
for umbrellas	756	684
for parasols	756	684
for sunshades	756	684
for whips	756	684
rough hewn or sawed only	223	679
Stilts for crockery	722	636
Still wines	336	244

	Paragraphs, present law.	Paragraphs, proposed law.
Stock—		
glue	606	506
paper	670	577
Stockings—		
cotton	352, 353	261, 262
clocked	353	262
Stone—		
burr	126, 723	638
cliff	723	638
pumice	723	638
rotten	723	638
ware	99, 100, 101	83–86
Stones	126–129	106, 107, 638
building	127, 128	638, 106
burr	126, 723	638
curling	552	462
flint	574	484
freestone	127, 128	106, 638
granite	127, 128	106, 638
grind	129	107
limestone	127, 128	106, 638
lithographic	636	538
load	638	540
mill	126	638
monumental	127, 128	106, 638
precious	454	338
sandstone	127, 128	106, 638
Storax	724	639
Stove plates	161	134
Straw	289	637
braids, plaits, and laces	518	417
and grass, definition of	460	352
manufactures of	460	352
Strip steel	148	124
Strontia—		
carbonate of	725	640
oxide of	725	640
Strontian, protoxide of	725	640
Strontianite	725	640
Strychnia	87	70
salts of	87	70
Strychnine	87	70
Styrax	724	639
Subacetate of copper	749	666
Suede gloves	458	343–350
Sugar	231–241, 726	182, 183, 611, 182½
bounty regulation on domestic	231–236, 241	182
repeal of	231–236	182
beet seed	699	611
box shooks	228	180
candy	238, 239	183
duty on, above No. 16 Dutch standard	237	182½
cane for seed	699	611
countervailing duty	237	
drainings	726	641, 182½
grape	240	183
machinery for manufacturing beet sugar	237	177
manufactured, in bond temporarily	241	
not above 16 Dutch standard free	726	641, 182½
maple	231–234, 726	182, 641, 182½
of milk	269	182
sorghum bounty	231–236, 241	182
sweepings	726	641, 182½
bone char for decolorizing	11	9

	Paragraphs, present law.	Paragraphs, proposed law.
Sulphate—		
of alumina	9	8
of ammonia	10	371
of baryta, unmanufactured	500	395
of barytes	51	39
of copper	12	405
of iron	23	455
of lime	680	588
of magnesia	34	24, 542
of potash	685	595
of quinia	690	601
of soda	85	622
Sulphide—		
of antimony	485	376
of arsenic	489	382
Sulphur	88, 727	71, 642
flowers of	88	71
lac	727	642
ore	727	642, 518
ore as pyrites	133	109½, 518
precipitated	727	642
refined	88	642
sublimed	88	71
Sulphuret of iron	727, 133	109½, 518, 642
Sulphuric—		
acid	5, 728	643
ether	25	17
Sumac—		
ground	89	72
extract	26	18
Sunken vessels, merchandise	Page 97.	Sec. 20.
Sunn	597	497, 399
Sunshade sticks	471	361
Sunshades and parts	470, 756	360, 684
Super-carbonate of soda	80	64
Surface-coated papers	420	308
Suspenders—		
silk	412	300
cotton	354	263
wool	398	286
Sweetmeats	303	218
Sword blades	166	139
Swords	166	139
Sycamore lumber	218	676, 178

T.

Table knives	167	140
Tacks	177	149
Taggers—		
iron	142, 143	118, 119
tin	143	119
Tailors' irons	161	134
Tallow	316	645
Talmas, woolen	397	285
Tamarinds	581	490
Tamboured articles	373	276
Tampico fiber	592	497, 399
Tank-bottoms	726	641, 182½
Tannic acid	6	5
Tannin	6	5
Tanning articles	26, 492	18, 386
Tapestry, Brussels carpets	403	291
velvet carpets	402	290
Tapioca	730	646
Tar, coal—		
crude	538	443
products of	18, 19	14, 443

	Paragraphs, present law.	Paragraphs, proposed law.
Tar, wood	731	647
Tartar—		
cream of	90	73
crude	487	380
partly refined	91	74
patent	90	73
Tartaric acid	7	6
Tartrate, soda and potassa	92	75
Tassels, wool	308	286
Tax, income	Page 122-129.	Secs. 54-68.
Tea and tea plants	732	648
Teazles	290	649
Teeth	733	650
Telegraph poles of cedar	219	684
Telephone poles of cedar	219	684
Terne plates	143	119
Terra-alba	734	651
Terra-cotta works	759	688
Terra Japonica	735	652
Textile grasses	597	497, 399
Thread—		
cotton	342, 343	250 251
cotton, spool	343	251
flax	370	274
hemp	370	274
of silver	196	162
of gold	196	162
of other metals	196	162
Thread, silk	410	298
Threshing machines, duty on	215	591
Thyme oil	661	568
Ties, railroad	755	673
Tile and fire brick	93, 94	76, 77, 78
Tiles—		
encaustic	94	78
glazed, ornamented or decorated	94	78
paving	94	78
roofing	94	78
Timber	216, 217, 754	672, 674, 675
for vessels	Page 90.	Sec. 7.
ship	755	673
hewn and sawed	216	674
used for spars	216	674
used in building wharves	216	674
squared or sided	217	675
Tin—		
articles of	215	177, 591
bars	209, 736	653
blocks	209, 736	653
boxes	328	
cans	328	
cassiterite	209	653
grains	736	653
granulated	736	653
manufactures of	143	119
ore	209, 736	653
oxide	209, 736	653
packages	328	
pigs	209, 736	653
plates	143, 145	119, 121
plates, limitation on duty	143	119, 121
plate drawbacks	328	
taggers	142, 143	118, 119
Tinsel wire	737	654
Tinware, articles of	328	
Tissue paper	410	307

T A——18

	Paragraphs, present law.	Paragraphs, proposed law.
Tobacco	242-246	184-188
leaf	242	184
stemmed	242	184
unstemmed	242	184
all other in leaf, unmanufactured and not stemmed	243	185
all other in leaf, unmanufactured and stemmed	243	185
manufactured	244	186
provisions for reimportation	493	387
stems	738	655
unmanufactured	243	185
Tires, iron or steel	185	156
Toilet preparations	77	61
Tonics	77	61
Tonka beans	739	656
Tonquin	739	656
Tonqua	739	656
Tools	156, 661	129, 568
Tooth and disk harrows, duty on	215	591
Tow waste	592	497, 399
Tow or flax or hemp	592	497, 399
Toys	100, 436	84, 321
Track-tools—		
iron or steel	156	129
Trade-marks, fraudulently copying	Page 90.	Sec. 6.
Tram-silk	410	298
Trees	282, 679	587
Trimmings—		
cotton flax	373	276
dress	398	286
for hats, bonnets, and hoods	518	417
Tripoli	740	657
Tubes	157	130
boiler	157	130
Turmeric	741	658
Turpentine, spirits of	743	660
Venice	742	659
Turtles	744	661
Twine—		
binding	362	268, 399
gilling	367	272
seine	367	272
Twist, silk	410	298
Type metal	208	171
Types, old	745	662
Tuckings	373	276
Turkey red oil	36	26

U.

Ulsters	397	285
Ultramarine	55	43
Umber and umber earths	54	42, 566
Umbrella sticks	471, 756	361, 684
Umbrellas, and parts	470	360
Undervaluation, penalty for	Page 121.	Sec. 50.
Unenumerated articles	Page 89.	Sec. 3.
United States—		
articles for	514	412
vessels	Page 90.	Sec. 7.
Unmanufactured articles not enumerated	Page 89.	Sec. 3.
Upper leathers	457	342
Uranium, oxide of salts of	746	663

V.

Vaccine virus	747	664
Valerian oil	661	568

	Paragraphs, present law.	Paragraphs, proposed law.
Valonia	748	665
Varnishes	56	44
Vases	100	81
Vegetable—		
excrescenses	24	470
ivory	402, 519	354, 418
wax	751	668
Vegetables	287, 288	198, 207
prepared, etc	271	198
substances, fibrous	592	497, 399
substances	653	558
ivory buttons	430	317
prepared or preserved	287	198
in their natural state	288	207
Vehicles of immigrants	483	374
Vellum	672	579
Velvet, cotton	350	259
carpets	402	290
Velvets, silk	411	299
Venetian chain carpet	404	292
Venice turpentine	742	659
Verdigris	749	666
Vermicelli	258	192
Vermilion red	57	45
Vermuth	336	244
Vessels—		
built in the United States, materials for	Page 90.	Sec. 7.
cast-iron	161	134
discriminating duty on	Page 95.	Sec. 14.
Vials, glass	103, 104	88
Vinegar	327	236
Vines	282	587
Vitriol, blue	12	405
oil of	5	613
W.		
Wads, gun	446	331
Wafers, unmedicated	750	667
Wagon-blocks	223	679
Wagons of immigrants	483	374
Walking-sticks	756	684
Walnuts	307	222
Warehouse, withdrawal from	Page 92.	Sec. 9.
withdrawals, on what based	Page 117.	Sec. 41.
Warps, or warp-yarn cotton	342	250
Wash blue	55, 58	43
Washers, wrought-iron	176	148
Waste	670, 472	362, 577
Waste composed wholly or in part of wool	756	685
cotton	549	458
top	278	388
slubbing	278	388
roving	278	388
ring	278	388
yarn	278	388
garnetted	278	388
carded	278	388
product	278	388
tow	592	497, 399
yarn	756	685
card	756	685
rope	670	577
bagging	670	577
bur	756	685
silk	705	617
woolen	388	278, 685

	Paragraphs, present law.	Paragraphs, proposed law.
Watches	211	173
Watch—		
cases	211	173
glasses	211	173
jewels	557	467
movements and parts of	211	173
parts of	211	173
Waters, minerals	311, 650	249, 555
Water-color paints	61	48
Waterproof cloth	369	273
Wax, manufactures of	459	351
mineral	751	668
vegetable	751	668
Wearing apparel	349, 396, 413, 752	258, 284, 301, 669
Wearing apparel, limit of value	752	670
Wearing apparel, rubber	349, 413	258, 301
Webbing—		
cotton	354	263
silk	412	300
wool	398	286
Wedges, iron and steel	156	129
Weeds	24, 560	470
manufactures of	460	352
sea	653	558
Whalebone—		
manufactures of	460	352
unmanufactured	753	753
Whale oil	46, 661	34, 568
Wheat	264	190
flour	265	190
Wheels—		
hubs for	223	679
or parts thereof	185	156
steel or iron	185	156
Whetstones	608	508
White lead	67	52
White, satin	51	39
White, Paris	59	46
Whitewood and white-pine lumber	218	676, 178
Whiting	59	46
Whip-gut	450, 529	351, 431
Willow—		
articles	459	351
sheets and squares, for hats, bonnets, and hoods	518	417
Wilton carpets	400	288
Window curtains, of lace	373	276
glass	112	91
Windows, stained or painted glass	122	101, 102
Wines—		
coloring for	22	16
prune	339	247
sparkling	335	243
sparkling, in bottles	335	243
still	336	244
still, containing 14 per cent alcohol	336	244
Wire—		
cloths	148	124
corset	148	124
crinoline	148	124
flat steel	148	124
drill rods	148	124
hat	148	124
iron or steel	148	124
coated with zinc or tin	148	124
of lead	201	167

	Paragraphs, present law.	Paragraphs, proposed law.
Wire—Continued.		
nails	175	147
needle	148	124
nettings	148	124
rope	148	124
for vessels	Page 90.	Sec. 7.
sheet steel	148	124
strand	148	124
additional duties	148	124
covered with cotton or silk	148	124
rods	147	123
Withdrawals from warehouse, on what based	Page 117.	Sec. 41.
Witherite	500	395
Women's hats	451	335
Wood—		
ashes	495	389
lye of	495	389
blocks of various kinds	223	679
bolts	755	673
box	220, 756	684
cabinet	220, 756	684
casks and barrels, etc	228	180
cedar	756	684
posts, etc	219	684
cabinet furniture	230	181
chair cane	229	179, 684
clapboards	221, 222	677, 678
ebony	220, 756	684
fence posts	755	673
fire	755	673
foreign export duties	218	178, 676
granadilla	220, 756	684
handle bolts	755	673
heading bolts	755	673
house furniture	230	181
lance	220, 756	684
laths	224	680
lignum-vitæ	220, 756	684
logs	754	672
mahogany	220, 756	684
manufactures	230	181
pickets and paling	225	681
Woods, poplar or other	670	577
pitch	731	617
Wood pulp, mechanical ground	415	303
chemical	415	303
unbleached	415	303
bleached	415	303
ties	755	673
rose	220, 756	684
round, unmanufactured timber not specially provided for	754	672
satin	220, 756	684
shingles	226	682
stave bolts	755	673
staves	227	683
timber	216, 217	674, 675
veneers of	220	684
tar	731	617
unmanufactured	220	683, 684
Woods	756	684
for dyeing	24, 560	470
Writing paper	422	310
Wool—		
classification of	381	685
definition of	376–378	

	Paragraphs, present law.	Paragraphs, proposed law.
Wool—Continued.		
different rates of, according to condition	383	685
duty of first class	384	685
duty of second class	384	685
duty of third class	385, 386	685
grease	316	645
brown	316	645
carbonized	389	278
of the sheep	389	278
manufactures of, felt for paper-makers' use	282	303
noils	388	278, 685
on the skin	387	685
roping, roving, or tops	390	279
slubbing waste, roving waste, ring waste, yarn waste, garnetted waste	388	278, 685
top waste	388	278, 685
unwashed	382	685
Wools	375–408	685, 278–296
class 1	376	685
class 2	377	685
class 3	378	685
standard samples	379	685
improved	380	685
on the skin	387	685
scoured	381	685
washed	382	685
Woolen—		
barrel buttons	398	286
braces, beltings, bindings, etc	398	286
braids, galloons, fringes, gimps, etc	398	286
blankets	393	282
bockings	406	294
bunting	395	283
buttons	398	286
carpets, Aubusson	399	287
carpets, Axminster	399	287
carpets, moquette	399	287
carpets, Saxony	400	288
Tournay velvet carpets	400	288
carpets, Brussels	401–403	289–291
carpets, velvet	402	290
carpets, velvet tapestry	402	290
carpets, tapestry Brussels	403	291
carpets, treble ingrain	404	292
carpets, Venetian chain	404	292
carpets, Dutch wool	405	293
carpets, ingrain two-ply	405	293
carpeting	407	295
covers, hassocks, bedsides, art squares	408	296
coat linings	394, 395	283
cords, cords and tassels, etc	398	286
cloaks, dolmans, jackets, talmas, etc	397	285
cloths	392	281
clothing, ready-made	396	284
dress goods	394, 395	283
dress trimmings, laces, embroideries	398	286
druggets	406	294
felt and felt fabrics	396	284
felt carpets	406	294
flannels	393	282
flocks	389	278
hats of wool	393	282
head nets	398	286
Italian cloths	394, 395	283
knit fabrics	392	281
manufactures of	391–408	280–296

	Paragraphs, present law.	Parographs, proposed law.
Woolen—Continued.		
mats, rugs, screens	408	296
mungo	389	278
pile fabrics	396	281
plushes	396	281
rags	389	278
rugs, oriental	399	287
Berlin, etc	399	287
shawls	392	281
shoddy	388	278
waste	388	278
yarns	391	280
nets, buttons, barrel buttons, etc	398	286
tassels and ornaments	398	286
webbing, gorings, suspenders, etc	398	286
Works of art	757, 758, 759	686, 687, 688
Worm gut, manufactures	459	351
Worm gut, unmanufactured	529	431
Worsted cloths	392	281
Worsted yarns	391	280
Woven fabrics of cotton—		
plain	257	190
in piece	257	190
figured	257	190
fancy	257	190
Writing paper	422	310
Y.		
Yams	760	689
Yarn—		
coir	545	450
cotton	342	250
flax	370	274
hemp	370	274
jute	361	267
silk	410	298
waste	388	685
woolen	391	280
worsted	391	280
Yellow metal	189, 195	159, 161
Yolks of eggs	561	471
Z.		
Zaffer	761	690
Zinc	212, 214	174, 176
blocks	212	174
pigs	212	174
sheets	213	175
old	214	176
oxide of	60	47

APPENDIX.

COMPARISON

OF

THE INCOME-TAX LAW OF 1864 AND 1867

WITH

THE PROVISIONS OF HOUSE BILL 4864 AS AMENDED BY SUB-COMMITTEE OF SENATE FINANCE COMMITTEE.

INCOME.

SEC. [116] *54.* [*And be it further enacted,*] That *from and after the first day of January, eighteen hundred and ninety-five,* there shall be levied, collected, and paid annually upon the gains, profits, and income [of every person residing in the United States, or of any citizen of the United States residing abroad,] *received in the preceding calendar year by every citizen of the United States and every person residing therein* whether *said gains, profits, or income be* derived from any kind of property, rents, interest, dividends, or salaries, or from any profession, trade, employment, or vocation, carried on in the United States or elsewhere, or from any other source whatever, a tax of [five] *two* per centum on the amount so derived over [one] *and above four* thousand dollars, and a like tax shall be levied, collected, and paid annually upon the gains, profits, and income *from all property owned and* of every business, trade, or profession carried on in the United States by persons residing without the United States [and not citizens thereof]. And the tax herein provided for shall be assessed, collected, and paid upon the gains, profits, and income for the year ending the thirty-first day of December next preceding the time for levying, collecting, and paying said tax.

SEC. [117] *55.* [*And be it further enacted,*] That, in estimating the gains, profits, and income of any person, there shall be included all income derived from interest upon notes, bonds, and other securities *except such bonds of the United States as are by the law of their issuance exempt from all Federal taxation* [of the United States]; profits realized within the year from sales of real estate purchased [within the year or] within two years previous to the year for which income is estimated; interest received or accrued upon [old(] all [)] notes, bonds, [and] mortgages, or other forms of indebtedness bearing interest, whether paid or not, if good and collectible, less the interest which has become due from said person *or which has been paid by him* during the year; the amount of all premium on [gold and] *all bonds, notes, or* coupons; the amount of sales of live stock, sugar, *cotton,* wool, butter, cheese, pork, beef, mutton, or other meats, hay and grain or other vegetable or other productions, being the growth or produce of the estate of such person, *less the amount expended in the purchase or production of said stock or produce and* not including any part thereof consumed directly by the family; *money and the value of all personal property acquired by gift or inheritance;* all other gains, profits, and income derived from any source whatever, [except the rental value of any homestead used or occupied by any person or by his family in his own right or in the right of his wife]; and the share of any person [of] *in* the gains [and] *or* profits of all companies, whether incorporated or partnership, who would be entitled to the same, if divided, whether divided or otherwise, except the amount of income received from institutions or corporations whose

281

officers, as required by law, withhold a per centum of the dividends, *interest, gains, profits, and income,* made by such institutions, *or corporations,* and pay the same to the officer authorized to receive the same; and except that portion of the salary, *compensation,* or pay received for services in the civil, military, naval, or other service of the United States, including Senators, Representatives, and Delegates in Congress, from which the tax has been deducted, *and except that portion of any salary upon which the employer is required by law to withhold, and does withhold, the tax and pays the same to the officer authorized to receive it. In computing incomes the necessary expenses actually incurred in carrying on any business, occupation, or profession shall be deducted, and also all interest due or paid within the year by such person on existing indebtedness.* And [in addition to [one] *four* thousand dollars, exempt from income tax, as hereinbefore provided,] all national, State, county, *school,* and municipal taxes, *not including those assessed against local benefits,* paid within the year shall be deducted from the gains, profits, or income of the person who has actually paid the same, whether such person be owner, tenant, or mortgagor; *also* losses actually sustained during the year, *incurred in trade, or* arising from fires *storms or* shipwreck, [or incurred in trade], *and not compensated for by insurance or otherwise,* and debts ascertained to be worthless, but excluding all estimated depreciation of values and losses within the year on sales of real estate purchased *within* two years previous to the year for which income is estimated; [the amount actually paid for labor or interest by any person who rents lands or hires labor to cultivate land, or who conducts any other business from which income is actually derived; the amount actually paid by any person for the rent of the house or premises occupied as a residence for himself or his family; the amount paid out for usual ordinary repairs:] *Provided,* That no deduction shall be made for any amount paid out for new buildings, permanent improvements, or betterments, made to increase the value of any property or estate: [And] *provided further,* That only one deduction of [one] *four* thousand dollars shall be made from the aggregate income of all the members of any family, composed of one or both parents, and one or more minor children, or husband and wife; that guardians shall be allowed to make [such] *a* deduction in favor of each and every ward, except that in case where two or more wards are comprised in one family, and have joint property interests [only one] *the aggregate* deduction [shall be made] in their favor *shall not exceed four thousand dollars: And provided further,* That in cases where the salary or other compensation paid to any person in the employment or service of the United States shall not exceed the rate of [one] *four* thousand dollars per annum, or shall be by fees, or uncertain or irregular in the amount or in the time during which the same shall have accrued or been earned, such salary or other compensation shall be included in estimating the annual gains, profits, or income of the person to whom the same shall have been paid, *and shall include that portion of any income or salary upon which a tax has not been paid by the employer, where the employer is required by law to pay on the excess over four thousand dollars.*

SEC. [118] 56. *[And be it further enacted,]* That it shall be the duty of all persons of lawful age *having an income of more than three thousand five hundred dollars for the taxable year computed on the basis herein prescribed,* to make and render a list or return, on or before the day [prescribed] *provided* by law, in such form and manner as may be [prescribed] *directed* by the Commissioner of Internal Revenue, *with the approval of the Secretary of the Treasury,* to the [assistant assessor] *col-*

lector or a *deputy collector* of the district in which they reside, *or to such officer or agent as the Commissioner of Internal Revenue may designate,* of the amount of their income, gains, and profits, as aforesaid; and all guardians and trustees, executors, administrators, [or any person] *agents, receivers, and all persons or corporations* acting in any [other] fiduciary capacity, shall make and render a list or return, as aforesaid, to the [assistant assessor] *collector or a deputy collector* of the district in which such person *or corporation* acting in a fiduciary capacity resides, *or does business, or to such officer or agent as the Commissioner of Internal Revenue may designate,* of the amount of income, gains, and profits of any minor or person for whom they act; *but persons having less than three thousand five hundred dollars income are not required to make such report,* and the [assistant assessor] *collector, deputy collector, or officer or agent designated by the Commissioner of Internal Revenue* shall require every list or return to be verified by the oath or affirmation of the party rendering it, and may increase the amount of any list or return, if he has reason to believe that the same is understated; and in case any such person *having a taxable income* shall neglect or refuse to make and render such list [or] *and* return, or shall render a false or fraudulent list or return, it shall be the duty of the [assessor or the assistant assessor] *collector, deputy collector, or officer or agent designated by the Commissioner of Internal Revenue* to make such list, according to the best information he can obtain, by the examination of such person, or his books or accounts, or any other evidence, and to add fifty per centum as a penalty to the amount of the tax due on such list in all cases of willful neglect or refusal to make and render a list or return, and, in all cases of a false or fraudulent list or return having been rendered, to add one hundred per centum, as a penalty, to the amount of tax ascertained to be due, the tax and the additions thereto as a penalty to be assessed and collected in the manner provided for in other cases of willful neglect or refusal to render a list or return, or of rendering a false and fraudulent return: *Provided,* that any [party,] *person or corporation,* in his [or] her *or its* own behalf, or as such fiduciary, shall be permitted to declare under oath or affirmation, the form and manner of which shall be prescribed by the Commissioner of Internal Revenue, *with the approval of the Secretary of the Treasury,* that he [or] she, or his or her *or its* ward or beneficiary, was not possessed of an income of [one] *four* thousand dollars, liable to be assessed according to the provisions of this act; or may declare that he [or] she *or it or his her or its ward or beneficiary* has been assessed and *has* paid an income tax elsewhere in the same year, under authority of the United States, upon *all* his [or] her *or its* income, gains [and] *or* profits *and upon all the income, gains or profits for which he she or it is liable as such fiduciary* as prescribed by law; and if the [assistant assessor] *collector, deputy collector or other designated officer or agent* shall be satisfied of the truth of the declaration, *such person or corporation* shall thereupon be exempt from income tax in the said district *for that year* or if the list or return of any [party] *person* shall have been increased by the *collector, deputy collector or other designated officer or agent* [assessor] such [party] *person* may [exhibit his books and accounts, and] be permitted to prove [and declare, under oath or affirmation,] the amount of income liable to be assessed; but such [oaths and evidence] *proof* shall not be considered as conclusive of the facts, and no deductions claimed in such cases shall be made or allowed until approved by the [assistant assessor] *collector deputy collector or other designated officer or agent.* Any person feeling aggrieved by the decision of the [assistant assessor] *deputy collector or any officer or agent other than the collector* in such cases may appeal to the [assessor] *collector* of the district, and his decision thereon, unless reversed by the Commissioner of Internal Revenue, shall be final. [and the form, time, and manner of proceedings shall be subject to rules and regulations to be prescribed by the Commissioner of Internal Revenue:] *If dissatisfied with the decision of the collector such person may submit the case, with all the papers, to the Commissioner of Internal Revenue for his decision, and may furnish the testimony of witnesses to prove any relevant facts having served notice to that effect upon the Commissioner of Internal Revenue, as herein prescribed. Such notice shall state the time and place at which, and the officer before whom, the testimony will be taken; the name, age, residence, and business of the proposed witness, with the questions to be propounded to the witness, or a brief statement of the substance of the testimony he is expected to give. The notice shall be delivered or mailed to the Commissioner of Internal Revenue a sufficient number of days previous to the day fixed for taking the testimony, to allow him, after its receipt, at least five days, exclusive of the period required for mail communication with the place at which the testimony is to be taken, in which to give, should he so desire, instructions as to the cross-examination of the proposed witness. Whenever practicable, the affidavit or deposition shall be taken before a collector or deputy collector of internal revenue, in which case reasonable notice shall be given to the collector or deputy collector of the time fixed for taking the deposition or affidavit:* Provided further, That no penalty shall be assessed upon any person for such neglect or refusal, or for making or rendering a false or fraudulent return, except after reasonable notice of the time and place of hearing, to be [regulated] *prescribed* by the Commissioner of Internal Revenue. [, so as to give the person charged an opportunity to be heard.]

SEC. [119] *57*. [*And be it further enacted,* That] The taxes on incomes herein imposed shall [be levied on the first day of March, and] be due and payable on or before the [thirtieth] *first* day of [April] *July*, in each year, [until and including the year eighteen hundred and seventy, and no longer]; and to any sum or sums annually due and unpaid after the [thirtieth of April] *first day of July*, as aforesaid, and for ten days after notice and demand thereof by the collector, there shall be levied in addition thereto the sum of five per centum on the amount of taxes unpaid, and interest at the rate of one per centum per month upon said tax from the time the same [became] *becomes* due, as a penalty, except from the estates of deceased, insane, or insolvent persons. [: *Provided,* That the tax on incomes for the year eighteen hundred and sixty-six shall be levied on the day this act takes effect.]

SEC. 58. *Any nonresident may receive the benefit of the exemptions hereinbefore provided for by filing with the deputy collector of any district a true list of all his property and sources of income in the United States and complying with the provisions of section fifty-six of this act as if a resident. In computing income he shall include all income from every source, but shall only pay on that part of the income which is derived from any source in the United States. In case such nonresident fails to file such statement, the collector of each district shall collect the tax on the income derived from property situated in his district subject to income tax, making no allowance for exemptions, and all property belonging to such nonresident shall be liable to distraint for tax:* Provided, *That nonresident corporations shall be subject to the same laws as to tax as resident corporations, and the collection of the tax shall be made in the same manner as provided for collections of taxes against nonresident persons.*

Sec. [120] 59. [*And be it further enacted,*] That there shall be levied and collected a tax of [five] *two* per centum on all dividends in scrip or money [thereafter declared due], wherever and whenever the same [shall] be payable, to stockholders, policy holders, or depositors or [parties whatsoever] *to any persons,* including non-residents, whether citizens or aliens, as part of the earnings, income, or gains of any bank, *banking institution,* trust company, savings institution, and of any fire, marine, life, [inland] *or other* insurance company, either stock or mutual, under whatever name or style known or called, *and doing business* in the United States [or Territories], whether specially incorporated or existing under general laws, and on all undistributed sums, or sums made or added during the year to their surplus or contingent funds; and said banks, *banking institutions,* trust companies, savings institutions, and insurance companies shall pay the said tax, and are hereby authorized *and required* to deduct and withhold from all payments made on account of any dividends or sums of money that may be due and payable as aforesaid the said tax of [five] *two* per centum. And a list or return shall be made and rendered to the [assessor or assistant assessor], *collector, deputy collector, or other officer or agent designated by the Commissioner of Internal Revenue,* on or before the tenth day of the month following that in which [any] *such* dividends or sums of money become due or payable as aforesaid; and said list or return shall contain a true and faithful account of the amount of taxes as aforesaid; and there shall be annexed thereto a declaration of the president, cashier, [or] treasurer, *or the principal accounting officer* of the bank, *banking institution,* trust company, savings institution or insurance company, under oath or affirmation, in form and manner as may be prescribed by the Commissioner of Internal Revenue, *with the approval of the Secretary of the Treasury,* that the same contains a true and faithful account of the taxes as aforesaid. And for any default in the making or rendering of such list or return, with such declaration annexed, the bank, *banking institution,* trust company, savings institution, or insurance company making such default shall forfeit as a penalty the sum of one thousand dollars; and in case of any default in making or rendering said list or return, or of any default in the payment of the tax as required, or any part thereof, the assessment and collection of the tax and penalty shall be in accordance with the general provisions of law in other cases of neglect and refusal : *Provided,* That the tax upon the dividends of life insurance companies shall not be deemed due until such dividends are payable; nor shall the portion of premiums returned by mutual life insurance companies to their policy holders, nor the [annual or semi-annual] interest allowed or paid to the depositors in savings banks or savings institutions, be considered as dividends.

Sec. [121] 60. [*And be it further enacted,*] That any bank [legally authorized to issue notes as circulation] *banking institution, trust company, savings institution, or insurance company* which shall neglect or omit to make dividends or additions to its surplus or contingent fund as often as once in six months, shall make a list or return in duplicate, under oath or affirmation of the president [or] cashier, *or principal accounting officer,* to the [assessor or assistant assessor] *collector or deputy collector* of the district in which it is located, *or to the officer or agent designated by the Commissioner of Internal Revenue* on the first day of January and July in each year, or within thirty days thereafter, of the amount of profits which have accrued or been earned [and] *or* received by said bank, *banking institution, trust company, savings institution,* or *insurance company* during the six months next preceding said first days of January and July *respectively;* and shall present one of said lists or returns and pay to the collector of the district a [duty] tax of [five] *two* per centum on such profits, and in case of default to make such list or return and payment within the thirty days, as aforesaid, shall be subject to the provisions of the foregoing section of this act: *Provided,* That ⋀when any dividend is made which includes any part of the surplus or contingent fund of any bank, *banking institution,* trust company, savings institution, *or* insurance [or railroad] company, which has been assessed and the [duty] *tax* paid thereon, the amount of [duty] *tax* so paid on that portion of the surplus or contingent fund may be deducted from the [duty] *tax* on such dividend.

SEC. [122] *61.* [*And be it further enacted*] That any railroad, canal, turnpike, canal navigation or slackwater company, *and any telephone, telegraph, electric light company, gas company, water company, and any street railway company, or other corporation or association, doing business in the United States and* indebted for any money for which bonds or other evidence of indebtedness have been issued, payable in one or more years after date, upon which interest is stipulated to be paid, [or coupons representing the interest,] or any such company *corporation or association* that may have declared any dividend in scrip or money due or payable to its stockholders, including non-residents, whether citizens or aliens, as part of [the] *its* earnings, profits, income, or gains [of such company], and [all] *when* profits of such company *corporation or association are* carried to the account of any fund, or used for construction, shall be subject to and pay a tax of [five] *two* per centum on the amount of all such interest, [or coupons,] dividends or profits, whenever and wherever the same shall be payable, and to whatsoever [party or] person the same may be payable, including non-residents, whether citizens or aliens; and said companies, *corporations or associations* are [hereby] *required to pay said tax and are* authorized to deduct and withhold from all payments on account of any interest, [or coupons,] and dividends, due and payable as aforesaid, the tax of [five] *two* per centum; and the payment of the amount of said tax so deducted from the interest, [or coupons,] or dividends, and certified by the the president or treasurer *or other principal accounting officer* of said company, *corporation or association* shall discharge said company, *corporation or association* from that amount of the dividend, or interest, [or coupon] on the bonds or other evidences of their indebtedness [so] held by any person or party whatever, except where said companies, *corporations, or associations* may have contracted otherwise. And a list or return shall be made and rendered to the [assessor or assistant assessor] *collector, deputy collector, or other officer or agent designated by the Commissioner of Internal Revenue* on or before the tenth day of the month following that in which said interest, [coupons,] or dividends become due and payable, and as often as 'every six months; and said list or return shall contain a true and faithful account of the amount of tax, and there shall be annexed thereto a declaration of the president, [or] treasurer, *cashier, or other principal accounting officer* of the company, *corporation, or association,* under oath or affirmation, in form [and] *or* manner as may be prescribed by the Commissioner of Internal Revenue, that the same contains a true and faithful account of [said tax] *the amounts so due and payable with the tax due thereon.* And for any default in making or rendering such list or return, with the declaration annexed, or of the payment of the tax as aforesaid, the company, *corporation, or association* making such default shall forfeit as a penalty the sum of [one thousand] *five hundred* dollars *and double the amount of the tax;* and in case of any default in making or rendering said list or return, or of the payment of the tax or any part thereof, as aforesaid, the assessment and collection of the tax and penalty shall be made according to the provisions of law in other cases of neglect or refusal: *Provided,* That whenever any [of the companies mentioned in this section] *company, corporation, or association* shall be unable to pay *all* the interest on [their] *its* indebtedness, [and shall in fact fail to pay such interest, that in such cases] the tax levied by this section shall [not] be paid to the United States [until said company resume the payment of interest on their indebtedness] *on the amount of interest only which the company pays or is able to pay: Provided further, That dividends or interest accruing to States, counties, or municipalities, and dividends, interest, or annuities accruing to corporations or associations organized and conducted solely for charitable, religious, or educational purposes, or to any trustee or other fiduciary on stocks, shares, funds, or securities held solely for charitable, religious, or educational purposes, or salaries due to State, county, or municipal officers, shall not be subject to such tax or deduction.*

SEC. [123] 62. [*And be it further enacted,*] That there shall be levied, collected and paid on all salaries of officers, or payments for services to persons in the civil, military, naval or other employment or service of the United States, including senators and representatives and delegates in Congress, when exceeding the rate of [one] *four* thousand dollars per annum, a tax of [five] *two* per centum on the excess above the said [one] *four* thousand dollars; and it shall be the duty of all paymasters and all disbursing officers under the government of the United States, or persons in the employ thereof, when making any payment to any officers or persons as aforesaid, whose compensation is determined by a fixed salary, or upon settling or adjusting the accounts of such officers or persons to deduct and withhold the aforesaid tax of [five] *two* per centum; and the pay-roll, receipts, or account of officers or persons paying such tax as aforesaid shall be made to exhibit the fact of such payment. And it shall be the duty of the accounting officers of the Treasury Department, when auditing the accounts of any paymaster or disbursing officer, or any officer withholding his salary from moneys received by him, or when settling or adjusting the accounts of any such officer, to require evidence that the taxes mentioned in this section have been deducted and paid over to the Treasurer of the United States, or other officer authorized to receive the same. *Every corporation which pays to any employee a salary or compensation exceeding four thousand dollars per annum shall report the same to the collector or deputy collector of his district and said employee shall pay thereon, subject to the exemptions herein provided for, the tax of two per centum on the excess of his salary over four thousand dollars:* [*Provided,* That payments of prize money shall be regarded as income from salaries, and the tax thereon shall be adjusted and collected in like manner: *Provided further,* That this section shall not apply to payments made to mechanics or laborers employed upon public works: *And provided further,* That in case it should become necessary for showing the true receipts of the government under the operations of this section upon the books of the Treasury Department, the requisite amount may be carried from unappropriated moneys in the treasury to the credit of said account; and this section shall take effect upon salary and compensation for the month of March, eighteen hundred and sixty-seven.]

SEC. 63. *That sections thirty-one hundred and sixty-seven, thirty-one hundred and seventy-two, thirty-one hundred and seventy-three, and thirty-*

one hundred and seventy-six of the Revised Statutes of the United States as amended are hereby amended so as to read as follows:

"SEC. 3167. *That* if any collector or deputy collector [or any inspector], or other officer *or internal-revenue agent* acting under the authority of any revenue law of the United States, divulges to any party, or makes known in any other manner than may be provided by law, the operations, style of work, or apparatus of any manufacturer or producer visited by him in the discharge of his official duties, *or the amount or source of income, profits, losses, expenditures, or any information obtained by him in the discharge of such duties,* he shall be subject to a fine of not exceeding one thousand dollars, or to be imprisoned for not exceeding one year, or to both, at the discretion of the court, and shall be dismissed from office and be forever thereafter incapable of holding any office under the Government."

"SEC. 3172. *That* every collector shall, from time to time, cause his deputies to proceed through every part of his district and inquire after and concerning all persons therein who are liable to pay [a special tax] *any internal-revenue tax,* and all persons owning or having the care and management of any objects liable to pay any tax, and to make a list of such persons and enumerate said objects.

"SEC. 3173. *That* it shall be the duty of any person, partnership, firm, association, or corporation, made liable to any duty, special tax, [stamp] or *other* tax imposed by law, when not otherwise provided for, in case of a special tax, on or before the thirty-first day of July in each year, *in case of income tax on or before the first Monday* [day] *of March in each year,* and in other cases before the day on which the taxes accrue, to make a list or return, verified by oath or affirmation, to the *collector or a* deputy collector of the district where located, of the articles or objects, *including the amount of annual income,* charged with a [special] duty or tax, the quantity of goods, wares, and merchandise made or sold, and charged with a [specific or ad valorem duty] tax, the several rates and aggregate amount, according to the forms and regulations to be prescribed by the Commissioner of Internal Revenue, [under the direction] *with the approval* of the Secretary of *the* Treasury, for which such person, partnership, firm, association, or corporation is liable: Provided, That if any person liable to pay any duty or tax, or owning, possessing, or having the care or management of property, goods, wares, and merchandise, articles or objects liable to pay any duty, tax, or license, shall fail to make and exhibit a list or return required by law, but shall consent to disclose the particulars of any and all the property, goods, wares, and merchandise, articles and objects liable to pay any duty or tax, or any business or occupation liable to pay any [special] tax as aforesaid, then, and in that case, it shall be the duty of the *collector or* deputy collector to make such list or return, which, being distinctly read, consented to, and signed and verified by oath or affirmation by the person so owning, possessing, or having the care and management as aforesaid, may be received as the list of such persons: Provided further, That in case *no annual list or return has been rendered by such person to the collector or deputy collector as required by law, and the* [any] person shall be absent from his or her residence or place of business at the time *the collector or* a deputy collector shall call for the annual list or return, [and no annual list or return has been rendered by such person to the deputy collector as required by law], it shall be the duty of such *collector or* deputy collector to leave at such place of residence or business, with some one of suitable age and discretion, if such be present, otherwise to deposit in the nearest post-office a note or memorandum addressed to such person, requiring him or her to render to such *collector or* deputy collector the list or return required by law, within ten days from the date of such note or memorandum, verified by oath or affirmation. And if any person on being notified or required as aforesaid shall refuse or neglect to render such list or return within the time required as aforesaid or whenever any person who is required to deliver a monthly or other return of objects subject to tax fails to do so at the time required, or delivers any return which, in the opinion of the collector, is false or fraudulent, or contains any undervaluation or understatement, it shall be lawful for the collector to summon such person, or any other person having possession, custody, or care of books of account containing entries relating to the business of such person, or any other person he may deem proper, to appear before him and produce such books, at a time and place named in the summons, and to give testimony or answer interrogatories, under oath, respecting any objects liable to tax or the returns thereof. The collector may summon any person residing or found within the State in which his district lies; and when the person intended to be summoned does not reside and can not be found within such State, he may enter any collection district where such person may be found, and there make the examination herein authorized. And to this end he may there exercise all the authority which he might lawfully exercise in the district for which he was commissioned.

"SEC. 3176. *That* the collector or any deputy collector in every district shall enter into and upon the premises, if it be necessary, of every person therein who has taxable property and who refuses or neglects to render any return or list required by law, or who renders a false or fraudulent return or list, and make, according to the best information which he can obtain, including that derived from the evidence elicited by the examination of the collector, and on his own view and information, such list or return, according to the form prescribed, of the *income, property, and* objects liable to tax owned or possessed or under the care or management of such person, and the Commissioner of Internal Revenue shall assess the tax thereon, including the amount, if any, due for special *tax, income or other* tax, and in case of any return of a false or fraudulent list or valuation *intentionally* he shall add one hundred per centum to such tax; and in case of a refusal or neglect, except in cases of sickness or absence, to make a list or return, or to verify the same as aforesaid, he shall add fifty per centum to such tax. In case of neglect occasioned by sickness or absence as aforesaid the collector may allow such further time for making and delivering such list or return as he may deem necessary, not exceeding thirty days. The amount so added to the tax shall be collected at the same time and in the same manner as the tax unless the neglect or falsity is discovered after the tax has been paid, in which case the amount so added shall be collected in the same manner as the tax; and the list or return so made and subscribed by such collector or deputy collector shall be held *prima facie* good and sufficient for all legal purposes."

SEC. 65. That *every corporation doing business for profit shall make and render to the collector of its collection district, in its return as to income tax required by section thirty-one hundred and seventy-three of the Revised Statutes of the United States as amended by this Act, on or before the first Monday of March in every year, beginning with the year eighteen hundred and ninety-five, a full return, verified by oath or affirmation, in such form as the Commissioner of Internal Revenue may pre-*

scribe, of all the following matters for the whole calendar year last preceding the date of such return:

First. The gross profits of such corporation, from all kinds of business of every name and nature.

Second. The expenses of such corporation, exclusive of interest, annuities, and dividends.

Third. The net profits of such corporation, without allowance for interest, annuities, or dividends.

Fourth. The amount paid on account of interest, annuities and dividends stated separately.

Fifth. The amount paid in salaries of four thousand dollars or less to each person employed.

Sixth. The amount paid in salaries of more than four thousand dollars to each person employed.

SEC. 66. That it shall be the duty of every corporation doing business for profit to keep full, regular, and accurate books of account, upon which all its transactions shall be entered from day to day, in regular order, which books shall, at all reasonable times, be open to the inspection of any internal-revenue officer or agent.

SEC. 68. That it shall be the duty of every collector of internal revenue to whom any payment is made under the provisions of this Act, to give to the person making such payment a full written or printed receipt, expressing the amount paid and the particular account for which such payment was made; and whenever such payment is made, such collector shall, if required, give a separate receipt for each tax paid by any debtor, on account of payments made to or to be made by him to separate creditors in such form that such debtor can conveniently produce the same separately to his several creditors in satisfaction of their respective demands to the amounts specified in such receipts; and such receipts shall be sufficient evidence in favor of such debtor, to justify him in withholding the amount therein expressed from his next payment to his creditor; but such creditor may, upon giving to his debtor a full written receipt, acknowledging the payment to him of whatever sum may be actually paid, and accepting the amount of tax paid as aforesaid (specifying the same) as a further satisfaction of the debt to that amount, require the surrender to him of such collector's receipt.

SEC. 71. That the Secretary of the Treasury shall have power to relieve and release from all forfeitures and penalties imposed by this act, in such cases as he may deem proper; but this shall not apply to any penalties imposed by law as the punishment of a misdemeanor or other crime.

O

www.ingramcontent.com/pod-product-compliance
Lightning Source LLC
Chambersburg PA
CBHW032054230426
43672CB00009B/1590